# GHOS
## *Of*
# St. Andr<

### A Ghost Tour of the Ancient City

Incorporating the 1911 Classic

## *St. Andrews Ghost Stories*

By

## W. T. Linskill

With 75 locations & over 100 ghostly encounters,
St. Andrews is not only the Home of Golf –
it is also the Home of Ghosts!

*To Alexandra,*
*Best wishes*

# RICHARD FALCONER 31/10/15

**1ˢᵗ Printed Edition**
Written in 1990, updated 2013

Please note
The enclosed Ghosts of St. Andrews Tour is a *Self Guided Tour* of the many Ghosts to be found in the town. The book is also an accompaniment to the Ghosts of St. Andrews *Guided Tour* around the town. Both are copyrighted and no part of this tour which includes the guided use of the material may be used for commercial purposes without written permission of the publishers and the author of this work.

www.obsidianpublishing.com
enquiries@obsidianpublishing.co.uk

## Dedicated

To the Citizens of St. Andrews

\*

To all who came forward in the 1980s from across the world with their own eyewitness accounts of the Ghosts of St. Andrews

\*

To the Dean of Guild W. T. Linskill

\*

And to Bob Miller who drove 800 miles in three days so I could take photos of the locations for this book and my companion books
*Ghosts of Fife* and *A St. Andrews Mystery*

# Table of Contents

# Part One
## A Self Guided Tour of the enduring Ghostly Residents of St. Andrews

# Part Two
## W. T. Linskill's Classic Work
### St. Andrews Ghost Stories
#### 1911

# Introduction

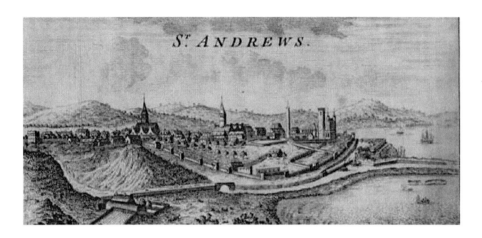

John Howie, a writer of the 18<sup>th</sup> century, described the City of St. Andrews as
"'The Metropolis of the Kingdom of Darkness.'"[1]

### *Included within this book*

- A Self Guided Tour of the enduring Ghostly Residents of St. Andrews
- Further Afield – More St. Andrews Haunts
- 'The Ghost Criteria', explaining the quantifiable nature of paranormal phenomenon
- *The Library Window* by Mrs Oliphant. A St. Andrews ghost story from 1896
- St. Andrews Ghost Stories by W. T. Linskill

This is a comprehensive look at the ghosts of St. Andrews forming the more elusive side of both town and gown.

With over 100 ghostly associations to be found within these pages in over 70 locations, St. Andrews for its size has one the highest concentrations of paranormal phenomenon to be found anywhere. This is why St. Andrews is not only the home of golf, it is also the home of ghosts!

This book is fully illustrated and can be read as a standalone or as a ghostly guide book of the town. Using the map on the back cover, the book will take you on a self guided tour of the many Ghosts of St. Andrews.

Documented here you will find an array of new ghosts to look out for. Far more than Linskill was aware of in his day. With previously unpublished eye witness accounts of poltergeist and ghostly activity in the Britannia Hotel. Now known as the West Port Bar & Kitchen, the activity seeped into a flat above the extension to the Bar causing it to suffer similar incidents. You will hear tell of a phantom car in Queen's Gardens, a floating head in South Street, fishermen appearing in a house in Lamond Drive and spooky goings on in the New Inn. The book also includes previously unpublished eyewitness sightings of the more traditional ghosts made famous by Linskill himself – the White Lady, Phantom Monks and the Phantom Coaches which have been heard careering through the ancient streets in the dead of night.

There is also a report here concerning the Phantom Piper of the Principal's House in the Scores where Prince William and Kate studied Art History together. The disturbance was highlighted by the Sunday Mail way back in 1980 and its legacy continues to this day. Also included are ghostly golfers, archbishops, martyrs, monks, royals, fairies, ghostly figures in black and an array of 'classic hauntings' to tingle the spine. They are all here! Appearing in and around haunted castles, mansions, flats, shops, hotels, bars, homes, student residences and the famed golf courses of St. Andrews as they roam, rattle, glide, fall, aid, stare and scare as they go!

Documented alongside these firsthand accounts and a wealth of history incorporated as a backdrop to the many locations, is a collection of fictional stories, legends and tales from the annals of local folklore. These are all drawn together by a wonderfully humorous ghost story about St. Andrews called *The House that lacked a Bogle*. The story is more than a children's tale and endearingly highlights the abundance of ghosts that are to be found in the town. In contrast, I have also included in the collection a few serious short fictional ghost stories interspersed between the accounts of the town. They include one written in 1896 by the famous Victorian Scottish author Mrs Oliphant. Entitled *The Library Window* this is a rare tale of young unrequited love, with its focus on the haunted James VI Library in South Street.

These rare apparitions blend seamlessly with one of the most dynamic and influential histories of any town. Whatever the political or religious climate, St. Andrews has certainly witnessed its fair share over the centuries, from the dizzying heights of vast wealth and power flowing through its sea and land ports, to the lows of an integral breakdown of the town, displayed by the ruins of its once prominent buildings.

I have given a few pages as a historical background detailing how close the town came to being wiped off the map of importance when the money from the church stopped flowing, and the merchants stopped coming. Entitled *Dung Hills and Herring Guts* it becomes easy to see why there has for many a year been such a wealth of ghosts lurking in timely fashion to startle the unwary.

John M. Leighton in his History of the County of Fife of 1840 wrote; 'To the east upon the sea coast is the venerable city of St. Andrews....with how many names of Scotland are these hallowed ruins associated! And how intimately connected is its history with the early civilisation and improvement of our country!'[2] W. T. Linskill in his inimitable style says 'the history and atmosphere of St Andrews lent itself to an all-pervading presence of ghosts, spooks, and spirits.'[i]

It is certainly difficult to be in St. Andrews without feeling nostalgic when its past reveals itself in the present at every turn. This all serves to create an atmosphere conducive to romantic associations – although not always in keeping with the historical reality of tragedy, violence and hardship to have blighted the towns past. It is nonetheless wholly in keeping with the ghostly phenomenon to be found here. With this, I begin the book with a somewhat retrospective and romanticised narrative of the town from 1911 entitled *Seekers after a City*. While it is not a ghost story as such, it conveys these atmospheric associations of its history. Associations, which I am sure, mirror the sentiments of so many wandering its precincts. If you have never been to St. Andrews it sets a tone that lends for a visit and is why I have included it at the beginning of this book more as an introduction to the town.

At the end of the book is an appendix explaining in brief a perspective on the various types of ghostly phenomenon – including that of poltergeist activity. I then hand the book over to W. T. Linskill and his classic 1911 publication *St. Andrews Ghost Stories,* which I have annotated and cross-referenced throughout with my *Ghosts of St, Andrews*.

As a lead up to his story *The Veiled Nun of St. Leonards* Linskill says of St. Andrews; 'now, from legends we learn that St. Andrews is possessed of a prodigious number of supernatural appearances of different kinds, sizes, and shapes – most of them of an awe-inspiring and blood curdling type. In fact, so numerous are they – 80 in number they seem to be – that there is really no room for any modern aspirants who may want a quiet place to appear and turn people's hair white.'[ii]

In *The Monk of St. Rules Tower* Linskill also conveys the scope of the many ghostly inhabitants of the town when he says of Captain Chester an old Cambridge friend: 'In Scotland he followed the scent of various ghosts, and finally landed in St. Andrews.

---

[i] Refer to W. T. Linskill's *A Spiritualistic Séance* p.275
[ii] Refer also to Linskill's *The Veiled Nun of St. Leonards*, p.344

"By Jove, sir," he said, "that's the place for ghosts. Every blessed corner is full of them – bang full. Look at those fellows in the castle dungeons, and Beaton and Sharpe and the men that got hanged and burned, and the old dev -- – I mean witches.

*I saw my ghost there.* Years and years ago I took an old house in St. Andrews, which was a small place then. Very little golf was played, and there was very little to do. But, gad, sir, the ghosts were thick, and the quaint old bodies in the town were full of them. They could spin yarns for hours about phantom coaches, death knells, corpse candles, people going about in winding sheets, phantom hearses, and Lord knows what else. I loved it; it took me quite back to the middle ages."[iii]

### The Early Researches for this Book

We have always been drawn to those shaded areas of reality where we cannot stop ourselves from taking a peek at what we dare not look at. How many times have you been told "don't look" and found the words to be an utterly irresistible invitation or challenge? Or said to yourself when watching a horror film "I can't look!" then somewhat half uncontrollably and half voluntarily - you do anyway!

Supernatural fictional stories and firsthand paranormal accounts are as old as humanity. Conversations, stories, books and films are filled with supernatural tales, legends, folklore, superstition and factually based experiences. All serve to kindle our childhood curiosities and maybe our own vague memories of early encounters. Whether we believe in them or not, they capture our imagination and form part of a cultural heritage we have each grown up with.

I was brought up in St. Andrews and its tales were commonplace in my mind. With seeing spirits from an early age I have always had an interest in the paranormal and an especial passion for St. Andrews and Fife. So numerous were the stories that in 1977 at the age of 13, I began spending many a night roaming the precincts of the Cathedral ruins of St. Andrews. I have incorporated some of my early experiences and encounters including the Phantom Coach in this present book, along with accounts in brief of appearances of the White Lady. The latter accounts can be found in full in my book *A St. Andrews Mystery* (2014).

---

[iii] Refer to Linskill's, *The Monk of St. Rules Tower*, p.323

*Published Material*

In 1987 I set about correlating what I could of the tales, the stories and the many legends and accounts of St. Andrews and Fife forming them at that time into one book. During the course of research I endeavoured to unearth as many sightings as possible through firsthand accounts as well as published material. Beginning with the published material in the town's Hay Fleming Library and the University Library in the autumn of 1987, I spent nine months pouring through books and papers spanning some 400 years on all aspects of St. Andrews and the Kingdom of Fife; as well as researching all the copies of the local newspaper *The St. Andrews Citizen* and a number of Victorian periodicals.

*Firsthand Accounts*

With no internet in the 1980s I placed ads in the *Readers Digest*, the *Scots Magazine, Dundee Courier* and the *St. Andrews Citizen* for any to come forward with their own paranormal experiences either in St. Andrews or across the Kingdom. A few weeks after publication I began receiving postmarks from across the world; Europe, America, Africa, Australia and Scotland.

There were letters of experiences and stories from all walks of life; from retired ministers and those in business, to doctors, cleaners, teachers and even a retired general. These were reports spanning back to the 1950s with a few of the reported occurrences correlating with one another.

I also received the same from local residents and students including a few from a local St. Andrews medium – Great Boyd, which are also incorporated throughout. ‡

*Early Submissions*

With computers still in their infancy, I originally wrote up this book on an old word processor in 1990. Once finished I submitted it to a number of publishers, but interest in the paranormal was at a general low at that time. It wasn't until around the mid 1990s with the advent of TV programs such as the 'X Files' series taking hold that interest once more grew around this subject. Added to this the specialist location wasn't deemed commercial enough at the time for the publishers. So one Christmas in the early 1990s I set it aside and gave a hard copy of the manuscript to a couple of dear friends I was staying with in Perth at the time and thought little more of it.

## A Book Rediscovered!

It wasn't until early 2013 whilst looking for something unrelated that I came across two floppy discs in a box, each marked with the title of this book. This renewed my interest for what I had completed over twenty years earlier. All was nearly lost however as the discs were so old, nothing I could do would recover them and I felt sure I had no other copy, but an impression came to mind which took me upstairs to a thick pile of papers stored on a shelf in the hallway. On looking through them, low and behold there it was – a copy of the manuscript I had previously submitted to one of the earlier publishers.

## This Current Publication

Life certainly has many interesting twists and turns. St. Andrews has become more popular than ever, especially with it being the location of the early romance of Prince William and Kate. Plus the Ghosts of St. Andrews have captivated the imaginations of generations, and with this the opportunity is open for new generations to be equally captivated by the towns many ghostly tales.

The popularity is such that in 2012 a slim volume was published by Geoff Holder entitled *Haunted St. Andrews*[3] as part of a national series, which naturally carries a modicum of crossover through the more well known of ghosts to be found in the town. Here however will be found more recent accounts of some of those classic tales and a wealth of unpublished material to be found alongside many snippets not having seen the light of day for a great many years which I have recounted in full.

So the manuscript and the valued eye witness testimonies, accounts, stories, legends and tales have all been salvaged for publication after so many years of lying on the shelf near forgotten. After refreshing the contents to bring it all up to date and incorporating W. T. Linskill's *St. Andrews Ghost Stories* I realised the wealth of information for St. Andrews and Fife was too great to be incorporated into one book, so I have split it into two works; *Ghosts of St. Andrews* and *Ghosts of Fife*. So after some 24 years it is all now in print.

## The Ghosts of St. Andrews Tour

The first part of this book comprises the *Ghosts of St. Andrews Tour* taking in the mainstay of the towns many haunted locations. Over 60 locations are to be found within easy walking distance. With the aid of the map on the back cover and the accompanying legend of the ghostly locations of the town on p.20, this is a fascinating way to explore St. Andrews in an alternative way. The tour correlates with the order each are placed in the book, and holds the same integrity when read without a physical tour.

Starting with the Rusacks Hotel Poltergeist, the tour moves clockwise around the town and finishes at the West Port Bar and Kitchen, where as I mentioned earlier ghostly activity took place when this was the Britannia Hotel a number of years ago. It was also where Prince William and Kate spent time relaxing and getting to know each other whilst in the town, but royalty aside, could the building still be haunted? You will have to spend time wining and dining to find the answer to this, or treat yourself to an overnight stay perhaps in one of its lovely rooms.

Also included are another 10 locations sited slightly further from the centre of town.

### W. T. Linskill's St. Andrews Ghost Stories

In the *St. Andrews Citizen* I found W. T. Linskill cropping up on a number of occasions. He corresponded in this newspaper up until his death in 1929, writing a number of generally short articles never published in his book. So although brief, they have also been incorporated throughout.

The second part of this book comprises of W. T. Linskill's *St. Andrews Ghost Stories* itself. First published in 1911 and having been out of print since 1978. A low quality scanned hard copy appeared in 2010, also in that year a poor online scanned version appeared as part of the continual drive to put everything now out of copyright onto the internet, but there is little in the way of quality with them. For this volume I have hand transcribed the book so the quality is the same as the original. I have also annotated it with additional information where appropriate and cross-referenced it with the relevant information in my book and vice versa. Just look out for **Linksill at a glance** and to footnotes in both books referring back to the same. There are also a few references to places, people and historical associations in Linskill's work wherever it was possible to do so. Although nailing down much of his tales has been quite an impossible task, there are some references correlating to modern day hauntings in the town. Also mixed in is the odd photo of association relevant to his writings and a photo of Linskill himself from his golfing days in Cambridge – in case you have ever wondered what this famous St. Andrews gentleman of the macabre ever looked like!

In 1896, J. G. Mackay the Sherriff of Fife and Kinross knew Linskill at the time when he was Dean of Guild for St. Andrews; he wrote 'A legend is not an invention, but a distortion of facts.'[4] His words ring true of Linskill's book and he could easily have written this with Linskill's work in mind.

I shall not linger too much here on Linskill or his work as I have covered this as an introduction to his book later. Suffice to say here, being an antiquarian Linskill cleverly incorporated what he read and heard into his fictional stories and tales, which he then wove around fictional characters. He gives a distinctly humorous Dickensian touch to their names, as they relate their experiences in convivial surroundings. By capitalising on the tiny nuggets of truth to be found in the anomalies of reality, Linskill had found a way of giving the legends a more significant impact upon his readership.

## Ghosts of Fife

For further afield I mentioned a companion volume I have written to this book entitled *Ghosts of Fife* (2013). This is also an exciting work. There are many books that feature the odd occurrence in Fife, however, this is the first time a book has been written exclusively devoted to the Ghosts of Fife. Like the *Ghosts of St. Andrews* the book is illustrated throughout, and includes many previously unpublished firsthand accounts from those who have stayed in Fife over the years. I have also conducted fresh research and brought the book up to the present with new unpublished material.

On par with the number of haunted locations in St. Andrews, the Ghosts of Fife has over 80 haunted places from all across the Kingdom, embodying over 100 locations and many more occurrences. The book incorporates firsthand previously unpublished eyewitness accounts, tales, legends and stories spanning the length and breadth of the Fifeshire landscape. Accounts include the infamous Pitmilly Poltergeist and the Tay Bridge Disaster of 1879 killing over 70 people after it left the shores of Wormit one stormy night. In the book, I explain the myth of the ghost train, and include a rare photo of the actual train that went down on that fateful night. Few are aware that this train was salvaged from the depths of the Tay and given the nickname of 'the Diver'; not only that, it then continued in service for another 39 years after it went into the Tay.

Also included in the book are numerous sightings of 'Green Jean', Fifes most popular ghost and a Ghost Trail of 25 Haunted Castles, (22 in Fife, with 3 fringing its border in Perth and Kinross). One of Fife's gems is Balgonie Castle. For those who have not heard of this fine 700 year old dwelling situated just outside Markinch, this is the Kingdom's most haunted castle. It is open to the public all year round and is one of the locations of the famed 'Green Jeanie' as they call her. I had the privilege of seeing her face when I visited September

2013. For its size, Balgonie Castle is one of the most actively haunted castles in Scotland.

## A St. Andrews Mystery

I have also written a book called *A St. Andrews Mystery* (2014). This is an intriguing story partly about the Haunted Tower in the Cathedral Precincts, which in itself is one of St. Andrews most enduring mysteries. It is also about the female ghosts who roam this quarter. In the book are new revelations about the ghost of the White Lady, together with more recent sightings of her and a firsthand account of a Green Lady which has never been disclosed before and which I give brief mention to later in this book, but the account itself will be found in *A St. Andrews Mystery*.

The book was originally also part of this present work, but it covers over 100 pages of itself, so it was necessary to publish it separately. It features all the current accounts together with the history and many speculations from the 19th century to the present day. Traditionally everybody thinks there is only one female ghost here, there are however seven in the area!

The book also incorporates W. T. Linskill's article to the St. Andrews Citizen in the 1920s called simply *St. Andrews Haunted Tower* and is cross referenced with additional material which ties in the White Lady, the Veiled Nun and the Green Lady.

## The Present Work

So now to the present book *Ghosts of St. Andrews*. Either sit back, relax and enjoy the many haunts St. Andrews has to offer, or take yourself off to the Rusacks Hotel and begin one of the most unusual and enjoyable tours you could ever have of the town – hopefully you will find yourself doing both.

If you know any stories or legends or have the privilege of witnessing any type of phenomenon, I will be most interested and grateful in hearing from you for future editions of this and the *Ghosts of Fife*. Especially once you have encountered one of the famed ghostly residents you may find awaiting your arrival around the next corner, as you explore the historic and haunted town of St. Andrews!

Richard Falconer

# Part One

## A Self Guided Tour
### of the enduring Ghostly Residents of
# St. Andrews

Samuel Bough – Off St. Andrews, 1856

*"St. Andrews by the Northern Sea,*
*a haunted town it is to me!"*
Lang, 1862[1]

# Information about the Ghosts of St. Andrews Tour

### Timesaver

If you don't have time to read the background to some of the locations, just look out for the monk to guide you straight to the goulish details. Then read the passages until you see the symbol at the end of this sentence marking the end of the piece or section. ❧ By just reading these sections the tour will take around 2 hours to complete, but with many additionally interesting things around the town to see en-route it is always best to allow for more time.

This symbol of the ghost tour highlights further information about the tour in this book.

This is a suggested self-guided tour, either virtual or physical of 65 haunted locations right in the centre of St. Andrews. All are in easy walking distance. The tour forms a very enjoyable way to experience all the major historic sites of the town, together with a little of its fascinating history; from its golf, its ruins, to its university and of course, it's many ghosts.

Moving in a primarily clockwise direction around the town, the tour starts at the top left of the map on the back cover and encompasses all bar 10 of the haunted sites of St. Andrews found in this book. Simply follow the reference numbers on the back cover map noting the occasional (→) marking the direction of travel when it may not be so obvious. Each reference has a page number where information for each location can be found. There is also a Map legend on p.20 with brief details of each marked location.

### The Tour

Your tour begins at the Rusacks Hotel (Ref. 1) on the Links overlooking the beautiful and challenging Old Course. Here you can enjoy a coffee or perhaps a hot toddy as you find yourself about to explore the history of St. Andrews in an unusual way. With quite a number of ghosts and hauntings in locations having never been published before, the chance is upon you to familiarise yourself with the route and its many ghosts. Before moving to the next location, it is worth reading the fictional piece from 1911 at the start of this book entitled *Seekers after a City*, to put you in a frame of mind conducive for a tour of the old town.

The halfway point for the tour after a visit to Kirkhill is an optional stop off for lunch or refreshments at the haunted New Inn in St Mary Street, which is only a 5 minute walk from the harbour. The tour then continues up the Pends Walk and concludes at the West Port Bar & Kitchen (Ref. 64-5).

## *Accessibility*

Kinburn Castle (Ref. 66) is the St. Andrews Museum and is well worth a separate visit. Although only a 5 minute walk from the centre of town it can take a while to wander around, so I have not incorporated it into the main body of the tour for this reason. Of course, you are free to roam as your fancy takes you, and this tour is a guideline to maximise a visit to its many haunted and historical locations. The Rusacks Hotel (Ref. 1) is open to non residents, so too is the Hamilton Grand's 'Hams Hame' Pub and Grill on the corner of the building (Ref. 3). The University buildings such as the King James VI Library of the St. Mary's College (Ref. 48) and those of St. Leonard's such as Queen Mary's House (Ref. 43) and Chapel (Ref. 31) generally require permission to enter. Others are private residences such as Strathtyrum House (Ref. 68); although it does have a vibrant and I have to say very popular and busy café in the grounds open to the public during the day. McIntosh Hall (Ref. 60) and Dean's Court (Ref. 36) are only open to university residents and the Principal's House (Ref. 14-15) and Castlecliffe (Ref. 16) are private university owned buildings and should be respected for being such. The Castle (Ref. 19) and Cathedral ruins (Ref. 37-42) are open to the public during the day and are run by Historic Scotland.

Location Ref. 67-75 encompasses the more outlying areas of the town's haunts (Ref. 69 and Ref. 72 being the closest). The Pipers Cave and Lady Buchan's Cave are both included on the map as a reference to their location and correspondingly to information about their hauntings in this book. They are not accessible as part of a regular tour from the Scores. To reach them requires a daylight coastal walk at 'low tide' from the Step Rock, Castle Sands or the Harbour. If venturing along to see either of these locations you should take great care. The seas around here are deceptively dangerous and the rocks are nearly always very slippery and treacherous.

If you plan on taking a ghost tour in the hours of darkness, a number of places such as the Castle, the Cathedral ruins and Kinburn Castle etc will be closed, but your enjoyment of their atmosphere as viewed from the outside will be just as pleasurable. Ghosts can appear at any time of the day or night and at any time of the year. Everyone has the ability to see ghosts, maybe now it is your time to experience something, as we all share the same space with the unusual side of a reality. I look forward to hearing from you when you do.

# Map Legend

* Private Residences

# An Introduction to the Old Grey Town

A St. Andrews Story
## Seekers after a City
1911

The following is a short fictional story by Robert L. Mackie, author also of a ghostly tale featuring Mary Queen of Scots and St. Andrews in *The Fair Woman* found in my book *A St. Andrews Mystery (2014)*. It isn't known what period he wrote this or *The Fair Woman,* only that they were both published in 1911, the same year as the appearance of Linskill's *St. Andrews Ghost Stories.*

### i

'THE wind howled about the gables, and at intervals I could hear the dull roar of the sea. My work was over for the night, but I still lingered beside the fire, for I felt as if I were trembling on the verge of some great experience. I started as a carriage rattled past my window, for who could tell, it might be no ordinary carriage, but the phantom coach of the great Cardinal's, or that other coach which drove furiously from Magus Muir with a dead man's body within it. Footsteps passed my window, halting as if one were battling with the wind, and I asked myself if they belonged to a living man; perhaps one who had walked these streets five hundred years ago had come back to gaze on "the dear city of youth and dream." Who would it be? Constantine, who did off his royalty and took on the white robes of a monk, the war-weary King Robert, or the inscrutable Mary? Or it might be Claverhouse, "the last of Scotsman," or he who was called "the Admirable," at whom all Europe wondered, or perhaps someone whose name has been forgotten, but who loved the worn old city with the love which one has for a mistress. Why should it not be as I thought; were those men who had been so lifted above change and emotion that no longing ever possessed them to walk once more under the shadow of the broken Cathedral?

It was a commonplace and foolish enough fancy, you say, but I am one who cannot see things simply, and here, at least, I have always lived a double life. All my time here I have spent among crowds of men, living their life and speaking their language, but often they are only dim far-off shapes to me, and I find myself among strangers who are closer to me than my friends, in a city which is and yet is not St. Andrews. In it there is no shattered Cathedral, but a glorious bulk rises up smooth and unbroken into the sunlight, the spire of St. Leonard's etches itself against the sky, and in the chapels of the Dominicans and the Franciscans the painted windows glow like jewels. Holy Trinity Church is again beautiful, and in St. Salvator's Chapel delicately tinted windows shine upon soft grey stone. Men walk about this city, some glittering in steel, some robed in grey; they are Franciscans, some in the Dominican black, some in the white of the Cathedral Canons, and some again in the red which yet flashes in our streets. This is the city in which I live, and these are the men with whom I converse. Sometimes I am a grey friar who has renounced the world, with music and love and all its vanities, till one day a scent of roses is blown into my face and I find myself weeping. Sometimes I am one of the builders of the Cathedral, and I labour at the hard stone until it flowers into a capital at which my fellow-workers wonder. Sometimes I am a knight, and in my battered armour I stand behind the Bruce, watching how the incense-smoke is lost in the dimness of the Cathedral roof, or I kneel and tremble as the Bread which is not bread and the Wine which is not wine is held up before the silent multitude. I have walked in the cloisters beside the Priory, I have made one of the four hundred priests who went in procession to the Cathedral when Bishop Wardlaw's University was founded, and I have marked Chastelard as he gazed on the Queen and crossed myself. You say that this is mere dreaming, and that I am losing touch with reality no, this is my true life, it is the other that is a dream.

## ii

These were my thoughts on the night when the wind whistled about the gables, and at such times the dream-city is securely built in my heart. I fancy then that if the city which others see were to be destroyed I should be moved but little, but at other times it is not so, for I see that the city un-built by man is but our own old grey town made perfect. It is walking about these streets that the image of the other city has blossomed in my heart, and I tremble, for the time seems at hand when these tangible buildings will be so altered that they can no longer be the symbols of an imperishable beauty. It will not be enough if Trinity Church is restored and the Cathedral and St. Salvator's Chapel are left; every gaunt, weatherworn mansion, every cottage with its crow-stepped gables and tiled roof helps to make our town what it is. We may tamper with them a little, a very little, but some day after a hot burst of "restoration and improvement" we shall walk the streets to find them dull and empty, and we shall know that the soul has vanished from the place. Here, for twelve hundred years, a dim light of mystery and beauty has burned who are we that we should gaily quench it?

Two buildings there are in St. Andrews on which I loved to gaze, but now I tremble and burn as I pass them. You all know them. One of them stands in a garden beside St. Salvator's Chapel, and on an April day it is good to watch the sun gleaming on the tossing lilacs, and lighting the worn old stone of the little tower with subtle shadings of gold. Men could build in the days when that stone-capped tower was fashioned, run your eyes over it, and they rest as lovingly on it as on the great spire of the College. But the garden must be dug up and the lilacs levelled with the earth, for there is no room in St. Andrews for a thing that is merely beautiful. Someone has whispered that the house itself is doomed. I believe much, but this I cannot believe, unless it be that the worthy who threw down the Chapel porch has come to life again. The other building is better known to us and better loved, for we have wandered about its tortuous stairs and moved through its panelled rooms.[iv] It is not so beautiful as it once was, for a modern architect in his wisdom has masked the expressive old stone with a facing of plaster, but I for one find it a joy to gaze at the round of the corner tower. It has its memories too, memories more to be cherished than the doubtful tradition which links it with the boy-scholar Crichton,[v] and here when we are gone down we shall come back in dreams and talk with friends half a world away, or listen as a faint sound of music and dancing feet comes borne along the twisting passages. The image in the side of the tower remained untouched at the Reformation;[vi] from its windows men watched the martyrs burning; while Queen Mary and Knox, Charles II and the traitor Sharpe, the great Montrose, Argyle his deadly enemy, and Dundee, King James' too faithful servant, have all passed underneath these walls. One would think that those who have charge over this place would not lightly touch a stone of it, but the lust of destruction is something which civilisation cannot eradicate, and the shapely old building must be destroyed. If only I could but words avail nothing.

---

[iv] Queen Mary's House

[v] Crichton was a boy genius who obtained a Batchelor of the Arts Degree aged 13, and a Master of the Arts Degree aged only 14 at St. Andrews University. He was murdered in Italy aged 22.

[vi] Referring to the mysterious face on the tower of St. Salvator's.

We are all seekers after a city which no human hand has built. As much as we can live as citizens of that state, it matters little to us whether this city does exist or ever did exist. Our duty of citizenship is no less plain. In different ways it comes, but the vision comes to all. Plato saw a city with broad white streets and austere dwelling-places and shining temples. Men moved about there, stately, with firm proud faces, who spoke graciously but not often. At times the shouts of the watchmen went about the walls, at times a music, deep and thrilling, sounded about the streets; and as one watched, the deep music, the severe beautiful buildings, the noble white-robed figure, and the blue sky of Greece above, all seemed to build themselves up into a harmony whose beauty made one tremble and feel ashamed. For Bernard of Morlaix the city was set above the clouds and built of topaz, sardonyx, amethyst, and jasper; for the dreaming Middle Age it was "the town of Sarras, the spiritual place," where weary knights bent in reverence before the mystery of the Holy Grail. But I know what my dream-city is. On one side of it is a great wall of rock broken again and again by slopes of bracken, on the other side a great stretch of sand; round it the sea is always sounding, and above it soft mists, purple and rose and golden love to float or rest. The houses are grey and worn, and behind them stretch long gardens, where all spring long the apple blossom falls like snow. The churches are unshattered, perfect prayers done into stone, and no raw new masonry affronts one as one stands in the silent quadrangles or paces the cloister by St. Salvator's Chapel. Figures move about the streets, ladies whose loveliness is such that the beholder grows faint with great joy, soldiers marching to muster at the Blue Stone, friars black and grey, and Cathedral priests all in white. I move at ease among the company, for they are my own friends in a different shape, just as the city in which they dwell is our own town made perfect.

This is the city after which I seek; and as stone by stone the St. Andrews which we see crumbles away, so much the more do I strive to build up this dream-city. I cannot build it of stone and mortar, of rich woods and curious cloths; I am but weak, and all my wealth is a handful of words. I have the will; could I but have the cunning, then the spires of that city would raise themselves up, built of my words, and all men would come and bow before my dream.'[1]

Robert L. Mackie

# The Ghost Tour

## The Rusacks Marine Hotel
### Now the Macdonald Rusacks Hotel
#### *Ghosts of St. Andrew Tour ref. 1*

With its prestigious location the Rusacks Hotel opened its doors in 1887 on the Links Road overlooking the 18th Green of the Old Course.

In 1958 between the early hours of September 13th and the 14th a small two storey building adjoining the hotel was the subject of poltergeist phenomenon witnessed by three members of a dance band. A thick leather belt, a book, a salt cellar and two scarves were thrown across the bedroom and a cup, a dish and an ink-bottle were thrown off the mantelpiece. The objects mostly seemed to fly from the free end of the building towards the hotel. The bedroom in which the incidents took place was only occupied during the season and was empty after the 14th of September when the hotel closed for the winter.

This is a case where earth tremors had been postulated as a cause, but this should be dismissed because of the nature of disturbances. Tremors can cause objects to fall from shelves etc but not fly across a room in the manner they have been experienced here.

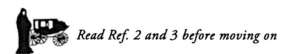

*Read Ref. 2 and 3 before moving on*

# The Ghostly Golfers of the Old Course
*Ghosts of St. Andrews Tour ref. 2*

**'Young' Tom Morris with his father 'Old' Tom Morris.**

A book on the ghosts of St. Andrews wouldn't be the same if there were no mention of the ghostly associations with the game of golf.

W. T. Linskill, author of *St. Andrews Ghost Stories* was a very keen golfer and spent many an hour playing the game on the Old Course, stretching some two miles northwards along the coast from St. Andrews. The course runs alongside the unspoilt golden shoreline of the West Sands, which is where the game was originally played before the course we know and recognise today was developed.

The above photo was taken the year of Young Tom's death in 1875.

## The Ghosts

One legend of the Old Course 'has it that a nobleman playing golf on the Old Course stopped mid-game, claiming to have seen the *Bodach Glas*,[vii] or grey haired man, which warned of impending death in his family. He died later that night. Now, to see the grey haired man playing on the course is said to be a dark omen.'[1]

There are many legends hereabouts having done their own rounds by the old Links Caddies of the Old Course. The only surprise really with 11 courses in the area, and one of those carrying the prestige of the game above all others, is perhaps their apparent lack of ghostly associations. However there are a few legends to be found. There is heard tell of a ghostly figure on the Old Course who comes to the aid of the stressed golfer by helping him look for his stray ball in the rough. The ghost is said to be that of Young Tom Morris, son of Old Tom Morris. ✝

---

[vii] Grey spectre, or dark grey man

Born in St. Andrews, Young Tom Morris was an extraordinary golfer, winning his first Open Championship aged only 17; a record that has never been beaten. Another unbroken record which he shares with his father is winning the Open Championship four times. His name was the first to be inscribed onto the famous silver claret jug and in 1868 and he also had the first recorded hole in one. W. T. Linskill knew Young Tom Morris, he was Linskill's golfing tutor and he prided that his golfing host was a championship winner.

In 1875 tragedy struck the Morris household. Tom's wife had died in labour along with their baby whilst he and his father were playing golf in North Berwick.

4 months later on the morning of Christmas Day and aged only 24 years, the heart broken Young Tom died of a heart attack in his home at 6 The Links overlooking the 18th hole of the Old Course, which had also been the home of his father.

He, along with his father are buried in the graveyard of the Cathedral ruins in the shadow of St. Rules Tower, and with them both being golfing legends, they are regularly visited by many golfers coming to the town to pay homage.

Young Tom was the greatest golfer of his age and to this day, he is still one of the all time greats. In pondering over the accolades he amassed in such a short space, I am sure each wonder at the golfing achievements he would have continued to make if his life had not been taken at such a young age. So if you lose your ball in the rough and a young golfer in Victorian attire should come to your assistance, maybe you can politely ask Young Tom for a tip so you don't end up there again!

The game of golf or *gowf* as it is known in the Scots has been played in St. Andrews in one form or another since the 15<sup>th</sup> century. In today's terms the game of golf pits nation with nation for title and trophy, but in the 15<sup>th</sup> century the bow was more important than the swing in defending the realm. So with political uncertainty James II of Scotland in 1457 recognising the importance of archery over the sport's popularity banned both golf and football through an act of the Scottish Parliament. It would be another 45 years before the game of golf would be reinstated. In 1502 a canny golfing enthusiast gave clubs and balls to James IV of Scotland whilst visiting Perth. It led to him playing the game himself in St. Andrews and to him repealing the 1457 law, but the game on the Links wouldn't be played on a Sunday – that was still reserved for archery practice. His granddaughter Mary Queen of Scots is reputed to have been the first woman to have ever played the game of golf and this was at St. Andrews. She is known in golfing circles as the 'Mother of Golf'. The 'father of Golf' is traditionally Old Tom Morris because of the advancements he made for the game we know today.

Known as the Links Course at one time it only had nine physical holes although 18 holes were played. The back nine were played using the same holes with etiquette dictating those playing out having precedence over those playing in. Not an easy arrangement, especially with so much scope to hit those playing in opposite directions! As the game grew in popularity and the course became busier, another nine holes were made, which is why to this day some share the same greens. The present layout of the Old Course was completed by Old Tom Morris in 1863, making changes to the 1<sup>st</sup> and 18<sup>th</sup> greens. His old golf shop where Young Tom Morris died is still in existence by the 18<sup>th</sup> fairway of the Old Course just along from the Rusacks Hotel, and it is still making clubs to this day.

Royal & Ancient Club House, Dunhill Cup 2013

Being the home of golf, St. Andrews is where the rules for the game are administered. Over the years the game has enticingly drawn many thousands of golfers from all over the world to play its shores and watch the numerous international championships being played out here. With this it has also attracted many celebrities. One of the latest at the time of bringing this work up to date being Bill Clinton, the former President of the United States, who came here on midsummer's day (June 21$^{st}$) 2013 for a round of golf on the Old Course. His low key visit greatly surprised a few locals and tourists milling around the first tee of the Old Course, just by the Royal and Ancient Club House. With no real security impacting the morning they easily received his autograph, along with a picture taken beside him. I remember seeing 'Charlie' Bronson wandering down Bell Street many years ago, and it wasn't uncommon to see Charlton Heston, Sean Connery, Bill Murray or Michael Douglas in the town. Maybe it will be Hollywood royalty or even the odd president who will haunt the town in the future.

## An Eye off the Ball!

Briefly while we are on the subject of the Old Course – being a golfing 'toun' and all. When I was a caddy myself for a time after leaving Madras College in St. Andrews I would be nearing the end of a round with my golfer teeing off to the 17$^{th}$. Now this is a blind hole with the fairway and flag being famously obscured by large dark green sheds on the corner of the Old Course Hotel grounds. These are used as offices for the hotel and are representative of the old railway tram sheds. The Old Course Hotel was built on the site of the original 1852 railway station in St. Andrews, which then became the goods junction when the station for the town moved near to the current bus station in 1887. The station was closed in 1969 as the final round of Beeching's merciless cuts of the UK's railway network.

On teeing off from the 17$^{th}$ tee the ball would go high into the air as it was sent (hopefully) over these symbolic railway sheds and disappear from view. With shot taken, on commencing the walk round the sheds with the hotel on the right, if it wasn't obvious to see the ball on the fairway myself and other caddies would exclaim… "oh my word, look, there it is!" pointing to the window of the hotel's restaurant. Sure enough, inset into this very large and *very* expensive plate glass window was a golf ball – complete with fake cracks, although it certainly looked the part. It must have been there for over thirty years at least for that very purpose, and it worked every time. Maybe a mean trick to play, but to look at the golfers face you would have thought he had seen a ghost alright!

Refer also to *Kinkell Castle & the Castle Golf Course*, p.191
Refer also to *Strathtyrum House*, p.205

# Hamilton Grand

*Ghosts of St. Andrews Tour ref. 3*

**Hamilton Grand with the R & A Clubhouse in the foreground**

Formerly the Grand Hotel and the Hamilton Halls of Residence, this formidable red (Dumfries) sandstone building has remarkable views overlooking the 1st Tee, the 18th Green of the Old Course, the West Sands and the sparkling North Sea. It stands as one of the most famous 'incidental' landmarks in the world, with it being seen by millions each time the Open and other Golf Championships come to St. Andrews.

A great many students stayed here over a 56 year period while it was owned by the university, so it has a place in many memories, and with this, there are a number of tales and accounts of ghostly associations within its walls. It became one of those places where the ghosts became larger than life, with the resident students over the years passing on the tales through generations of occupancy.

In September 1976 I was studying at Kilrymont School in St. Andrews around one mile from the centre of town, when we saw large flames extending 15 to 20 feet above a building, silhouetted against a clear blue sky. I found out later in the day that part of the top floor of Hamilton Hall had gone up in flames and due to its height it had taken the fire brigade many hours to bring under control. The large lead cupola, the bell shaped dome; the 'pepper pot' or the 'salt cellar' as it has been known on the roof of the building had been completely destroyed. The fire had been started by a painter's blowtorch. He had set fire to the curtains during a refurbishment of one of the rooms below the cupola. After the fire a replacement cupola was made for the building out of fibreglass, but the floor was never reopened again. The building continued as a student hall of residence on five floors instead of six, and the fire along with the empty floor was to spur even more rumours of ghostly goings on in the building than before. With students leaving and new arrivals being told the embellishments of the last to leave, stories were rife and would include tales of ghostly occupants having died in a fire. Fortunately these are rumours that remain such.

Mysterious fires or ghosts associated with fires seem to be a running theme with the myths of this and other student residences in the town. A visit to the empty – and 'out of bounds' 6th floor was certainly a creepy experience with its chard walls and general state of dilapidation. It was easy to see how it would spur or reinforce its own tales of ghosts. The building though did indeed have its ghostly residents. In the summer the building was let out as a residence for holiday makers, who reported among other disturbances, seeing an old man

looking out of the window of one of the rooms. Students had also seen the figure in the same location and all described the same figure as being an old man. There have also been reports of poltergeist activity on the 4th and 5th floor with objects moving around, unaccounted for noises such as footsteps in the corridors and areas of extreme cold to set the nerves on edge.

The building has an interesting history as it now commences a new chapter. Hamilton was built over a five year period from 1894 -1899 with the first stage being opened in 1895 by an American businessman by the name of Thomas Hamilton. He had applied for membership of the Royal & Ancient Club House in the early 1890s but his application was refused as he didn't fit with their requirements. There was a perceived snobbery about who the R&A

would admit in late Victorian times. Rumours abounded that it was his Jewish descent, or that he was American. Whatever the reason, it wasn't because he was lacking in money. Infuriated at the decision he decided to build the grandest hotel in Scotland. He built the hotel on the corner of Golf Place and the Scores, being sure to place the building as close to the Royal & Ancient Club House as he could get away with – so as to overshadow it. In this, along with the grandeur of the hotel he succeeded, once finished it also became the largest hotel in Fife. It was built on the grounds of the first golfers' club house in St. Andrews. He must have enjoyed this also as it had been known as the Union Parlour and was the original home of the R & A Golf Club. They met here between 1835 and 1854 when they then built the existing Club House.

Official meetings of the R & A between times until the new building was opened were held in one of three public houses in the town, including the Cross Keys Inn in Market Street which still exists, and the Black Bull Inn which faded from local history a long time ago. This Inn stood at 29 South Street near the corner of South Street and South Castle Street. This was a major hub for the town in the early to mid 1800s with solicitors, bankers and merchants all conducting official business on its premises. Not surprisingly it is why they would also meet here to discuss R & A business, as most of the businessmen of the town were also keen golfers.

The building Thomas Hamilton built was called the Grand Hotel. This was indeed a grand hotel, and instantly became one of the world's most luxurious hotels when it opened. It was also the first building in Scotland to have hot and cold water in all the rooms. This attracted King Edward VIII who had exclusive occupancy of the hotel during his visit to St. Andrews. As a hotel it was also home to all the top golfers, tourists and early Hollywood celebrities visiting the town of the time including Bing Crosby.

Ironically the hotel was so successful the R & A had to build another golf course to accommodate the additional influx of interest having been partially created by the success of the hotel. So they built the 'New' Course and the existing Links Course became known as the 'Old' Course.

When the Second World War broke out the hotel was requisitioned by the RAF. Then in 1949 the university bought it and turned it into a hall of residence for its student populous, renaming it Hamilton Hall. The last university occupants to stay here were in the first half of 2006 when this tired old building was then sold by the university to an American Real Estate Company for £20 million. This was a canny move by the university, selling it just before the financial bubble burst. With the ensuing global financial turmoil the building lay empty for another three years and the proposed project for time share flats never materialised.

In a state of dilapidation and of increasing worry to the townsfolk the building was then purchased in 2009 by the US billionaire bathroom company Kohler. They paid £11.5 million from the administrators of the building, with the intention of providing 26 exclusive luxury private flats, together with a bar

Hams Hame Pub and Grill

and a restaurant that would then be open to the public. The same company also own the Old Course Hotel and the Dukes Golf Course, two miles out of the town at Craigtoun.

The internal structure has undergone extensive redevelopment. Little remains internally now baring the ornate staircase, the pneumatic elevator (the original and first in Scotland) and some of the ornate plaster work from the original hotel. All else was more or less gutted and rebuilt, so only the façade primarily remains the same. The new owner Herb Kohler went the extra mile in refurbishing the building by even replacing the makeshift cupola to its original lead covering, which to his credit shows the attention to detail he has put into its subsequent redevelopment.

Whether the refurbishment will lay the disturbances to rest or increase the levels of activity remains to be seen. The new exclusive residence opened in July 2013, heady days since it was a student residence with its new golfing residents paying up to 4.3 million for an apartment.

Whoever stays here is set to enjoy the location with its outstanding views over the course and the North Sea. Once they have played a round of golf maybe as a bonus they will experience something else, something money could never buy, and witness one of the enduring ghostly residents the town is renowned for. It certainly would be a bonus for the residing golfers to see the ghost of the old man in the building peering out of a window overlooking the Old Course, especially once they realise local legend attributes the ghost to Old Tom Morris himself! ♟

# A Haunted House on the Scores
*Ghosts of St. Andrews Tour ref. 4*

### The 'Trixie Spirit!'

Just around the corner from Hamilton Grand along the Scores, and a few doors along from the Scores Hotel, a beautifully furnished house overlooking the Bow Butts and the North Sea had been the residence of an elderly American woman. She was on vacation in St. Andrews for a few months in 1988 after her husband passed away.

Whilst here she began to notice some strange things beginning to happen. Some of her personal effects would disappear and reappear days later from the living room, bathroom and her bedroom. The disturbances were slight and not at all obvious at first, but she became increasingly aware of a strong presence in the living room in the mornings. Just as she was relaxing over breakfast she would have an intense impression of something watching her.

I met her one evening in the Scores Hotel just before she was due to fly back to the States. "The rooms can become very cold, very quickly" she said "and when this happens, I know something is about to happen." She continued, "when I became used to it I would mentally try and remember what I had lying around so I would know what might have disappeared."

She was a strong headed and light hearted society woman from Dallas, and just took the incidences in her stride. She actually felt herself lucky and jovially said "a trip to your beautiful country wouldn't be the same if I didn't experience something!" Although she did joke about her "trixie spirit" as she called it, she got wise to its antics and with a slightly more serious tone to her voice, accompanied however still with a smile as if to reassure my concerns, she continued "It's a little difficult to be too fond of it though, my 'trixie spirit', disposables are one thing, my keys and cards, now I keep those very close by."

There is talk of poltergeist activity at a house in Gillespie Wynd with things disappearing and moving around. In all probability this is the place, it is in the right location and the activity sounds very similar. I have kept the exact house location quiet as the present occupants don't wish to be disturbed by potential 'ghost hunters', but the spontaneous areas of cold are still present at times – even when the sun is shining through the large windows in the morning. ⱡ

# Bow Butts

*Ghosts of St. Andrews Tour ref. 5*

## *Fairy folk on the Scores*

Just in front of Hamilton Grand and the Scores Hotel is this area known as the Bow Butts. This is a grassy area on the Scores between the Martyrs Monument and the Royal & Ancient Club House. Its main feature today is the St. Andrews bandstand where some gather to sit with their ice cream and listen to bands playing on lazy summer days.

I spoke earlier that James I in 1424 decreed it compulsory for the males over the age of 12 to practice archery, and in 1457 James II of Scotland banned the game of golf through an act of Scottish Parliament. Grierson in 1807 wrote: 'James II, ordaining that no such game should be permitted, but that *Bow-marks* should be made at every parish-church, and that whoever did not repair thither on the appointed days, and shoot at least six shots, should be fined in *twa pennyes*, to be given to those that came, to drink.'[2]

An old postcard of the Bow Butts with the bandstand
and Martyrs Monument.

Until 1457 this area of the Scores had been a stone quarry for the towns buildings, hence it's cut through shape. In the above photo this is far more pronounced than it is today with its smooth slopes. The quarry then became the Bow Butts, taking its name from the archery practice that took place here by the able bodied men of St. Andrews.

Eventually as weaponry and times changed archery became more a university sport than a compulsory requirement for the town's folk, so in 1618 a St. Andrews Archers Club was established. The first silver arrow was won in this year, with the last being won in 1751 when the club folded. This was about the time when golf became the more popular of sports, with the first golf club or society that was to eventually become the R & A Golf Club of St. Andrews (rather than the club house mentioned earlier) being established in 1754. In 1833 archery had a brief comeback and was especially popular with the ladies while their husbands played golf. It had been revived in part by the Provost Hugh Lyon Playfair who was a keen archer himself. As part of Playfair's bid to clean up the town the area was eventually given a degree of landscaping. They cleared away the rubble and covered it over with grass, making it more in-keeping with how we now see it today.

St. Andrews folklore attributes this quarter to the haunt of fairies. The area where the Martyrs Memorial now stands was once called Methven's Tower, it was also known as Fairy Knowe, and a more sinister association where it is popularly known as Witch Hill.

There is certainly a magical quality to be found hereabouts as the sun rises in the summer months over the horizon of the sea with a clear sky. The spectacular golden-blue light shines through the morning ha'ar or sea fog, enveloping the land in a haze of warmth. The sparkling of the dew highlights the bright greenery, and a glance from the early riser as the rays hit the eye, is all there is required to understand why this area is known for these traditional inhabitants of folklore. This is the one moment of the day when the appearance of their forms cast no doubt on the minds of those who see them, and to those who do, they are not noticed as being out of character on the Bow Butts of the Scores.

## The Poltergeist and the Pavilion
### Ghosts of St. Andrews Tour ref. 6

The Pavilion in St. Andrews was a small shed like building situated by the Bow Butts down the Bruce Embankment at the foot of a small concrete amphitheatre. It put on variety shows for 100 years, from the 1850s to the 1950s and was a very popular attraction in the summer months. It then underwent changes and became a tea room for quite a number of years.

In the late 1980s whilst conducting initial researches for this book I had the pleasure of meeting a local St. Andrews woman by the name of Greta Boyd. Her natural mediumistic abilities have drawn occurrences to her from an early age. The conviction behind her firsthand accounts as she relived her paranormal experiences through the retelling of them to me, was both spontaneous and detailed, and a testimony to how strange reality can really be. Greta worked in the Pavilion one summer and would often witness the aftermath of disturbances within the Pavilion.

On her arrival early in the morning when opening for business, the sight often greeting her after unlocking the door and pushing it aside was a puzzling one. "It would invariably be a real mess" she said, "cans of soft drinks would be laying all over the floor in front of the counter. It was as if they had been flung and kicked around during the night." She continued "they couldn't have fallen from the shelves and rolled to where I would find them in the morning, as they were kept on shelves behind the counter, making it impossible for them to end up on the other side of the room. There were never any signs of a break in, the locks were always intact and nothing was ever missing. Yet the Pavilion was like a small boat having been violently rocked in a storm during the night."

There are theories about the effects of earth tremors being a cause of disturbances, as I mentioned one had been put forward as a theory for the Rusacks Hotel poltergeist, and while this is true of a few known 'poltergeist type' cases, what she found when she opened the door was far too regular and violent to have been tremors.

The Pavilion was demolished in 2003, with the site being redeveloped as The Seafood Restaurant. Commanding panoramic views of the West Sands and the North Sea this is one of the most idyllic locations for a restaurant to be found anywhere. Even

The Seafood Restaurant, formerly the Pavilion

though this ghost tour has only just begun, the temptation is to definitely stop and relax here for a time. That is one of the charms of St. Andrews. The environment is so aesthetically pleasing and conducive to relaxation at every turn. This is certainly a place to come back to once you have 'bagged' a few more of those ghosts on the tour, and I have a feeling by the end of it I will have recommended half of St. Andrews for you to return to!

Refer also to Greta's experiences, p.128 & p.184

## Martyrs Monument Ghost
*Ghosts of St. Andrews Tour ref. 7*

There is a fairly sinister ghost who lingers around the Martyrs Monument area. That of a tall man dressed all in black, who, like some of the other apparitions of the town follows those who see him along the Scores. ♦

## Witch Hill and Lake
*Ghosts of St. Andrews Tour ref. 8*

The name Witch Hill comes from a time when those poor unfortunates from the late 16ᵗʰ to early 18ᵗʰ centuries were tried and convicted of supposed 'witchcraft' and were garrotted then burnt at the stake. It stands overlooking what has been known for many years on the old maps of the town as Witch Lake.

In 1856 during a tremendous storm the battering waves of the rough seas dislodged stone and sand around the cliff area of Witch Lake coving round the shore beneath the scores. With this a large number of human bones were exposed on the beach. This occurred on a number of occasions as the powerful seas eroded more of the land. It happened again in the 1980s. At the foot of the rocks is the St. Andrews Aquarium, once this was called the Sea Life Centre and before that the Step Rock Swimming Pool. The pool built in the 1903 was originally an open sea gentleman's bathing pool and eventually became a mixed pool. Amazingly this was the town's only municipal swimming pool until an indoor pool opened at the East Sands Leisure Centre in the 1980s. The Step Rock Pool was filled everyday when the tide came in with the icy waters of the North Sea, and with one glimmer of the sun through the clouds we all happily stripped off and threw ourselves at its mercy. Such were the days – a hardy bunch we were indeed!

When the Step Rock Swimming Pool was being transformed into the Sea Life Centre in the 1980s many human bones were also uncovered in a small section of hill being cut into to make way for a restaurant and bar.

Witch Lake encompassing this area is where the notion in the town comes from that the ducking of witches took place. Stories state how their arms were crossed and the thumbs and toes tied together forming a St. Andrews cross, and how they were then ducked in the lake. We have all heard that those who drowned were innocent and those who floated were guilty and were burnt accordingly. There is however, no evidence that this happened at all in St. Andrews, and the poor unfortunates who were burnt at the stake were not burnt alive. A noose was placed over the stake and their neck. They were strangled before they were burnt. The lower part of a wooden tie-post embedded in masonry was found in the 1960s, which local folklore attributed as being one of the stakes used during those gruesome executions.

There is also no evidence to suggest the quantities of bones found were the remains of those unfortunates having been tossed back into Witch Lake once the flames were out. In reality, the bones were the remains of plague victims, as this area was also known for its plague pits or mass graves in 1605.

It is also highly unlikely many, if any who were burnt at the stake knew the first thing about what they were being executed for. The granny knowing a little about herbal remedies to cure a cold was an intellectual world away from any correlation with the Devilish archetypes they were being accused of consorting with by the church. Under torture and extreme duress the inquisitor's soon extracted confessions relating more to their own theological understanding and paranoia, than to there being any tangible basis in reality of such activity ever taking place. This was nothing more than an active portrayal by the church to keep a tighter rein on its congregation by generating paranoia for anything not in-keeping with its own imposed conditions of control. It was also a way of them 'legally' ridding areas of supposed undesirables and in this they were very effective, 'accuse before you are accused' seemed to be more the order of the day. Just along the coast, some ten miles from St. Andrews, the small fishing villages of the East Neuk of Fife were particularly unforgiving. Their methods were often the most brutal and it wasn't uncommon for villagers to take the law into their own hands.

I have recorded a particularly gruesome episode in Pittenweem where a mob decided the fate of an unfortunate woman in my companion book *Ghosts of Fife*.

John Knox who you shall hear more of shortly was particularly zealous when it came to harnessing convictions. The persecutions in St. Andrews and Fife as a whole were particularly brutal and fanatical.

The ghostly form of a woman roams this area of the Scores, either wandering aimlessly over the grassy slopes or standing by the railings overlooking the sea. Linskill in relation to this in his story *Related by Captain Chester* and relayed by the same mentions 'My brother met the ghost of a horrible looking old witch, quite in the orthodox dress, on the Witch Hill above the Witch Lake. It upset him terribly at the time – made him quite ill – nerves went all to pot – would not sleep in a room by himself after that. He made me devilish angry, sir, I can tell you."

So in this same short area of the Scores we have two separate ghosts, poltergeist activity and legends of fairy folk roaming the grassy banks. **I**

### The Murray Place Ghost
*Ghosts of St. Andrews Tour ref. 9*

At the other end of a narrow lane running alongside the St. Andrews Hotel from the Scores to Murray Place, a house on the corner, above the highly popular Ziggy's Restaurant, is haunted by the ghostly form of a woman. She is dressed in what has been described as "the shabby clothing of someone very poor, living around the turn of the twentieth century."

The proprietor many years ago told me the apparition was first seen in the early 1980s by a chambermaid at the entrance to the premises. She is believed to have been a servant of the house between the late Victorian and early Edwardian period. Various members of the household have also seen her in successive years. They have witnessed the apparition in the living room, hallway and the attic of the house. At times, these areas have become characteristically very cold, even on the warmest of days. **I**

### The Crawford Arts Centre's Ghostly Girl
*Ghosts of St. Andrews Tour ref. 10*

**Crawford Arts Centre
with the roadside cottage on the right**

The Crawford Arts Centre situated at 91 North Street used to be the preparatory school of St Leonards – St Katherine's Junior School for girls, opening in 1894. In 1970, the school moved to the Sanitorium Building in the grounds of St Leonards – which is in the expansive grounds of the old Cathedral priory.

The Arts Centre itself was established in 1977 by the University and is now run as an independent charitable company.

The roadside cottage has the ghost of a girl who has been known to move furniture, cause objects to disappear and reappear sometime later. She is often accompanied by odd sweet smelling scents and out of the corner of the eye she has been seen flitting almost as a wispy shadow across the walls.

This small cottage can also be a cold place in summer as well as in winter. Always thought of as a 'benign presence' she has also been felt within the main Arts Centre building itself, and especially in the rooms to the left. She is believed to have been one of the pupils of St. Katherines Junior School many years ago.

## The Old Cinema House & the Ghost of John Knox
*Ghosts of St. Andrews Tour ref. 11*

The Cinema House in St. Andrews at 90 North Street - not to be confused with the New Picture House which is still standing, used to be alongside Muttoes Lane, running between North Street and Market Street. It stood opposite St. Salvator's Church and the Crawford Arts Centre which before then was the St. Katherines Junior School for girls.

The Cinema House was known locally as the 'Old Cinema House' distinguishing it from the 'New' Picture House built later, and was opened in December 1913. After serving St. Andrews with entertainment for 66 years it unexpectedly closed for the last time early in December 1979, partly through financial issues and partly due to the retirement of the long serving Manager Mr Jack Humphries, who had worked at the cinema for 51 years. He can be seen on the far right of the following picture, taken some 40+ years earlier.

It closed just after the cinema had a refurbishment of new plush seating, so the announcement in the *Citizen* came as a great surprise to the residents of St. Andrews, especially as attendance appears to have increased following its refurbishment.

It seems however that the cinema in general in the late 1970s was going through a crisis with attendances at an all time low, so a revitalised attendance at that stage still wasn't enough to keep the doors open. The last film to be shown at the Cinema

**The Cinema House in the 1930[3]**

House was the Buddy Holly Story – fairly appropriate in some ways.

The building was demolished in the early 1980s and the site redeveloped as residential flats called Muttoes Court. Once the cinema had been demolished

and the rubble removed, an archaeological team temporarily moved in to find what they could of the history of the site. Chelsea Wassel reported: 'A 1984 archaeological dig revealed 14th century remains including a

**Muttoes Court, site of the Cinema House**

well, a hearth and furnace, pottery, and a bronze horse pendant.'[4]

The ghostly figure of a man used to haunt this old cinema and people would feel the odd icy chill brush by them when watching a film. It was believed to have been the ghost of John Knox, the Protestant preacher who also features in this next account at the same location.

John Knox

The following story from sometime after 1894 also concerns the ghost of John Knox. Seen in the same area opposite St Katherines School – which places it outside what would in 1913 become this Cinema House. 'A lecturer many years ago spent a Sunday evening with a professor in an old house not far from the Pends.[viii] They sat engrossed in conversation so long that one o' clock sounded from the tower of Holy Trinity ere they were aware. The visitor started up, bade his friend good night, and was shown out into the silent and deserted moonlit street and sped on his homeward way, while the professor closed the door and prepared to retire. Little more than a quarter of an hour elapsed ere he was disturbed by an agitated peel at the door bell. All the other inmates being wrapped in slumber, he answered it in person.

On the doorstep stood his friend, breathless and excited. He had a strange tale to tell.

He had reached a point opposite St Katherines School in North Street without encountering anyone, when he was startled to see coming towards him a man with a stern and commanding countenance. He was garbed in a German gown, and the ministerial bands worn with it peeped out beneath a long dark beard beginning to be seemed with grey. Behind him at the distance of a few paces marched a halberdier, clad in partial armour – breast plate and steel cap. The strange visitants passed without a sound of footfall, each fixing the bewildered lecturer with their eyes. Those of the minister chilled him to the marrow, so awful was their cold and penetrating power. The lecturer instantly recognised the face and form as being that of John Knox. Andrew Lang[ix] a resident in St. Andrews at the time was greatly interested by the story, but he found the attendant man at arms puzzling. It was only later that in the course of researches into records of Reformation years, he found a statement that the reformer was accompanied for his protection by one of the City Guard.'[5]

---

[viii] Possibly Deans Court
[ix] In a footnote to this Wilkie says: 'It was said that he [Lang] kept an open mind towards manifestations of the supernatural.'

# The Mystery of the St. Salvator's Chapel Face
*Ghosts of St. Andrews Tour ref. 12*

When you next pass by St. Salvator's Chapel and College in North Street take a look at the cobbled ground directly in front of the main arched entrance, there you will see the initials PH inset into the cobbles. This marks the spot where at only 24 years of age Patrick Hamilton, a student at St. Andrews was horrifically burned to death on the 29th of February 1528 as Scotland's first martyr of the reformation, and indeed as one of the only Lutheran sympathisers in Scotland at the time.

When you look up at the wall of the tower above the arched entrance way to the quad, a face can be seen on one of the stones which local tradition believes to be that of Hamilton himself.

Patrick Hamilton

Along with being a student, Patrick Hamilton was also a young Catholic Abbot and had facilitated mass in the Cathedral. Well educated he had gone to study at the University of Paris and had graduated at the age of 17. Whilst there, he picked up new ideas being propounded by Luther and became a young Lutheran. On his return from France he continued his studies at the University in St. Andrews and in 1524 his preaching drew attention to himself. Archbishop James Beaton on hearing of Hamilton's heretical doctrines had him brought forward for questioning. He absconded to Germany for a year where he met others of like mind and on his return continued to preach. He published a book on reformed theology about the difference between Law and Gospel early in 1528. Preaching these doctrines without consent of the clergy he was once again summoned by Archbishop James Beaton.

At the Cathedral under pretence, Friar Campbell from the Blackfriars Monastery in South Street tried in earnest to find out what Hamilton's doctrines were, by it would seem, pretending to be a convert himself then attempting to make Hamilton renounce his 'heretical opinions.' The tactics he deployed were totally against his better nature, being a man of sympathy he didn't enjoy the undertaking given to him. It is also possible from what subsequently transpires that while initially his tactics may well have been under pretence, he began to believe some of what Hamilton was saying to him. On hearing Hamilton's religious views and his unshakable convictions, Archbishop James Beaton had no choice but to order that he be taken to the castle and as John Foxe writing in 1563 put it 'be confined in the most loathsome part of the prison.'[6] Basically he was slung into the infamous and dreaded Bottle Dungeon for the night hoping this would make him see 'their' sense. The following morning he was brought before Archbishop James Beaton in the Cathedral once more. Following a cursory trial, he was swiftly condemned to the stake for heresy on the 29th of February 1528. James Beaton did what he could for Hamilton, given the constraints of his own church, at least that is until he was suitably angered by Hamilton's stubbornness and refusal to renounce his newfound faith. The last thing Beaton wanted however was to see him die, you see they were related through marriage, and being only 24 years of age he would far rather have seen him renounce his beliefs than to burn at the stake. Unfortunately, by this time, the process had gone too far, and he could do nothing other than move with procedure. The whole process from trial to prosecution had been an expeditious one, unlike what was to follow. It had lasted less than a morning and the judgement was for Hamilton to be executed.

After his trial he was taken in the pouring rain from the Cathedral, along North Street to St. Salvator's Chapel. A gathering crowd saw him being chained to a stake outside the entrance of the chapel tower. Being only a young man and of the church, the town's folk initially thought all they were going to do was to scare him and turn his views once again to Catholicism. They had no idea they were going to do anything more drastic; they certainly didn't think they were going to kill him. It must be understood how new this all was to the church. While many Protestant reformers were to follow in Patrick Hamilton's terrible fate at the hands of the Catholic church of the time, he was the first one to suffer in Scotland as a martyr of the reformation.

Foxe in 1563 also writes; 'A quantity of gunpowder having been placed under his arms was first set on fire which scorched his left hand and one side of his face, but did no material injury, neither did it communicate with the fagots.'[7]

A great storm raged on this day. The high gales and torrents of freezing rain whirling around from the North Sea made the faggots placed about him wet and hard to take light. When they did eventually light, the weather soon extinguished them again. In vein, bundles of straw were thrown onto the pyre to aid in what the canons and friars acting as his executioners were trying to do – which basically was to roast him alive. With straw being of no use, the inexperienced clergy given with the task of burning him had to go for more powder and combustible matter from the Cathedral. Hamilton was conscious all the way through the process. Their inadequacies coupled with the downpour of rain throughout this gruesome episode of human history made the affair a very long and painful process for many concerned, not least for Hamilton himself. They fetched bags of gunpowder from the Cathedral three times during that day. In desperation, they hung them round Hamilton's neck to blow him up. The first faggots and bags of gunpowder they had tried to light had been at midday. It was not until some six hours later – at 6pm when he was finally reduced to ashes!

As he was slowly and painfully being scorched and burnt in stages it would appear with flame, smoke and gunpowder explosions, Grierson in 1807 wrote of his speech to the increasingly large gathering "Lord Jesus, receive my spirit! How long shall darkness overwhelm this realm? And how long wilt thou suffer the tyranny of these men?" He then addressed his inquisitor – Friar Alexander Campbell who was present at these proceedings as follows: "Wicked man, thou knowest I am no heretic, and that it is the truth of God for which I suffer; so much did thou confess to me in private. I charge thee therefore to answer before the judgement – seat of Christ."[8] This had a lasting impression on Campbell's mind for currying favour with Hamilton's beliefs with which to use as a confession against him.

Referring to the sickening event, John Howie, a writer of the 18th century wrote in 1775 describing the city where such scenes could take place as "'The Metropolis of the Kingdom of Darkness.'"[9]

Canon Alexander Alane wrote an account some thirty years after the event stating that 'Friar Alexander Campbell, an inquisitor that Hamilton converted during private conversations and a man of placid nature did not survive long after and died insane or in a state of delirium.' The ghost of Alexander Campbell in remorse for what he had done as his part in Hamiltons death still appears around the ruins of his dwelling – Blackfriars Chapel in South Street.

Refer to *The Unhappy Dominican of Blackfriars*, p.166

The initials PH on the cobbles marking the spot where he burned to death were once emblazoned in brass and are still deemed by the students of this quarter as unlucky for their exams if they are stood on.

Patrick Hamilton was a student of the University and the Student Room – an internet service for students has the following: 'According to student tradition, stepping on the PH will curse you, the consequence of which is failing your degree. On one of the blocks on St Salvator's tower, it is said there is the face of Patrick Hamilton immortalised in the stone, looking down on the PH cobbles which curses the student.

There are two ways to lift the curse. One is to run backwards, naked, 3 times around St Salvator's Quad at the change of class. The other is to participate in the May Dip.

On May the 1st every year, students gather on the beach at the East Sands to run into the North Sea at dawn to rid the curse.'[10]

Another student ceremony for the Mayday celebrations in St. Andrews is a 6am walk in their undergraduate gowns to the end of the pier, followed by the washing of the face in the dew from the grass on the hallowed hill of Kirkheugh or Kirk Hill.

The dawn undergraduate pier walk on Mayday

Like the dramatic plunge into the cold North Sea or the potentially embarrassing task of running backwards three times around the quad naked, washing the face in dew represents a way of purifying the self to bring good luck by warding off any negativity without suffering either embarrassment or catching a cold.

One of the other associations of Mayday and the PH curse comes from the tradition of sunrise on Mayday. Marking the beginning of summer (not to be confused with Mid Summer's Day marking the longest day) and so the idea of light and liberation contrasting against the darkness and oppression suffered by the student Patrick Hamilton. So if you inadvertently step on the spot where he was burnt you now know how to banish the curse set upon you by Hamilton's awful gaze!

~ 47 ~

For those lucky enough not to stand on the PH, washing the face in the Mayday morning dew is said to promote beauty - leading to love and romance.

Along with Mayday, the Pier walk takes place each Sunday after the morning service. At one time this was a major weekly event, with a great many taking to the pier. When viewed from Kirk Hill the sight to behold is like a procession of red ants marching in single file. Unfortunately not so many take part today unless it is a special occasion, or an extraordinary amount have stepped in the PH initials and fear for their forthcoming exams.

*The Identity of the Mysterious Face*

An article about the mysterious face was published in the *St. Andrews Citizen* dated August 4th 1928:

'The face has been sculptured out of the rock. One legend runs that during his prolonged agony Hamilton looked up at the tower and the form of his face by some miraculous means was impressed on the stone, and has remained there to this day. Another legend says that the face of Christ appeared on the stone to comfort Hamilton in his agony and that the stone retained the image. The simple explanation for the face is that it was a little bit of an ornamentation when the tower was built or of some person associated with the building of the tower. Or simply just decoration.'[11]

We will probably never know the origins of the face unless records of its sculpture are found. It might well be an elaborate mason's mark, which is still unlikely as there would probably have been more of them around the town, or at least of a similar elaborate ilk. The chances of it having no meaning or it just being 'ornamentation' is very slim, more so in fact than it being the miraculous impression of Hamilton in his final moments of agony which is as good an explanation as many, and more so than some.

I find it interesting when it comes to anything concerning the unknown, rather than saying "no one knows", or "I don't know?" the words 'ornamentation' and 'decoration' seem to easily spill into our vocabulary as a substitute for any additional information. Interestingly the head appears to be wearing a hat, similar to that of Patrick Hamilton in the earlier painting.

Whatever its origins the face is one of the most unusual features in the town, but it is not the only feature to be inscribed on this south facing wall.

Another oddity etched into the stone here is what is known as a Mass Sundial. These are rare to find in Scotland. They were used up to around the 1600s – but were not for telling the time like a conventional sundial, these were to mark the church services – hence the name Mass. They were generally situated on the south facing wall of the

The Mass Sundial

church, just to the right of the entrance and a few feet from the ground. This one sits on the south facing wall, just along to the right of the arched entrance on the second buttress – and is easily missed. Like so many examples, the gnomon is long gone but it is still believed to be one of the finest examples of its kind to be found.

## St. Salvator's College Ghost
*Ghosts of St. Andrews Tour ref.13*

Moving through the arched entrance to St. Salvator's, the following reference is to a ghost at St. Salvator's College that is little known and only appears to be recorded as a reference in an almost missed description about St. Salvator's from 1875. It was included as part of a quote amongst details of the college that Hay Fleming was writing about in 1897. The piece is proceeded with an earlier short description of the college he included, which I have incorporated here also as it then dates the second piece: 'Writing in 1728, William Douglass says: "The common hall and schools are vastly large; and the cloysters and private lodgings for masters and scholars have been very magnificent and convenient"; but, he adds, "the fabrick has of late become very much out of repair. "Dr J. W. Taylor, who knew it well a century later, thus describes it [1875]: "Dingy and decaying and old-world like it seemed, but it was full of interest. On its east and south sides were the ruins of the houses in which the College bread was baked, and the College beer brewed.

St. Salvator's Quad

Along the north side extended a range of barrack-like buildings, supplying in its upper stories rooms for the collegians, and from which the last occupant was driven by the nightly invasion of a ghost; and affording under the piazzas class-rooms for Greek and Logic.'[12]

For many years, the ghost of Patrick Hamilton has been reputed to roam this area of St. Salvator's. Standing in the archway, and frequenting the rooms of the buildings themselves, which may well be the same apparition mentioned in that almost illusive piece of 1875. A local St. Andrews legend has it that around the site of his execution the sounds of a crackling fire and the smell of burning flesh have also been experienced, although I have found nothing thus far to substantiate this as reported testimony beyond imagination and rumour.

The next haunted residence is the Principal's House. Leaving St. Salvator's Quad through the arch, turn right then right again down Butts Wynd. On reaching the Scores, the Principal's House is in front of you. Please remember this is a private university residence. Refer to p.60

*Ghost Tour continues on p.60*

# The Curios Tale of the Devil and the Unfortunate Student of St. Andrews

Tests and exams are some of the most stressful periods in anybody's life, coped with by most they are an accepted way of determining the advancement of our abilities. We all know there are no shortcuts to success other than the hard work we put in to get the breaks we look for. But how many of us at times wish an easier solution could be found. This next story is a ghost story, maybe it is an account. It was first told by Wodrow a great many years ago and was related also within the pages of James Wilkie's *Bygone Fife*. It involves a student at the University of St. Andrews who fell unwittingly for an easier option with his exams.

'The events in which this young man figured took place in the latter half of the seventeenth century, or in approximately the same period as that in which Sir Robert Redgauntlet died. They were written down in 1707.

The minister of the Kirk of the Holy Trinity who was a prominent member until his removal from his charge and confinement to Musselburgh and elsewhere after the Restoration, had reluctantly admitted a certain student to trials for a licence. This was a youth whose university career, it would seem, had been far from brilliant. In conformity with practice a text was given him whereon to discourse at their next meeting. The unfortunate student brooded over it by day and night, but could make nothing of it, nor could any of the friends to whom he appealed for help. Melancholy and dejected he walked alone "in a remote place" from St. Andrews – doubtless "the Muir of Fife"[x] – wondering what was to become of him, and seeing all his prospects darkened by impending failure.

Readers of Pitcairn's 'Criminal Trials', familiar with the adventures of Alisone Peirson in Byrehills and others of her sisterhood, will not be surprised to learn that as the young man paced with slow and heavy step that heathery expanse of evil repute, where witches and warlocks were wont to forgather, there overtook him a stranger "in habite like a minister," with black coat and band.[xi]

---

[x] Magus Muir, the scene of Archbishop Sharpe's murder.
[xi] This is Archbishop Sharpe, whom the presbytery were quick to claim was in league with the devil.

The stranger gentleman saluted him courteously, and inquired the cause of his melancholy. Like Steenie Steenson in similar circumstances, he told his trouble. The gentleman naturally inquired as to the text that was so puzzling. Perhaps it is well that this has not been recorded, as the story might, in later years, have led to unfounded suspicion of estimable clergymen who with greater resources preached brilliantly from it.

The minister on the moor was able to dispel the gloom which had settled upon his companion. By a singular coincidence he had in his pocket at that very moment a sermon on the difficult text. It gave him the greatest pleasure to present it to one in distress.

So generous an offer could not be refused. It was, indeed accepted with heartfelt gratitude. All the benefactor asked in return was a written promise to oblige him should such services ever be required. This was willingly given, and since ink was not available the student signed it with his blood. Where the pen was procured is not stated, but in days when the scholars of St. Andrews made their own quills and in a locality where moor-fowl were numerous, the problem presents no insoluble feature.

It is hardly necessary to say that when the Presbytery were gathered in the hour of trial, they were astounded by the brilliance of the discourse. In the words of the minister at Eastwood's correspondent, they were "pleased and amazed."

The Reverent Robert Blair,[xii] experienced beyond his brethren in the wiles of Satan, though himself protected by his sanctuary from falling a victim to the most subtle onslaught, smelt brimstone. He took the gifted student aside, and by skilful interrogation elicited the truth.

"Did you not get the whole of this discourse written and ready to your hand from one who pretended to be a Minister? …Did not you give him a written promise subscribed with your blood?"

Then with an awful gravity Mr Blair revealed to the trembling culprit the identity of the stranger with whom he had entered into a compact. "It was the Devil!"

Overcome by terror, convinced that he had sacrificed all in time and eternity, the unhappy lad was on the verge of collapse.

---

[xii] Authors note: Blair was a covenanter who opposed Sharpe, for his convictions he was banished from St. Andrews and lived out his days at his residence – Couston Castle on the banks of Otterston Loch by Dalgety Bay, which is also where he died in 1666. The loch is haunted by a woman and a baby. Refer to my *Ghosts of Fife*. (2013)

The Presbytery resolved to save him if possible. They kept him with them lest a malign fate overtake him did he venture from their midst. They completed their business, and remained at St. Andrews all night. Then on the morrow they adjourned with him to one of the most retired churches in the district. Dunino rises before the mind's eye, but the exact locality is not specified.

In that holy place the student was set among them, and each in turn wrestled for his soul in prayer: Mr Blair came last. His strenuous and fervent supplications were almost overwhelmed in a wild burst of storm that surged about the hill. It tore the branches from the trees in the den. It shook the little lonely Kirk to its foundations, rattling doors and windows and howling round the walls till those within feared lest the building should fall about them. Strange demonical laughter and shrieks of rage mingled with the blast.

Mr Blair had triumphed. The powers of evil were vanquished.

There dropped from the roof into their midst the covenant signed in blood.

The storm was instantly stilled.

What became of that paper? Had it been preserved, it had surely been not the least interesting of the treasures contained in the library at S. Mary's. Was it cast into the fire in the manse? We have no record; but we have, at least, Steenie Steenson's account of the exit of the unhallowed document which he obtained:-

"Wi that my guidsire readily agreed that the receipt should be burnt, and the Laird threw it into the chimney with his ain hand. Burn it would not for them, though; but away it flew up the lum, wi' a lang train of sparks at its tail, and a hissing noise like a squib."[13]

# The House that lacked a Bogle

The following is a lovely short fictional children's ghost story from the folklore of St. Andrews entitled 'The House that lacked a Bogle.' A light-hearted tale I found within the pages of a Scottish folklore compilation entitled 'Gaelic Ghosts' by Sorche Nic Leodhas, her real name was Leclaire G. Alger (1898-1969). The story was relayed to her by her father.

I have included it here because it is a ghost story concerning the town of St. Andrews and because it humorously typifies the profusion of the town's ghostly activities. Leclaire's father was certainly aware of this and by now I imagine also the reader of this work. St. Andrews I would like to think would not have quite the same charm if it were not for its additional inhabitants; who from time to time appear when the conditions are appropriate. To give a more technical appreciation for a moment of 'appropriate conditions,' in St. Andrews this translates to mean when one is alone and the moon is full!

'There once was a house that lacked a bogle. That would be no great thing for a house to be wanting in the ordinary way, but it happened that this house was in St. Andrews. That being a town where every one of the best houses has a ghost or a bogle, as they call it, of its own, or maybe felt the lack sorely. They were terribly ashamed when their friends talked about their bogles, seeing that they had none of their own.

The worst of it was that they had but lately come into money and had bought the house to set themselves up in the world. They never thought to ask if it had a bogle when they bought it, just taking it for granted that it had. But what good was it to be having a fine big house if there was no bogle in it? In St. Andrews anyway!

The man of the house could be reckoned a warm man with a tidy lot of money at his banker's, while his neighbour MacParlan had a hard time of it scraping enough to barely get by. But the MacParlan's had a bogle that had been in the family since the time of King Kenneth the first, and they had papers to prove it.

The woman of the house had two horses to her carriage, and Mrs MacNair had no carriage at all. But the MacNairs' had three bogles, being well supplied, and Mrs MacNair was so set up about them that it fair put one's teeth on edge to hear her going on about them and their doings.

Tammas, the son of the house, told his parents that he couldn't hold up his head when chaps talked about their bogles at his school, and he had to admit that there weren't any at his house at all.

And then there was Jeannette, the daughter of the house (her name was really Janet but she didn't like the sound of it, it being so plain). Well, she came home one day, and banged the door to, and burst into tears. And when they all asked her what was amiss, she said she'd been humiliated entirely because they hadn't a bogle, and she'd never show her face outside the house again until her papa got one for her.

Well, it all came to this. Without a bogle, they could cut no figure at all in society, for all their money.

They did what they could, of course, to set the matter right. In fact, each one of them tried in his own way, but not letting on to the others, however, lest they be disappointed if naught came of it.

The man of the house kept an eye on MacParlan's house and found out that MacParlan's bogle liked to take a stroll by night on the lead of MacParlan's roof. So one night, when all the MacParlan's had gone off somewhere away from home, he went over and called up to MacParlan's bogle. After a bit of havering, the man got down to the point. 'Do you not get terribly tired of haunting the same old place day in and day out? He asked.

'What, why would I be doing that?' the bogle asked, very much surprised.

'Och, 'twas just a thought I had,' said the man.

'You might be liking to visit elsewhere maybe?'

'That I would not,' said the bogle flatly.

'Och well,' said the man, 'should you e'er feel the need o' a change of scene, you'll find a warm welcome at my house any time and for as long as you're liking to stay.'

The bogle peered down at him over the edge of the roof.

'Thank you kindly,' said he, 'but I'll bide here wi' my own folks. So dinna expect me.' And with that he disappeared.

So there was naught for the man to do but go back home.

The woman of the house managed to get herself asked to the MacNairs' house for tea. She took with her a note to the MacNairs' bogle, telling them she was sure three of them must be a bit cramped for room, what with there being so many of them and the MacNairs' house being so small. So she invited any or all of them to come over and stay at her house, where they'd find plenty of room and every comfort provided that a bogle could ever wish.

When nobody was watching, she slipped the note down behind the wainscoting[xiii] in the MacNairs' drawing room, where she was sure the MacNairs' bogle would be finding it.

The MacNairs' bogle found it all right, and it surprised them. They didn't know exactly what to make of the note when they'd read it. But there was no doubt the woman meant it kindly, they said to each other. Being very polite bogles, they decided that she deserved the courtesy of an answer to the note, and since none of them was very much for writing, the least they could do was to send one of themselves to decline the invitation. The woman had paid them a call, so to speak. So one of them went to attend to it that same night.

The bogle met up with the woman of the house just as she was coming out of the linen press with a pile of fresh towels in her arms. The maids had left that day, being unwilling to remain in a house so inferior that it had no bogle in it. She'd have been startled out of her wits had she not been so glad to see the bogle.

'Och then!' said she, ''tis welcome you are entirely!'

'Thank ye kindly,' said the bogle.

'You'll be stopping here I hope? Questioned the woman eagerly.

'I'm sorry to be disappointing you,' said the bogle, 'but I'm not staying. I'm needed at home.'

'Och now,' said the woman, 'and could they not make do without you just for a month or two? Or happen even a fortnight?'

But she could see for herself that the bogle was not to be persuaded. In fact, none of them could accept her invitation. That's what the bogle had come to tell her. With their thanks, of course.

''Tis a sore thing,' complained the woman, 'what with all the money paid out for the house and all, that we have no bogle of our own. Now can you be telling me why?'

'I would not like to say,' said the bogle.

But the woman was sure he knew the reason, so she pressed him until at last the bogle said reluctantly, 'Well, this is the way of it. The house is too young! Losh! 'Tis not anywhere near a hundred years old yet, and there's not been time enough for anything to have happened that would bring it a bogle of its own. And forbye…' The bogle stopped talking at that point.

'Och! What more?' urged the woman.

'We-e-ell,' said the bogle slowly, 'I'd not be liking to hurt your feelings, but your family is not, so to speak, distinguished enough. Now you take the

---

[xiii] Wooden panelling

MacParlans and the MacPhersons and the MacAlisters – their families go back into the far ages. And the MacAlpines is as old as the hills and rocks and streams. As for the MacNairs,' he added proudly, 'och, well, the MacNairs *is* the MacNairs. The trouble with your family is that there is nothing of note to it. No one knows exactly where it would be belonging. There's no clan or sept o' the name. Losh! The name has not even a "Mac" at the front of it.'

'Aye,' said the woman slowly, 'I can see that fine.'

And so she could. For the truth was that they had come from Wigtown and were not a Highland family at all.

'Well,' said the bogle, 'that's the way it is. So I'll bid you good night.' And away he went like a drift of mist, leaving the poor woman of the house alone and uncomforted.

The daughter of the house had taken to her bed and spent her time there, weeping and sleeping, when she wasn't eating sweeties out of a pink satin box and reading romantic tales about lovely ladies who had adventures in castles just teeming with ghosts and handsome gentlemen in velvet suits of clothes.

So there was no one left to have a try but the son, Tammas. It must be admitted he did the best he could, even if it turned out that he was maybe a little bit too successful.

Tammas had got to the place where he kept out of the way of his friends on account of the shame that was on the family; he being young and full of pride. He only went out by night, taking long walks in lonely places all by himself.

One night he was coming back from one of these walks, and he came along a kirkyard. It was just the sort of spot that suited his gloomy thoughts, so he stopped and leaned over the wall to look at the long rows of gravestones.

'All those graves lying there,' he thought, 'with many a bogle from them stravaging[xiv] through the town and not one of them for us. 'Tis not fair on us.'

He stopped to think about the injustice of it, and then he said out loud, 'If there's a bogle amongst you all who's got no family of his own, let him just come along with me. He can bide with us and welcome.' And with a long, deep sigh he turned back up the road and started for home.

He'd not gone more than twenty paces past the end of the kirkyard, when all of a sudden he heard a fearful noise behind him. It was so eerie that it near raised the hair right off from his head. It sounded like a cat yowling and a pig squealing and a horse neighing and an ox bellowing all at one and the same time.

---

[xiv] Scots dialect – meaning to wander aimlessly.

Tammas scarcely dared turn and look, with the fright that was on him, but turn he did and he saw, 'twas a man coming towards him. He was dressed in Highland dress with kilt and sporran, jacket and plaid showing plain, and the moonlight glinting off his brooch and show buckles and off the handle of the dirk in his hose. He carried a pair of bagpipes under his arm and that was where that noise was coming from.

'Whisht, man,' called Tammas, 'leave off with the pipes now. The racket you're making's enough to wake the dead.'

'Twill do no such thing,' said the piper. 'For they're all awake already and about their business. As they should be, it being midnight.'

And he put his mouth at the pipes to give another blow.

'Och, then ye'll wake all the folks in St. Andrews,' protested Tammas. 'Give over now, that's a good lad!'

'Och nay,' said the piper soothingly. 'St. Andrews folk will pay us no heed. They're used to us. They even like us.'

By this time he had come up to Tammas where he stood in the middle of the road. Tammas took another look at him to see who the piper was. And losh, 'twas no man at all. 'Twas a bogle!'

''Tis a strangely queer thing,' said the piper sadly. 'I've been blowin' on these things all the days of my mortal life till I plain blew the life out o' my body doing it. And I've been blowing on them two or three hundred years since then, and I just cannot learn how to play a tune on them.'

'Well, go and blow somewhere else,' Tammas told him. 'Where it's lonely, with none to hear you.'

'I'd not be liking that at all,' said the piper. 'Besides, I'm coming along with you.'

'With me!' Tammas cried in alarm.

'Och eye,' said the piper, and then he added reproachfully, 'you asked me, you know. Did you not?'

'I suppose I did,' Tammas admitted reluctantly. 'But I'd no idea there'd be anyone listening.'

'Well, I was there,' the piper said, 'and I was listening. I doubt that I'm the only bogle in the place without a family of my own. So I accept the invitation, and thank ye kindly. Let's be on our way.

And off he stepped, with his kilt swinging and his arms squared just so and the pipes going at full blast.

Tammas went along with him, because there was nowhere else he could go at that hour but back to his home. When they got home, Tammas opened the door and into the house the two of them went. All the family came running to see what was up, for the pipes sounded worse indoors than out since there was less room there for the horrible noise to spread.

'There!' Tammas shouted at them all, raising his voice over the racket of the bagpipes. 'There's your bogle for you, and I hope you're all satisfied!'

And he stamped up the stairs and into his room, where he went to bed with his pillow pulled over his ears.

Strange to tell, they really were satisfied, because now they had a bogle and could hold their own when they went out into society. Quite nicely as it happened, for they had the distinction of being the only family in the town that had a piping ghost – even if he didn't know how to play the pipes.

It all turned out very well, after all. The daughter of the house married one of the sons of the MacNairs and changed her name back to Janet, her husband liking it better. And she had a 'Mac' at the front of her name at last, as well as her share of the three MacNair bogles, so she was perfectly happy.

The mother and father grew a bit deaf with age, and the piping didn't trouble them at all.

But Tammas decided he'd had all he wanted of bogles and of St. Andrews as well. So he went off to London where he made his fortune and became a real Sassenach. In time, he even got a 'Sir' before his name, which gave him a lot more pleasure than he'd ever have got from a 'Mac'.

The bogle never did learn to play the bagpipes, though he never left off trying. But nobody cared about that at all. Not even the bogle.'[14]

# The Pipers Cave, the Principal's House & Surrounding Controversies
*Ghosts of St. Andrews Tour ref. 14-15*

Just opposite Butts Wynd stands the Principal's House. Set amid its own grounds on the Scores Road between the golf courses and the ruins of St. Andrews Castle. The wonderfully elaborate Victorian mansion at 9 The Scores overlooking the North Sea is also known as University House, and has been the residency of the University Principal's here at St. Andrews for over one hundred years.

This large picturesque Scottish baronial style mansion lies almost directly above the Piper's Cave, and in 1980 the controversy over a ghost on the premises connected to the cave, was to spark a debate not about its reality, so much as a financial row that has continued to this day.

## The Pipers Cave
*Ghosts of St. Andrews Tour ref. 14*

The cave entrance is at sea level, between the St. Andrews Aquarium and the Castle. The Piper's Cave was at one time believed to travel some distance under this ancient city. With the Principal's house towering some 100 feet above, the large entrance to this cave still remains and is easily found, but the cave is only accessible at times of low tide. This whole area has suffered from many landslides over the years. Some minor and some quite dramatic. With this, there have been numerous cave-ins so it is only possible to go into this cave a few feet before hitting a wall of fallen rock.

W. T. Linskill was fascinated throughout his life by the possibility of there being a network of passages running under St. Andrews. Cathedrals when built often have a series of underground passageways carved for the easy access of monks wishing to traverse from one place to another undetected. They were also used for hiding important treaties, papers, valuable treasures, and perhaps the monks and those they wanted to protect in times of trouble. St. Andrews Linskill felt was no exception.

There is an old tale concerning Culross Monastery which the author David Beveridge wrote about in 1885, and which Linskill will have been aware of. The tale follows the same formula as Linsill's story *The Smothered Piper of the West Cliffs,* p.331. Beveridge says 'Of Culross Monastery… the usual tale is recorded of mysterious subterranean passages and communications. In one of these, a man is said to be seated on a golden chair, and has doubtless prizes of regal magnificence to present to the courageous adventurer who may succeed in penetrating to his secret retreat. The story is told of a blind piper and his dog who entered the vaults at the head of the Newgate, and was heard playing his pipes on his subterraneous march as far as the West Kirk, three quarters of a mile distant. But the gnomes or subterranean demons got hold of him, and he never again emerged to the upper air. His dog managed to effect his escape, but the faithful animal of course could tell no tales.'[15]

Linksill spent a great deal of time and energy in trying to discover entrances to such places with the hope of perhaps finding lost treasures from the old town. Hs stories teem with tales regarding them. Although there are indeed a few remaining entrances to caves around St. Andrews, the accessibility to them is now somewhat prohibited. This is due to the sheer profusion of landslides and the natural decay that befalls any un-kept location. Deemed unsafe, some have been blocked off completely by the council to prevent the unwary from venturing into their own tomb. Of the cave entrances and the onetime depths that were to a degree explored, there have never been any reports of any treasure having been found within them. If the Cathedral had manmade passageways, which it linked to a natural cave network under the town, it would now be of such an age it is hard to see how anything of substance can remain. As there appears to be no written record of subterranean passageways under the Cathedral and elsewhere for an ecclesiastical purpose, it would ironically be only by a chance landslide which typically fills in such cave's that could also expose one in the cliff face. One entrance to the caves is situated under the stage of Madras College in South Street. The entrance was bricked up a number of years ago as it was deemed far too unsafe for inquisitive school pupils (me included) and others alike to venture into.

Another may be found under the Scores Hotel just up from the Royal and Ancient Club House. I ventured down this one a few years ago. The part I ventured into appeared to have been manmade, around 7 feet in height and 6 feet wide. Its direction of travel is towards the sea. Again due to landslides it wasn't possible to go very far along this tunnel. I made it to underneath the pavement outside the front entrance. Here I was met with the long dangling roots of a large tree, hanging down with clumps of earth from the roof of the tunnel. The roots had caused a lot of the cave to fall in just beyond, so unfortunately it wasn't possible to go any further. The tunnel runs below the Golf Shop of the Hotel and out to the tree which stands just to the left and a few feet in front of the hotel entrance. It extends from the kitchen area of the hotel, so it is possible this was a smugglers tunnel from the cove of the Step Rock. Alas many landslides over the years have filled in any sign of an entrance from that direction – but with the way the land shifts in this area, it is always worth as I mentioned keeping a look for any signs of the weather revealing an opening in the cliff face. However with knowing the decay suffered by these caves, they are all far too dangerous to explore.

In a later introduction to Linskill's book *St. Andrews Ghost Stories* a piece called *Note on the Author* had the following:

'The search for Underground St. Andrews by the "howkers" was to a large extent inspired by him. He was convinced through his visits to the Catacombs of Rome and to Cathedrals and other ecclesiastical buildings on the Continent that there must be an underground passage or passages connecting St. Andrews Cathedral with the old castle or some of the former ecclesiastical buildings in the vicinity of the Cathedral. The discovery of the Subterranean Passage at the castle in 1879, when workmen were demolishing the old red-tiled cottage of the Keeper of the castle, seemed to favour the theory of the existence of Underground St. Andrews, but no further discoveries of this nature have been made.'

This last sentence is quite odd really, as it seems to suggest they were unaware of the purpose of their discovery.

At the Piper's Cave just along from here, the ghostly figure of a crouching woman has been seen around its entrance, along with the sounds of strange pipe music being carried by the wind; sometimes accompanied by the form of a piper himself, walking on part of the rock that has long since been reclaimed by the sea. A lot of the cliff face in this area has been reclaimed over the centuries, so when he is seen he appears to be walking in the air above ground level – not by the cliff face but slightly further out toward the sea. ‖

## Linskill at a glance

Linskill in his book on speaking of the Piper's Cave says: 'it has had many names among them being the "Jingling Cove," "The Jingling Man's Hole," "John's Coal Hole" and later "The Piper's Cave or Grave."' Later he introduces it as the 'West Cliff Cave' which also forms part of the title of the story *The Smothered Piper of the West Cliffs* which he devotes to the legend of the Phantom Piper.

The following short extract from Linskill's tale leads us seamlessly into the next intriguing story.

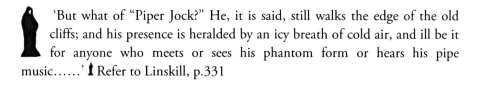

'But what of "Piper Jock?" He, it is said, still walks the edge of the old cliffs; and his presence is heralded by an icy breath of cold air, and ill be it for anyone who meets or sees his phantom form or hears his pipe music......' ¶ Refer to Linskill, p.331

## The Principal's House & Surrounding Controversies
*Ghosts of St. Andrews Tour ref.15*

In 1980, Mr J. Steven Watson, the Principal of the University and his family moved out of the Principal's House. They had lived there since he became Principal of the university some 14 years earlier in 1966, but his family had been disturbed once too often by the building being haunted. The ghostly activity even courted some national press activity at the time. The Sunday Mail ran a story about it on the 15th of June 1980.

Written by Gavin Goodwin the story commenced with the following headline:

'The Mail investigates one of the year's biggest mysteries
### THE £200,000 GHOST
Wife flees from the 'haunted'
mansion...and starts a row!

**A PHANTOM piper has driven a university head
and his family out of their home.**

But the ghost story has upset district councillors in St. Andrews, Fife. For the total cost of re-housing the family could amount to **£200,000**.

Mrs Heba Watson, wife of the Principal of St. Andrews University, fled from the town six months ago. And she refused to return until her husband found a new home.

She vowed she would never again set foot in their old house at 9 The Scores – which has been the residence of university principals for a hundred years.

*So the university leased a luxury mansion and the Watsons will stay there until a new home is built for them.*

Yesterday I spoke to Mrs Watson at the mansion – Wayside House[xv]. And she told me of her life of misery with her unwanted supernatural lodger.

"I have lived there for 14 years, but finally I could stick it no more. I went off to our cottage in London and told my husband I would never return to the house.

"I came home when I was told about this place, and frankly I have fallen in love with it. I cannot recall being so happy and at ease.

"My husband refused to believe me when I told him about the ghost.

"He told me not to be silly. But the ghost opened and closed doors and there was bagpipe music.

"There is a cave that runs directly beneath the house.

"Folklore has it that a piper had a bet with friends about playing his pipes from the depths of the cave.

"Locals were afraid of the cave because it was close to what they called the witches pool.

"They heard him playing from deep inside but suddenly the music stopped and the piper was never seen again.

"I know people will say I am letting my imagination play tricks on me, but I heard the pipe music on several occasions."

The Principal, Mr J. Steven Watson has never heard the ghost, but he told me that his wife and son Paul had both complained the house was haunted.

He added: "The house was too large for us in any case, particularly with me being away so much. It would be enough to get anyone down."

The university have now finalised plans to build a new residence for the principal – in the grounds of the house Mrs Watson says is haunted.

And the 36-room former residence will be converted into offices and classrooms.

The principal's new home will cost about £120,000 and the conversions could add another £80,000 to the bill.

And this has upset some North East Fife district councillors.

One of them, Mr James Braid, hit out: "It is scandalous to spend so much public money on a house for the Principal. We are talking about a £200,000 ghost."

Liberal councillor Derek Barrie also attacked the project.

---

[xv] 96 Hepburn Gardens

"There is a ghost story attached to most houses in St. Andrews. It is absurd that so much is to be spent to exorcise a woman's imagination," he said.' [16] ↟

*** 

Principal, Mr J. Steven Watson continued to be Principal of the university for another 6 years, living as it mentions in the above article at Wayside House for a time. A mansion designed by Sir Robert Lorimer in 1902 at 96 Hepburn Gardens. He died shortly before his planned retirement in 1986, having been a much liked Principal for 20 years.

### *The £200,000 Ghost gets richer!*

The building was converted into classes and offices and in 2001 the building became the residency for the School of Art History, where both Prince William and Kate came and studied together whilst at the University of St. Andrews, before William switched to Geography. Rather than building a new residence for the Principals, all subsequent Principals have lived here, upholding a tradition spanning back to 1891. With a lot of the building being modified the third floor was refurbished as the Principals private dwelling.

In 2009 the Art History Department requiring more space was moved to North Street and following on from the financial controversies of 1980, the mansion was reinstated back as the Principals 'official' residence - meaning they converted the building once again back to a Principals residence. This time they converted the classes and offices into reception rooms and guest accommodation at a cost of some 1.18m. With so many financial and strategic knock on effects taking place since it all started with a ghost in 1980 it is interesting to see how the ripples of an incident can accelerate over time. The piper had become an expensive catalyst for the university.

In an article for The Scotsman dated 25th of May 2010 it was stated: 'The overall cost to the university has now reached close to 4m, as the School of Art History, which had occupied the building, was forced to move to new premises. This triggered a "domino effect" due to the refurbishment of other suitable accommodation for displaced staff.' [17]

The £200,000 ghost was now getting richer! The University had gained 20 million to add to their coffers in 2004 from the sale of Hamilton Hall but like the ghost itself, the decision for the future of the building has been controversial and financially it put the hackles up the backs of many! The justification for the 'upgrading' of the new 'official' residence was in order to entertain visiting academics, dignitaries and potential sponsors of the university. They were converting it for the long term with a greater picture in mind despite its timing during a recession. A counter argument given the financial climate of the time stated how in times of austerity other buildings were available that could have served this purpose just as effectively. The article in the Scotsman continued: 'Politicians and student leaders said the university could not "afford to be out of touch with their students' lives, operating in an entirely different world" and said the spending needed to be examined.'

Following the initial sparks of the 1980 controversy, the only publicised disturbances today seem to be of this occasional financial variety connected with the mansion. The purpose it serves is back to what it was originally intended to be up until 1980 and despite the financial controversies, the building itself is certainly assured its place on the haunted map of St. Andrews.

## Castlecliffe & the Phantom Soldier
*Ghosts of St. Andrews Tour ref.16*

Castlecliffe

The area of land stretching round the Scores from the Catholic Church to the west and the castle across the cliffs toward the east with the Principal's House in the middle was once known as Sea Street, Castlegait and Swallowgate before becoming the Scores, so named from the markings of the geological strata around the base of the cliffs below. The Scores runs the length of coastline from the start of the West Sands to the Pier. The last building along the Scores toward the castle on the cliff side is the large mansion known as Castlecliffe. Dating back to 1869 the mansion has served a number of functions through its history. It was the Victorian residence of a chemist, a WWI Auxiliary Hospital, a St. Leonards girls boarding school, the Spanish department for the University and is now home to the University's School of Economics and Finance.

The full background to the story of the ghost may be found in *The StAndard*, the Universities staff magazine. In brief, when it was the Spanish Department 'a student, apparently on their way to the Head of Schools office – now the main school office – saw a soldier, dressed in uniform dating from the First World War, nonchalantly waiting outside the door. He subsequently disappeared, and had been seen by no one else in the building at the time, but has been seen by others since…' The article proposes the identity of the ghostly figure as possibly being that of John Ripley, a Corporal of the First Battalion of the Black Watch in the First World War. He had returned to St. Andrews after the war with the Victoria Cross, and 'had apparently been killed whilst cleaning the windows of Castlecliffe.' The article then goes on to say that; 'unable to deal with the notoriety he gained from being something of a local hero, he had turned to drink and had fallen from a ladder.'[18]

## Phantom Figures in Armed Conflict
### *Ghosts of St. Andrews Tour ref. 17*

'In a somewhat narrow way that emerges near the castle and probably once ended at a port,[xvi] there are (or were) houses which tales are told. A dwelling which need not be more closely identified was sometimes disturbed by the sounds of armed conflict, and shadowy figures of Highland clansman and Hanoverian troopers were seen crossing swords. The tradition is that after Culloden some of the fugitives succeeded in reaching the east coast not far from Inverness and escaped by sea. They arrived at St. Andrews, but were tracked to this house where they had found shelter, and were slain or taken prisoner after a fierce fight.'[19] It is possible the dwelling mentioned here is Castle Wynd House featured in the next article, although they have not reported any associated incidents with above account.

## Castle Wynd House
### *Ghosts of St. Andrews Tour ref. 18*

Castle Wynd House is situated midway along from the castle in North Castle Street. It was built in the 17th century and harbours the apparition of a woman seen flitting around the

---

[xvi] The port or gate was situated at the north end of Castle Street.

rooms. Described by the household as benevolent she never causes any alarm when making an appearance.

Fishing was of great importance to the early settlers of this area. This street was originally called Fishergait, with access to the harbour along the coastal route. In the 15th century its name changed to Castle Wynd and it then became North Castle Street in 1843. As relatively unassuming this street may appear to be it is one of the oldest streets in St. Andrews, with the town growing westwards from this area. In 1975, a couple and their son were disturbed by poltergeist activity. ♟

# The St. Andrews Castle Ghosts
### Ghosts of St. Andrews Tour ref. 19

Drawing by the author, 1983

## Ghosts of the Castle Ruins

With such a bloody history you might suppose the grounds of St. Andrews Castle to be overrun with ghosts. Certainly a keen eye will pick up more flitting amongst the ruins than the mind can ignore.

The possible ghosts here include James Hepburn, 4th Earl of Bothwell – the third husband of Mary Queen of Scots (p.70), George Wishart (p.73), Cardinal David Beaton (p.77), Marion Ogilvy (p.78), Archbishop John Hamilton (p.81) and a number of unidentified apparitions (p.84). ♟

The following pages comprise of a potted history of the castle directly related to each of these apparitions as a background to those often complex events leading up to their deaths, or the tragedies to have befallen them whilst alive. It focuses primarily on one of its darker periods being 1546 leading up to the reformation of 1559, which is also the time period from which most apparitions seen in the castle today originate.

All is designed hopefully with effect to give a clearer picture of why they may still linger in these iconic grounds, as a little of the historical complexities surrounding them is unravelled.

## Early History and the Ghost of James Hepburn

Known also as the Archbishops Palace the castle sits perched on a cliff top promontory overlooking the North Sea. What remains today of this building – in like manner to that of the Cathedral, gives little away of its former grandeur and importance.

The stronghold was built in the 13th century by Bishop Roger de Beaumont. It is difficult to believe today that at its height this ancient dwelling was thought to have been able to house around 1600 people within its walls, including servants, guards and guests alike, which lends an idea of the scale it must have once commanded.

The castle has been rebuilt at least four times as a result of attacks by the English and French, and incredibly it was rebuilt twice after the Scots demolished it in 1337 and 1447 to prevent its recapture, firstly by the English and latterly by the Protestants. The rebuilding of the 1337 episode was in the early 1400s by Bishop Walter Trail, who imprisoned Thomas Platter for the murder of Prior Robert De Montrose, the monk who now haunts the area of St. Rules Tower mentioned later.

The bloody past of the castle has included countless murders, executions and plots. In 1319 it was the seat of the Scottish Parliament under King Robert the Bruce. It has also been a prison, a garrison, and a residence of the Archbishops and Cardinals of Scotland including Archbishop James Beaton who died here in 1539 aged 66. James Beaton you will recall had Patrick Hamilton burnt at the stake outside St. Salvator's. It was also home to James Beaton's nephew, Cardinal David Beaton on his inauguration after his uncle's death.

Within the Sea Tower is a deep bottle shaped pantry, hollowed out of the rock it forms the shape of a large upright rounded flask or bottle and was used for the storing of food and the preservation of meat. It has also been used for the storage of valuables but this has almost been forgotten by a reputation it acquired for another use. Patrick Hamilton, Henry Forrest, George Wishart and Walter Myln[xvii] were each incarcerated in what became a most unusual and gruesome dungeon before being taken from this place and burnt at the stake for heresy. They are each commemorated at the Martyrs Memorial erected on the Scores in 1842.

Once within it was impossible to escape. Its depths are only accessible by rope thrown down its 11 foot well like neck, reaching into a larger near rounded stone cavity. When any found themselves here they knew they were about to die a most abhorrent death. Some of those unfortunates to perish here died of starvation.

### The Ghost of James Hepburn

Now known as the 'Bottle Dungeon' it still exists today and the depths of this cold stark place is now lit by electric light to highlight the confined extent to which those trapped within had to endure. The dungeon is housed in the Sea Tower and one of Linskill's stories speaks of the ghostly figure of James Hepburn, 4th Earl of Bothwell – the third husband of Mary Queen of Scots being glimpsed by Captain Chester in his story *Related by Captain Chester*, p.287 leaning against the door of the Sea Tower.

**The Kitchen Tower**

Another ghost in period costume is to be seen here momentarily looking across the bay near the Kitchen Tower of the castle, standing to the north east. He has been witnessed by those who have been on the Castle Sands in summer evenings after the castle has been closed to the public. This might be the same apparition Linskill also refers to, but being in a slightly different location, it was either this location he was meaning or he may well have been seen in both locations.[xviii]

---

[xvii] For more about Walter Myln refer to *Deans Court* p.121

[xviii] Refer to his chapter *Related by Captain Chester, p.287*. Refer also to *Two Appearances of James Hepburn, 4th Earl of Bothwell*, p.144

George Wishart was in his time the most famous Protestant preacher in Scotland and the mentor of John Knox. Cardinal David Beaton believed Wishart was also a spy for Henry VIII and had him arrested. On his capture he spent some time in the prison of Edinburgh Castle before being brought to the Archbishops Palace of St. Andrews. Following a token trial by David Beaton he was condemned and imprisoned in the Bottle Dungeon to await his fate. He followed his uncle's example with regard to burning Patrick Hamilton and carried on the zeal the Roman Catholic Church had for the violent persecution of supposed heretics. He had already condemned another heretical reformer to the Bottle Dungeon – a Friar by the name of John Roger who was murdered in the castle. Officially he seems to have 'died whilst trying to escape'. If he did try to escape it certainly wouldn't have been from the bottle dungeon, with no doors or windows it is probably the most secure of its kind.

On the 1ˢᵗ March 1546 George Wishart was taken from this living tomb to meet with his destiny.

George Wishart and a woodcut of his martyrdom
in front of the castle in 1546

'It is averred by some writers, that he prophesied in the midst of the flames, not only the approaching death of the cardinal, but the circumstances also, that should attend it. Buchanan's account is as follows: After relating the manner in which Mr. Wishart spent the morning of his execution, he proceeds thus: "A while after two executioners were sent to him by the cardinal; one of them put a black linen shirt upon him, and the other bound many bags of gun-powder to all the parts of his body. In this dress they brought him forth, and commanded him to stay in the governor's outer chamber, and at the same time they erected a wooden scaffold in the court before the castle, and made a pile of wood. The windows and balconies over against it were all hung with tapestry and silk hangings, with cushions for the cardinal and his train, to behold and take pleasure in the joyful sight, even the torture of an innocent man; thus courting the favour of the people as the author of so notable a deed. There was also a great guard of soldiers, not so much to secure the execution, as for a vain ostentation of power: and beside, brass guns were placed up and down in all convenient places of the castle. Thus, while the trumpets sounded, George was brought forth, mounted the scaffold, and was fastened with a cord to the stake, and having scarce leave to pray for the church of God, the executioners fired the wood, which immediately taking hold of the powder that was tied about him, blew it up into flame and smoke.

The governor of the castle, who stood so near that he was singed with the flame, exhorted him in a few words to be of good cheer, and ask pardon of God for his offences. To whom he replied, 'This flame occasions trouble to my body indeed, but it hath in no wise broken my spirit; but he, who now looks down so proudly upon me from yonder lofty place (pointing to the cardinal) shall ere long be as ignominiously thrown down, as now he proudly lolls in ease.' Having thus spoken, they straitened the rope which was tide about his neck, and so strangled him; his body in a few hours being consumed to ashes in the flame.'"[20]

The potential for distortions in the detail of the history from this period is high. Much depended on the particular religious fever of the author of the time as to the viewpoint they would have on the incidents they were writing about. Perhaps nothing has changed in this respect. Wishart may or may not have made what would become a traditionally eloquent martyrs speech whilst in the process of being blown up – and just before being strangled, and in this instance the side you were on would influence or shadow whether Wishart's prophesy was actually stated or not. If indeed he did say those words, it would just as easily induce others to take the initiative from his idea as it would be to fulfil itself as a prophecy.

Certainly after a hearty meal and entertaining his guests, Beaton, like an emperor waiting for the games to begin in Rome's Coliseum had got his way with the burning of Wishart. This was despite some reservation by the other prelates he had summoned to St. Andrews as to what to do with such a famous prisoner. The minds of these other prelates were more in line with limiting the potential repercussions back onto the clergy – or more the point back onto themselves than they were to questioning their own morality. A suggestion by a prelate from Glasgow was to appoint some nobleman to conduct the trial to deflect any repercussions. The cardinal however would have none of it despite a number of potential niggling legalities that may or may not have been taken care of by the time he went ahead with his trial by prosecution.

## The Ghost of George Wishart

A ghost was seen in the early 1960s standing on the road looking towards the castle. A report believed it to be a young looking John Knox, but it is far more likely to be that of George Wishart. His horror highlighted the call for a major religious change in the climate of many Scottish minds that was mirrored in various parts of Europe at the time.

**The Initials of George Wishart marking where he was burnt to death**

His extreme suffering at the hands of this catholic prelate had emblazoned his energy on the spot where he was tied to the stake, and like Patrick Hamilton, his initials are displayed on the ground where he so callously died.

Once Wishart was dead 'the cardinal was pleased with himself, imagining he had given a fatal blow to heresy.'[21] How wrong he could be, the decision to burn him created exactly the kind of fervour the other prelates had been looking to avoid, especially as Beaton already had a reputation for both lavish excess and excessive cruelty. The following is an account from Perth in 1544, some two years earlier. It was included in a Historical Gazetteer of Scotland written in 1856. I have included it here as the circumstances typify the mounting air the citizens of Scotland were developing for changes to be made in the religious and political system. Beaton had to be stopped from committing the persecutions and atrocities he was conducting across the country under the banner of his church. The following puts into perspective more of the reasons why he had to go, as well as retribution for Wishart's death it gives a contextual frame, one that would spur the common and decent folk into rebellion, and culminate in the eventual reformation:

'Perth, as to a considerable number of its citizens, early received the reformed doctrines; and suffered more severely than most places from the truculent wrath of the blood-drinking priests of Rome. That the Perthensians, and our readers, in general, may prize the respect now paid to the sacred rights of conscience, and see from how horrible a thraldom the Reformation was the means of delivering the "fair city" and Scotland at large, we must quote in full, from the historian of the town, the narrative to the leading incident of one year – the year 1544. "This was a busy year. Cardinal Bethune, in the last convention, having obtained an act in favour of the bishops and clergy, to persecute and punish heretics to death, came in January this year to Perth, with the Regent Hamilton, Earl of Arran, who was a weak man. Friar Spence accused Robert Lamb and his wife Helen Stark, William Anderson, James Ronald, James Hunter, and James Finlayson. Lamb and his wife were accused of interrupting Spence in a sermon, in which he taught that there was no salvation without intercession and prayers to the saints. They confessed the charge, declaring that it was the duty of everyone who knows the truth to bear testimony to it, and not suffer people to be abused with false doctrine, as that was. Anderson, Finlayson, and Ronald, were indicted for nailing two ram's horns to St. Francis' head, putting a cow's rump to his tail, and eating a goose on All-Hallow even. Hunter, a butcher, simple and unlearned, was charged with haunting the company of the heretics. Helen Stark was further charged with refusing to pray to the Virgin Mary when in child birth and saying that she would only pray to God in the name of Jesus Christ. They were all imprisoned in the Spey tower, being found guilty and condemned. Great intercession was made to the regent for them, who promised that they should not be hurt. The citizens, who were in a tumult, relying on a promise of Arran, dispersed and went peaceably home. The cardinal, who had the regent in his power, had taken his measures. Determined to make an example of these heretics, he brought them forth next day to the gibbet, January 25th, being St. Paul's day, and feasted his eyes from the windows of the Spey tower with their execution.[xix] The men were hanged, and Helen Stark was drowned. Robert Lamb, at the foot of the ladder, made a pathetic exhortation to the people, beseeching them to fear God, and forsake the leaven of popish abominations. Helen Stark earnestly desired to die with her husband, but her request was refused; however, they permitted her to accompany him to the place of execution. On the way, she exhorted him to constancy in the cause of Christ,

---

[xix] This is exactly as has been described when Beaton then watched the death of George Wishart at the castle some two years later.

and, as she parted with him, said, 'Husband, be glad, we have lived together many joyful days, and this day of our death we ought to esteem the most joyful of them all, for we shall have joy for ever; therefore I will not bid you goodnight, for we shall shortly meet in the kingdom of heaven.' As soon as the men were executed, the woman was taken to a pool of water hard by, where having recommended her children to the charity of her neighbours, her sucking child being taken from her breast, and given to a nurse. She was drowned, and died with great courage and comfort." This atrocious murder of excellent persons, under the pretext of serving the cause of religion, exerted a powerful influence, along with the kindred martyrdom of George Wishart and Walter Mylne at St. Andrews, to render the character and superstitions of the popish priests an object of public execration, to fan the ignited elements of ecclesiastical, doctrinal, and moral reform, and to push up to a crisis the silent but powerful process of antagonism which was at work between a large portion of the people and their cowled and ghostly oppressors.'[22]

## Retribution!

Fuelled by anger at the barbaric murder of George Wishart and amid growing tensions 'over the Cardinal's property transactions rather than by politics or religion,'[23] the Protestant reformers on the 29th May 1546 did something that would change history. Everything came to a head on this particular day. In fact the whole future of how religion was to play its course in Scotland came to a head on this day in May. Norman Leslie, Master of Rothes with four separate parties of men comprising Fifeshire Lairds went to the castle at dawn. In order to gain entry a few posed as stonemasons, others that an appointment with the Cardinal had been arranged.

After killing the Porter on the gate, and dealing with the guards, eight others gained entry, allowing the servants and some workman to leave the castle. According to John Knox, Beaton's mistress or wife Marion Ogilvy also left the castle by the privy postern (a private backdoor or gate).

Leslie and his men having secured the castle and by all accounts having done so expediently and in relative silence, went straight to Beaton's quarters and found the Cardinal was still asleep in his chamber. Hammering on his door they forced entry and despite his imploring they repeatedly stabbed and mutilated him in his bedchamber. The whole process from start to finish was swift and efficient.

Word spread quickly of what was happening, probably by the workmen and servants having been banished from the castle. Before long it is said 400 of the town's people led by Provost James Learmonth of Dairsie, a supporter of

Beaton had gathered outside the castle demanding to know what had happened to their Cardinal. Having dealt with the Catholic garrison in the castle and to stop any attempts at a rescue, they hung his naked body by an arm and a leg from the window he had been gloating from for all to see. Like a rag doll Beaton's body bloodied by his wounds now hung in the form of a human St. Andrews Cross, and with this the castle was now in the hands of the reformers.

As can be imagined, the Protestants now in charge of the castle were in no hurry to see Cardinal Beaton buried. So as some small retribution his body is believed to have been incarcerated within the Bottle Dungeon for a few months where he had himself imprisoned George Wishart and numerous others. Beaton's body was either pickled in a barrel of brine or as John Knox had stated; 'they covered his body in salt, wrapped it in lead and buried it in the Sea Tower'[24] until arrangements were eventually made for his burial. These arrangements were done in strictest secrecy by John Beaton of Kilrenny and Silverdykes lest the mob found him and desecrated it. He was taken to Kilrenny near Cellardyke and was buried at Kilrenny Kirk yard in the tomb of the Beaton's of Balfour. The tomb still exists but is now a ruin. Being such a cold place, among all its uses, the bottle dungeon had been used a number of times to preserve bodies having met their end within its walls before burial.

An ancient local folk saying from East Fife in 1546 is associated with the body of Beaton whilst interred in the Bottle Dungeon and runs as follows:

> "'Marry now, maidens,
> Maidens, marry now;
> For stickit is your Cardinal,
> And sautit like a sow."

Robert Chalmers writing an article in 1829 relating to this piece states: 'I am informed that the boys of St. Andrews, and also of other towns in the east of Fife, are in the habit of singing this stanza to an air, as they perambulate the streets in bands at night. It is evident, in my opinion, that it must have been composed in 1546, immediately after the assassination of the Cardinal, while he was still lying pickled in the dungeons of the castle.'[25]

The Reverend James Kirkton in 1817 records another version from the 17th Century:

> "'Maids be merry now,
> maids be merry now,
> For stickit is our Cardinal,
> and saltit like ane sow."[26]

### The Ghosts of Cardinal David Beaton[xx]

There are various ghostly appearances of Cardinal David Beaton, looking out of the window at the front of the castle from where he watched the execution of Wishart; and from where his body was subsequently hung. He has also been observed walking or standing in various parts of the grounds wearing his red robe and biretta.

The following is one such account of the ghost of Cardinal David Beaton published in a longer article in the National Observer dated January 7th 1893, entitled *St. Andrews Ghosts*:

Cardinal David Beaton – Murdered 1546

'Long ago on the evening of Midsummer's day three masons were sitting relaxing by the drawbridge within the castle ruins, they were waiting for a friend to arrive, after a while they heard footsteps approaching – but deliberately. 'Jocks takin his time the nicht,' said one. The steps came slowly nearer, passed the ford of the ruined stairs, and began climbing them one by one, 'I'll go and meet him,' said one, he started forward but his feet recoiled, and he stood with the rest. And turning to greet their friend, now on the last step of the staircase, they saw it was not he but a woman; for who but a woman would wear that trailing gown, that big red hat?

She approached them and they realised it was a man. He said no word and went straight by them seeming to be unconscious of their presence 'he aye looked out to sea,' said one of them afterwards. 'The face was ghastly – one set in a look of dreadful sadness. One man started sobbing.' It was now on the opposite staircase, slowly it went down. They then ran to the steps but it had gone.'[27]

---

xx Refer also to *Cardinal David Beaton and the Devil – East Sands*, p. 203

## The Ghost of a Woman – Marion Ogilvy?

The ghost of a woman has been seen here which might be Beaton's wife or mistress – Marion Ogilvy, as she also haunts Claypotts Castle across the Tay in Angus. This would fit with the following account recounted by James Wilkie in 1931. He makes no suggestion as to who she might be, but Marion Ogilvy was 80 when she died.

'A sojourner sat within the courtyard watching to the eastward the great breakers roll in and dash in spray upon the cliffs. The tide was nearing the fall and the nor easter [wind] blew strong and salt. It was the hour between one and two in the afternoon when the castle and cathedral alike are left to a stray visitor. No footfall sounded on turf or gravel, but the mortal became aware he was not alone. Over the grass in a diagonal line from the gatehouse and past the draw-well came a lady of old years "gazing straight on with calm eternal eyes. "She pressed steadily forward to the boundary rail where there is no exit. "The unspoken question formed itself "whither?" and the unspoken answer was flashed back, "it matters not to you." She passed on through the rail to where the sea broke in foam below, and turning to her left where no foot can now tread disappeared beyond the masonry.'[28]

Her exit was into the Great Hall that once stood by the Castle Sands and had finally collapsed into the sea in 1811. ⚊

## Claypotts Castle Anniversary Ghost

Situated across the Tay to the east of Dundee, there was a ferry landing site here in 1546 before the castle was built. The ghostly figure which appears on this site is the ghost of Marion Ogilvy. She makes her appearance here every 29th of May, on the anniversary of Beaton's death. Dressed all in white she is seen waving in the direction of St. Andrews Castle.

Although Claypotts Castle wasn't built at the time she is also attributed as being seen peering out of one of its windows.

The dress of the female ghost at St. Andrews Castle isn't stated but Linskill makes reference to a White Lady being seen at the castle which could be another connection with Marion. ⚊

## The Siege of 1546-47 and the Ghost of Archbishop John Hamilton

Following Beaton's death amid panic amongst the Catholic Church in Scotland they immediately succeeded him with John Hamilton, appointing him as the new Archbishop in the same year. With this he took over all of Beaton's legacies – both good and bad. It was Archbishop John Hamilton who granted the right for the people of St. Andrews to play the game of golf on the links of St. Andrews in 1552.[xxi]

With the reformers including Leslie and Knox now occupying the castle it became a centre for the Protestant cause, forming the first Protestant congregation in Scotland with John Knox preaching from within its walls. In the winter of 1546-47 the Governor of Scotland laid an unsuccessful siege to the castle for three months, during which a siege mine had been dug out of the rock to gain entry into the castle. The reformers on finding out about this, dug a successful counter mine to meet them. The work involved in this task on both sides must have been incredible. The mines were big enough for ponies to enter and fetch out the rubble. After a false attempt they were successful in meeting with the incoming mine and thwarted plans that would have otherwise blown up part of the castle.

The mine was rediscovered in 1879 and as I have mentioned earlier in *The Piper's Cave* it mistakenly bolstered Linskill's conviction that St. Andrews was festooned with subterranean passageways. He didn't know at that time what the reason and purpose of these mines were. [xxii]

Mines such as that of the castle are rare to see, the techniques used in its creation was the same as that adopted by the British soldiers in the Somme when they dug tunnels under the German defence lines to blow them up. These castle mines are open to the public and are well worth a visit. In fact many who come here are pleasantly surprised they are actually allowed in them. The mine and countermine certainly adds to the dramatic nature of the siege at the castle, the lengths the Catholics were going to in order to claim back their residence, and the lengths the protestants were going to retain it! It also gives an impression of what an underground passageway system in St. Andrews might be like, and there certainly are tunnels, passageways and caves under the town.[xxiii]

With a number of the protagonists of the Protestant reformation being contained in this building, and with it symbolising the increasing rise of the reformation stronghold in Scotland; in 1547 at the behest of King Francis II of France and in assistance to the government of Scotland, he sent a French fleet of 21 galleys headed by Leon Strozius - a priest and warrior to recapture the castle. They arrived in the Bay of St. Andrews to put pay to the Protestant's and their reformation and immediately began bombarding the castle from the sea. The mêlée lasted for 20 days and although impressive, it had little impact on

---

[xxi] Refer to *Strathtyrum House* p.205
[xxii] Refer to The Pends Gatehouse, p.120
[xxiii] Refer to *The Principal's House, the Pipers Cave & the surrounding controversies*, p.63

~ 79 ~

the castle itself. So on the 30th July 1547 they conducted a land assault. They brought 14 French canons onto the land. The artillery of the Scots Catholics also included two uncommonly large Scottish cannons nicknamed Crook-mow and Deaf-Meg which they trundled through the old cobbled and earthen streets of St. Andrews to the castle. They also placed cannon on top of both the Cathedral roof and St. Salvator's Tower to cover better vantage points. The constant bombardment of the castle that was to ensue lasted for six hours, it only stopped when heavy rain began to fall. The lairds of the Castle and the other reformers – including a few who were now struck by the 'plague' as it was put – meaning an illness, had had enough and duly surrendered. The French apprehended John Knox and the Protestant garrison at the castle, taking Knox and others as galley slaves, while others were sent to languish in French prisons.[xxiv]

After the eventual near ruin of the castle to the French, at the beginning of August 1547 Lyon writing in 1838 says; 'the governor, by the advice of the council, [took it a stage further and] demolished the castle, lest it should be a receptacle of rebels.'[29] Shortly after its near demolition Archbishop John Hamilton who was building St. Mary's College at the time just off South Street, then set about rebuilding and strengthening it as a defence against any future attacks! Despite all efforts, the Protestants some twelve years later in 1559 would again have their way, but this time not only in taking the castle once more, every catholic building in Scotland would feel the unrest of the people.

So to recap slightly; the Protestants seize the Bishops Palace, they then retake it and after destroying it further so the rebels wouldn't recapture it again, they decide to rebuild it the following year. Only to find the Protestants retaking it again anyway – and who says history is dull!

This time they took the building with ease and it was left relatively intact, but this time, the money for its upkeep wouldn't last for much longer. Following the reformation it became the residence of the Protestant Archbishops, and at one point it was occupied by the constables who were in charge of the town's security. One of its last residents was Archbishop Patrick Adamson who, suffered like a number of his time after being accused of consorting with a witch by his enemies.[xxv]

---

[xxiv] Refer also *to The Old Cinema House & the Ghost of John Knox*, p.41
[xxv] Refer to *The Knights Templar, Mary Queen of Scots and a Witch!* p.156

## The Ghost of Archbishop John Hamilton

The purported ghost of Archbishop John Hamilton has been seen in the castle grounds. For all his accomplishments with building and renovating many of the town buildings, he met his end by being hanged in 1571 beside the Mercat Cross in Stirling. He was executed through association. His nephew had assassinated James Stewart, 1st Earl of Moray from Hamilton's residence in Linlithgow. James Stewart was an illegitimate son of James V of Scotland and half brother to Mary Queen of Scots. The Earl of Moray among his darker dealings had hung his arch enemy William Stewart – a former Lord Lyon King of Arms in 1569 for crimes of necromancy. With one against the other, there was no end to the rumours and reasons for handing down judgement. No one was safe when all had enemies. The hanging of Archbishop John Hamilton was also retribution for his 'severe misjudgement' in continuing the execution of Protestants by burning Walter Myln, an 82 year old man outside Deans Court a number of years earlier.[xxvi]

Linskill in his book only gives one reference to the ghost of a Cardinal [Beaton], but it is to the ghost of Archbishop John Hamilton where he relates the story of him being seen within the castles now near derelict walls. It was related by the butler of his fictitious Lausdree Castle: 'I was in the castle one evening, and I was sitting on the parapet of the old wall when I saw a head appearing up the old broken steps on the east side of the castle that once led down to the great dining hall. I knew no one could now come up that way without a ladder from the sea beach, and when the figure got to the level ground it came right through the iron railing just as if no obstruction were there. I stared hard and watched the advancing figure. It looked like a woman. I had heard of the Cardinal's ghost, and wondered if it could be his Eminence himself. Nearer and nearer it came, and although it was a gusty evening, I noticed the flowing garments of the approaching figure were quite still and unruffled by the wind. It was like a moving statue. As it passed me slowly a few yards away, I saw they were not the robes of a Cardinal, but those of an Archbishop. I am a Churchman, and know the garments quite well. I saw all his vestments clearly, and I shall never forget the pale, ashen set face, and the thin determined mouth. Then I noticed one very very strange thing – the statuesque tall figure had a thick rope round the neck, and the end of the rope was trailing along the grass behind it, but there was no sound whatever. On it went and began to climb the stairs to the upper apartments.'[xxvii]

---

[xxvi] Refer also to *Novum Hospitium*, p.102 and to *Deans Court*, p.121
[xxvii] Refer to Linskill's *The Spectre of the Castle*, p.335

There are two main notes of interest or observations in this report. Firstly the apparition appears on the same broken piece of stairway once leading to the Great Hall as the ghost of the woman. Secondly the description of the ghost being statuesque is a very unusual but precise way of describing what has been seen, kind of reminiscent of Dr Who and the Weeping Angels. The Lairds wife at Balgonie Castle in the heart of Fife near Markinch who saw the ghost of Alexander Leslie in the Great Hall there, described him in the same way "grey like a statue". Generally ghosts appear human and are often mistaken for being physical beings. With this the only way of knowing they are a ghost is if they do something that defies the laws of physics such as ascending or descending stairs no longer in existence. Having corpse like unanimated features is quite uncommon – but they do exist as recorded anomalies on the fabric of a location, and form an aspect of paranormal criteria I call Impressionistic Ghosts.[xxviii] ✝

## End of Days for the Fortified Palace of St. Andrews

Moving back to the castles history: By the early 1600s Hamilton's reconstruction of the castle was showing major signs of decay. In 1635 the Protestant Archbishops switched from the castle to the Novum Hospitium – the 'New Inn' in the Pends. The decay of the castle this time was not through war, but through the ravages of long term neglect. This coupled with Hamilton's reconstruction which was proving to be an 'inferior structure'[30] led the castle to suffer from the same deterioration that was also taking place at the cathedral and the monasteries of the town after being abandoned following the reformation. So the castle fell this time with no bloodshed or any such attempts to repair or rebuild it. It had simply out-served its purpose. How easily these buildings can fall without the aid of canon when they no longer provide a haven of importance. Some of what remains today is Hamilton's reconstruction work. His coat of arms can be seen above the castles south gate entrance, which was one of the areas he reconstructed.

Although in a fairly ruinous state the castle was still substantial. The ruinous state we see today is partly the result of the council in 1656 decreeing that the stones of the castle be taken and used in the building of the pier and a few of the nearby buildings. A great storm had completely destroyed the original pier the year before. With a rebuilding of the pier commencing in 1656 using the stonework from the castle the new pier we see today was completed in 1668.

---

xxviii Refer to The Ghost Criteria, p.243

The decree of the council came seven years after they authorised the use of the cathedrals stones for the construction of the town's buildings.

Because of the castle's position, the sea also had a big part to play in its final destruction. Grierson in 1807 writes; 'Martine[xxix] says that in his time (1683) there were people living in St. Andrews who remembered to have seen bowls being played on the flat ground to the east and north of the castle, and that…cattle were driven between the castle and the sea.'[31] This report gives an idea of the area the castle once commanded in the seaward flanking directions and how it could house 1600 people within its walls at its height.

The rocks lying beneath are forever a reminder of how even a fortress is at the complete mercy of the tremendous North Sea tides. So much so that the cliff face has been gradually eroded by the powerful waves receding the land around the castle estate, crumbling away whole sections. The Great Hall that once entertained Kings, Queens and Great Nobles stood in that section where the sea now breaks and swirls between the Castle Sands and the Kitchen Tower. It finally crashed into the sea in 1801. The only remains today of its existence are those few haunted steps off the existing edge, leading the unwary to a perilous end.

The Great Hall until that moment was a substantial building, and its collapse was indeed another loss to the town. So much so the that Reverend James Playfair, Principle of the University of St. Andrews and the Historiographer Royal for Scotland, in recognising the potential for a lot more to fall into the sea 'obtained on a representation to the barons of the Exchequer in 1803, a grant of 211 pounds to be laid out in pointing and repairing those places of the castle most likely to give way. This was accordingly done under his direction, and will doubtless be the means of prolonging very considerably the existence of the ruin.'[32] So at least some of the historical value of the castle was preserved thanks to his early foresight and efforts. James Playfair was the father of Hugh Lyon Playfair who was to continue his father's work in the town, and as I mention shortly in the piece called *Dung Hills and Herring Guts!* p.91, he was to turn the fortunes of the town around from one of neglect and destruction to one of preservation and eventual prosperity.

Around this period a clearing amid the ruins of the castle was even being used by a tenant for the planting of tatties (potatoes). Such was the extent of its transformation, one where a residential symbol of pre-reformation decadence that many had lost their lives in fighting for or against, now had no other purpose or position than to be a simple allotment for vegetables!

---

[xxix] Archbishop Sharpe's Secretary

## *Unidentified Ghosts*

The castle houses the ghosts of a number of unidentified figures. Whilst bringing this book up to date and conducting further research into the details of Mary Queen of Scots first visit to St. Andrews, I found a post on a blog by 'Geri, the History Lady' from May 2012. As interesting is it was, I didn't find what I was looking for, but with the nature of research taking some interesting turns, at the end of her post was an account by Chris, a former student at the university about ghosts he and a few others saw in the castle ruins around 1982. The following post which is about these unidentified ghosts was dated October 2012.

'When I saw your reply this morning I added up the years since I saw this phenomenon and I couldn't believe thirty years have passed since then. I was newly matriculated at the university. I was recently turned twenty and studying ancient history for a year abroad. My newly met mates from the residence hall, all of dubious quality, and I were returning home from an evening gaudy, an impromptu pier walk, and for one of our party, a dip into the sea. He scurried back to the hall immediately claiming hypothermia since none of us would give the coat off our backs for him. Needless to say we were young and we were very merry. As you know the castle ruins are not far from the old pier, at least that is what I remember, and in passing them at midnightish we thought it a great idea to explore the environs of our new college town. Back then the only hurdle separating us from our goal of viewing the castle green was a simple spiked iron fence. In true first year reasoning, if we were sober enough to climb over the fence we were qualified to view the grounds. I remember walking out onto the green space and seeing the ruined walls all around. One of my group initially spotted something and called our attention to it. What I saw were two figures suspended in space about a foot above the ruined walls and moving towards each other. They were wearing what I would now describe as clothes possibly from the Restoration [period of Charles II, 1660 to 1685]. They met and embraced. At which time, my friends and I came to the end of our courage. We bolted from the grounds, raced back to the RH sobered and somewhat relieved to be there. We all knew and confirmed we had seen something, but being guys, we found it very hard to verbalize what we had seen. This is how and what I remember seeing, as silly as it sounds. Chris.'[33]

By the time of the restoration period much of the castle had virtually been reduced to a quarry, but enough would have remained to walk on levels not now in existence. Lovers or long lost friends? The former sounds more appealing and the seclusion of ruins have always been a favourite trysting place of lovers. ⚊

# The Castle Sands Entity
*Ghosts of St. Andrews Tour ref. 20*

The Castle Sands with the open sea bathing pool

The Castle Sands lies at the foot of the castles eastern side. This is a picturesque area with its golden sands and impressive rock strata coving round the castle and shore line. Along with the golden beach it has an old open sea tidal swimming pool within an enclosed wall which disappears with the high tide. This was a bathing pool for ladies in the 1800s so long as they could pay a sum for the privilege.

On a good day when the tide is low it is possible to walk around the coastline west from the castle to the nearby haunted 'Pipers Cave' in one direction, and eastwards along the rocks to the haunted Lady Buchan's cave toward the pier in the other.

The effects of the harsh weather beating upon this area is seen at times when the heavy rain and driving seas cause landslides of the cliff face along the entire sea front. The council have had to close the Castle Sands on a number of occasions over the years until repairs have been carried out to make the area safe again.

Along with being a vantage point for catching sightings of the ghostly form of Hepburn near the castle wall above the sands, a strange oppressing presence has been felt on the sands by the old bathing pond. Sometimes there is an inexplicable feeling of fear, especially when swimming in the pool itself, as if a great danger is about to befall those swimming around. Perhaps it is the presence of one who drowned here many years ago and they are alerting those who swim here of the dangers. A legend has it a Phantom Coach containing David Beaton careers down to the Castle Sands and into the sea. ᛏ

Refer also to *Cardinal David Beaton and the Devil,* p. 203

# The Ghost of Lady Buchan and her Cave
*Ghosts of St. Andrews Tour ref. 21*

View from the castle sands round to the pier, with the cave midway. The ghost of Lady Buchan wanders this stretch and the scent of her perfume pervades the air.

Lady Buchan was an 18th century local St. Andrews lady who refurbished the cave and held tea parties there.

The ghost of Lady Buchan haunts the area between the Haunted Tower and the castle. She has been seen on the Kirkhill pathway between the castle and it's merging with the path from Gregory Place, and especially along the rocky shore front highlighted in the photo above. Wearing white, she has been mistaken for being the White Lady of the Haunted Tower – especially by Linskill. †

The cave of her name is now blocked off. The site of it is only accessible at low tide and during daylight hours either from the castle sands or round the pier towards the castle. Also known as St. Rules Cave, this is where St. Rule is believed to have stayed for 6 months when he first arrived at the site of St. Andrews with the relics of St. Andrew himself. Along with St. Rules Tower, this cave was a venerated site of pilgrimage for many thousands coming to the town each year.

Further information can be found in my book *A St. Andrews Mystery*. (2014)

## The Mysterious Head on the Scores
*Ghosts of St. Andrews Tour ref. 22*

The following is a very short and entertaining article written by W. T. Linskill for the *St. Andrews Citizen* in November 1928. The short tale typifies Linskill's imagination – or does it? As exuberant as he is in embellishing most of what he puts to print he has on many occasions startled the reader with more than a hint of truth. It has a habit of peering tentatively at you from behind his often humorous fiction, laced with a liberal coating of his gentlemanly Victoria manner. The following is much like a great deal of the information in this book, which has either never seen the light of day in the case of the firsthand accounts, or never seen the light of day since the material was originally published many years ago. The article is only a few lines; these can so easily be lost and forgotten so there is a value here. The above title is also the title of the article. The location of the article is by the haunted tower along part of the east side of the Scores, but it is not related to the apparitions roaming that exposed rocky outpost of the town with a melancholic fervour. So it is more appropriate to place it here where it can remain relatively undisturbed:

'It was brought back to my mind the other day. Someone roaming along the Scores between the gloaming[xxx] and the mirk[xxxi] sighted lying near the Haunted Tower what they thought was a big turnip. This person picked the object up with both hands, when it revolved in his grasp, and there gazing up was a human skull, with gleaming lights in the cavernous depths of the eye sockets. Needless to say, such an unexpected object was speedily dropped – and the finder fled! Sculls with incandescent red eyes are no canny.'[34]

## The Kirkhill Green Lady
*Ghosts of St. Andrews Tour ref. 23*

There is a ghost who roams Kirkhill or Kirkheugh as it was once known. This is a very special ghost, seen by a woman studying at the university in 1988 and related to me shortly after. It was given to me during my researches for these books and this disclosure is its first time in print. The ghost further confirms the tales having caused fear to build over many years in the hearts of so many locals of the town venturing past this area after nightfall. It is of a green lady on account of her wearing a long green dress. The fascinating account in full can be read in my book *A St. Andrews Mystery* (2014).

---

[xxx] Twilight or dust
[xxxi] Darkness

# The New Inn

Official halfway stop on the self guided Ghosts of St. Andrews Tour

*The Tour Continues p.99. Ref. 24*

 If you fancy a short break and a refreshment stop before continuing with your tour along the haunted stretch of road known as the Pends, this is the place to do it. The New Inn is haunted and is well worth a visit for the few minutes it takes to walk to the Inn from the Kirkhill and Harbour. They serve food and drinks. They have accommodation, children are welcome and they also have a resident ghost!

## Directions:

From Kirkhill turn right and follow the harbour road to the end, then left onto St. Mary Street. You will see the Inn 100 yards on the same side.

The New Inn is a three star Inn and public house named after the former haunted New Inn in the Pends. Run by local proprietors John Marini and Heidi Orr, a more welcoming environment would be hard to find.

John and Heidi have had this Inn for a number of years now and are fairly used to the paranormal activity taking place here. As John says, "whatever it is, it is looking to cause the most disruption it can." Among the disturbances the taps for the gas and the beer in the cellar are frequently turned off. The only way to get to the cellar is through a hatch in the floor behind the bar, so they know that no one is down there when it happens. ❦

John Marini on the right with the current author

I have known John now for around 36 years. We were best friends at Kilrymont School in St. Andrews and this was the first time I had seen him since a school reunion 13 years ago. He is down to earth, sincere and wouldn't talk of ghosts if they were unfounded. If another explanation could be found, John would have found one… but there are certainly ghosts at The New Inn. Whilst I was visiting John and we were talking about the disturbances, the barmaid called over to him that one of the taps to the beer lines had been switched off – "again". I went down with John to the cellar just after it had happened.

John pointing to the tap of the beer line in the cellar that had just been switched off

John explained "There are taps for the gas bottles and taps for the beer lines. It isn't possible for them to switch off by themselves." He continued "it takes physical pressure to turn them, but they can be turned off sometimes a few times a day." A few seconds after I took this photo of John he was changing a gas bottle when a full bottle fell on his foot, he is a hardy soul and put a brave face on it but the pain must have been quite extreme.

Often when John is in the kitchen, he has a hard job of lighting the industrial gas cooker. John said, "There is nothing wrong with the flow of gas but it just won't light. So I say to whatever it is 'I am too busy today, leave me alone – thank you!' Once I have said this, the cooker always lights straight away."

In the bay room upstairs, John, Heidi and the staff would hear the television in the room blaring away with the volume on full blast – this is when no one is in the room and the door is locked. So they are forever going into the room to turn the TV off. There is also a presence in the room – a resident ghost.

Whilst I was at the pub I was told about a local chap, Colin Henderson who around 20 years ago for a bet had slept in the cathedral ruins for the night. The next morning a few of his friends went to the ruins to find him, but all they could find was his sleeping bag covered in blood. This got them very worried. They eventually found him and he had been to the nearby cottage hospital. During the night he was so scared that at one point he felt something crawling up his chest. When it reached his face he bit hard on whatever it was.

It had been his own hand crawling up his chest and he had bitten his finger off! Apologies Colin, it shouldn't really be humorous but the retelling of it was hilarious.

There are three kinds of spirit here, the ghost, the whisky, and the real sense of community spirit. The latter two I am sure are the ones everyone prefers.

Although my visit was brief I had a great time, with you all and look forward to seeing you all again. My thanks to John and the locals of the New Inn for their hospitality. The Inn has a great environment and this is a great place to stop off for refreshments before continuing your tour.

While you are here it is worth taking time to read the article on the following page I have written entitled *Dunghills and Herring Guts!* It has nothing to do with the Inn I might add, I have placed it here to give a brief and hopefully fascinating background to the old town of St. Andrews and how close it came to desolation up to as recently as the early 1800s. It gives an eye opening perspective to the increasing problems of the town in the years following the reformation of 1559, and with this an additional insight into the turmoil's having contributed to the appearance of so many spectres over the years.

If you are in the New Inn, just backtrack along the harbour to the large stone archway on the left. This marks the beginning of the Pends from the Harbour to South Street. After passing through the archway the Pends walk looms. The tour continues on p.99 with *The Angel and a Supernatural Entity*. Ref. 24

# Dunghills and Herring Guts!
### *The ruins where ghosts doth tread*

It is important to give a brief historical background of the town as a contextual framework for the many ghosts who now roam these ancient precincts, and who in their own time shaped the fabric of the town we recognise today.

Ghosts can be both the historical imprints of a bygone age and the spirits of the past locked as a legacy into distant events. Seen in the present as anomalous impressions they are cast upon the fabric of wherever we choose to roam as we wander the old town of St. Andrews.

Whenever I speak of the ruined Cathedral or the castle of St. Andrews I am always reminded of the odd tourist, who in not being aware of the fate suffered by the ruinous buildings, exclaims on seeing such devastation; "what a pity they were bombed during the war!"

Although a few residential buildings in St. Andrews sustained direct hits in the 1940s with a number of fatalities, these historical edifices weren't touched by the German forces. The castle was certainly bombed on a number of occasions by the English, the French, incredibly once by the Scots in 1337 to prevent its recapture by the English, and as I mentioned in the section above regarding the castle, this was a tactic the Roman Catholic Church in Scotland would replicate some 200 years later in 1547 to prevent its recapture by the Protestants.

The history of this period around the reformation of the mid 16th century in St. Andrews was complex, with events changing extremely rapidly. In many ways they are difficult to keep up with or fathom. There is so much we know and so much more we don't as we grapple with existing historical records, complete with all the religious, political and romantic fabrications and associations of their age. Finding records that were actually recorded at the time they speak of becomes an increasingly rare commodity the further back in time we go. Even accounts written thirty years after an event is enough to suitably distort the picture of the day they were speaking of.

Whatever took place in St. Andrews was almost guaranteed to create waves across Scotland and beyond. There are a number of ruins in St. Andrews and along with their ghosts they all have important histories to be discovered. To understand what happened to the Cathedral and other ecclesiastical buildings in the town we need to go back to a crucial period in St. Andrews history, when the reasoning of God through the Catholic and emerging Protestant faiths collided as opposing corridors of power looking to crush the opposing ideologies of the day, and the Devil was always on the side of the enemy.

John Knox once free from the trappings of the French Fleet having captured him following the siege of the castle in 1547 travelled to England, Germany and Switzerland before returning to his native country once more. On his travels he made quite an impact preaching Lutheran ideas. In 1559, some twelve years after his capture he preached in Perth, bringing about the ideas for the revolt against idolatrous images of the Catholic Faith. After another rousing sermon preached in the Holy Trinity Church in South Street, the wellbeing of the citizens swung between persecution and liberation, depending if you were of the new Protestant movement or the Old Catholic faith – for this was the time of the Reformation. This affected all in its path as many lost their lives or livelihoods through conviction and belief, while others profited from the same. The bloody games man played were long fought out battles for power as they used conviction to brandish their own brand of justice. 'Led by the Provost and magistrates, the inhabitants, in June 1559, removed all the "monuments of idolatrie" from the churches, and burned the "idols" of the Cathedral on the site of Walter Myln's martyrdom.'[35] These 'inhabitants' included the influential landowner Norman Leslie and his men – who had already killed Beaton at the castle and sparked the upheaval of the Scottish reformation with a switch from words to action.

They also ransacked the other Catholic buildings in the town including the Kirk Hill Chapel, Blackfriars Monastery in South Street, and Greyfriars Monastery – at that time situated just outside the town at the end of Market Street. Accounts have it that of the 51 Bishops or Archbishops to have been previously buried in the Cathedral – many of which had expensive monuments erected to them in the Cathedral, there were also 200 plus canons of the priory who were known to have also been buried here over the years, the graves of only three canons were found to remain intact.[xxxii] This was the same across Scotland. Wherever Knox went 'Monasteries and cathedrals were certain to perish sooner or later, for the lead of every such roof except Coldingham had been stripped and sold by 1585, while tombs had been desecrated for their poor spoils, and the fanes were afterwards used as quarries of hewn stone.'[36]

We could well think the reformers had done a good job in destroying everything in their path and believe such was the discriminatory extent of the destruction served by them. The destruction was greatly accelerated with the lead from the roofs being taken. The resultant decay of the buildings was then inevitable. The historian Lyon in 1838 goes one stage further however by saying 'when the Protestant party, which had then assumed the reins of government, [1560-1561] issued an order "for demolishing cloisters and abbey churches, such as were not yet pulled down," in all probability it [the Cathedral] would be reduced nearly to the condition in which we now see it.'[37]

In contrast and closer the mark we have the historian Hay Fleming in 1898 giving a different picture 'there is not a single scrap of contemporary evidence to prove that the Cathedral was demolished at the Reformation. The ablest historians now acknowledge this, yet the old fable is repeated and perpetuated by the tongues and pens of those who are either too prejudiced to receive the truth, or too indolent to inquire into it. A careful inspection of the ruins not only reveals the fact that this Cathedral had shown signs of weakness; but that means had been taken to strengthen the great central tower, and that buttresses had been erected to stiffen the north wall.'[38]

Fleming then goes on to recount 'As Carlyle has said, "Knox wanted no pulling down of stone edifices; he wanted leprosy and darkness to be thrown out of the lives of men."'[39] It is true that wherever Knox preached destruction would shortly follow, although as Fleming continues 'the real cause of destruction was neglect, not violence.[xxxiii] Had there not been such a large parish church in St Andrews [The Holy Trinity], the Cathedral might have been carefully preserved; but, as it was not required, it was allowed to decay. People who have kept their eyes open must have been struck by the rapidity with which a building goes to ruin after the roof fails. The absence of a few slates, or tiles, permits the rain to enter, the woodwork rots and speedily collapses, frost soon rends the soaking walls, and renders them an easy prey to the howling

---

[xxxii] Refer to Lyon: *History of St. Andrews*, 1838, p.193
[xxxiii] Refer to St. Andrews Castle Ghosts; *The End of Days for the Fortified Palace of St. Andrews*, p.82

tempest. In the case of the Cathedral, the lead was probably stolen from the roof — secretly or openly — and the destruction would be hastened by the heavy groined roofs over the chancel and side-aisles, and the weakness of the central tower and north wall.'[40]

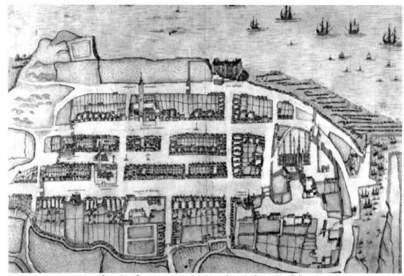

St. Andrews circa 1580 by John Geddy,
shortly before the central tower of the Cathedral collapsed.

A few years later, in the latter part of the 16th century the rapid neglect of the building had taken its toll, the main central tower of the Cathedral with a height of some 200 feet came crashing down and took with it the north wall of the Cathedral building. The Cathedral was now itself in a semi ruinous state. The south transept of the Cathedral had already been blown down by a storm in 1409. 'A strong wind struck down the south gable of the transept, crushing by the fall of great stones the dormitory and 'under chapter-house' and had to be rebuilt.'[41] The job of the weather had been made all the easier as some of the stones being used in its construction were of a poor quality. This becomes somewhat of a running theme with not just this building but with many of the ancient buildings of old St. Andrews including the castle, and gives an idea of how fragile this immense structure was, and how fragile the existing remains still are today.

In the 1650s following a visit by Charles II and the great storm of 1655 which had destroyed the pier; 'the importance of the town rapidly diminished, and its affairs had become so bad by 1655, that in that year the council humbly represented to General Monk, Commander-in-chief in Scotland, that in consequence of the total failure of trade the town was utterly unable to pay the assessment of £43 imposed by him.'[42] This was partly because of the collapse of the pier which had been 'constructed of wooden branders, with great stones inlaid.'[43] 'Rebuilding work from the ruins of the existing buildings was common place in the town. In 1649, Parliament authorised the Town Council to use all the stones of the decayed buildings, walls, and dykes of the Abbey in fortifying the Town. The destruction at that time may have been enormous; but it was a ruin before that.'[44] In 1668 the pier was reconstructed in this way from the stonework of the castle.

'From this time [1697] its deserted condition became still worse.'[45] the process of decay had become so bad that a proposal was made to remove the university to Perth, some of the reasons given by a professor of the university in this year being that the 'place being *now only a village,* where for the most part farmers dwell, *the whole streets are filled with dunghills,* which are exceedingly noisome and ready to infect the air, especially at this season (September) when the herring guts are exposed in them, or rather in all corners of the town by themselves; and the season of the year apt to breed infection, which partly may be said to have been the occasion of last year's dysentery, and which from its *beginning here, raged through most part of the kingdom.'[46]

So an unhappy picture is portrayed at this time of St. Andrews, one we would barely recognise from the description alone as being the town we know and love today and it was all further compounded by the unfortunate state of the Cathedral. Being once the symbolic seat of the Catholic Church in Scotland and the location for the pilgrimages of so many thousands over the centuries, parts of what was left of its structure were becoming very dangerous. Aside the remains we see today, both the western pinnacles that stood between the entrance archway to the Cathedral were still standing at this time. Today however, only one pinnacle along with the entrance arch survives. Of the other pinnacle John Geddie in 1894 relates 'it was reported in the 17th century that one of the western pinnacles of the Cathedral fell, narrowly missing a funeral party that had just entered through the gateway.'[47]

Thomas Pennant, an early travel writer and antiquarian, on visiting St. Andrews in the 1760s was quite shocked when he saw what John Knox and his reformers had done to the town. Writing about it in his *Tour through Scotland* in 1769 he says: 'A foreigner, ignorant of the history of this country, would naturally inquire, what calamity has this city undergone? Has it suffered a bombardment from some barbarous enemy? Has it, like Lisbon, felt the more inevitable fury of an earthquake? But how great is his horror in reflecting that this destruction was owing to the more barbarous zeal of a minister, who, by his discourses, first inflamed, and then permitted, a furious crowd to overthrow edifices dedicated to that being he pretended to honour by their ruin?'[48]

It must be remembered that while the destruction of the buildings were due to the elements, their ultimate decay was due to the neglect caused by the ousting of those who valued them most. So while Knox didn't want any buildings pulled down, with no physical intervention his ideology was all it took to seal their fate from stature to ruin.

The English writer Dr Samuel Johnson in his letters about his visit to St. Andrews in 1773 said: 'the city of St. Andrews, when it lost its archiepiscopal pre-eminence, gradually decayed: one of its streets is now lost; and in those that remain, there is the silence and solitude of inactive indigence, and gloomy depopulation.'[49] The street that was lost might have been the Pends, which was reconstructed in the early 1800s, being surrounded by priory and Cathedral ruins it would barely have been accessible.

Interestingly during all this an attempt had been made to preserve and improve the ruins of St. Regulus Tower even when the surrounding grounds were either falling down or covered with great mounds of cathedral rubble. Lyon writes: 'This beautiful specimen of ancient architecture has lately (1789) been repaired at the expense of the Exchequer, and a winding stair built from the bottom to the top, which is covered with lead, with a parapet of some feet in height.'[50] This is a reference to a steep stone spiralling stair which runs the length of the tower baring the bottom which had been made of wood, before this access to the top of the tower had been by a series of ladders between wooden floors. Its replacement may have been partly in recognition of the significance of the 11th century church which housed the relics of St. Andrew and gave the town its name. With all the stone rubble the stone stairs would probably have been constructed from these cathedral ruins themselves.

'Unhappily, the example thus shown of utilising it [the cathedral] as a quarry [in 1649] was long followed by the citizens, who freely took the stones, once deemed sacred, to erect the humblest edifices.'[51] This was a reference to 1801 when the council officially backed the town's folk to make use of not only the Cathedral but also the castle and the priory as quarries for the rebuilding of dwellings. Many, if not the majority up until then had lived in poor quality timber homes. With this they were able to replace their dwellings with that of stone. Many dwellings of the town and stone edifices we see today were constructed from these make shift quarries.

Other buildings had come from the ruins of Blackfriars and Greyfriars, and of the latter, the only remaining feature is part of its boundary wall and a haunted well in what is now Greyfriars Gardens.

By the early 19th century after so many years of abandonment by the towns former wealthy sponsors, 'the stone and rubbish [that was still left following the rebuilding of nearby buildings and the pier] produced by the demolition of the Cathedral lay where they fell till so recently as the year 1826, when they were then removed by order of the Exchequer, and the floor and the bases of the columns laid open. On this occasion, three stone coffins were discovered projecting from under the stone floor of the high altar. They still remain as they were found, excepting that the bones which they contained were taken out of them and buried.'[52] These were the three mentioned earlier as being the only ones found out of over 250 entombed within its walls.

The Haunted Tower in Hepburns wall

Whilst removing loose stones from one of the towers, workmen noticed something that was to spark an enduring St. Andrews mystery. As well as being different in design to the others, this particular tower had at some point been hermetically sealed. A great deal of interest arose that lasts to this day, with talk of a ghostly White Lady and plenty of speculation as to what lay beyond the

South Street in the 1840s facing North-West towards the West Port. Notice the amount of rubble in the street.

sealed entrance to this somewhat 'odd' tower, which shall be explored further shortly.

With St. Andrews by 1830 becoming little more than a village due to the destruction, neglect and the general level of abandonment, the town was left 'with only the spacious streets and fine ruins to serve as marks of its former grandeur… It was then quite neglected by tourists, and deemed too secluded and bleak to be thought of as a watering-place.'[53] The easiest way to get to St. Andrews had been by boat.

**Sir Hugh Lyon Playfair (1786-1861)**

The state of the town had become untenable and all was very nearly lost, had it not been for the primary work of an individual whose father had already preserved the castle. So it was then that St. Andrews 'was revived by the vigorous exertions of Sir Hugh Lyon Playfair'[54] who became the Provost of the town. A leading political figure he changed the fortunes of St. Andrews from one of decimation and dereliction, to that of consolidation and preservation.

St. Andrews had been saved from the dunghills and the herring guts! With his efforts the history of the town was preserved, and it soon became a pleasant and thriving place to live and do business. With a reputation for being the home of golf, having the third oldest university in the world (oldest in Scotland) and becoming a bastion for tourism by 1855, there was such a change. So much so that on 'the 1st of January of that year Provost Playfair was able to tell the citizens that "In consequence of the cleanliness of the streets and the taste displayed in ornamenting the houses, the fame of St Andrews has spread abroad. This well-deserved celebrity is rapidly extending. Strangers from every quarter are induced to reside amongst us."'[55]

So let us now explore further the mysteries, the ghosts and the legends of this old quarter of St. Andrews made famous by W. T. Linskill, as we explore the Precincts and ruins that captured the imagination of Playfair and a handful of antiquarians looking to preserve what so many over the centuries had lived and died for.

# The Pends Ghosts

James K. Robertson writing in 1973 has a wonderfully romantic piece about the Pends. It becomes especially poignant when dark and misty and you find yourself strolling up this often-lonely stretch of road:

'Even more to-day a feeling of time-in-suspension pervades the crumbling remains of the Cathedral and the massive torn walls of the Priory as the Pends hill is climbed from the harbour. In that haunted quarter of the 'old grey toun' of a shadowed evening the sensitive mind responds with primal instinct to the atmosphere of agelessness. Where else should dwell the ghostly legions of St. Andrews' tortured past? No reason is apparent why panic should surge, but reason retreats and the mind's disorder conjures up what dread visions?

Yet, the St. Andrean scorns the superstition of his ancestors never more bravely than the moment the narrow Pend is passed and he reaches the comforting familiarity of the main street.'[56]

## The Angel and a Supernatural Entity
*Ghosts of St. Andrews Tour ref. 24-25*

*Ghosts of St. Andrews Tour ref. 24*
Within the Eastern Cemetery on the Pends, there is a statue of a white angel. Keeping watch over the cemetery, the angel stands serenely against a wall at the top of the hill marking a grave. An old legend has it that the angel flies by night seeking out victims by strangulation. The wind blowing the dust around this old graveyard has collected a residue of dark earth near the right hand of the angel and lends the impression that the hand has moved. ⚊

*Ghosts of St. Andrews Tour ref. 25*
Stewart Lamont in his ghost book *Is Anybody There*, published in 1980 has the following account which may tie in with the above legend: 'Betty Willsher of St. Andrews was once knocked off her bicycle by what she is certain was a supernatural entity while cycling up the Pends. She got to about the entrance to the graveyard [Eastern Cemetery] when something white flew at

her, eventually when she got to the top of the Pends she noticed a few spokes were missing from one of the wheels. Apparently she had been attending a debate on whether ghosts exist, at which she voted for the negative.'[57]

If indeed it was the angel that flew at her that night she had a lucky escape with only having a few spokes of the wheel of her bicycle being broken. ⟟

## The Pends Presence
*Ghosts of St. Andrews Tour ref. 26*

Russell Kirk writing in 1954 in his book *St. Andrews* on speaking of the Pends Walk mentions:

 'Just past midnight on autumn, when walking up the Pends road from the harbour I became conscious of some being on the opposite side of the road, so shadowy as to be more movement than definite form, in this black place between high stone dykes; and trying though I would, I could not make out the face – nor indeed the sex or substance of my companion, though we kept pace right into the Pends. Upon emerging into the lurid mercury – vapour light which illuminates South Street just at the mouth of the Pends, I halted, waiting for my fellow traveller to emerge; but he never did; and then it occurred to me that he had made no sound, though my feet had scuffled in the gravel of the road. No moon was out that night nor were there shadows.'[58] ⟟

## Two Accounts of the Phantom Monk on the Pends Walk
*Ghosts of St. Andrews Tour ref. 27*

There have been at least two accounts of the ghostly monks in the Pends Walk, 1977 and 1981. The later is being published here for the first time.

'A St. Andrews' businessman saw the monk in the Pends during the winter of 1977, nothing more though has been ascertained concerning this brief encounter.'[59]

The following is a previously unpublished account experienced in 1981 and given to me by Robert Bell, a local St. Andrews citizen and an old school friend from Madras College. Of Robert, all I can say is that he is a fine spirited character, when I knew him all he needed was a break in life. I hope he has received a number of them since we were at school together. His company in the history lessons always brightened those days when the curricula was dull –

so he made me laugh every day. He could take a serious mood though, and this is his account of something that happened to him he couldn't explain.

Walking to the harbour one night Robert noticed a figure in front of him on the opposite side of the road. It was a man of heavy stature, dressed in the attire of a monk; walking the same direction as he and keeping the same pace as himself.

He followed the figure partway down the road until when opposite the Eastern Cemetery by part of the high stone wall of the Priory the monk turned his head, glanced back at him and disappeared through the wall.

"There were no entrances in the wall for the figure to disappear into" he explained. He was somewhat puzzled and perplexed by his experience. As with so many cases of this nature he never thought of the figure as being supernatural in origin until it vanished before his eyes, and it wasn't the kind of story he would just come out with if it didn't happen. †

 *Read the following account also at the same location:*

## The Phantom Rider
*Ghosts of St. Andrews Tour ref. 28*

Helen Cook in her article *Haunted St. Andrews* in the Scots Magazine of November 1978 wrote about the same spot to Roberts with a different ghost. A figure wearing a green riding habit on horseback was seen by a police sergeant in the 19th century. The horse and rider rode down the Pends before disappearing through this same part of the Priory wall where there was no entrance.[60]

The point at which Robert's monk and the 19th century policeman's account of the horse and rider disappeared through a wall makes complete sense. Behind this wall is where the stables were located for Archbishop Sharpe when he resided at The New Inn. The point where they disappeared is where the original entrance to these stables was located. ⬩

## Novum Hospitium
### (The New Inn or New Hospice)
*Ghosts of St. Andrews Tour ref. 29*

*The History*

Heading up the Pends past the Cathedrals Eastern Cemetery on the right is an archway midway up the Pends on the left, this is the last remnant of a Palace adjoining the gardens of St. Leonard's College. Its name was the Novum Hospitium (The New Inn) or the New Hospice. Linskill calls it the 'haunted house in the Pends Road'.[xxxiv]

It is often quoted as being the last building erected in connection with the Priory before the reformation, which is quite possible, but in all likelihood the building is of an older origin than most desire to attribute to it. This is because the popular notion promoted in books skirting its history state it was constructed in the space of only one month by an army of workmen and masons in 1537 on the instruction of James V. He certainly commissioned the building as a residence for Madeleine of France after his marriage to her in the same year. David Hay Fleming who built the town library says of this building '...Bishop Lesley calls the building "the new Pallice in the Abbey."[61] Continuing he says 'a considerable portion of the structure survived until the early part of this [19th] century.'[62] In 1807 Grierson who was around at the time describes firsthand the last remnants of The New Inn; 'The eastern gable of it is still standing, and appears on the right as we proceed from the principal gate of the abbey to the shore. It has been vaulted below, and the gateway, a fine semicircular arch, is still entire. Part of the wooden floor also, of this structure, yet exists. A person now living in St. Andrews remembers to have seen it complete. The Teind Barn[xxxv] is still in use, and stands a few yards to the south of this ruin. The Abbey Mill [Flour Mill] stands a little on the east of it, and is in use also. The Granary stood to the north-east of the New Inn, about twenty or thirty yards, but there is now no trace of it to be seen, except a small part of the east side-wall.'[63] Another Tiend Barn stood further down the grounds of

---

[xxxiv] Refer to my book; *A St. Andrews Mystery, Concerning More Appearances of the White Lady, (2014)*

[xxxv] The Tiend Barn is where the local farmers would give ten percent of their crop to the priory.

The New Inn opposite what is now the Eastern Cemetery which as mentioned, Sharpe used as a stable during his stay here.

The New Inn itself was eventually demolished in stages and was finally laid bare not long after. It was believed to have been a highly impressive structure and was with little doubt of an older origin. So for the time even an army of builders had to complete their task it makes more sense for an existing building to have undergone structural repair and major refurbishment than a new building being erected in the space of only one month.

The only remaining feature of The New Inn is its arched gateway on the southern side of the Pends road. Even though this is the original gateway it was itself taken down and moved twice in the 1800s, once in 1845 as part of Hugh Playfair's redevelopment of the area which saw the footpath of the Pends being lowered and the road straightened.[64]

In 1893 the archway was moved to its current position during a major development of the Pends. At this time the arch was slightly enlarged and during development 'In March 1893 one of the foundation walls, four feet thick, was laid bare.

Its appearance was inconsistent with the tradition of its rapid erection'[65] and pointed to a greater antiquity, as does the coat of arms of Prior John Hepburn on the arch next to that

**Hepburn's coat of arms is on the right**

of the arms of Scotland as Hepburn died some fifteen years before the commissioning of the building by James V.

In 1860 Fleming says of a find of skeletons discovered at nearby Kirkhill; 'several rude stone cists containing skeletons were discovered, very similar to those found in the contiguous extremity of the Cathedral burying ground, in the so called New Cemetery [Eastern Cemetery], and in the neighbourhood of *Novum Hospitium.*'

This whole vicinity, in fact a large part of the old town of St. Andrews itself, with its many religious developments and redevelopments spanning so many centuries is steeped with the burial sites of the dead. It is no wonder there are so many ghosts here.

On the former site of The New Inn another hospice was built, this time the Hospice for the girls of St. Leonards School.

Hospice for the girls of St. Leonards,
Note The New Inn Archway in background

*The Residents*

Before moving to the paranormal accounts associated with The New Inn, it is worth noting a little of the actual history of The New Inn in terms of its occupants, as the background to these residences is all important in understanding more of who or why they may be haunted. I mentioned earlier how in 1537 on the instruction of James V the building was to be made ready as a residence for Madeleine of France after his marriage to her in the same year. Madeleine, daughter of the King of France, Francis I, was only 16 when she married James V in Paris. Suffering from poor health she was advised by her physicians to head for St. Andrews and Balmerino Abbey as they had the most suited air in the Kingdom for her condition. So with this recommendation in hand as to where she should reside she came to Scotland. Unfortunately as the brisk Scottish air worked its course she never made it to the Palace that had been so hastily fashioned for her stay in St. Andrews, she died in Edinburgh's Holyrood Palace six weeks after her arrival.

One year after Madeleine's death James V married again. The Roman Catholic Mary of Guise was his new bride to be. It was to Mary that Henry

VIII had offered his hand after Jane Seymour had died a couple of weeks after giving birth to the future Edward VI.

James V and Mary (the future parents of Mary Queen of Scots) were married on the 18th of May 1538 at Notre Dame in France – the same Cathedral where James had married Madeleine. He then married Mary again in June that year within the Cathedral of St. Andrews. After landing in the small picturesque fishing village of Crail some ten miles south of St. Andrews, she journeyed to the town where she was lavishly welcomed to Scotland outside the gates of this Palace. They stayed in The New Inn all summer along with Mary Queen of Scots half brother James Stewart Earl of Moray who I mentioned earlier[xxxvi] concerning Archbishop John Hamilton. An illegitimate son of James V born by Margaret Erskine in 1531 at the age of only seven he was made the Prior of St. Andrews Priory and studied at St. Andrews University. He was Mary Queen of Scots chief advisor, but after irreversible differences James Stewart would travel to York and Westminster, and take part in the investigations eventuating in his half sisters death. He was desperate to have the throne for himself but this was never to be. Making many enemies from his involvement in her persecution, rough justice was served when he was murdered on the 23rd of January 1570 at the very place where Mary Queen of Scots and her father were born – Linlithgow. His assassination was the first from a gun, and was fired from Archbishop John Hamilton's residence in Linlithgow by his nephew. As I mentioned earlier in *St. Andrews Castle Ghosts* Hamilton was hung as a result of the murder in Stirling and now haunts St. Andrews Castle with a rope around his neck trailing along the ground.

The New Inn continued to be one of the many residences of the royals for 21 years, including further visits by Mary of Guise following her husband's death at Falkland Palace in 1542. He had sustained fatal wounds at the battle of Solway Moss and had died only six days after the birth of his daughter Mary Queen of Scots in Linlithgow Palace, making her the new Queen of Scotland at the tender age of only six days old. She was dually shipped to the French Court in 1548. Mary of Guise being of French Catholic blood and the regent of Scotland in her daughters absence fled from The New Inn of St. Andrews to Edinburgh in 1559 after John Knox's rousing reformatory speeches marking the advent of the reformation.[xxxvii] She died in Edinburgh Castle the following year in 1560.

---

[xxxvi] Refer to *St. Andrews Castle Ghosts,* p. 68
[xxxvii] Refer also to *Deans Court,* with regard to Mary, Archbishop John Hamilton and the burning of Walter Myln p.121

The Palace of The New Inn being a royal rather than an ecclesiastical residence had been untouched during the ravages of the reformation, consequently it became the Presbyterian residence of John Knox himself, quite a turnaround of events! He also stayed here with his wife and three daughters 12 years later from April 1571 to the following July, when he then journeyed to Edinburgh and died peacefully four months later in November 1572 aged 58 – still preaching with the last moments of his breath.

The next famous occupant to stay here was the son of Mary Queen of Scots – King James VI who was here in July 1580.

**Bishop's Castle, Glasgow, 1560**[xxxviii]

Regarding the New Inn, 'In 1732, Loveday[xxxix] describes it as '"now much decaying."' He also says '"it had something of the look of the Bishop's Castle at Glasgow, though not so good."'[66]

The central building in this engraving on the left is the section Loveday was referring to. Also known as the Bishop's Palace and depicted from the same era, this is probably the closest we shall ever be to seeing what The New Inn actually looked like. The building on the right is Glasgow Cathedral.

Eventually with the final demise of the Palace of the Archbishops at St. Andrews Castle in 1635, The New Inn having already been a residence of Protestants became the Archiepiscopal Palace for the Protestant Archbishop John Spottiswoode until 1638, when the episcopacy - or the rule of the bishops was abolished and wasn't restored again until 1661. This is when James Sharpe became Archbishop of St. Andrews, Primate of Scotland and Chancellor of the University. He took his official residence here as well as having the large estate of Strathtyrum. When he was murdered The New Inn passed to Archbishop Alexander Burnet, in 1683. 'Martine says of the Novum Hospitium 'it is very well in repair, and of late much bettered than formerlie.'[67] It became one of the

---

xxxviii From the Mitchell Library, Glasgow Collection

xxxix Loveday, John of Caversham: Diary of a tour in 1732 through parts of England, Wales, Ireland and Scotland.

residences of Archbishop Ross in 1684. By this time it had been a residence for Kings, Queens, Princes, Princesses, nobles and notoriety for 147 years.

## The Paranormal Phenomenon of The New Inn

This was a place destined to have its ghosts and it is believed to have been a Palace with a great deal of apparent disturbance within its walls even leading up to 1684. David Hay Fleming, a local historian who built the town's library, writing in 1897 in reference to the Palace says that 'Even in Archbishop Ross' time (1684-88), one of the apartments was believed to be still haunted.'[68] There is very little recorded detail of the hauntings here, yet the allusion of what is written has a way of portraying an air of great disturbance spanning a long period of terror for those who came here. Indeed the severity of paranormal phenomenon was alleged to have been one of the main factors for its eventual demolition. James Wilkie in 1931 wrote; 'in its later years it was inhabited by a ghost which so terrified those who ventured within the gates that there remained no other course than to demolish the ill-starved building stone by stone.'[69] This may have been taken from Linskill who wrote in the *Fife Herald and Journal*, dated 13th January 1904, '…the terrible ghost in the Novum Hospitium, which so alarmed the people that it had to be pulled down; and only a fragment now remains.'[70] That fragment being the archway. He also incorporated this piece in his 1911 book. Refer to Linskill's *The Smothered Piper of the West Cliffs* p.331. If indeed this were true it would almost certainly point to the 'classic haunting' incorporating poltergeist type activity for it to be quite so alarming; unless that is, the inference was more to a gruesome encounter than to the unexpected we find with most poltergeist phenomenon. It did have a haunted room but as romantic as it is for its disturbances to be the cause of its eventual demise in-keeping with the mysteries of say Pitmilly House,[xl] there is no supporting documentation that this was the case. To any I imagine this must strike the mind as being a little strange, disturbance of this magnitude would have created quite a stir and somebody of the day would have recorded it. In all likelihood the building like many properties of the time, fashionably out served its purpose and fell into ruin through decay and neglect, and of its ghosts, although maybe not the reason for its eventual demise, records are thin on the ground for these types of supernatural events. They tended to be more recorded as part of an official enquiry into the exploits of suspected witches, especially when this was a time when the witch trials were still in full sway.

---

[xl] Refer to my companion book *Ghosts of Fife* (2013) and to the chapter Pitmilly House.

There are however two recorded incidents here from the 1600s but neither are on par to warrant such a reputation a number of authors have subtly attributed to the place. Linskill calling it a 'haunted house' for instance when one of the incidences concerning a doppelganger mentioned shortly was probably a one off occurrence. In its favour we have already heard two accounts of ghosts in the Pends disappearing through the wall where an entrance once stood leading to Sharpe's former stables. These are important as they give an indication there might yet be more here to ponder on that only further research and time given to more sightings in the area will reveal.

Of the two recorded incidents within the building one account concerns Archbishop Sharpe, the other with Archbishop Ross. Linskill remarks on both of these but the latter is an acknowledgment only with no further details given by him. There is however an account recorded by Wodrow which I have reproduced below.

### The Doppelganger of Archbishop Sharpe

Doppelgangers have been with us for a long time. The word doppelganger is of German origin meaning; *look alike* – a literal translation would be a *double walker*. We think of them as sinister supernatural entities, but they can just as well mean a spitting image or body double. The paranormal variety is generally viewed as a bad omen. When seen by others they denote misfortune, illness or a danger of some description to befall the person in question, but when seen by the same person they are said to be portents foretelling their own death, however Simpkins quoting F. A. Rorie in his book *Folklore of Fife*, 1914 adds: 'I have come across those who believed they saw the apparitions of absent friends at the moment of their (the friends') death. One case I came across of a woman who saw her own wraith. She was engaged in bed-making, and, looking up through the window, saw "herself" passing. She knew that it meant either sudden death or long life. In her case it was the latter (she lived to be 92) Rorie. F. A.'[71]

Robert Wodrow 1679-1734. A Scottish Historian and Parish Minister with no less than 16 children to his name hands down to us an account posthumously published on his behalf by the Maitland Club in 1842. The club surviving until 1859 specialised in the publication of early Scottish texts. This particular account concerns a doppelganger seen in The New Inn of St. Andrews and is one of only a very few early accounts to have been written about this type of phenomenon:

'Upon a time, when Archbishop Sharpe was at Edinburgh, a member of the Privie Councell, and active in prosecuting criminally some men who had been at Pentland[xli], he wanted a paper which tended to a further clearing of the lybel, which was in his cabinet at St. Andrews; and so dispatches his footman in haste to bring it, giving him both the kye of his closet and cabinet, directing him to the shotle where it lye. The footman came off about ten a – cloak in the afternoon, having run very fast. When he opened the closet door and looked in, he saw the Bishop sitting at a table near the window, as if he had been reading and writing, with his black gown and tippet, his broad hat, just as he had left him at Edinburgh, which did surprise the fellow at first, though he was not much terrified; for being of a hardie frolick temper, or a little hollowed, as we called it, he spake to him myrrily thus, "Ho! My Lord! Well ridden indeed! I am sure I left you at Edinburgh at ten a – cloak, and yet yow are here before me! I wonder that I saw yow not pass by me!" The Bishop looked over his shoulder to him, with a sure and frowning countenance, but spake not a word; so that the footman runs downstairs, and tells the Secretare or Chamberlane, that the Bishop was come home. He would not believe him; he averred he saw him in his closet, and that he was very angry; and desired the Chamberlane to come up stairs; but before they were fully up, they both saw the Bishop standing upon the stair – head, stairing upon them with ane angry look, which affrighted them in earnest. Within a little, the footman came up to the closet, and there was nobody there; so he opens the cabinet, and takes out the paper, and comes away in all dispatch to Edinburgh, and was there the next morning, where he meets the Bishop and delivered to him the paper, and told him the former story. Upon which the Bishop, by threats and promises, injoyns him secrecy.' [72][xlii]

'Martine, Sharpes faithful secretary does not record this story of his masters double.'[73]

Another story concerning Archbishop Sharpe and The New Inn involves a woman by the name of Janet Douglas, not to be confused with Janet Douglas, Lady of Glamis who was burnt at the stake over 100 years before on the 17th July 1537 at Edinburgh Castle for witchcraft. She was accused of plotting to poison James V. The accusations were unfounded, but she had reason enough

---

[xli] These were Covenanters he was prosecuting.

[xlii] These were deeply troubled times, if word had spread chances are he would have been accused of sorcery and witchcraft. Such was the popular fervour of the day as shall be found later in regards to Archbishop Adamson p.156 and to Sharpe in this section and paragraph 4, p.199

to confess. In order to obtain information against her James V had her family and servants tortured.

'Janet Douglas, who was accused of Sorcery and Witchcraft was brought before the Privy Council. Sharpe wished to banish her to the West Indies.

"My Lord," said she, "who was gone with you in your closet on Saturday night last, betwixt twelve and one a clock?" The Archbishop 'turned black and pale' but said nothing. On Rothes afterwards promising to warrant her at all hands, and that she should not be banished, she gratified his curiosity by telling him the dread secret – "My Lord, it was the meekle black Devil!" Sharpe had made himself so obnoxious by his treachery and tyranny that the people then and long afterwards would believe anything to his prejudice, no matter how absurd it might be.'[74]

An assassination attempt had been made on Archbishop Sharpe in 1668. However the failed attempt saw its conclusion 11 years later when he met his tragic end by being murdered on Magus Muir in 1679. ☥

### *Phantom Coach on the Pends Walk*

 Andrew Green mentions a phantom coach being seen in St. Andrews, although the exact location isn't mentioned in his article, the coach in question was seen along the Pends Road:

'When on an assignment here in 1973 I was assured by a local historian, a Mr. McKenzie that on "the road down to the bay one or two people, including some golfers, have seen what appears to them to be a coach drawn by two horses. There is on record an incident in the 1800's in which a coach travelling up to the Cathedral tipped over and the passengers and the driver were killed. As far as I know the last time it was seen was last year, in 1972, but people are a wee bit canny about talking on such things." The time the vehicle was seen was somewhere between four and five in the afternoon.'[75] ☥

Archbishop Sharpe was murdered on Magus Muir and his phantom coach is one of the most famous to be witnessed in and around the St. Andrews area. It would however be easy to think this phantom coach was a different one to that of Sharpe's, as only two horses were seen driving the coach along the Pends and Sharpe's coach was driven by four horses. But when we look again at the records of the time of the murder at Magus Muir, we find the coachman could not be touched because his whip affrighted the Covenanters horses, the postilion was wounded in the head by a sword and pulled down, then the two foremost horses were disabled by swords hacking their hamstrings to finally stop the coach. This meant that from Magus Muir the coach carrying the dead body of Sharpe, his wounded daughter and battered entourage etc., eventually completed its journey to his Palace of the Archbishops midway down the Pends being pulled not by four but by only two horses.[xliii]

There is also a tie in with Sharpe's murder at Magus Muir and the following account at The New Inn:

### The Spectral Coachman and the Postilion in The New Inn

The last Archbishop in St. Andrews was Archbishop Arthur Ross, holding the position from 1684 to 1688. He stayed within The New Inn and one night slept in a haunted bedchamber. A ghostly account of the event originally written in 1718 is included here from the pages of Lyon's History of St. Andrews Vol. II – 1843. Firstly I have included a summary of the account by Russell Kirk in 1954:

'A spectral coachman and a spectral postilion awfully affrighted Andrew Berrage, principle servant to the Archbishop. Archbishop Ross, to disprove their delusion, resorted to sit all night in the haunted chamber; but about the middle of the night, the bishop comes down stairs, with all speed possible, and thought it convenient to bring nothing with him but his shirt, barefooted, calling for his servants; but what he saw he would reveal it to non.'[76]

On the following page is the more detailed account of the apparition described in a letter to the Rev. John Warden, and by him communicated to the Rev. Robert Wodrow in 1718. It is fairly difficult to read the original without missing some of what is being relayed. It has a little of the Scots language but it is more that it has been written phonetically and with incorrect spelling etc. This is commented on further by Lyon in a footnote to this piece which is also included below this piece. So I have transcribed a more user friendly version on the left and included the original on the right for reference. My transcribed version is not meant to be definitive; it is more to grasp the detail in the story without being distracted by trying to work out some of the words in the content.

---

[xliii] Refer to *The Bloody Murder of Archbishop Sharpe at Magus Muir*, p.196

**Transcription**

"Alloa, 14th January 1718

"Rev. Sir, - I mind some time ago, I had the occasion to speak with you regarding something which happened in that house in St. Andrews where Bishop Ross lodged, which is as follows":-

""Andrew Berrage, my wife's brother, was principle servant at the time to the bishop. He was a young man who was very apt to dispel any thought of apparitions before that time. Andrew Berrage told me and his sister, that there is a chamber in the lodging which was in possession of the bishop; that neither family nor stranger would lay in that room, because of an old superstition about apparitions frequenting that room. So many strangers arrived one day that all the rooms were taken up with them except that suspected room. My brother-in-law, endeavouring to banish such a Chimera (as he called it) out of the family, decides along with the Paige, a young lad, that they should both stay together in that room; and accordingly started a good fire in the chamber, the bed being near to the middle of the room. My brother-in-law lay down with his face towards the door, the Paige with his back to his, which allowed one to look to one end of the chamber, and the other to the

**Original**

"Alloa, 14th January 1718

"Rev. Sir, - I mind some time ago, I had the occasion to converse with you anent sume thing which fell out in that house in St. Andrews where Bishop Ross lodged, which is as followeth":-

""Andrew Berrage, my wife's brother, principell servant at the time to the bishop, a young man who was verie apt to crush anie surmise of aperitions befor that time. Andrew Berrage told me and his sister, that there is a chamber in that lodging possest then by the bishop; that neither family nor stranger lay in that roome, by reason of ane ould suspition of aperitions that frequented that roome. It fell out, there comes so many strangers one day, that all the other rooms was taken up with the strangers except that suspected roome. My brother-in-law, indevoring too banish such a Himera (as he called it) out of the family, prevails with the paige, a young lad, that both should ly together in that roome; and accordingly set on a good fire in the chamber, the bed being neere to the middle of the roome. My brother-in-law lies down with his face towards the dore, the paige with his back to his, which obliged the one to loke to one end of the chamber, and the other to the other end of the chamber.

"About the middle of the night came an apparition of a coachman at the entrance of the chamber where my brother-in-law's face was pointing; at the same time, a postilion appears at the other end of the chamber. My brother-in-law and the Paige both being awake, the coachman advances towards my brother in his bed; my brother-in-law starts scolding the coachman, calling him a drunken rascal and questioning him why he was not in bed at this time;[xliv] the apparition continues advancing towards him until it comes close to the bed, and the other apparition on the other side of the bed advances towards the Paige; the Paige all the time was smiling at what my brother-in-law was saying, he was mistaking as he thought, the coachman for the postilion that was advancing towards him. My brother-in-law rose on his elbow, swearing he will ring the devil out of the coachman, and thrusts at him with a full stroke. Until he sees his arm through the apparition, and his hand on the other side of him. After the thrust at the apparition, the coachman and the postilion each went back to either end of the room and disappeared like smoke.

other end of the chamber.

"About the middle of the night [comes] ane aperition of the coatchman at the entrie of the chamber where my brother's face was pointing; at the same time, the postiline appears at the other end of the chamber. My brother abd the paige being both awake the coatchman advances towards my brother in the foreside of the bed; my brother fals a scowlding of the coatchman, calling him drunken rascall, questioning him why he was not in bed ere this time; the aperition still advances towards him till it comes close to the bed, and the other aperition in the back side of the bed advances towards the paige; the paige all the time smyling at my brother taking, as he thought, all the time, the coatchman for the postiline that advances towards him. My brother-in-law riseth on his elbow, and swears he would ding the devil out of the coatchman, and thrusts at him with a full stroake. Till he seeth his arme through the aperition, and his hand on the other side of him. After the thrust at the aperition, the coatchman and the postiline each of them went back to each end of the roome and disappeared like smoak. Then, he said, instead of cursing, he fell a

xliv As with so many appearances of ghosts – he thought the coachman was real and this gives a certain authenticity to the story.

Then, my brother-in-law said instead of cursing, he fell praying; he then touches the Paige asking if he was awake. The Paige answered, 'Yes,' – 'Did you see the coachman?' he asked; the Paige answered, 'I saw the postilion.'

"After some discussion between them, they found with their backs facing each other in the bed their faces were looking to each end of the chamber, they then relayed to each other what they had seen above. They instantly arose and sat at the fire until morning, talking to one another and swearing not to divulge what they had seen in case they frightened the rest of the servants.

"However, the secret broke out and it soon reached the ears of Bishop Ross, who in looking to persuade his servants there were no apparitions, would prove it himself by laying in that chamber alone. His servant said to him, in a joking manner, 'My Lord, allow me to be in the chamber below your Lordship.' So the fire is put on, candles placed on the table and in a little time his Lordship went to bed. My brother and the Paige sat up in the room below him. About the middle of the night the Bishop came downstairs with all speed possible and thought it convenient to bring nothing with him but his shirt. Barefooted he called for his servants; but what he saw in that

praying; then tutches the paige, asking if he was waking, who answered, 'Yes,' – 'Saw you the coatchman?' said hee; who answered, 'I saw the postiline.'

"After some conference betwixt them, they fand that their backs being towards other in the bed, and accordingly their faces looking to each end of the chamber, declared to each other what they saw as above. They instantly arose and sat at the fire till morning, taking wan another ingaged not to devilge what they saw, for frightening the rest of the servants.

"However, the secret breaks out, and comes to Bishop Ross his ears, who industeruslie laboured to desuad his servants, and for proof thereof he would ly in that chamber alon. His servant says to him, in a joking manner, 'My Lord, alow me to be in the chamber below your Lordship.' The fire is put on, candels placed on the table, and in a little time his Lordship goes to bed. My brother and paige sets up in the roome below him. About the middle of the night, the Bishop comes down stairs with all speed possible, and thought it convenient to bring no thing with him but his shirt, barefooted, calling for his servants; but what he saw he would reveal it to non.

"Sir, this is the reall account my wife and I had from her brother's room he would reveal to no one.

"Sir, this is the real account my wife and I had from her brother's mouth; and next to seeing it myself I could confirm it no better.

"My dutiful service to you, your wife and family. Your Own,
        "THO. HARLAW."[77]

mouth; and next to seeing it myself, I could confirme it no better.

"My dewtiful service to you, your wife and family. Yours ain,
        "THO. HARLAW."[78]

The following is the footnote to this written by Lyon in reference to the above:

'Mr Wodrow was fond of collecting idle gossip of this kind from all quarters, on which he often founded the gravest accusations against those to whom he bore an antipathy. The house here said to be haunted, had been previously occupied by Archbishops Spotswood and Sharp; but a more clumsy or worse described apparition, it is difficult to conceive. If Andrew the servant could not describe accurately, his brother-in-law the clergyman might at least have written intelligibly. From a comparison of dates it will be seen that the narrative must have been written at least thirty years after the event occurred. Archbishop Ross was deprived in 1688, and died in 1704.'

Is it possible for the ghosts of the coachman and the postilion to be of those who were driving Sharpe's horses and coach through Magus Muir less than 10 years earlier? It would only figure if they were either doppelganger's themselves or had both died by then. I have not found a record of them being killed during the Magus Muir assassination; in fact the records for this part of the proceedings are quite scant, although certainly the Postilion had suffered badly in the first stages of the proceedings and may well have died of his injuries. Wodrow records in 1829: 'When the Covenanters caught up with the Archbishops coach, as the coach drove furiously away, they shot their muskets at it, but could not stop it, til the person upon the fleet horse came up to the coach, crying out, 'Judas, be taken.' The primate called the more violently to the coachman, 'Drive, drive, drive.' The coachman kept off the gentleman's horse from him with his whip; but he came up with the postilion, and called him to stop; and he driving on, he struck him over the head with a sword, and dismounted him....'[79]

With the Postilion sustaining a head injury [the injury was to his face] with a sword and no doubt having sustained more from having been pulled from his horse at great speed when they were trying to get away from them, it is possible he had died. But of the coachman we do not know.

Since the site of The New Inn became the Hospice of St. Leonards School there doesn't appear to have been any apparent reports of ghostly activity from the residents having occupied the building over the years. But this doesn't mean there have been no incidences.

Refer to *A background story of the Phantom Coaches, The Bloody Murder of Archbishop Sharpe, at Magus Muir,* p.196
Refer also to *Strathtyrum House* p.205

## The Veiled Nun of St. Leonards
*Ghosts of St. Andrews Tour ref. 30*

By far the most famous ghost of the Pends is of the Veiled Nun made famous by W. T. Linskill. So much so the Nuns Walk was named after his 'creation'.

The walk is located just off the upper part of the Pends and leads to St. Leonards Chapel, St. Leonards College and Queen Mary's House. It is along this quiet unassuming avenue that the apparition of a Nun is said to appear and whose sad story is recounted by Linskill.

In brief, around 400 years ago during the time of Mary Queen of Scots a young woman living in South Street decided that instead of marrying a young man with whom she had been courting she would escape the trappings by becoming a nun. When her courtier

**Nuns Walk from the Pends**

discovered her intentions he came to St. Andrews at full speed, but upon arrival he found he had been too late. The young woman in a bid to rid herself of her husband to be, mutilated her once beautiful features by slitting her nostrils, cutting off her eye lids, cutting off her lips and if that were not enough she branded her cheeks with hot irons. Irreproachably devastated he shortly after went back to Edinburgh where in a state of despair took his own life. She too died shortly after...

According to Linskill's story 'Her spirit with the terribly marred and mutilated face still wanders o' nights in the peaceful little avenue to old St Leonards iron Kirk gate down the Pends Road.

She is all dressed in black, with a long black veil over the once lovely face, and carries a lantern in her hand. Should any bold visitor in that avenue meet her, she slowly sweeps her face veil aside, raises the lantern to her scarred face, and discloses those awful features to his horrified gaze.'

Seeing her is a grave ill omen and if she chances to lift her veil revealing the grotesque features she so grimly inflicted upon herself – death or madness is almost a certainty. ⚊

Refer to Linskill, *The Veiled Nun of St. Leonards* p.344 for the full story
Refer to the authors book *A St. Andrews Mystery* (2014)

**Entrance to the Nuns Walk from the Chapel**

## St. Leonards Chapel Apparition
*Ghosts of St. Andrew Tour Ref: 31*

A small figure in black clothes has been seen either wandering into the chapel or within the chapel itself. It is believed to be the ghost of a nun and is almost certainly part of the inspiration behind Linskill's story *The Veiled Nun of St. Leonards* roaming along the nearby approach to the chapel. ⚊

David Henry writing in 1912 says 'The conclusion is not unwarranted that the church of 1413, then recently built, was for the old ladies who succeeded the pilgrims – a church or convent chapel being for them a necessity. Other meetings are mentioned as being held in the church, but the Canons who built it, and who administered the affairs of the sisterhood, may very well have had the use of it when they required....'[80] Further details can be found in *A St. Andrews Mystery* (2014) by the present author.

Refer also to *The Ghosts of Queen Mary's House*, p.140

## St. Leonards
### *Ghosts of St. Andrews Tour ref. 32*

St. Leonards is one of the finest private schools in the world. Founded in 1888 as a school for girls it only started admitting boys in 1999.

'Stories circulate that the last headmistress of St. Leonards (built on the site of the former St. Leonards College) had to change her bedroom because of a ghost. However, the lady in question cannot substantiate the story, nor can her successor.'[81]

## The Masked Maiden
### *Ghosts of St. Andrews Tour ref. 33*

James Wilkie in his book *Bygone Fife* tells of a maiden seen down the Pends: 'A lady who studied manners and costumes of men and woman from early times whilst walking through the Pends was surprised to pass there a figure in a garb of long ago with a face concealed. When at her destination she explained she had met a masque in a dress worn in the 15th century and had been struck by the accuracy of certain details.'[82]

The woman in a dress with face concealed fits with the description of both the Veiled Nun and one of the appearances of the White Ladies. With the apparition wearing a masque or a fancy dress costume it doesn't determine the time period the apparition is from. However, being a very fashionable pastime in the court of Mary Queen of Scots, the apparition could be placed around the 1560s and wearing a costume of a century earlier. This would be much in the same way as dressing up today in Victorian or Edwardian attire for a period party. It was believed that Mary Queen of Scots had around 30 such costumes for her 'masques' or balls where she loved to dress up and dance the night away. Does this lead credence to the story of the Veiled Nun or to the White Lady, or is it another apparition independent of either? While it harks of the others by association of her concealed face, the apparition wasn't described as a nun. 'A lady who studied manners and costumes of men and woman from early times' would have easily stated this rather than say she wore a dress worn in the 15th century. The appearances of the White Lady with a veil are all on the other side of the Cathedral precincts, and again if she had been all decked in white it would surely have been mentioned. So this is a different apparition to both the White Lady and the veiled nun and a rare experience it would be indeed to see her. ⚑

Refer also to my book A St. Andrews Mystery (2014)

## The Uncanny Pig
### *Ghosts of St. Andrews Tour ref. 34*

The following story involving the Pends Walk is one of the more unusual and fanciful ghostly tales, published in the National Observer, January 7, 1893:

⚑ 'Around 1863 the family of a St. Andrews Professor had staying with them an English nurse; a woman strange to the place, yet singularly sober minded, sensible and sane. One summer morning this woman unable to sleep arose and went forth into the dawn. Street after street, lane after lane were empty, as she wandered simply letting her feet bear her where they would. Eventually she arrived at the mouth of a lane leading from the Priory to the sea. As she stood, heedless of all things but the joy of the early riser, she was aware of a patter of feet, and looking up she saw a pig. He was running down the lane towards her, so she turned aside to let him pass, and presently he ran by. But even as he went a great terror and a deadly sickness seized upon her and she sought to cover her face. For in truth the thing had turned its head as it ran and the eyes were the eyes of a man – entreating, desperate, shamed. It was gone when she dared look up; but she went home and being seriously ill, was moved to tell her mistress what she had seen. She was laughed at – kindly; but the Professor told her tale abroad, and an old woman came forward and declared, that on a certain morning of the year a pig with mans eyes runs down the lane from the Priory to the sea.

Condemned in the Bible and Koran as unclean; the pig has for many years been associated in some way with Satan or some other such demon, this tradition also presenting itself in the annals of various folklore traditions may in consequence account for the description of the aforementioned pig.'[83] ⚑

The association of the pig with the Devil or Satan comes from the fact that pigs cannot sweat. They are by nature very clean animals but when subjected to hot climate countries they roll around in mud to cool themselves down. They then get the reputation of being unclean and un-god like and hence the association with the Devil.

# The Pends Gatehouse

*Ghosts of St. Andrews Tour ref. 35*

**The Pends, photo circa 1840s[84]**

The 14th century gatehouse serving as the main entrance to the former Priory grounds at the top of the Pends is the most splendid of its kind in Scotland. Some 78 feet long and originally vaulted it included porter's lodgings that stood above. The lodgings have since disappeared and like so many other ancient edifices the ruined gatehouse now only has the heavens as a cover.

This was the location of the end of one of Linskill's stories *The Beckoning Monk* in which the main character finds himself here after being in the subterranean passageways. The inspiration was spurred by the discovery of a mediaeval latrine which he mistook in his enthusiasm for one of these illusive passageways under the cathedral grounds: '"Next time I came to myself and opened my eyes I was out of the accursed passage. I saw the sky and the stars, and I felt a fresh breeze blowing. Oh! Joy, I was back on the earth again, that I knew. I staggered feebly to my feet, and where on earth do you think I found I had been lying?"

"I cannot guess," I said.

"Just inside the archway of the Pends gateway at St. Andrews," said Ashton.

"How on earth did you get there?" "Heaven knows," said Ashton. "I expect the White Lady helped me somehow.'[xlv]

---

[xlv] Refer to Linskill *The Beckoning Monk*, p.303

# More Phantom Monks

A large number of apparitions within St. Andrews are of the monks who for many years outnumbered the town's folk. Two sightings of monks have already been encountered as you journeyed along the Pends Walk. So we continue here with a few more, starting with two unpublished accounts of a Phantom Monk encountered in Deans Court, before heading to the Cathedral ruins and the monk of Robert de Montrose of the famed St. Rules Tower.

## Deans Court
*Ghosts of St. Andrews Tour ref. 36*

Deans Court – formerly the Archdeacon's Inns or Manse

When coming out the Pends to South Street across the road overlooking the entrance to the Cathedral is a wonderful old building with a picturesque draw well in the front courtyard adding to its attractive charm. Once called the Archdeacons Inns or Manse, it is now called Deans Court and was one time home to Sir George Douglas, the man who helped Mary Queen of Scots in her escape from Loch Leven Castle. It was he who saved this building from destruction by the reformatory mob in 1560. This is one of the oldest surviving residences in St. Andrews, although not much survives today of its original structure. In the first part of the 1900s it was residence to the Dean of Guild, magistrate, antiquarian, author and early ghost hunter W. T. Linskill himself.

Since 1951 Deans Court has been the home to postgraduate students studying at the University. It was originally built in the 12th century as home to the Archdeacons of the Cathedral, with its vaulted chamber being used today as the dining hall for its postgraduate residents. The building has undergone various transformations, additions and restorations over the years, being extended and modified to suit its occupant's needs.

In the second half of the 1500s Archbishop John Hamilton who we met earlier at the castle restored parts of it. It was Hamilton who although being against persecution, tried and burnt an 82 year old man for heresy outside the front of the building in 1558. His name was Walter Myln or Mill and he became the last martyr to be burnt before the reformation a year later. Myln is one of the four martyrs to be remembered on the Martyrs Monument along the Scores. Although against his principles Hamilton did this it would seem in a bid to appease Mary of Guise – the Regent of Scotland at the time and who was becoming very unsettled with the protestant uprising. Regarding the murder of Walter Myln, John Knox said of Hamilton 'that cruel tyrant and unmerciful hypocrite,'[85] which about sums up the sentiments which then led to him hanging for his involvement in the assassination of Mary Queen of Scots half brother James Stewart.

## The Accounts

A retired military man living in Africa wrote to me during researches for this book with an experience he had in Deans Court during the month of May in the early 1950s. He was spending his third year in these residences and it was during this term when he saw the ghostly figure of a monk.

He shared a room at the time with a fellow student and was studying hard for his forthcoming exams. Late one evening his roommate after making the customary adieux's retired to bed leaving him to work on for a while. Beside his bed was a deep but small recessed window looking across to the old Cathedral grounds. Eventually he finished his studies and was about to fall asleep when he had a very clear vision of a monk in a grey habit, his cowl thrown back from his tonsured head, standing within the window alcove and bending over him. The young academic told the figure in strong language to "take himself off", whereupon the figure without any sound turned and faded through the wall beside the head of his bed. This rebuke startled his roommate who awoke and was told what had happened. That next morning after having had little sleep the night before, they joined the small community of Deans Court for breakfast, whereupon his roommate informed the others that his friend had been visited by a ghost during the night. Immediately the two students who occupied the neighbouring room became very excited and asked for a description. The figure described fitted exactly in appearance and time with a figure that passed into their room through the adjoining wall. The apparition then crossed the room and faded through the opposite wall.

 Another incident similar in nature to this was briefly related to me by a woman who had a student lodging with her in St. Andrews a few years ago. She related that her lodger had walked into the ghost of a monk one fine mid-May morning within the courtyard precincts of Deans Court.

Maybe the sightings of the monks happen at any time of the year, but always being one to look for possible correlations I find it interesting that both the above accounts occurred in May.

## The Moonlight Monk

 Another story mentioning a ghostly monk tells of a lady who stayed in a house somewhere around St. Andrews and was woken during the night to find a monk standing in her room surrounded by moonlight…

'Among the many tales of monkish figures still manifesting themselves in the environment they knew so well of old is one concerning a lady of position in the county who took rooms in a house which, though not of itself of any great antiquity, succeeded an earlier building. She entered on possession at a time when night was left to the stars. Some hours after retiring she awoke to find the room flooded with the pale light of a full moon which shone in at the window – despite the calendar. In its silver radiance stood a monk.

She switched on the electric lamp beside her. Moonlight and monk alike were gone. She shut it off again, and their appearance was repeated. She had no feeling of fear, simply of wonder, and that chiefly because she remembered there could be not even be a crescent in the sky for an evening or two to come.

In a casual way she made an inquiry to her landlady as to the monastic associations of the site. The other showed embarrassment and a desire to evade direct reply. The vision was then mentioned. It was elicited that the phantom and its accompaniment were occasionally seen, and an undertaking was given that the house should not be identified lest the story interfere with the letting of the room.' [86]

### *Phantom Dogs*

 Mrs Batchelor of Strathkinness related to me in 1989 that this vicinity is also said to be haunted by a black spectral dog wandering outside the confines of the court, it seems though that the level of the ground has dropped over the years or thick snow lay on the ground at the time when the dog originally roamed the area, for when seen it paces around a few feet above the ground!

This legend also had a mention on a student internet forum which had an entry by the user name 'Princess' in late 2004 – "Has anyone heard of the ghost dog that is 'walking' above the floor in Deans Court (I think it is) because they changed the height of the rooms, but the dog is still 'walking' on the old floor … or was that just a random story I was told when I visited two years ago?"

A reply to this from 'Rae' early in 2005 says: "I heard something like that when I was living in Deans Court – apparently the courtyard is haunted by a big black dog who walks a few inches off the ground because it has receded. Which doesn't make much sense, but there you go – that's it as I know it."

The level of the ground in this area like the buildings occupying it, have undergone many transformations over the centuries, not least Deans Court itself. Work carried has lowered as well as heightened the level of ground in different areas. An example of this was mentioned earlier, [xlvi] in 1845 the footpath of the Pends was lowered and the road straightened.[87] In 1896 the roadway near the top of the Pends was raised and a concrete footpath introduced.[88]

## A Phantom Dog in the Cathedral Precincts
*Ghosts of St. Andrews Tour ref. 37*

 A legend across the road from Deans Court has it that a phantom three legged black dog roams around the Cathedral ruins.

### Linskill at a glance
Among the many supernatural curios Linskill intimates as being in St. Andrews is a phantom bloodhound,[xlvii] but as with some of his other 'bogles' as he calls them, there is no further information to be found. The closest are the aforementioned accounts and with Linskill living in Deans Court for a time, he would have been aware of the stories of its resident phantom dog. ♦

---

[xlvi] Refer to *Novum Hospitium* p.102
[xlvii] Refer to Linskill *The Veiled Nun of St. Leonards*, p.344

# St Regulus Monks and the White Lady of the Haunted Tower
## *Ghosts of St. Andrews Tour ref. 38-42*

Yes, Yes, I love that sombre scene,
When weary daylight seeks its pillow,
When up to thee with notes serene;
Ascend the song of darkening billow;
For then there comes, evoked by thee,
A host of memories, sweet and holy.
O friends who loitered there with me,
Who round thy base are lying lowly.

*St. Regulus Tower. Anon*
*St. Andrews Citizen,*
*Saturday January 28, 1871*

After negotiating the dark worn spiralling stone steps, the top of this tower standing at a height of 108 feet commands breathtaking views of the surrounding landscape and of St. Andrews old and new lying below.

Situated within the Cathedral grounds the tower, also known locally as St. Rules or the Square Tower, is believed to have been the work of Bishop Robert during the 11th or 12th century. As time elapsed there became a need for a more substantial structure to replace this building. This had been the first Cathedral of St. Andrews. It now proved too small for the worship of so many travellers making pilgrimage to the town to see the relics of St. Andrew.

This was realised by Malcolm IV, the first King of Scotland and Bishop Arnold who began laying the foundations for the much larger Cathedral in 1160. Through them and their various successors it took a highly impressive 158 years to build the structure. In July 1318 it was finally consecrated in a lavish ceremony by Bishop William Lamberton. Many Bishops, Abbots and Scottish Nobility were present at the ceremony including King Robert the Bruce who made his entrance into the Cathedral on his horse. Due to the victory at Bannockburn he gave 100 merks a year in gratitude to St. Andrews.

This was an immensely impressive and important structure - the largest of its kind in Scotland with the central tower standing at a height of some 200 feet. It soon attracted very large numbers of pilgrims to its doors before the reformation took hold in 1559 and stripped it of its glory. So although very little remains of its past stature it still retains an almost overpowering and grand quality.

## The Phantom Monks
### Robert De Montrose and Thomas Platter
*Ghosts of St. Andrews Tour ref. 38*

*The background stories to one of St. Andrews most famous ghosts*
Two major fires occurred during the Cathedrals history. One in 1378, the other in 1604, the fire of 1378 was due to lightning or as one source states 'a jackdaw carrying a lighted twig to its nest in the Cathedral eaves.'[89] The Prior of the monastery in 1386/7 was Robert De Montrose, a Lord of Parliament who had precedence over all other Priors and Abbots in Scotland. By all accounts he was a gentle and well respected man who humbly carried out extensive work on the monastery following the 1378 fire. He loved the Cathedral and St. Rules Tower, and enjoyed ascending the wooden ladders of the tower after night fall on moon lit nights to admire the stars, the precincts and the settlement of the town below.

Being devout and energetic he spent much time reforming the discipline of the canons – but with one exception; a black sheep by the name of Thomas Platter. Complete with an undisciplined nature Thomas was prone to rebelling when confronted by authority. During the year 1394 Montrose found the monk had been cavorting with a woman and banished him to the Priory dungeon for a few days hoping this would discipline him. Far from succeeding in this Platter taking a grievance to the Priors punishment plotted his demise. One version of the story has it that one evening after vespers, on deciding to gain his revenge, he waited until the Prior was on his way from the darkened cloisters to the dormitory of the Canons,[xlviii] noticing he was alone he emerged from the darkness, and seizing his opportunity drew a dagger from within his cloak and drove the blade clean into the poor Prior. Leaving Montrose slumped to the floor he then attempted to flee the scene, but was later seized in trying his

---

[xlviii] A few of the stone wheel steps which once led up to the dormitory from the south transept can still be seen, they are near the south transept archways leading to the cloisters. The canons descended these steps from the dormitory to the church to perform their midnight services.

escape. The Prior only survived for three long days after this atrocity and was able to identify his assailant before his life was extinguished.

### Linskill at a glance

Another version offered by Linskill has it that 'One evening just before Yuletide, when the Prior, as usual, was on top of the tower, the contumacious monk slyly followed him up the ladders, stabbed him in the back with a small dagger, and flung him over the north side of the old tower.'

Refer to Linskill, *The Monk of St. Rule's Tower, p.323*

Two days after his body was buried in the New Chapter House, Thomas Platter was brought forth and after a long discourse from Bishop Walter Trail[xlix] to the clergy and people he was thrust bound into prison. Prison conditions were harsh and he too died soon after. His body was cast onto unhallowed ground or the 'dung hill'[90] as Lyon records in 1838 and I imagine quite accurately so.

Nothing more was heard of this incident until over '500 years later when an employee of one of the hotels in St. Andrews had two visions, both connected with the above incident they were of a monk who appeared beside his bed. During the second visit the monk said he was Thomas Platter, who for his crime had fed on the bread of grief and the water of affliction till he died and his body cast onto unhallowed ground. As he had never received a Christian burial and the stonemason at work in the Priory had disturbed his remains, he entreated that his bones might now be interred with the rights of the Holy Church through the instrumentality of Lord Bute. So on the 15th July 1898, the bones of Thomas Platter were exhumed. Carried by the visionary they were laid to rest in the consecrated grounds of the Cathedral. Also present at the re-burial were a local priest, Lord Bute and a prominent Benedictine monk who performed the last rights.'[91]

 Over the years the ghosts of Robert De Montrose and his assailant Thomas Platter have been sighted within St. Regulus Tower and also wandering the grounds of the Cathedral ruins.

Michael Elder a young actor from the Byre Theatre had a peculiar experience within the tower one summer's day in 1948:

---

[xlix] He rebuilt the castle in the early 15th century after the Scots demolished it to stop the English from recapturing it again!

'I paid my three pence and was climbing the wooden stairs near the bottom when I noticed the legs of a man standing above me clad in a sort of cassock. I didn't think of the strangeness of the dress at the time and when he asked if I was going up I said yes. "You can follow me up," he said, but when I got to the top and looked round, there was no one in sight. There was no way that I could have squeezed past him on the narrow stairs, I got a cold shiver, panicked and ran down the stairs as fast as I could. When I got into the sunshine, the custodian was standing watching two men mowing the grass. I asked him if he had seen anyone come out of the tower. "There has been no one in or out since yourself," he replied.'[92]

A local St. Andrean had a similar encounter a number of years later: When 14 years of age Greta Boyd, the St. Andrews medium you met earlier concerning the Pavilion Poltergeist visited St. Regulus Tower with some friends. The old worn steps tightly and steeply spiralling within the tower were precarious and dark, so her concentration had been directed toward them. When nearing the top a figure wearing a brown skirt appeared from around the corner above her, before carrying on she moved to one side to let the woman pass. Once at the top her friends asked what had taken her so long. After explaining about the woman they looked at her astonished and informed her there had been no one else on the stair at all. What Greta had assumed to be a woman wearing a brown skirt had in fact been the habit of the famed monk of St. Rule! It was only then she realised it wasn't possible for the figure to have squeezed past her on the narrow stair, and there had been no physical contact.

Refer also to Greta's experiences, p.36 & p.184

A few sources state the apparition of a monk appears during the time of a full moon. Linskill rather fancied the ghost of Robert De Montrose may be seen from time to time peering over the edge of the tower on moonlit nights and to the horror of those chancing to see, he appears to fall over the edge. (Refer to Linskill, p.323)

The tower has certainly not been without its more recent misfortunes in that respect. In 1978 an unfortunate student jumped from its top falling to his death due, it was believed to the pressures of his forthcoming exams. Following this incident, students were dissuaded from ascending the tower around the time of the university exams and new barriers were placed around the perimeter of the top to deter any accidents.

Local legend has it that in the dead of night if one dares ring the bell hanging at the entrance to the tower, push aside the large heavy wooden door and step inside, a helpful and willing monk will be waiting to guide the curious up the steep narrow steps to the top of the tower. Having tried this method on numerous occasions I must admit I am still awaiting the presence of the helpful monk.

Peter Underwood – one of the foremost authorities on ghosts, wrote in his book *Scottish Ghosts* published in 1973: 'The monk appears at the time of the full moon, he is friendly and helpful, frequently appearing on the treacherous dark and twisting stairway of St. Rule's tower to help a visitor who is in danger of slipping. He is reported to have helped people in this way on occasions in 1948, 1952 and 1970.'[93]

St. Rules Tower

Lights like the flickering of candles have been seen in recent times shining through the windows of the tower late at night when all is silent and locked.

## The Monks Face

*Ghosts of St. Andrews Tour ref. 39*

'One summer afternoon around 2:30pm a monk was seen looking from one of the windows in the left hand tower of the ruined Cathedral itself by a woman who described him as being between 40 and 50 years old but with a face that seemed younger.'[94] I am imagining she meant he looked youthful for his age.

# The White Lady of the Haunted Tower

*Ghosts of St. Andrews Tour ref. 40*

Drawing by the author, 1984

A very special and unusual tower is to be found along the precinct wall of the Cathedral. Situated in the shadow of St. Rules Tower it once housed the body of St. Andrews most famous ghost, the White Lady herself.

Over the years, there have been at least 11 sightings of the White Lady in this vicinity and a great deal of speculation as to her identity.

In 1868 the tower had been opened by a few eminent men of the town. What they found was to spark an enduring mystery in the town. Anciently crafted coffins and preserved corpses were discovered, including that of a young woman with long dark hair. She was said at the time to have been a very beautiful young woman wearing white with long dark hair. Her description complied with some of the apparitional sightings of her around this tower. The tower was hurriedly resealed following an injunction from the Lord Advocate of prosecution if this was not carried out immediately. 20 years later in 1888, the tower was opened again, this time by W. T. Linskill and a few others; including one of the original stonemasons present at the first opening. The scene which met their gaze was completely different to 20 years earlier. A fair amount of desecration had occurred which was coupled with what amounted to rapid decomposition. The White Lady and other bodies had disappeared and all that remained were a few skeletons, a number of skulls and fragments of the coffins. The decomposition was attributed to it being exposed to the air when the seal was broken first time round. The desecration and missing body or bodies were attributed to grave robbers or medical students of the time. What secrets they may have been buried with was never known.

When they opened the tower the first time they didn't carry out a search so anything that might have contributed to identifying them, anything they were buried with was now lost.

The opening of 1888 reached the national press of the time and captured the imagination of the Victorians across the British Isles. It started a wave of correspondence with debates in press columns as to who the occupants might have been, including plenty of speculation as to the identity of the preserved beautiful young woman. With no possible way of identifying them speculation was rife. Theories ranged from the occupants being plague victims of 1605. That it was perhaps a mausoleum for an ancient Fife family, or the occupants were connected in some way with royalty. The relics of St. Andrew himself also got a mention. This was all compounded by white calf skin leather gloves which the White Lady was observed wearing, one of which may have been taken by John Grieve the apprentice Stonemason. The mystery of their identities, not to mention the level of preservation was compounded by the coffins themselves. There was no consistency. They were believed to have dated from very different periods in history up to the 16th century.

## A St. Andrews Mystery
### Ghosts of St. Andrews Tour ref. 41

I have conducted a fair amount of research into this mystery, the findings of which include new correlations with new evidence to support there being 4 separate female apparitions in this quarter alone with 3 being of the White Lady. I shall not dwell on the findings at this stage as this mystery is quite involved, but there are 7 ghostly female figures in all and with a number of twists and turns it is over 100 pages in length. So I have published everything separately as a wee book entitled *A St. Andrews Mystery*, (2014), which is all about these female ghosts of the Haunted Tower and surrounding area.

The book includes previously unpublished sightings, including accounts from myself in the early 1980s, with sightings of her standing on two occasions by the pillar on the far right archway in this photo.

These archways are part of the west side of the south transept. The book also includes a rare sighting of a Green Lady seen on Kirk Hill by a student at the University in 1988, together with a wealth of material from Linskill, newspaper correspondence of the time, and published research conducted in its day. It all leads to a gradual unveiling of a fascinating mystery that also links in Linskill's apparition of the Veiled Nun of St. Leonards and Mary Queen of Scots.

Refer also to Linskill, *Concerning More Appearances of the White Lady*, p. 283

## A Visionary Experience
### *Ghosts of St. Andrews Tour ref. 42*

 A visionary experience connected with the Cathedral involved Mr Russell Hunter, a spiritualist medium from Aberdeen who was on holiday in St. Andrews…

'Standing in the ruined cloister, it changed before his eyes to its former ecclesiastical glory – monks were bustling to and fro. One of them who introduced himself as Brother John beckoned him to follow but he held back as he had a strong impression that if he went after the monk he would not be able to return. Brother John was clad in a black habit and there were student types in grey. There was a bustling trade on the slope from the Cathedral to the harbour and the monks seemed to be dealing with important export business.'[95]

It was often stated by Martine, Archbishop Sharpe's secretary in the 17th century that the turrets were 'furnished with many fair, great, and excellent bells, which, at the razing of the church (during the reformation), were taken down and put aboard of a ship, to be transported and sold. But it is reported, and certainly believed in this place, that the ship which carried off the bells sunk in the bay on a fair day, within sight of the place where the bells formerly hung.'[96]

In an article to the local newspaper *The St. Andrews Citizen*, Linskill wrote that 'some greatly favoured mortals have been able to hear the once beautiful bells of St. Andrews Cathedral.'[97] Linskill also incorporated the sound of the bells of the Cathedral into his ghost story *The Beckoning Monk*, p.303 which contains a whole plethora of famed spectral visitations of the Cathedral area.

*The tour continues p.140*

A South Street Ghost Story
## The Virgin's Necklet
By
David Scott
Published in 1911

The following is a short fictional ghost story of St. Andrews, centred in a residence at the east end of South Street. When I read this story I was struck by the similarity it has in part to the ghostly encounter of the fishermen in a Lamond Drive council house related later.[1]

'AN Academic Bunk: it was an expression we often used in my student days at St. Andrews to indicate a bunk possessing furniture and pictures above the common run of such things. Did a bunk possess an oil painting, a high-backed, carved chair with red-plush seat, an old-fashioned sideboard or bookcase, it was an academic bunk, and one such as to excite the envy of those whose lot it was to sit in a threadbare armchair and have nothing to divert their thoughts from work but a hideous tarnished engraving of Cromwell dissolving the Long

---

[1] Refer to *The Lamond Drive, Fishermen,* p.189

Parliament, or, it might be, the portrait of some straight-haired Calvinistic divine. Now, when a student, it was my lot to be classed among those latter people; I never had an academic bunk. But when, after having been "down" for some four years, I returned in the capacity of Assistant to the Professor of Greek at the munificent salary of 150, I determined to gratify my heart's dearest desire and be academically housed. Accordingly I made a long and systematic search for suitable quarters, and at last came upon something that more than gratified my curious whim. It was an old, commodious house at the east end of South Street, into which one entered by a low, wide door. As I rang the bell a fear stole over me that I had made some mistake, that this palatial residence could not be a bunk; but yet there, sure enough, was the sign, "Apartments to Let." My summons was, after some minutes, answered by an old lady dressed in black, of stately mien[li] and erect carriage. On my inquiring whether she let rooms, she answered simply, but with something of a quiver in her voice as if it were an effort for her to say it, "Yes, it has come to that. Will you just step in and see them?" With that she turned and led the way to my future abode. It was a long, low room, and, to my surprise and delight, I observed that it was heavily panelled in black oak. Devoid of pictures or any species of ornament, the only thing that relieved the monotony of the panelling was a rack filled with old china at the end of the room. Against the wall, opposite the great open fireplace, with its quaint wrought iron dogs, stood a kind of sideboard, walnut it seemed and curiously carved, while in the middle of the room was a large oval table polished to such a degree that it returned an almost true reflection of the vase of fragrant chrysanthemums that graced the centre of it. Here, surely, was an Academic Bunk, if ever there was one! Why, one felt in it as if one had been whirled back over a hundred and fifty years and set down among one's Jacobite forefathers in the brave days of the '45.

With my new landlady I very quickly came to terms, for although her charges were high I was determined to secure the rooms, and besides I felt it would be insulting this poor unfortunate lady, for lady the reader will have guessed her to be, and lady she was to "haggle " with her over a few shillings. Well, to cut a long story short, I found myself in a few days comfortably settled down in my new quarters, and each evening, when the hard part of my work was over and an hour or two of leisure opened before me, I would settle down before a cheerful blazing fire with a favourite author. Or there were times when, amid my old-world surroundings, I would sit and ruminate on the past and let my imagination fashion for itself pictures of incidents that had happened in this

---

[li] A persons character or mood

grand old room of mine. One night in November, the 6th of November it was (how clearly I remember it!) I was engaged in the latter ploy, and while the rain beat and the wind howled outside, rattling the shutters in the deep-embrasured windows, strange shadowy visions of men in plum-coloured coats and great curled perukes, men who drank Canary out of bulging green glasses and swore by "Od's Fish," kept coursing through my brain. At last, tired of my somewhat profitless pastime, and conscious that the hour was already late, I made a move to retire for the night. Now, I should have explained that my bedroom opened off my sitting-room, and was in its furnishings in keeping with the latter apartment, a great old-fashioned four-poster bed being the principal feature of it. I have already said that the night was stormy and bitterly cold, and I felt a natural disinclination to forsake the warm glow of the fireside for my cold bedroom. However, by dint of a little exercise of will-power I did retire thither, undressed quickly, and got into bed. In order, however, to make the most of my fire, I left the door connecting the two rooms ajar, and, being healthy and tired, I soon fell asleep. I must have slept for some two hours when consciousness began once more to supervene. I lay for some time half in a doze, getting gradually wider and wider awake, when I was suddenly brought up sharp by a noise in the next room. Raising myself on my elbow, I peered through the door, and my eyes met a sight which I shall never forget. Reader, believe it or not as you like, I will swear it to my dying day that there around my table were seated four such figures as I had been picturing to myself but a short two hours before. Having ascertained that I was fully awake, which I did by pinching myself vigorously and rubbing my eyes, my first impulse was to make a dash into the next room and find out at closer quarters what was afoot. But I could not move; it was as if "the weight of twenty Atlantics" were pressing upon me, and I lay inactive, a compulsory and evidently an unnoticed spectator of the strange drama that was going forward in my sitting-room. As my eyes grew accustomed to the light for there were candles on the table, though where they came from I never knew I saw that the four ghostly figures were playing some game with cards and dice, and, further, that they were gambling. I could only see two of them properly, for of the other two the one had his back to me and the other sat in shadow. Let me describe, then, the two that I saw. The one who sat opposite to where I lay, and whose face and every movement I could mark, was a young man of some three-and-twenty summers, handsome and nobly proportioned. His fine aristocratic face was framed amid a lot of beautiful auburn hair, which waved away from his high forehead and was tied at the back with a bow of black ribbon. From his movements I judged that he was the host of the party, for every now and then he would take upon himself to replenish the empty glasses of the others from a large wicker-covered flask which stood on the table. I noticed, further, that his face bore a troubled expression, and now and then his hand would shake violently: he was, in fact, losing at the game, losing heavily. His companion on his left hand was of a less pleasing aspect, and though in feature and figure handsome, his eyes wore a look of cruelty and cunning which was far from prepossessing. Still, as I say, he was in all points a "proper man," a man that, having once seen, one was not likely to forget. From his dress and bearing, his bronzed countenance, and the large sailor's ear-rings which he wore in his ears, I judged that he "followed the sea," and the nautical phrases which I afterwards heard him use confirmed me in that opinion. The time had evidently just come for a fresh deal, and while silence reigned the sailor dealt, four cards to each man. This done, he threw down the rest of the pack and, in a peculiarly disagreeable tone of voice, said, "Stakes this time, gentlemen, a hundred guineas." I noticed the young man wince, but quickly covering his confusion he said airily, "Hey, Captain, but you fly too high for me. Fortune has been but finished with me tonight, and has now left me but seventy-five. Make it seventy five and I'm with you."

"Done!" said the other; "seventy-five be it. I had forgotten, Herries lad," he went on, "that you were in that case. Earlshall's last broadside carried away your main-sail? Eh? Rake him this time, boy, rake him. He's the wealthiest pirate on the high-seas this night. Here's luck!" And with that he drained his glass to the dregs.

The fall of the dice gave the order of play first to Herries, next to the man on his right, to wit Earlshall, third to the little rat-headed man with his back to me, whose name I afterwards gathered from their conversation to be Bethune, and last to the Captain. Herries accordingly played, laying out a king, a queen, a five, and a three. As he did so I noticed his hand shake more violently than ever, and he blanched visibly. A curse, however, from Earlshall, as that individual laid down a hand containing no royal cards, brought the blood back to his face with a rush. Bethune's luck was no better, and all now lay with the Captain. How things stood with him I had known from the beginning of the round, for I had noticed his eyes light up with a momentary gleam of pleasure as he glanced over his cards. But it was only for a second, and his face was all impassivity again. Herries was now violently excited, his eyes shone in his head like live coals, and his chest seemed to heave as if he were being choked. Suddenly the Captain turned to him and said, in an aggravating tone, "My ace, king, jack, and ten does for you, lad! But, look you, as your locker's nigh empty, we'll cry off and have another hand with stakes at a hundred, for the odd twenty-five of which I'll be your banker." The other, whose face had grown white as marble when he saw the Captain's cards, became suddenly cool and collected, and with a haughty curl of the lip he turned to him and said, "Captain Nicholls, your charity is entirely misplaced. Remember that a Herries always pays his debts of honour." With that he pushed his little pile of gold over to the Captain, filled himself a huge bumper from the flask, raised it to the health of the company, and draining it at a single draught sat down. The Captain, stupefied, as it were, at the unexpected way in which his offer was received, sat silent a minute and then burst out, "So be it, Master Hellfire, or whatever your name is. Die in poverty if you like for all I care. "Gentlemen" (turning to the others), "as we can't play with paupers, I think we'd better take our leave." With that he rose, but Herries, who was now considerably flushed with wine, leapt up and prevented him moving further.

"By Heaven," he thundered, "you shall not go. You talk of paupers, Sir Pirate! But you shall see who is the pauper. What would buy you – body and soul, if I thought your soul was worth bargaining with the devil for." With that he strode to the corner of the room, and taking a small knife prised open the top corner panel of the end wall, put in his hand, and brought out a superb necklet of diamonds and rubies. "This," he said, holding it up to the light, "shall be my stake, and I put it against three hundred guineas from each of you. I warrant you it is worth it. Let me tell you its history.

"Close on three hundred years ago a priest came from the Low Countries to be chaplain in the house of my ancestors. Little was known of him except that he had been a monk in Antwerp, and for some political reason had been forced to flee the country. Coming to Scotland, where the Pope was held to have but little sway, he wandered about for some time, a beggar, until one day he happened to come asking alms at Herrieshaugh. The then baron, learning that he was a priest, and being at that time in want of a chaplain, without more ado gave him the post, and for sixteen years he held it, performing the duties faithfully and quietly. At the end of that time he fell sick and died. But the day before his death he called the baron to his side, and asked to be taken to the chapel. To the chapel they took him, and at his direction bore him right up to the effigy of the Virgin that stood there. He gazed at it in mute adoration, and then taking from his cassock pouch this necklet, he hung it round the neck of the image, saying, 'O holy Virgin, in Antwerp I robbed thee, but now do I restore to thee thy due. Let me die in peace.' With that he fell back in a swoon. They carried him away, and next day he died. Such is the story of the monk. For years the necklet hung where he had placed it, none of my pious ancestors daring, or indeed wishing, to remove it, for there was an old wives' tale that a curse would follow whoever diverted it again to secular uses. Gentlemen, I have diverted it to secular uses, and I dare the curse. Shall we play?"

The others were by this time examining the necklet, which from their admiring exclamations I judged to be of chaste workmanship. They all nodded assent to Herries' suggestion, and the game began just such a process as I have already described. It would be vain for me to try to give the reader any idea of the awful suspense that reigned as the various parties played. Suffice it to say that Herries was knocked out from the first, and, whether by fair means or foul I know not, the Captain gained the entire pool jewels included. After a few minutes' silence, during which Herries sat drumming aimlessly on the table with his fingers, Earlshall rose to go, and the others following his example made ready to depart also.

"We part friends," said Nicholls, going up to his young host with outstretched hand.

"Friends," said the other, taking the hand; "friends, if so you can forgive my hasty words, Master Nicholls. They were hasty words, and I now take them back."

The Captain signified his forgiveness by an impatient gesture, and the three guests moved towards the door, and were escorted downstairs by Herries, who took with him one of the candles, which were by this time burning low.

As I gazed into the empty room I began to wonder again if it was not all a dream. But no! There was the other candle still burning, and here was Herries coming back. He walked over to the table and laid down the candlestick. For a while he gazed at the scattered cards with eyes void of all expression. Then he took one up and tore it in two, and so with another and another till he had destroyed the whole pack. The fragments he gathered slowly together, and with a movement indicative of decision he deposited them in the heart of the fire. Then with a gesture of utter abandonment he threw himself into a chair and covered his face with his hands, and I noticed that his body heaved with great convulsive sobs. He was ruined!

So real and concrete did it all seem that my natural feelings of pity prompted me to rise and comfort him, but I could not move: the indefinable something that I spoke of earlier, still held me down. I had the will but not the power to act, and so lay still to await events. And now comes the last and most gruesome part of my tale.

Herries had not lain long in his chair ere sleep assumed dominion over him, and his head fell back and his arms dropped by his sides. The candles were by this time guttering in their sockets, giving a last flare-up before going out, and I felt, strange to say, that when they did go out the awful drama of which I was the sole witness would end too, but I knew not then what the last act was to be.

Suddenly, from out of the darkness of one of the window embrasures, I saw a tall figure emerge. With swift cat-like movements it glided across the room to where the young man lay, and as it passed by the candles I observed that it was habited after the fashion of a monk. The cowl falling away from one side, displayed features whereon was imprinted a look of the most implacable hate, and the teeth, were bare like an angry dog's and gleamed horribly. Certain that this strange visitant could only have evil intent towards the sleeping man, I made a last effort to rise, but it was as if my limbs were frozen, and I dropped back on my elbow, helpless and almost out of my wits with terror. I would have hidden my eyes, but I was as one fascinated, and gazed on, straining eye and ear. One candle had now gone out and the other was giving a last flare-up. By its light I saw the monk's fingers suddenly hook, and with a swift dart, like that of a hawk on its prey, he seized the sleeper by the throat and wrenched. ... A gurgle ... a groan, and then all was dark. I opened my mouth to cry for help, and to my astonishment was able to emit a sound, though ere its echo had died away in my ears, the world had fallen away from me and I had fainted.

When I came to myself, the morning sun was streaming in through the blinds, and as I tried to gather up the broken, scattered threads of consciousness, I felt cheered and strengthened by its beams. Then I remembered all, and was straightaway filled with a desire to find out what had really happened, and as I rose to go into the sitting-room a fear seized on me that I should there be confronted with a corpse. But no; all was as I had left it when I went to bed the night before. Herries, monk, dice, candles all gone. Was it then a dream after all? I had one way of proving it still: the corner panel. Taking my penknife I went over to the place whence I had seen Herries take the jewels the night before, and slipping it in under the wood I exercised just a little force. To my surprise shall I say? (for I had really begun to fear that the whole thing was some trick of the fancy) it opened. I put in my hand, and then I very quickly knew it was not a dream. Lying in the bottom of the little hiding-place were a piece of paper and a silk handkerchief, the former underneath the latter. Taking these out I carried them to the window and examined them. Of the handkerchief I could make nothing, for it was just a plain silk one, rather yellowed with age. But the paper told me all I needed to know, for on it were written these words: "The Virgin's Necklet J. Herries, 1717."[98]

# An alternative stroll along South Street

1896 Postcard of South Street

*Ghost Tour continued...*

The Ghosts of Queen Mary's House
*Ghosts of St. Andrews Tour ref. 43*

From 1562 up until 1566 Mary Queen of Scots stayed at Scrymgeor House. So named after Hugh Scrymgeor; an influential merchant who built this three storied mansion in 1523 on the site of a 15th century house called Smalmonth. This was a privately owned property and had been rented out around the turn of the twentieth century. In 1926 St. Leonards Girls School bought the property and after restoration it was opened in 1927 as Queen Mary's Library for the Girls of St. Leonards School by the Duchess of York; future Queen of George VI, where it become known also as Queen Mary's House.

Charles II's stayed here nearly a hundred years later when he visited St. Andrews in 1650 just one year after he was proclaimed King of Britain and Ireland in Edinburgh – which was denounced by Cromwell favouring a republic in England. Part of the grounds had a coach works and during Mary's stay of 1562 she had a coach repaired from damage caused by the inadequacy of the roads, or more the point the lack of them at the time. It is doubtful she used this mode of transport often unless it was for excursions within the town, much preferring the practicality of horseback for the travels of herself and her often quite sizeable retinue as they journeyed across Scotland.

The mid to late 16th century stands out in particular as one of the most fascinating and complex periods in Scottish if not international history as the course of events were changing so rapidly. This was a period of great turmoil and in Scotland it was Mary Queen of Scots and John Knox who took centre stage. Roman Catholics and Presbyterians battled for what they both saw as their God given rights. It was a time where only one thing was for certain; survival depended on how useful each were as a resource to others, politically the crown and the church were the most heavily fought for prizes.

Queen Mary's House

Symbolising the influence of countries and nobles, the tide was to have in power whoever would favour the greater aspirations of the jostling elite looking to benefit. There was a constant shuffling of positions through the chain of power and influence between allegiance and plots with all looking to sway opinion in their direction. The involvement was a heady and volatile mix of politics and power, wrapped in a culture of manipulation and espionage, and with this it became all the more difficult to stay alive. Everyone from royalty, to court, clergy to layperson were looking over their shoulder in these difficult times. This was a time when ideologies and the spoken word killed more than the various plagues and deadly diseases to ravish the town's folk. No one was safe in St. Andrews or beyond its precincts and no one was immune to ridicule. Sharp wits were a necessary prerequisite for survival when treachery and manipulation walked hand in hand with agreement and favour.

Mary Queen of Scots felt it important to be kept informed of what was going on, politically, religiously and socially, but while in St. Andrews she had no time for the political infighting and backbiting that always accompanied it. Despite St. Andrews being a hub of conflict when she arrived and a seat for the reformation in overthrowing the dynasty of the Catholics, St. Andrews for Mary was still a catholic town and very much a haven for her when she was here – albeit a relatively temporary one. This was a place she could retreat to from the difficulties of the day and the constant of these political sparing bouts taking place in Edinburgh and London. As Lang puts it; 'Queen Mary, escaping the formalities and ceremony of her unhappy court, loved to come and live for a while the simple busy life of a 16th century bourgeois housewife of a little grey city. The panelled room in the west wing with a corner oriel[lii] is the room associated with her.'[99]

Mary and her four 'Maries' despite the protestations of John Knox were able to carry on the practice of the Catholic faith and attend Mass amid the turmoil's of the reformation, which had now become the governance of Scotland. If the rumours which were rife at the time were to be believed Knox had something of a soft spot for Mary, but then if this was the best the propaganda of the time could do to try and smear his name, it would have fallen well short. By all accounts her charm was such that there were few who didn't succumb to it. Elizabeth I was Mary's cousin

Queen Mary's House from the garden

and eventually had her imprisoned for a staggering eighteen and a half years for the threat she posed to her crown. In all this time she never met Mary choosing instead to always send envoys on her behalf to deal with whatever business or occasion arose. It must be wondered, would Elizabeth have executed her if they had met. Elizabeth was aware of Mary's grace and charm and feared her potential for a Catholic uprising, which was realised in numerous thwarted plots by the enemies of Elizabeth. Mary had a greater tolerance for the Protestant faith than for Knox, but her views favoured the reformers own

---

[lii] A bay window projecting from the house

tolerance – such was the intrigue and games played on all sides. Elizabeth became so wary of espionage that in 1584 she drew up a Bond of Association, creating a no win situation for Mary. Essentially any plots against the Queen connecting any member in line to the throne, whether they were aware or not of the plot would be executed. It didn't take long before another plot against Elizabeth was discovered, Mary was implicated or framed depending upon the angle of the historian and executed at Fotheringay Castle in 1587.

Her chamber within Queen Mary's House has been preserved, and the Queen's insignia may still be viewed in one of the windows. The building she stayed in for each of her annual visits from 1562 to 1566 also houses some of the oldest furniture remaining in Scotland.

### The Ghost of Mary Queen of Scots and a Dark Figure

Dressed in white the apparition of Mary Queen of Scots has been seen either seated at her tapestry or flitting around the building 'with noiseless steps'.[100] The ghostly figure of a little woman in dark clothing has also been seen throughout the building and garden.

### Ghost of a Minister

The garden also has the ghostly figure of an old minister dressed in black. The figure has been seen pacing around the grounds between the house and the chapel of St. Leonards and is thought to be one of the apparitional sightings of John Knox. He enjoyed walking through the garden and grounds of St. Leonard's College when he stayed in The New Inn just nearby.

### The Blue Girl

There is heard tell of a house in central St. Andrews believed to be haunted by a ghostly figure known as the 'Blue Girl'. In the report the exact locality is not known, but the ghost of a woman has been seen in St. Marys House wearing a blue dress. Linskill fancied the woman was the weeping woman of the Maiden Rock from where he says it received its name. So there are currently three reports of an apparition in the town wearing blue and this is the only house to my knowledge where one has been seen. So maybe this is the location Linskill's story speaks of.

Refer also to *The Maiden Rock and the Weeping Woman* p.190

The building was or perhaps still is the subject of what may be termed the 'classic haunting'. There have been many ghostly inhabitants and associations with this old house. The following short account mentions a figure I spoke of just now: 'The library was haunted most disturbingly and girls who sat here to read, in the gloaming, were terribly oppressed by some presence. Sometimes the figure of a little woman in dark clothing was seen scurrying out of the building into the garden, of an evening – seen by various people on various days. All this was vexatious; the Bishop was brought, with bell, book, and candle; now, it appears, Queen Mary's and the adjacent house are undisturbed.'[101] In reality however, the exorcism succeeded it seems in allaying more the fears of the occupants for a time than the disturbances.

A reference to the building being haunted by the Queen's Maries is as follows:

'On the north side of South Street is or was an old building which at one time may have been 'Glass's Inn'. A house in the locality is said to have been haunted by "the Queen Maries."'[102] ❧

The Glass's Inn was probably the most famous hostelry in St. Andrews in its day. Boswell and Samuel Johnson stayed here when they arrived in St. Andrews on their tour of Scotland. The address was 5 South Street, directly opposite Queen Mary's House.

The four Maries along with Mary Queen of Scots are important to the ghostly associations of St. Andrews. With Linskill's help one of the Queens Maries, albeit a fictitious one has become associated with the White Lady. Mary Queen of Scots was nearly 6 feet tall and by the majority of accounts she was far more beautiful than her contemporary portraits give her credit. With her appearing in this house wearing white it gives more credence to the association with the white lady and is one of the theories I explore in my book *A St. Andrews Mystery* (2014). Refer to the chapter entitled *The Identities of the White Ladies*.

## *Two Appearances of James Hepburn, 4th Earl of Bothwell*

A few ghost stories are in circulation concerning Mary's third husband James Hepburn 4th Earl of Bothwell. Although the locations are not stated they almost certainly also concern Queen Mary's House. Although Mary and James were not married until the latter stages of her reign, being a year after her last visit to St. Andrews, Bothwell had been on the Privy Council since Mary's arrival in Scotland in 1561, and eventually became her closest advisor. So it is possible he stayed here also during her visits to St. Andrews.

'In a certain venerable dwelling the noble whose influence wrought doom, has, it is told been encountered on more than one occasion. There in the boudoir of the lady of the house a friend sat at the piano, idly running over the keys. A feeling that she was not alone impelled her to look round. She was astonished to see a stranger, evidently from an earlier century, entering the room. She watched spellbound for a few moments, and noted that he was of tall stature, that his dark hair was tingeing with grey, that his eyes were a vivid blue and that his cheek was marred by a scar.

On another occasion a relative of the family met the same figure on the stairs, he was identified as being James Hepburn, Earl of Bothwell 3rd husband of Queen Mary. She said I have seen Bothwell, she identified him from his portrait in the National Portrait Gallery in Edinburgh.

James Hepburn, 4th Earl of Bothwell

A certain old house in the City was on one occasion let for a few months to an American lady who moved out sooner than she would have liked.

She was sitting in the drawing room on the first floor looking out upon the garden, when a tall man in a garb seen only in pictures of later Stewart Scotland walked in through a great mirror on the wall. In earlier years the banqueting hall of the mansion comprised the room itself and the apartment adjoining, now separated from it by a partition to which the mirror was affixed.

In the same house the proprietrix had on one occasion a child of about five years old staying with her. They were sitting in the drawing room when the child pointed to the door, trembled and burst into tears. The lady herself could see nothing, but was told in faltering tones "a man was standing there." The girl was too young to give any coherent description of him.' [103]

### Ghostly Monks and a Spectral Dog

'In the house that Bothwell made his appearance[liii] a lady saw in one of the rooms a small table, seated at it were two or three monks, while another stood with his back to the fireplace. She was accustomed to abnormal experiences and after contemplating the scene quietly withdrew.

For many years there was the form of a dog stretched out in front of a fireplace, it seemed to enjoy the heat whether a fire burned or not. An eminent churchman, who saw it, said some words of blessing and the apparition was seen no more.'[104]

## Linskill at a glance:

Linskill speaks of James Hepburn, 4th Earl of Bothwell haunting the castle.

Refer to p.70

Refer to Linskill's Related by Captain Chester p.287

### The Poltergeist of Queen Mary's House

In the late 1980s a workman carrying out minor repairs within the building vowed never to enter again after an incident there. He was working late one night after everyone had left the building and had nothing more to disturb him than the faint sounds of traffic outside. Around 11pm though he was suddenly startled by the loud constant banging of doors slamming shut throughout the building, and the sounds of footsteps echoing all around. Knowing that he was alone in the old building the commotion immediately brought him to his senses and a shiver ran down his spine. He stopped what he was doing and cautiously surveyed the rooms for its source but found nothing to account for the noises. Somewhat bewildered he felt the commotion must have been his imagination and decided to resume working. But soon after the noises started up again in the same manner as before, loud banging and almost equally as loud footsteps echoed throughout the building. Becoming very unnerved he looked around again but still found nothing to account for what he was hearing. On his return a second time to the room where he was working however, the furniture within had been left untouched but he was startled to see that his tools had now been scattered all over the room and his pots of paint although in the same place as before were now standing upside down. This was all too much for the workman who panicked and fled the building never to return.

---

[liii] So far as I can tell it can only be Queen Mary's House

# The Exotic Woman and the Dwarf!

*Ghosts of St. Andrews Tour ref. 44*

'It is narrated that a lady reported to Andrew Lang that she had been struck by seeing in South Street a very handsome "foreign – looking girl" talking excitedly to a man in "fancy dress." Her surprise was intensified when she became aware of a dwarf running up to them and uttering some words which at a distance were inaudible. The communication seemed to shock the lady beyond measure, for she buried her head in her hands and burst into passionate weeping.

Dr. Lang questioned the tale, and could then throw no light on the matter. It is understood, however, that when in Paris at a later date, examining manuscript records in preparation for a work he had undertaken, he chanced upon old writings relative to St. Andrews. These he naturally read through, and was struck in the course of his perusal by a statement that the news of Cardinal Bethune's murder was communicated to a fair Spanish lady whose friendship he prized – by a dwarf!'[105]

Andrew Lang (1844-1912) was a Victorian collector of folk and fairy tales and had been nominated for the Nobel Prize for Literature. Living in St. Andrews he was famed for the publication of 12 books with the series title; *Andrew Lang's Fairy Books of many colours.* Now much sought after, each book has a different colour for the cover and they comprise a comprehensive collection of 437 tales from many countries.

# The Phantom Coaches

## *Reports of Phantom Coaches - Locations*

Phantom coaches are a perpetual talk of the town when it comes to the ghosts of St. Andrews. There have been various sighting over the years alongside even more reports of the unmistakable sounds of a coach and horses being heard in the still of the night. The locations have been in the quite outlying areas towards Strathkinness and around the precincts of the old town itself, especially along the cobbled east end of Market Street. Near to where the old Tolbooth once stood which saw various body parts being displayed from executions here and elsewhere. The occupants of these large black coaches range from Archbishop Sharpe and Cardinal David Beaton, to Hackston of Rathillet. All are being driven to hell with the Devil beside them as their final companion!

There are a number of locations where a Phantom Coach has been reputed to have either being seen or heard in and around St. Andrews. It is not until the list is put together that the extent becomes apparent:

Legend also tells of it being heard in Hepburn Gardens. With such a profusion of locations it is more a case of where hasn't the coach been seen or heard in St. Andrews than where it has been. Although it will be noted there is nothing random here, the reported locations of the coach with unidentified occupants are all from the direction of Magus Muir running towards St. Andrews Bay.

## The Phantom Coach of Abbey Walk
*Ghosts of St. Andrews Tour ref. 45*

Abbey Walk is one of those locations, mentioned by Linskill in his story *Related by Captain Chester*, p.287, "...my nephew and I saw that phantom coach in the Abbey Walk one windy moonlit night. It passed us very quickly, but made a deuced row, like a lifeboat carriage."

"What was it like?"

"Like a huge black box with windows in it, and a queer light inside. It reminded me of a great coffin. Ugly looking affair; very uncanny thing to meet at that time of night and in such a lonely spot. It was soon gone, but we heard its muffled rumbling noise for a long time."

"What were the horses like, eh?"

"Shadowy looking black things, like great black beetles with long thin legs."

"And what was the driver like?" I asked.

"He was a tall thin, black object also, like a big, black, lank lobster, with a cocked hat on the top. That's all I could see. On the top of the coach was an object that looked like a gigantic tarantula spider, with a head like a moving gargoyle. I can't get at the real history of that mysterious old coach yet. I don't believe it has anything whatever to do with the murdered prelates, Beaton or Sharpe. However, the coach does go about.' ‡

## The Haunting of the Byre Theatre
*Ghosts of St. Andrews Tour ref. 46*

Awarded the MBE for services to the theatre, playwright A. B. Paterson together with a few theatrical enthusiasts founded the Byre Theatre in Abbey Street in 1933. As the name suggests the theatre began its existence as the Abbey Street Dairy Farm of St. Andrews followed by a merchants potato store; not the type of place one would readily expect to be suitable for productions to take place, but the thespians of the day having vision for its potential constructed a stage, and with plenty of shared enthusiasm transformed it into a centre for the arts.

The success of this small theatre was soon noticed. Charles Murford – a former actor with notable achievements including stage director of the Old Vic in London, came to the theatre and successfully ran it until his retirement to Devon. Before his death in 1950 he came to St. Andrews on a number of occasions taking part in and running a number of its plays.

It was he who had managed to keep the theatre open and running throughout the Second World War after most of the able bodied had been called into service.

The last performance in the old Byre as it was known was January 3rd 1969[106] after which parts of it were incorporated into the New Byre that opened in its place in 1970. The Old Byre had been one of the smallest theatres in Britain for 35 years.

It is the ghost of Charles Marford or 'Chas' that is believed to haunt this locality. Having been heard or seen over many years since his death it seems fitting that someone who loved the theatre so much should make the occasional appearance from time to time.

'In 1959, the author Ian Curtis was directing a play at the Byre, "one night after the show I had to go back for a script I'd left at the theatre." He said later. "The place was deserted but as I went through the stage door I heard heavy footsteps, I had been told the theatre was haunted by Charles Marford, and in my panic I called out as loud as I could – "All right Charlie, if you're up there, stop that noise and come down!" The clumping footsteps stopped instantly. Then there was silence. Eventually I plucked up enough courage, and had a look round. Nobody!"

Perhaps the most intriguing incident was in the new theatre when the company was working on a change-over late on a Saturday night. Suddenly the familiar mix of scenery and lighting changes was punctuated by the record/tape player which started to play one of Charles Marford's favourite pieces of music. Nan Eagle, the caretaker who is still with the company[liv], remembers those startling few seconds vividly-although she cannot recall the title of the music.

The backstage team stopped, transfixed, and when it ended Andrew Cowie,[lv] the stage manager went over to the player to investigate. On it he found, not the tape they had heard – but the one that had originally been set-up for the interval earlier – a totally different piece. Yet years later Nan remains convinced that what they all heard was Marford's favourite – however it was relayed!'[107]

'In 1973 a ghost was seen at the theatre by an American couple, Mr and Mrs Herman Josephson which may have been Marford or the founder A. B. Paterson as some believe. They had just come down the little passageway from South Street when they saw standing near the entrance to the theatre a man – dressed in tight trousers, a white shirt with a frilly front and leather boots. He had one foot on the step as if he was reading the theatre program.

Mr Josephson took a few photographs saying that he could clearly see him through the viewfinder. When they moved nearer – Mrs Josephson said she could see right through him – she felt quite sick and sat on a nearby bench.

When they looked again the figure had gone, and on getting the film developed the figure wasn't in the print.'[108]

There is a marked difference between photographs traditionally developed from negatives and there more recent digital counterparts. Digital seems to pick up phenomenon more readily. From orbs to apparitions, the difference in what is revealed in an exposure can really be quite profound.

---

[liv] Nan Eagle performed in some of the plays within the theatre and together with her husband was a caretaker in the Byre Theatre for many years. She passed away in the latter half of the 1980s.
[lv] Andrew Cowie passed away in 1980

# No.49 South Street

*Ghosts of St. Andrews Tour ref. 47*

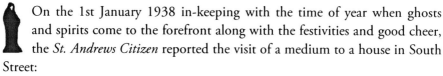 On the 1st January 1938 in-keeping with the time of year when ghosts and spirits come to the forefront along with the festivities and good cheer, the *St. Andrews Citizen* reported the visit of a medium to a house in South Street:

'The story is told of a lady who paid a visit to No.49 South Street. She asked the owner (Miss Rotherham) to let her walk through the house, and as she did so she said, "a Royal personage has dwelt here; I think he must have been a Charles."

At the time the owner had no idea of such being the case, but recently this has proved to be true.

In the attic a large quantity of painted panels were found, a painted roof was discovered after an electrician had put his foot through the ceiling above and struck something solid – an oak roof. These finds were all attributed to the 15th or 16th centuries. The owner traced through the title deeds that the house once belonged to Robert Blair, being one who signed the National Covenant. She also found out that when Charles II visited St. Andrews he visited Blair at his home.'[109]

This house is only yards away from Queen Mary's House on the opposite side of the road where Charles II stayed in 1650 when he visited St Andrews. 'He was received at the West Port by the provost and magistrates, who presented him with silver keys; and afterwards Dr Samuel Rutherford made him a long address in front of St Mary's College.'[110]

# St. Mary's College
*Ghosts of St. Andrews Tour ref. 48*

Drawing by the author, 1984

Archbishop James Beaton who committed Patrick Hamilton to the stake outside St. Salvator's secured a papal foundation for this college in 1538 and began construction of the college for religious studies in the same year. This was shortly before his death in 1539 where he died peaceably within the castle walls. Following his death his nephew Cardinal David Beaton became his successor, followed then by Archbishop John Hamilton after Beaton's murder. Hamilton continued the work of building the college and a considerable sum was spent on its construction and development.

Construction of the old university library called the King James Library began here in 1612 and was repaired or rebuilt in 1764. Initially it was built to house a number of rare Greek and Latin books from Mary Queen of Scots personal library. She had bequeathed them in her will to the University in 1566 whilst in labour with the future king. However following her forced abdication of 1567 in favour of her one year old son, many books disappeared.

With numerous changes occurring both architecturally and academically over the years to the buildings, the north and west sides still remain today and form part of the St. Mary's Quadrangle. Continuing the tradition of theological teachings at St. Mary's College, it now houses the School of Divinity at the University of St. Andrews.

Two ancient trees stand here; one is a huge Holm Oak dominating the main precinct, the other a hawthorn tree known as Queen Mary's Hawthorn. It was believed to have been planted by Mary Queen of Scots in 1563 as a commemoration to her French uncle Francis Duke of Guise who had just been assassinated.

Overall this particular area is one of the most charming and attractive to be found anywhere in St. Andrews. Maybe it is because it is just off South Street and the contrast is more pronounced, but it is also one of the most tranquil. I am sure in part at least this was the intention of its architects being a place of spiritual learning. It is described beautifully in the following piece written some time before 1911.

## *Alma Mater*

'THE Moon looks down upon Queen Mary's thorn,
And lines each leafless branch with silver light,
Until 'twould seem as if some thievish sprite
Had stolen radiance from the sleeping morn
To cheer the night.
Eke did he then adorn
The grey-hued College walls with subtle grace
Of white and ebon, so that the age-worn place
Is robed in moonlight charm, no more forlorn.
Even so, when Memory's orb lights up the past,
In mingled gloom and gladness stand the years;
The College girt with friends, or 'midst foes cast,
Now fair with hope, now dark with hopeless tears.
Oh, Alma Mater! may a kind moon play
On thy loved form, till dawns the gladsome day.' [111]

## *The Library Ghost*

The room above Parliament Hall in the northern building is the Long Gallery that housed part of the library mentioned as follows:

'In an upper hall is an inlaid line crossing the floor diagonally, following the line traditionally stated to have been scratched by James Gregory as Scotland's first meridian line. Gregory, inventor of the reflecting telescope, carried out many of his experiments in this hall. In the recesses behind the bookcases on the north side – where once were windows – a ghost is reputed to have constantly appeared.' [112] James Gregory was a Professor of Philosophy in St.Salvator's College, a mathematician and astronomer of the 1670s.

A short Victorian ghost story of 1896 written by Mrs Oliphant, a popular Scottish writer of the 19th century concerns the appearance of this ghost in the King James VI Library. Her story, is a somewhat melancholic a tale of obsession and unrequited love, called *The Library Window – A story of the seen and the unseen* it can be found in full on p.208 🕯

Although the identity of the ghost in the library is not known, it is possibly that of a former 'carrier' for the university and is mentioned as follows:

## The University Postman

Russell Kirk in 1954 relates to us a gruesome piece of local history associated with this quarter:

'One of the most macabre touches in old St. Andrews formerly clung to this gallery. In 1707 the University porter hanged himself from the balustrade of the stairway to the gallery; and the senatus,[lvi] then still possessed of remarkable powers and being wrathful at this sacrilege, resolved that the suicide should hang in perpetuity "and be forever without a name." The wretched man's bones, suspended in a case above the stairway, languished after the fashion of Mahomet's coffin[lvii] until 1940, when they were given decent burial. He may or may not haunt this area.'[113]

In a more recent times Norman Reid, Keeper of Manuscripts and Muniments and Head of Special Collections at the University wrote an article for the 13th edition of the University Staff Magazine *The StAndard* in 2008. In brief it seems the suicide was the university messenger, possibly by the name of David Murray who took the position in 1704. Although this cannot be verified as true to their word his identity was never disclosed. The senatus had paid for his body to be dissected and turned into a skeleton and a case was commissioned to house it. The display then hung in view above the stairway to the library, at some point it had been placed in the loft above the stairway and in 1940 or 1941 'it was removed on the instruction of the University Librarian and Mr J B Salmond, a member of the University Court. The skeleton was passed to the Professor of Anatomy, who (having first studied the method of articulation used in the early eighteenth century) arranged for the proper disposal of the bones.'[114]

## A Commotion in St Mary's Quad!

Lyon writing in 1838 tells of an incident in St. Mary's Quad in 1592 and how both the Catholics and the Protestants of the day would have the other

---

[lvi] A senatus is Latin for a chamber or parliament

[lvii] Mahomet's coffin refers to a legend where Muhammad's coffin was suspended in mid air by load stones from the ceiling of his tomb

cavorting with the Devil in anything they were involved in. None were immune to these allegations including Cardinal David Beaton, Archbishop Sharpe and John Knox. Although the following doesn't involve a ghost, it is a worthy account for inclusion as it bears important insight into the continuing tensions in St. Andrews of the time. It was these same tensions that had previously resulted in the ransacking and destruction of the Catholic places of worship in the town; including the Cathedral, Blackfriars Monastery and Greyfriars Monastery and directly created the ghosts we see today of the towns bloody past:

"'In that summer (1592) the devil stirred up a most dangerous tumult of the people of St Andrews against my uncle, (the famous Mr Andrew Melville,) to the extreme peril of his life, if God had not been his protection. The wicked malicious rulers of the town hated Mr Andrew, because he could not bear with their ungodly and unjust dealing; and they incensed the rascally mob, by false information, against him and his college, (St Mary's,) making them believe that he and the college sought trouble of the town. They being thus prepared, the devil furnishes them with an opportunity of falling to work. There were some students of theology, who, wearying to go out of the college to their exercise, erected a large pair of butts in the college garden, adjoining to a wynd of the town. At these they were shooting one afternoon, when one of them, (Mr John Caldcleuche, a master of theology, but scarcely a scholar in archery,) missing the butt, and some thatched houses beyond, shot his arrow down the wynd, and hit an old honest matman of the town, and hurt him on the neck. This coming to the ears of the foresaid malicious rulers, they rung the common bell, and stirred up the mob, who attacked the college, broke open the gate, and with great violence tried to force an entrance into the hall, crying for fire to burn it. But the Lord, assisting his servant with wisdom and courage, enabled him to deal mildly with some of them whom he knew to be misled, and sharply with others whom he knew to be deceivers of the people. By the exertions of Mr David Black, and Mr Robert Wilkie, Principle of St. Leonard's with other masters and scholars of the university, after long vexation and much ado, the uproar was quelled." It must be borne in mind that both the Melville's were keen party men, and that they made no scruple of ascribing to the devil whatever was contrary to their own preconceived notions of propriety.'[115]

Interestingly at the time of this incident it was reported that theology students were exempt from taking part in the compulsory archery practice at the Bow Butts.

# The Knights Templar, Mary Queen of Scots and a Witch!
## No.69-71 South Street
*Ghosts of St. Andrews Tour ref. 49*

71 South Street is a very special building, yet it attracts little attention from the passing tourist in search of the established attractions of the town. It is located just before the main shopping thoroughfare of the street and aesthetically blends in with the stretch of town houses in this relatively peaceful quarter of South Street.

69-71 South Street

It is believed to be the oldest surviving inhabited dwelling in St. Andrews and running along its eastern edge is Baker Lane. Formerly known as Baxter Wynd this is believed to be the oldest Wynd in the town.

Of its historical occupants, there are the Knights Templar, Mary Queen of Scots and Archbishop Adamson who was cured here of his maladies by a witch and became a pauper for his trouble.

The popular residential associations in the town with Mary Queen of Scots is Queen Mary's House by the Cathedral, however she didn't reside in that building until her second and subsequent visits to St. Andrews. For her first visit it is believed she stayed here for a week. This has only been noted by a few. Hay Fleming in a footnote wrote; 'Another fine old house – 71 South Street – is also traditionally associated with Queen Mary... She did not like Edinburgh, but seems to have liked St. Andrews; and, between September 1561 and September 1565, she paid several visits to it and to the immediate neighbourhood, two of these visits being of considerable duration.'[116]

On taking her seat as the Scottish Queen shortly after arriving in Scotland for the first time since she was taken to France at the age of six, she 'must have found it difficult with both her parents being dead and her husband Francis II also dying the year before. In September of that year on her first tour of Scotland she came to St. Andrews with her four Maries and a large primarily French retinue. Enjoying the town so much they stayed here for a week. The

Cathedral had been abandoned by the time she arrived, but it was all still intact.'

*The Knights Templar, Mary Queen of Scots, an Archbishop and a Witch!*
The Knights Hospitallers, the Knights Templar, Knights of St. John had temple land granted to them in a number of locations in the centre of St. Andrews by Malcolm IV in 1160. They were given three tenements occupying the lands running from South to North between South Street and Market Street, Market Street and North Street, and North Street and The Scores. Covering an area from east to west running from Baxter Wynd now Baker Lane westwards along South Street to parallel what is now Kennedy Hall on the Scores. The most important of these Templar tenements was the South Street to Market Street tenement of 71 South Street. This old Templar building now encompassing 69-71 still remains to this day, complete with its almost hidden garden called St. John's Garden to the rear, which is known as a secret garden being hidden away, and is generally open to those who find it. The garden forms the larger part of what originally existed when it was an early Templar tenement and is accessed through a black iron gate partway way along the narrow lane of Market Street – once off the main Market Street area. The building was originally part of a larger structure and its vaulted chambers which are also intact were originally used as stables for the Templar's horses.

One of the connections between this residence and Mary Stuart, Mary Queen of Scots, was that she knew Sir James Sandilands, Commander or Prior of the Knights in Scotland and the Preceptor of Torphichen which oversaw the Templar's and the Templar lands. He met Mary in France back in 1553. It may have been as a result of this meeting which led to an invitation for her to stay at the residence in South Street should she find herself in St. Andrews. It was known they got on well with each other, and that she favoured the Templar's, and whilst staying here in 1561 she played archery in the St. John's Garden. Enjoying court favour, Sandilands became the first Lord of Torphichen – the headquarters of the Templar's by her hand in 1563.

By 1614 the tenement lands of the Templar's had a new owner. They came to the possession of the Earl of Haddington – the richest man in Scotland, who rented the tenements out for many years. In 1576 the Archbishop of St. Andrews and Scotland was Archbishop Patrick Adamson. His position came with many enemies who were quick to accuse him of anything they could to secure his downfall. In 1578 amid Presbyterian fervour he was accused of consorting with witches. This never amounted to anything at the time but ten years later in 1588 it became a different story. A woman from Boarhills became a pawn in the post reformation politics through her involvement with Archbishop Adamson. It was believed that at 71 South Street a witch called Alison Pearson cured the Archbishop of various maladies by transferring his illnesses to a white pony.

The enemies of the Archbishop also fabricated a story that he was himself a witch saying 'the Archbishop, like other witches, had a familiar in the form of a hare, which once ran before him down the street.

These were the beliefs of men of learning like James[lviii], the nephew and companion of Andrew Melville.'[117] [lix]

**Archbishop Patrick Adamson**

Sir Walter Scott writing in 1830 says; 'Alison Pearson, in Byrehill, [Boarhills] was, 28th May, 1588, tried for invocation of the spirits of the devil, especially in the vision of one Mr. William Sympson, her cousin and her mother's brother's son, who she affirmed was a great scholar and doctor of medicine, dealing with charms and abusing the ignorant people. Against this poor woman her own confession was the principal evidence.' [At her trial all manner of stories were given by her, no doubt these were given in agreement to fantastical allegations during torture, which was still being practiced in Scotland after the reformation.]

Scott continues: 'Alison Pearson had a familiar in the court of Elfland. This was her relative, William Sympson, born in Stirling, whose father was king's smith in that town. William had been taken away, she said, by a man of Egypt (a Gipsy), who carried him to Egypt along with him; that he remained there twelve years, and that his father died in the meantime for opening a priest's book and looking upon it. She declared that she had renewed her acquaintance with her kinsman as soon as he returned. She further confessed that one day as she passed through Grange Muir she lay down in a fit of sickness, and that a green man came to her, and said if she would be faithful he might do her good. In reply she charged him, in the name of God and by the law he lived upon, if

---

[lviii] James Melville (1556-1614)
[lix] Andrew Melville (1545 to 1622) a noted preacher and theologian he was Principal of St. Mary's College in 1580 and Rector of the University in 1590

he came for her soul's good to tell his errand. On this the green man departed. But he afterwards appeared to her with many men and women with him, and against her will she was obliged to pass with them farther than she could tell, with piping, mirth, and good cheer; also that she accompanied them into Lothian, where she saw puncheons of wine with tasses or drinking-cups. She declared that when she told of these things she was sorely tormented, and received a blow that took away the power of her left side, and left on it an ugly mark which had no feeling. She also confessed that she had seen before sunrise the good neighbours make their salves with pans and fires. Sometimes, she said, they came in such fearful forms as frightened her very much. At other times they spoke her fair, and promised her that she should never want if faithful, but if she told of them and their doings, they threatened to martyr her. She also boasted of her favour with the Queen of Elfland and the good friends she had at that court, notwithstanding that she was sometimes in disgrace there, and had not seen tile queen for seven years. She said William Sympson is with tile fairies, and that he lets her know when they are coming; and that he taught her what remedies to use, and how to apply them. She declared that when a whirlwind blew the fairies were commonly there, and that her cousin Sympson confessed that every year the tithe of them were taken away to hell. The celebrated Patrick Adamson, an excellent divine and accomplished scholar, created by James VI Archbishop of St. Andrews, swallowed the prescriptions of this poor hypochondriac with good faith and will, eating a stewed fowl, and drinking out at two draughts a quart of claret, medicated with the drugs she recommended. According to the belief of the time, this Alison Pearson transferred the bishop's indisposition from himself to a white palfrey [pony], which died in consequence. There is a very severe libel on him for this and other things unbecoming his order, with which he was charged... The margin of the court-book again bears the melancholy and brief record, "Convicta et combusta."'

He then says 'she is more to be pitied as, whether an enthusiast or an impostor, she practised her supposed art exclusively for the advantage of mankind.'[118]

She was tied to a stake on Witch Hill and strangled before being burnt on the 28th May 1588. Patrick Adamson was excommunicated and died a pauper in 1592.

So with a history of the Templar's, Mary Queen of Scots, Archbishop Adamson being excommunicated because of his involvement here with a purported witch, and with it perhaps being the oldest inhabited building in the town, it is a very special building indeed. Maybe now it will command a few moments of time to admire the architecture of this ancient structure when wandering along South Street en-route to other more well known landmarks of the town.

This building is now home to the University's Institute of Mediaeval Studies – a fitting compliment indeed for a gem with quite an extraordinary history having been hidden in plain sight all these many near forgotten years.

## The Phantom Coach – East End Market Street
*Ghosts of St. Andrews Tour ref. 50*

In the early 1980s myself and another sharing a first floor flat towards the east end of Market Street heard the phantom coach. We were in the living room of the flat facing onto Market Street. The time was around 1am. The windows were open to allow a cool breeze to enter from a hot summer's night. We were chatting away when we heard a coach in the dead of night. The sound was unmistakably as it trundled across the old cobbled stones, with the echoing sounds of a number of horses hooves accompanied by heavy rattling chains making its way along Market Street. It was all fairly brief and as the unusual sound began to register we looked at each other and flew to the window to see what it was, but there was nothing to see, the street was as deserted as it ever is at this time of night and the silence had returned, baring the faintest sound of a distant car in North Street or South Street. Immediately we went out the door of the flat and down the steps excitedly describing to each other what we had heard and both coming to the conclusion it was definitely the sound of an old horse drawn coach, it was unmistakable. Once in the clean fresh air we looked up and down the street. My flatmate looked down Union Street and I looked down Church Street but there was no sign of any horses let alone a coach or any sign of movement to be found. There was no other explanation than it being the Phantom Coach we had heard that night.

Independent of our encounter with the coach and with a description correlating with the same, a local resident of St. Andrews, when living also in the east end of Market Street heard the Phantom Coach on a number of occasions. The first time she heard it was before hearing any of Linskill's stories or indeed hearing any tales of the coach at all.

At night when all was still she heard the loud clattering sounds of the horses hooves accompanied by the echoing trundle of a heavy carriage travelling at some speed across the cobbled road; only lasting a few seconds the sounds died out as rapidly as they started. She could give no physical explanation for the eerie sounds and saw nothing that could have made them when she looked out of her window. After each experience with the coach she always felt ill and slept uneasily.

The east end of Market Street continues down the long narrow cobbled lane to South Castle Street, then turning to the left it is only a short distance to the castle itself. We heard the sounds of coach and horses around 1am which is also the time when one of the legends states that Beaton makes his appearance in his coach as it speeds its way down to the Castle Sands and into the sea.

## Linskill at a glance

Linskill in his usual manner relates to us three stories concerning the Phantom Coach; two stories of the Strathkinness to St. Andrews Road where one ends its journey in St. Andrews Bay, and a third giving mention to a Phantom Coach also being seen in St. Andrews Abbey Walk. ⚑

Refer to Linskill: *The True Tale of the Phantom Coach*, p.340
*Related by Captain Chester*, p.287
*Concerning More Appearances of the White Lady*, p.283

## The Star Hotel Haunting
*Ghosts of St. Andrews Tour ref. 51*

The Public Bar of the Star Hotel stood on the right and extended to the hotel part at the back of Logies Lane and across the pavement to the gully on the pavement.

An account given to me many years ago by a barman concerns the Star Hotel that stood at 92-94 Market Street. The hotel ran from Market Street through the length of Logies Lane to Church Square beside the Hay Fleming Library. The hotel part faced onto Market Street, while the entrance to the public bar area was accessed from Church Square facing the South Street end. Before its closure and demolition in the early 1980s it served great bar meals and was a popular haunt of locals, students and tourists alike.

The public bar of this hotel was called 'The Star'. A long dimly lit public house of no little character from the décor and the locals who regularly drank there. Ah, those were the days! It was here about two years before closure that we now concern ourselves.

 The barman of the public bar one night after last orders and once everyone had left, locked the main entrance door and had cleared everything away as usual. He then briefly went through to the hotel and on his return all the tables and chairs throughout the pub had been disrupted. Some were lying on their sides; others had either been upturned or were now piled on top of each other in the middle of the room. The door to the pub was locked and there was no one else present. No sound had been heard and no one could have entered the bar through the hotel without passing by him first. His absence from the pub was for only a minute or two and there was not nearly enough time for any physical person to have rearranged everything in the given time. The sound alone of all the furniture moving to where he now found it would have alerted him, but all was silent.

Also around the time of this disruption the ghost of a lady had also been seen within the hotel by staff and guests flitting along some of the corridors. ✝

The *St. Andrews Citizen* in 1982 concerning the site of the Star Hotel following its demolition reported: 'Remains of three individuals were recovered during rebuilding at the Star Hotel. Workmen stated that they had found others, one at least being undisturbed. These burials lay along the N edge of Trinity Parish church Burial ground, and show the burial ground extended some 2 to 2.5m N of the present property boundary. Shards and glass fragments were found round the perimeter of the Star Hotel property and above the burials. All were in secondary positions and indicate disturbance of earlier domestic activity.'[119]

Archaeologists were given a brief period with which to make a study of the grounds before making way for the construction of a small shopping precinct on the site (pictured) of the former hotel and the area of Church Square that was to be pedestrianised. They also found a sealed up well in the heart of where the hotel stood. If you stand anywhere in the vicinity of Church Square and wonder what happened to the graveyard of the Holy Trinity Church – chances are you would be standing on it! This whole area was built over the graveyard of the Holy Trinity stemming back to before 1412. The tower is original but the rest of the church occupies the site of an earlier structure.

When Church Square itself was in the course of being pedestrianized it laid bare more of these ancient bones, only a few feet below the present level of ground. Finds of this kind have always been an attraction, so a few of the graves were left open for a time for the locals and visitors to view them. Provisions were made at the time to alter the plans of the area, so the graves would not then be disturbed by any future work being carried out in this location. So they still remain today where they were originally buried, under the pedestrian area of Church Square and the surrounding buildings.

Holy Trinity Church is the last resting place of Archbishop James Sharpe murdered on Magus Muir.[lx]

## The Phantom Car of Queen's Gardens
### *Ghosts of St. Andrews Tour ref. 52*

The accounts earlier of the *Poltergeist and the Pavilion* and an account of the monk of St. Rules were both given to me by Greta Boyd of St. Andrews, I continue here with another one of her experiences in St. Andrews.

### Queen's Gardens

"I was on my way to work at the Bute Buildings in St. Andrews (part of the University). It was dark and rainy, but there wasn't anything unusual about this particular evening; well, so I thought anyway. I drove along a few roads in the town to South Street, along this road then turned down Queen's Gardens following a car in front of me to the bottom. Nothing struck me as being unusual about this car, I remember it was a saloon but felt no need to pay any more attention to detail. Its lights were on and when nearing the bottom it indicated to turn left along Queen's Terrace, it then turned the corner leaving my view for a very brief moment. Upon turning the corner myself though, all I saw was an empty stretch of road – the car had completely vanished into thin air! I really couldn't believe it. There was absolutely nowhere for it to have disappeared to. No parked cars lined this stretch as they sometimes do and there was nowhere for it to turn off given the time it was out of my sight."

---

[lx] For more details of Sharpe and for something interesting about his last resting place refer to *The Body Snatchers* p.204

Stories of phantom cars are very few in number around the British Isles. It is more likely that you will see a spectral coach than a phantom motor vehicle – despite the numbers on the roads. The most famous account of a disappearing car in Scotland is set on the lonely misty roads of the Isle of Skye. The car is a 1934 Austin which makes no sound as it travels at great speed (well, relatively speaking for a 1934 Austin that is) with lights on full travelling along the road between Sligachan and Sconser. By all accounts there is no driver at the wheel and like the car Greta saw, it always vanishes abruptly. ¶

## The Haunting of John Menzies
### Now W. H. Smiths
*Ghosts of St. Andrews Tour ref. 53*

John Menzies was one of the larger shops in South Street standing opposite Holy Trinity Church. Now occupied by W. H. Smiths the building was occupied for many years by the Bank of Scotland.

The newsagents was delayed from opening by a few months in mid 1970s due to the engineering required to move a large vault from the former bank which proved to be an engineering feat in itself.

The top floor of this building used occasionally as a temporary stock room in the days of John Menzies was haunted by an unaccounted for invisible presence. Untouched by the refitting of the premises on the ground and first floors below, the largest of the rooms on this upper floor was the board room in the days of the bank. A picture still hung at one end of the room above the old fireplace. The picture was of official looking bankers from the turn of the twentieth century. This set the scene with the imagination to transform the room to its hay day and to the financial dealings of old St. Andrews life. With the floor being so high above South Street it is only the feint sound of the traffic from the town below that notifies as a reminder of which century you now find yourself to be in. It is within this beautiful walnut panelled room that the haunting of this building is particularly strong. Various members of staff over the years have felt the presence of somebody on this floor when no other has been present. Even to the extent that some of the staff would not venture up there again after experiencing the ghostly goings on, whilst others would not venture up there alone. The opening, closing or occasional locking of various heavy wooden doors adjoining the rooms has been experienced on numerous occasions without any physical intervention. The windows up there are kept tightly shut so there are no drafts to speak of that could have caused a vacuum or blow these great doors to and fro. It could get so bad that a member of staff would have to stay by the main fire door at the foot of the stairs which led up to this floor, whilst another went up to fetch some stock, lest the door lock itself and whoever was on the second floor find they are stranded up there!

The floor is decked throughout with old wooden floorboards in-keeping with the wooden panelling which creak and echo under foot when moving around this large primarily empty space - baring that of a few boxes of retail goods. The distinct sounds of slow and measured ghostly footsteps have been heard by most that have been up there at one time or another. These are the hollow sound of shoes walking slowly across the floorboards which could well be that of the old bank manager pacing around pondering on a deal. They are most distinct as they echo around these empty rooms. The sound is accentuated because it is so still and quiet up there. The footsteps are often heard almost straight away on entering this floor, as a reminder it would seem to any who enter that they are not alone. Occasionally these footsteps were accompanied at times with the noise of something slowly shuffling around a large heavy object - like a heavy filled sack being dragged across the bare wooden floorboards. These have all been attested to on many occasions by the staff. I have also witnessed the banging and locking of doors and the shuffling of a heavy object. Also the measured slow footsteps of a person who never appears from the room adjoining whatever room you happen to be in at the time. I worked there in the late 1970s and early 1980s and to my knowledge nothing of a physical manifestation has thus far ever been seen here. ⚑

## The Floating Head in a South Street Flat
*Ghosts of St. Andrews Tour ref. 54*

Along South Street from the West Port is an old flat above shops opposite Blackfriars Chapel. The flat is the haunt of a dark shadow like form drifting around the walls. The spectre is usually accompanied by areas of extreme cold and the large head of a bearded man has been seen floating around one of the rooms – much to the surprise and shock of those who have witnessed this gruesome spectacle. One night an occupant in one of the bedrooms of the second floor awoke to see the head hovering just above her face. On waking the other occupants with a scream they rushed in to see what had happened, but by the time they arrived the apparition had disappeared. Various people staying in this bedroom have experienced the same.

Dark shadows flitting across the interior walls of dwellings are a common feature of many disturbances. They are especially common as an accompaniment to poltergeist or the 'classic haunting' activities to be found in so many paranormal cases. Oppressive and often disturbing they have a menacing quality about them when witnessed, as if death itself is paying an unexpected and most unwelcome visit.

*Linskill at a glance*
There is a brief acknowledgment to the floating head in Linskill's book, but no further details are given. In his book he attributes a floating head to Lausdree Castle – a fictitious castle somewhere close by St. Andrews. Linskill used this as a showcase platform for some of the hauntings and oddities he had heard about across Fife, but had no further details for. It is my feeling he used Earlshall Castle near Leuchars as the setting for Lausdree. ⚱

Refer to *Ghosts of Fife (2013) By the author*

## The Unhappy Dominican of Blackfriars
*Ghosts of St. Andrews Tour ref. 55*

The vaulted chapel ruins of the Dominican Blackfriars Monastery in South Street sits on the green in South Street in front of Madras College where I spent my 5th year at school. The chapel forms the last surviving remnant of the monastery built by Bishop William Wishart of St. Andrews in 1274. The chapel which can be seen today was part of the northern transept, built beside the monastery in 1526 under the auspices of Archbishop James Beaton and formed the last completed section. One story runs that Cardinal David Beaton was said to have been finally buried here[120] after his murder at the castle and his body preserved or pickled in its infamous Bottle Dungeon which I related earlier. This appears to have been a decoy or perhaps one of a series of decoys of the time to thwart any desecration from the town's folk venting their anger. As we saw earlier in the section on the castle regarding his murder he was secretly buried in Kilrenny.

Following its vacancy during the reformation the land was eventually passed to 'Dr Patrick Young, Archdeacon of St Andrews, [who] granted the land to the town as a site for a grammar school. The late Dr Bell obtained it from the town, and upon it, with some other ground he had purchased the Madras College has been erected.'[121] The college was built in-keeping with the chapel's style.

In 1526 - the same year the chapel was built the clergy appointed a Dominican Friar by the name of Alexander Campbell who lived at Blackfriars to associate with one Patrick Hamilton, a young student at the university you will have met at St. Salvator's College above.

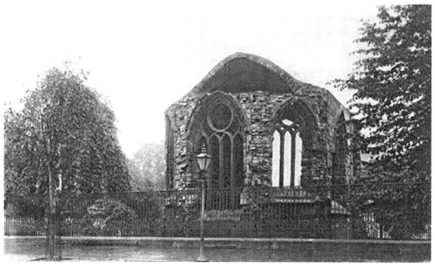

The North Transept of the Chapel of Blackfriars Church,
South Street circa 1927

*The Ghost of Alexander Campbell*

The ghost of Friar Alexander Campbell the Dominican Monk of Blackfriars to this day still haunts the ruined chapel at Madras College in South Street. He is seen as a shadowy figure in a long white cloak adorning the black cross. Those who pass by may chance to see the unhappy Dominican gliding noiselessly into the chapel ruins. Struck it would appear with a troubled conscience for sending a man to his death for beliefs he could not now deny were also his own. This is more than reason enough for his apparition to still haunt his former monastery. †

Refer also to *The Mystery of the St. Salvator's Chapel Face*, p.44

## South Street's Murdered Pedlar

*Ghosts of St. Andrews Tour ref. 56*

A cellar perhaps within a shop in the western quarter of South Street is haunted by a pedlar who was murdered many years ago. Which would more than likely place it in one of the shops on the north side of the street between the West Port and Bell Street.

***Linskill at a glance***

The pedlar is also referenced briefly by Linksill in his story *The Smothered Piper of the West Cliffs,* p.331 where he says he 'sweeps down with chilly hand the cheeks of invaders to his haunted cellar.'

# Last Leg of the Tour

## Market Street West End

*Ghosts of St. Andrews Tour ref. 57*

Near the site of the old Woolworths once lived Janet Young. She was a supposed witch and was the last to be burnt at the stake on Witch Hill. When the site was a Woolworths, the staff of the store often found stock had been moved around during the night and cold areas in the back area were common. The apparition of a woman has also been seen walking along the pavement.

## The Old Monastery of Greyfriars

*Ghosts of St. Andrews Tour ref. 58*

Founded in 1458 by Bishop Kennedy the monastery stood on the east side of what is now known as Greyfriars Gardens and was occupied by Franciscan Friars or Greyfriars appropriately named after their greyish brown attire. There pious order was relatively short lived, only surviving some one hundred years before it fell into ruin and decay.

The site of Greyfriars has since been developed with residential buildings and shops covering most of its traces. The chapel of the monastery stood on the corner of Greyfriars Gardens and St. Mary's Place with a draw well nearby. Sadly the chapel has disappeared also but the draw well dropping to a depth of some 48 feet still remains and by all accounts is kept in a state of good repair.

Half shrouded almost into obscurity in flowers and bushes depending the time of year, it lies tucked away in the corner of a residential garden by the roadside of Greyfriars Gardens. On its rediscovery in 1839 it was found to contain two inscribed stones, now to be found within the Cathedral museum.

### Linskill at a glance

 A curious tale is related by Linskill about the well which he associates with a screaming skull.

'In 1513 Neville de Beauchamp known as Flash Neville as he went in for racing, cards and drink, married a pretty girl, daughter of a silk mercer in Perth and who it seems dies (they say of a broken heart) two years later.

Neville seized with awful remorse shortly afterwards became a monk in Greyfriars monastery.

After his wife's death her relations blaming him for her death hunted him for revenge. The girl's brother eventually tracked him down at the monastery.

"It seems that one afternoon after vespers he forced his way into the Monastery Chapel, sought out Neville de Beauchamp, and slashed off his head with a sword in the aisle of the Kirk. Now a queer thing happened – his body fell on the floor, but the severed head, with a wild scream, flew up to the chapel ceiling and vanished through its roof."

The story continues with the screaming scull and may be found in full in Linskill's *The Screaming Skull of Greyfriars*, p.327

The site of the former Monastery is also the haunt of a phantom, a headless monk who wanders the former precincts from Greyfriars Gardens to the Students Union which ties itself in with the next account. ∮

## The University of St. Andrews Students Union
*Ghosts of St. Andrews Tour ref. 59*

Part of the eastern grounds occupied by the University of St. Andrews Students Union in St. Mary's Place was once encompassed within the gardens of Greyfriars Monastery. The grounds are haunted by the fleeting spectre or shadow of a male figure in dark clothing. Within the building an unaccountable oppressive atmosphere or force has been felt. Electrical equipment placed within the eastern area has a tendency to malfunction with uncanny regularity and the customary bouts of extreme cold associated with a haunting have been also been experienced. The origins of the presence are unknown but it is likely to be one of the Franciscan monks who inhabited the nearby Monastery. ∮

# McIntosh Hall

*Ghosts of St. Andrews Tour ref. 60*

McIntosh Hall in Abbotsford Crescent near the North Street entrance to Gillespie Wynd is so called from its nineteenth century owner William Carmichael McIntosh. He was Professor of Natural History at the University in 1882 who leased the property to tenants, including the military for a time around 1918. It was known then as Chattan House, which then became Chattan Hotel. The house was leased to the University in 1921 and like Hamilton Hall they turned it into a student residence. It is known by the students as 'Chattan' after its former name. Considerably smaller than Hamilton, the University over the years have both bought and been bequeathed the adjoining private residences right along the sweeping arc of Abbotsford Crescent to form the hall of residence it is today. The hall was a residency for woman only until 1982.

Rumours abound about this place being haunted, with tales of fires much like that of Hamilton Hall, including some which resulted in fatalities alongside student suicides, which of themselves carry no substance in fact. There are also reports of a presence being felt in some of its rooms, cold spots, lights turning themselves on in vacated rooms, toilets flushing with no assistance and books and papers being moved around in the rooms by unseen hands. It has always been difficult to substantiate many of the occurrences when the stories pass through so many generations of occupants. Speculation and embellishment are all too easily added to reports, which over the years have led to its own mythology, but there are some who have certainly felt, seen or heard phenomenon here. I did meet a student in the mid 1980s who said she saw the ghost of a male figure dressed in dark clothing move across her room in Chattan.

I wrote the above piece in 1989 and find it interesting that in 2005 a student internet notice board carried similar stories and accounts to some of the above, including the report of a ghostly male in black in one of the rooms. It is in many ways all too easy to dismiss potential phenomenon when it appears to be overshadowed by the ramblings of rumour and conjecture. It comes down once again to finding that nugget of truth hidden in the presented material. It takes time in some cases to do this and understand more of what might be occurring in some places. To sort the wheat from the chaff and to see if any patterns emerge that are not just the spontaneous antics of the imagination on an internet chat room. In some cases it is true there is no smoke without fire (to excuse the pun) and this seems to be the case with Chattan. Looking at the alleged incidences I had heard about up to 1989 and comparing them to those over the following 16 years up to 2005, aside alleged suicides and fires at Chattan the phenomenon appears to be uncannily similar to what I had previously found. The accounts can seem fanciful but the embellishments between the two periods are actually very slight, which points more towards these being the nuggets of truth that have sustained themselves above high spirited hearsay. Importantly no one has been harmed over the years in Chattan, and for all the disturbances there might be in this popular residence, they are, like the Venus fly trap, more the variety of the unusual than the disturbing. ⓵

## Alexandra Place - The Blue Stane
### Is a stone just a stone?
*Ghosts of St. Andrews Tour ref. 61*

The Blue Stane (stone) of St. Andrews almost hidden behind railings was for many years partially obscured by the foliage and hedges of the garden on the corner of Alexandra Place and City Road, opposite the Hope Park Church. Long forgotten by all but a few who knew of its significance, times have changed. Now the area around the stone has been cleared and a plaque giving details to some of its history sits proudly on the railings above it.

The stone is situated in the grounds of the public house running along the basement floor of the private residences above. The bar was once called Kate's Bar, and proved a very popular watering hole in its time for both residents and students. With an old murky feel and a dark wooden floor it gave a character in-keeping with its welcoming proprietor Mr Fotheringham and his two very large dogs!

Eventually the public house was sold around the late 1980s and has changed hands on numerous occasions with few – if any in the past finding the same successful formula it once enjoyed. The public house is now called 'The Blue Stane' after its namesake depicted here on the corner of its grounds.

**The Blue Stane**
**by the right post of the sign**

The stone is of no great size, indeed it can hardly be seen in this photograph and if the passing layman were troubled to notice it, there would be no great importance or value to be found attached, other than it now being the name of the public house. A stone is a stone many would say. Once however, this stone commanded a great deal of worth from all who chanced to pass by it, and in not letting respect for the stone go unnoticed they would each curtsy, nod or touch it as they passed. For it was long believed this stone was endowed with some long forgotten magical power that brought them good fortune should they acknowledge its presence.

As unassuming and as small this stone is, with its radius of only around 2 feet, it has a great long history attached to it. The stone has sat in a number of locations in the area, on the south side of Double Dykes Road and by the West Port before being moved to here by the Victorians.

In 1314 the pike-men of St. Andrews touched the stone to give them strength before heading for Bannockburn and the battle they eventually won. 'For hundreds of years it was also the rendezvous of the Whiplickers or Carters society, when they had their annual races the day after the Lamas Market.'[122] Whiplickers or Carters were horse and cart hirers – the equivalent of today's taxi service in the town. Meetings were held here with the stone as the central focus and it is believed it may go back as far as 843 AD as the coronation stone of Kenneth MacAlpine who united the Scots and the Picts.

Being the size it is, a custom of old would be for the men to display their strength by trying to lift it! A more realistic association had this as the trysting place of lovers.

An old legend has it also that fairies and elves once frequented this site and this is how it gained the magical powers that for hundreds of years and more the local folk believed would bring them to the door of good fortune. An old religious legend tells how a giant on Blebo Craigs or Drumcarrow Craig which is believed to be where it originated from, threw the stone at St. Rules Tower when it was erected, falling short of its mark it landed near to where it now resides. ↟

So is a stone always just a stone as many would say?

The picturesque fishing village of Crail also has a blue stane, somewhat larger than the one in St. Andrews but with a very similar folklore attachment. Rather than a giant throwing the stone it was hurled at the nearby Crail church by the Devil standing on the Isle of May. Such was the fashionable scope of the early Protestant reformers in using anything they could as propaganda against the Catholic Church at the time.[lxi]

## The Phantom Coach – Argyle Street
*Ghosts of St. Andrews Tour ref. 62*

The coach was also heard in the winter of 1987 in Argyle Street not far from the West Port. A resident heard the galloping of horses pulling a carriage outside her bedroom window. By the time she got out of bed and went across to the window the sounds had stopped and there was no sign of anything to have made them. ↟

Argyle Street is part of the B939. Heading out of town it turns into Hepburn Gardens, then Buchanan Gardens, and as it winds its way it becomes the Strathkinness low road which passes Bishops Wood and the site of Sharpe's execution.

Once known as the village of Argyle, the houses in this area were out with the precincts of the town. There is a letter written in the winter from a woman who lived here in the 19th century to her friend who lived in South Street. The letter says she hope the letter finds her well and she would visit her friend in the spring once the weather had improved. At the most the distance can't be more than a mile.

---

[lxi] Refer to *Crail – The Blue Stane* in the book *Ghosts of Fife*, (2013) by the author

## The Phantom Coach – South Street
*Ghosts of St. Andrews Tour ref. 63*

 Sharpe's phantom coach has also been seen in South Street making its way from Magus Muir along Argyle Street and into South Street towards the Pends or Abbey Walk. It is looking to complete its journey with the dead body of Sharpe, his badly wounded daughter and battered entourage as they make their way to his Palace of the Archbishops midway down the Pends. ⚑

## The Britannia Hotel
### Now the West Port Bar & Kitchen

## *Last Stop on the Ghosts of St. Andrews Tour!*
**Read both refs. 64 and 65**

*Ghosts of St. Andrews Tour ref. 64*
The West Port guarding the entrance to South Street at the west end in St. Andrews is one of the finest remaining city gateways in Scotland. It was built on the one time boundary of the medieval borough of St. Andrews and beckons the traveller to explore the treasures lying within.

It is believed to have been constructed in the early 1500s and reconstructed in 1589, then renovated in 1843. It has stood well over the years to the elements, but has suffered in more recent times to a fair amount of damage from heavy transport trying to fit under the low stone archway. With the corner of vehicles clipping and scraping the stone work, new blocks of sandstone are visible around the inside of the archway attesting to the visible repairs of various accidents.

The popular West Port Bar & Kitchen just by the West Port at 170 South Street has been well and truly put on the map of St. Andrews. It is known as the location where Prince William and Kate would come to socialise and get to know each other better during their university terms in St. Andrews. A number of years ago this establishment was called the Britannia Hotel. Built in 1870, there was nothing overtly special about the hotel. In fact it sat quite unassumingly by the West Port for many years. Having been relatively unchanged for many years the tourists would spot it, but the residents would pass it by without a thought. There was however something quite unusual about this hotel, and it wasn't because of its continental feel. It was something only noticeable once inside. Often the bar wouldn't open its doors until 7pm or 8pm. If I remember it was 7pm at the weekends and they tended to close around 10pm.

Once inside the customer and resident was greeted by two elderly sisters. When ordering drinks you gave your order to one who then took your money while the other poured your drink. Sounds simple, but this would turn into a process that would somehow take around 10 minutes to complete. One of their numerous quirks was refusing to serve alcohol in a pint glass, believing it would contain far too much alcohol for any to consume. So, ever being the resourceful types, we would drink copious amounts of half pints whilst pondering the solution to the pint glass problem.

In the winter our hosts would turn the portable calor gas heater on so it wasn't quite as chilly as outside, and once lit it was wheeled over to wherever you happened to be sitting. Needles to say if it got busy the dilemma presenting itself would be where to place the heater.

Nuts and quavers were always on the bar to nibble on. Or rather they weren't quite on the bar until you ordered a drink. Then one would supply a batch before taking your money which partly added to the reason why getting served took so long. A small black tube with coloured circles sat as a seventies icon at one end of the bar. This would come to life at the weekends and it was always a big deal turning it on. They would get more excited than the punters as it created whirling flashes of colour across the dimly lit room, transforming the bar and giving it a 70s disco ambiance. Despite this much anticipated entertainment extravaganza every weekend, nothing could top the ghostly phenomenon which took place here and was somehow in-keeping with the eccentricity of these two little elderly ladies. Who, if I didn't know better, could well have been ghosts themselves.

The ground floor and especially the garden area was the haunt of a well dressed middle aged gentleman wearing a dark suit. He would appear to residents around dusk, either standing or seated and would always appear quite motionless.

Some friendly faces from Falkland on the 28th September 2013, enjoying a Saturday stag afternoon in St. Andrews at the haunted beer garden!

Occasionally things in the bar would move around without any intervention and both the bar and the guest rooms were prone to an unnaturally cold chill. Sometimes a particular area on the right, at the foot of a few ascending steps to a restaurant area would become very cold, and no amount of heating would solve the problem. The two elderly sisters were aware of this. It is why they kept the heater here until someone came in. This was once the area at the end of the bar which ran along what is now a partition wall between the bar and restaurant. The lights in the bar, the toilet and other parts of the hotel would flicker or go off at times, as if something was trying to notify of its presence. It would happen just for a moment when someone was doing something they needed to see by, such as going to the toilet or walking up or down the stairs. No electrical faults were ever found. The ghostly gentleman was believed to have been a guest who died in the hotel many years previously. †

Eventually one of the sisters died and the hotel became too much for just one of them to run, so the doors were closed for the last time in the mid 1980s. It is believed the surviving lady took over Dairsie Inn for a number of years. They were undoubtedly a couple of real characters and those having the privilege to sample their hospitality missed them when the place closed down. They were always very pleasant and their old fashioned eccentricity gave them an endearing charm and a reputation for the unusual, which was so often taken for granted at the time. Subsequently their reputation has given them an almost folkloric stature in the town with their wee oddities I spoke of earlier, Their Victorian hospitality is rarely something we see anymore. I for one missed them when they went and I imagine so did their non paying guest!

As the Westport Bar & Kitchen, Prince William and Kate by all accounts were known to sit and relax of an evening in the window seats to the right of the entrance door of the bar area, The spot where the presence used to be felt and just by the cold area at the foot of those few ascending stairs. With the Bar and Kitchen's new found charm adding to their budding romance in this vibrant location, I imagine William and Kate were unaware of any disturbances, and the growing warmth between them would have dispelled any overt sensations of an icy chill when they were sitting engrossed in conversation.

Like its predecessor, the Westport Bar also has accommodation in the form of four first class double/twin rooms. Well worth a visit and an overnight stay!

 Read also the following account where the presence felt in the window seats and the other disturbances at the Hotel were also experienced in a flat above the new restaurant area at 172 South Street, which is the subject of the following account. If time is short read the *Account in Brief*, and if more time can be afforded *The Full Account.*

## West Port Poltergeist and Presence
*Ghosts of St. Andrews Tour ref. 65*

*Account In Brief*

In the autumn of 1988 the flat at 172 South Street came in for a bout of poltergeist activity and a presence affecting a student couple, lasting for a period of around three and a half months. The outbreaks were of a subtle nature rather than being overly dramatic, which is characteristically more common with this type of phenomenon than the extreme examples we tend to associate activity by. 

 If short of time, this marks the end of the tour, a full description of the activity continues on the next page.

Poltergeist activity of itself is bad enough with it always being spontaneous and unpredictable in how it manifests, but it is the unknown cause that is often found to be the more disturbing of factors. Our conscious mind is ill prepared for experiencing the great unknown typified by paranormal activity. When something happens we are unable to account for we try to make sense of it by searching our minds to find something to attribute it to – however unlikely it may be we try to find an answer – however tenuous. Often this isn't possible so we simply pass it off as a one off occurrence and rarely think any more of it. What I talk of here tends to involve small incidences which don't tend to raise that much of a concern for us – at least to start with. It is the frequency which tends to alert us to something more going on than simply a misplaced memory or a moment of enthusiastic imagination.

The subtle occurrences I am about to mention can and do happen to us, a great many of us. The couple staying in one of the flats at 172 South Street were in their early twenties and were both studying at the University in St. Andrews. After moving into the flat during the month of June 1988 everything went well for them - until the November of that year when the kind of odd and subtle occurrences I spoke of just now began to happen to them.

It all started with feelings of unease, feelings that they were not the only occupants in the flat, and with this a very strained oppressive atmosphere began pervading the air. The main areas to become affected by this unseen intrusion were the study and the bedroom. Both these rooms were also being subjected to sudden drops in temperature with no accounted for cause. On one occasion after going to bed, J (they have asked to remain anonymous) became extremely cold down one side of her body as if someone or something very cold had just lain down beside her. Startled she sat up to look, the sensation disappeared straight away and nothing was to be seen that could have accounted for what she had just felt. Her boyfriend slept on the other side of the bed so it wasn't he who could be attributable to it.

In the bedroom there were two mirrors, one of full length in the door of the wardrobe, the other a semi-circular dressing table mirror. Whilst looking in the dressing table mirror the other mirror could be seen, this gave rise to yet another view of the bedroom. After a while they both felt the presence of something almost tangible in this room with them. This room was above what is now the restaurant of the West Port Bar and Kitchen. In the days of the Britannia Hotel the room was above and adjoining wall of the bar area where the presence and sense of extreme cold would be felt.

When J looked into the wardrobe mirror through the dressing table mirror - even for a moment, a fleeting shadow was sometimes seen darting across one of the walls of the room. On turning round in her chair nothing would be seen. Thinking it was a trick of the light or her imagination, and with the usual array of things preoccupying her mind taking precedence, these were primarily dismissed as odd distractions. They did have thoughts sometimes as to the nature of the unusual experiences, with occasional fleeting thoughts of something not being quite right, but for the most part they thought nothing of it at all.

Soon though the feeling of not being alone in the room increased, so too did the shadow become more obvious, it was as if something could be seen, but only seen indirectly when looking at the room by reflection, or in this case a double reflection through two mirrors. The mirrors seemed to be acting in the same way as an obsidian scrying mirror, which allows the magician to see and commune with spirits of other realities. M her partner felt a presence in this room but he never saw anything other than his own reflection when looking into the mirror. Eventually the feeling and the distracting shadow became more pronounced, even to the point of whatever it was becoming unbearable, and the shadow becoming more a defined dark shape. This got too much for J, so they decided to conceal the wardrobe mirror with paper hoping this would help. This gave them both a little piece of mind and she found the presence didn't seem to appear in the dressing table mirror of its own. Unfortunately this didn't put an end to the feelings they were not alone. There was still a strong and very tangible presence and there were never any set patterns as to when they would feel it, or when they would experience a sudden bout of cold in one of the rooms.

After some time small objects began to disappear, a padlock was the first, then a tape measure; always small items and always relatively insignificant, but always with enough regularity to frustrate and annoy them, especially as they always needed what they couldn't find. After conducting thorough searches the objects would never reveal their hiding places. A few days later they would reappear again in obvious places they could not have possibly overlooked.

The proceedings became so subtle and numerous it would have been easy for each to have accused the other of moving something without thinking. However they trusted each other and knew each other well enough to know the other wasn't playing games. For a while they both believed their imaginations were to blame for what was happening around them, but on reflection they were never able to come up with any logical explanations.

In January 1989 the feeling of unease in the study and bedroom had further intensified. The feeling of another presence being there with them had grown enormously. They equated it to someone constantly standing behind them – looking at them intently. The regularity of the cold spots, especially in the study had also increased. Even with the heaters on full it would instantly become icy cold for no apparent reason, and it was now no longer localised to certain areas. The feelings got so dramatic and the atmosphere so oppressive, they decided to remove all their belongings from the study and keep out of that room altogether.

In the bedroom they had tried to ignore the bouts of cold that would suddenly stir up and disappear just as rapidly. Confined now to the living room and bedroom with which to study in and with things still disappearing, the final straw for them came in mid-February, just over one month later. M was in the kitchen when he heard his girlfriend let out a loud scream. He rushed through to the bedroom to see what had happened and saw J in a state of shock. She was just standing still, starring at her watch lying on the ground in front of her. She had been tidying up the bedroom when she saw her watch leap off the chest of drawers and land on the floor. It was lying about three feet in front of the chest. This part of the room had also become very cold, in fact "colder than ever."

Their nerves were already frail by now and the disturbances were affecting their relationship as well as their academic studies. After this incident they became even more frightened, not for what had already happened, but for the unknown of what could happen next. Things were really taking a turn for the worse and whatever the cause of these disturbances, it was doing a good job in attempting to drive them out of the flat altogether. They had thought about moving, but only had a few more months to go on the lease before the term was up for the summer. Also, they couldn't afford to move somewhere else in that short time, so they decided it would be best to stick it out and not now use the bedroom! Although this meant they now only had the use of the kitchen and living room it was their only option.

Once the study and the bedroom had been vacated the disturbances seemed to stop altogether. They said there was still a kind of menacing atmosphere hanging over the place, which may have just been their nerves in anticipation of something starting up again.

They were both relieved and began feeling better about things when they stopped using these rooms, but however much relief they did feel, it all paled in comparison to how they felt when they finally moved out of the flat for the summer break in June 1989.

On speaking with the couple about these disturbances I found it to be something they had not mentioned to anyone before. They stopped having visitors to the flat in February when they moved out of the bedroom and as I mentioned earlier they wanted to remain anonymous and didn't wish to make a fuss. They had contacted me after they saw my 1989 letter in the Scots Magazine for accounts for this book.

The phenomenon was relatively low key compared to the dramatic and more stereotypically glamorous of occurrences we tend to associate with hauntings, but they neither exaggerated nor bolstered their story to make it more credible. It had been given to me in a kind of embarrassed, almost sheepish matter of fact way, as though I would not believe what they were telling me, or that it had been their imagination and there was not really anything to report. They were keen to express that they didn't want to waste my time, but they had to know if it was them or if something had been present.

Because their experiences were not overly dramatic they thought I might be disappointed or was expecting a full blown haunting with all manner of things flying around and a cupboard full of ghosts to choose from. While that would have been nice I reassured them that what they experienced was more the realty, and more in-keeping with most cases. The 'classic' disturbances – although they can be a feature they fortunately happen with a lot less regularity than the minor incidents which they experienced, and which do tend to build over time. The haunted house on the Scores was like this.

These experiences had really affected them. When I was speaking with them they were still trying to work out if it was all their imagination and that they had been fussing over nothing. It had clearly upset them very deeply. They were still scared of the place and were clearly disturbed if not a little incredulous as to their own experiences.

Some relevant details emerged when speaking with them that may or may not have had some bearing or influence on the phenomenon which I can share with you. A short time before the phenomenon began J had been studying hard for her forthcoming exams. The pressure of these were giving her frequent bad headaches and making her feel quite ill. The growing feeling of a presence, the objects disappearing and the unnatural bouts of cold she experienced, were all coupled with growing problems with her health. This had resulted in her suffering from a form of depression which in turn was attacking her immune system. This all grew in measure to the disturbances becoming more prevalent over the winter months, and with all this the atmosphere in turn became consistently more oppressive.

Interestingly when we were speaking about this I could see by the way she was speaking that something was clicking into place, she was becoming increasingly pensive. It was as if she was remembering something. Then at the end of her speaking of her health and how it coincided with the trouble, she said she had been subjected to similar activity before, but until this moment she had never made any connection nor coupled what had occurred to her before with these experiences. She told me when she was eleven years of age the house she stayed in was disrupted for a short time by similar activity; her father's keys were discovered on the living room floor one evening after being missing for about a month. Bed clothes were frequently pulled off her bed at night by unseen hands, and her mother's leather coat was found badly slashed one morning with no apparent explanation as to how. With this she gasped, and on putting her hand to her mouth I could see what she was now thinking was terrifying her – as she then asked me if she might have been the cause of the disturbances.

You have to bear in mind some of what she was now saying had never come to light in previous conversations. She had never spoken with anyone about this until now, and for all the conversations she had had with her partner she had never mentioned to him about the activity from when she was 11. Also neither of them had seen a potential relationship between the increase of stress and ill health being concurrent with an increase in the phenomenon they experienced.

This is not a simple case, there are a few possibilities as to the cause, and there is a partial conclusion. One of the possibilities is the growing emotions and tension for her exams, coupled with severe headaches and stress, and the corresponding increase in phenomenon may in part have contributed to her generating enough PK energy to manifest itself – although unaware herself of the source of the disturbances. Most of the activity in the flat had centred about her and it was in the main confined to the study where she had spent most of her time under pressures for her exams. By the same respect the bedroom had been the place where she had been stressing over her ill health, and as her health deteriorated so too did the shadow across the wall increase, a shadow only she saw. Following this line it is possible the frustration of her health and her situation caused the watch to fly off the chest of drawers. This then marked the last straw for their occupancy of that room.

The study by association had become a symbol of pressure and the bedroom likewise with ill health. With the two significant rooms in her life now not being occupied, the symbolic associations were no longer present – at least not to the same degree. The pressure, the stress and the ill health were initially still present, but with the change of scenery and the calming of disturbances, she began feeling a lot better. Aside an apprehensive residue the disturbance almost immediately then disappeared.

Along with the potential for PK activity and it being caused by J, it has to be remembered the activity follows a similar pattern to what had been occurring in the Britannia hotel (now the West Port Bar and Kitchen). The presence, the poltergeist activity and possibly also the shadow which was gradually taking on more form, may well have been the ghostly figure of the gentleman dressed in a dark suit.

Through the wall of the flat were the bedrooms of the hotel, which had also suffered from their own disturbances. So it would appear the phenomenon had not been caused on this occasion by J as she was beginning to think, but she had been the catalyst for everything that was already present and had been making itself known next door. It would seem the energies of the presence had fed off the energies of her insecurities of the time and once alerted to the activity, the whole process of its manifestation became self generating. Her heightened emotions had accelerated the energies looking to find their release, which in turn may then have accentuated the disturbances. Although she was the only one who could see the shadow they both felt the presence.

In the Britannia Hotel account I wrote 'Occasionally things in the bar would move around without any intervention and both the bar and the guest rooms were prone to an unnatural chill. Being through the wall from one another it is more than a possibility for the activity to have stemmed from the same source. The couple here were unaware themselves that there had been any disturbances next door.

Activity of this kind can put such a strain on a relationship. They didn't go down the accusation route with each other which would have destroyed their relationship very quickly. They did well to be there for each other and gave each other the strength and support to get through those terrible months. As I say they wanted to remain anonymous and I thank them for the courage they had in coming forward with an account of what for them had been a very difficult ordeal. ⚑

## *This ends the Official Ghosts of St. Andrews Tour*

 If you would like to continue to other haunted locations in St. Andrews the next stop is only a 5 minute walk away to Kinburn House – Now the St. Andrews Museum.

*Details on the next page*

# The Kinburn House Ghost
## Ghosts of St. Andrews Location Ref: 66

Since 1991 Kinburn has been the home of the St. Andrews Museum. It is not part of the main tour as the museum can take a while to go round, so it is well worth a separate visit. The Museum is signposted and is only around a 5 minute walk from the West Port. It is free entry, and opening hours apply.

The house was built in 1856 by David Buddo as a mansion in the style of an ornate castle and named after the victory of Kinburn during the Crimean War, in which Buddo had been a medical officer in the Indian Army.

The landscaped grounds have lawns, tennis courts and a putting green. In 1872 it was bought by an ironmonger by the name of John Peterson and was later inhabited by the Provost of the Burgh from 1887-93. In 1920 the town council bought the premises and while workmen were redeveloping the building, they discovered a large number of stone coffins or cists which were found to contain human remains. The building once housed the library of David Hay Fleming the Scottish antiquarian and St. Andrews historian 1849 – 1931.

### A St. Andrews Medium

By far the most intriguing experience relayed to me by Greta Boyd, the St. Andrews medium who has relayed a number of experiences to me for this book was one that began with this house.

In 1975 whilst working in Kinburn House she heard heavy footsteps in the corridors at times when nobody else was in the building. Occasionally this was accompanied by the feeling of a presence standing behind her. It got so bad that on one occasion she rapidly left the building because of the awful feeling she had of a "fearful presence."

Her daughter saw the ghostly figure of a woman one evening in one of the upper stories of the building. They had just finished work and were the last to leave. After locking the door of Kinburn they began to make their way along one of the gravel paths spreading its way around the grounds when her daughter turned and saw a woman staring down at them from a window in the building.

Around the same time these disturbances were presenting themselves to Greta and her daughter at Kinburn, Greta held a party at her home for a group of children that were in her company for the evening. After a few party games they all decided to sing a few songs, so Greta brought out her tape recorder to

~ 184 ~

record the event for them. Afterwards Greta rewound the tape as everyone earnestly gathered round with big grins at the novelty of hearing their own voices. On playing it back however, instead of there being the merry sing-along having been so eagerly anticipated, there was only a menacing voice. Greta didn't know what to make of it at all; she had pressed record so the singing should have been picked up, but instead there was this singular, very intrusive, very menacing and very strange voice. She didn't know if it were of a male or female but it kept repeating a message, the same message over and over again in a slow staggered voice:

"A---g---n---e---s…..H-e-l-p….m-e…..B-a-b-y….

A---g---n---e---s…..H-e-l-p….m-e…..B-a-b-y….

A---g---n---e---s…..H-e-l-p….m-e…..B-a-b-y….."

There was a short pause between each word and the word 'AGNES' sounded longer and more drawn out than the other words. It was almost the voice of someone in distress, someone very weak or dying. Upon hearing this, the silence of anticipation turned to a silence of confusion, disappointment and partial dread for some of those gathered who knew it was impossible for whatever it was to be on the recording. She forwarded it, rewound it and each time she played it the same voice with the same creepy message was heard. The children present soon became quite alarmed and frightened and Greta was quite lost for words as to what to say to them. There was no rational explanation at all for this being on the tape. Shortly after, the confused and somewhat bemused children left the house leaving Greta to ponder on the tape and its eerie message.

She tried a number of times to record over the voice, but every time she played it back – there it was, this same message being repeated over and over:

"A---g---n---e---s …..H-e-l-p ….m-e …..B-a-b-y…."

A few days after the message appeared on the tape she went out for a stroll and found herself in the Eastern Cemetery of the Cathedral ruins. Strolling around the many tombstones her curiosity was aroused by a leaf dropping down in front of her onto a grave. Leaning forward she looked at the inscription of the stone it had fallen by. To her astonishment, the grave was for a relation of a Provost who had lived in Kinburn house in the late nineteenth century. The woman's name on the grave was Agnes!

Now the correlation of all this isn't known other than there may be a connection between the plea for help on the tape and the woman who Greta's daughter saw at the window of Kinburn House, and the presence Greta had felt on a number of occasions whilst working within the building.

Greta kept the tape in a drawer at the house. It played heavily on her mind and eventually after around 8 or 9 months it finally got the better of her. Feeling it too spooky to keep anymore she threw it out. She had been thinking about this recording and the associations with Agnes and Kinburn for far too long, once she threw it out she felt a weight had lifted from her shoulders. Although it had been her only real evidence of the strange occurrences she was glad she got rid of it.

***

In September 1975 at the Cross Keys in Peebles there was a similar occurrence to the one above. Room 3 was subjected to ghostly phenomenon and a radio interviewer came hoping to make a recording of a ghostly human voice, in this he got an intriguing result, although not the kind he was probably expecting. The voice was of Donald Duck recorded at high speed![123]

### Ghostly Pets

Whilst lying in bed at night Greta has been visited by a dog she once had, a white poodle. The first time it happened she felt it crawl up the bed beside her and rest by her side, she opened her eyes and said a few kind words to the animal, to which it then disappeared. It wasn't until then that it struck her the animal had passed over a while before.

A number of years ago I had a similar experience myself whilst staying at my parent's home in Winram Place in St. Andrews. The family pet was a small collie dog. Now showing signs of great age he had steadily become worse and on contracting rheumatism in his back legs wasn't able to walk with the ease he once knew. On this particular day I had been out for the most part and hadn't arrived back until all was in relative darkness and everyone asleep. On entering the house I greeted the dog in the kitchen as I always did before retiring myself. He appeared very frail and weak lying there, I said "everything will be alright" as I crouched down and stroked him in his wicker bed.

Next morning I awoke to be told he had been taken to the vets the previous day and put to sleep.

My thanks to Greta for her testimony, and for the lovely hospitality she extended to me in her home on that cold winters evening all those years ago, as we recounted to each other our own supernatural experiences of the many ghosts we have found in St. Andrews.

For more of Greta's experiences refer to *The Poltergeist and the Pavilion* p.36
Also to p.128

# Further Afield
## More St. Andrews Haunts

### The Lade Braes Spirits
*Ghosts of St. Andrews Location Ref. 72*

The woodland walk of the Lade Braes runs from Bogward through the west side of the town to near the back of Madras College. It runs by the course of the Kinness burn, a stream running through the town. Up until the late 19th century the burn marked the southern boundary of the town from just south of the West Port to its outlet at the harbour.[lxii] It is formed from three streams; one from the neighbouring Clatto Hill to the west of Strathkinness, another from the lake at Craigtoun Park, and the other from Cairnsmill Reservoir. They all meet at the haunted Hallow Hill, then as one burn it continues its course and runs right through the town to the Harbour. The Kinness burn was once diverted by the monks to run mills which were found along the Lade and down the Pends. It also supplied a constant fresh water supply for the Cathedral priory. The Lade Braes walk cuts through the town marking the western part of the town for about a mile, but it is easy to forget you are in the town at all, as the plush woodland occasionally opening to expanses of parkland obscures most of the surrounding houses.

This is a popular local walk and local folklore tells of it being the haunt of fairies and earth spirits. It can certainly have an eerie feel to it around dusk and many have reported feelings of constantly being watched when walking through the Brae on their own. Shapes and shadows, sometimes human and corporeal, sometimes more wispy and fairy like have been glimpsed. Earth and water spirits are also known to haunt this stretch and so too is a figure that stands by the parkland along the walk.

There is a real timeless feel to be found about this stretch, with the remnants of various mills dotted along its course, it is suitably filled as it would appear, with both benevolent and malevolent spirits. One thing is assured however; walk from one end of this 'between the worlds' place to the other and chances are by the time the other end is reached all the stresses of the day will have

---

[lxii] Refer to p.94 for a map of St. Andrews circa 1580, showing the Kinness Burn boundary running across the south of the map

dissolved. Along the end of Lade Braes is Law Park Wood by an ancient Mill Pond. This was used for curling from 1846 then a skating pond from 1905 and just near here is the famed Hallow Hill.

### Linskill at a glance
Linskill gives a mention of Law Park Wood in his story *A Spiritualistic Séance* p.275 'The next spirit that turned up was one Jaspar Codlever. He alluded to me as "the Cambridge man in the chair with the cigar." He said that if excavations were made between the two last trees in Lawpark Wood a stone cist would be found full of Pictish ornaments.'

## The Hallow Hill Figures
*Ghosts of St. Andrews Location Ref. 73*

This grassland hill just off Law Park Wood is haunted by shadowy figures and an ominous presence which sweeps over any when walking this way by night as a short cut through to the Lade Braes below. In fact, few walk this way by night for this reason.

Hallow Hill or Holy Hill has a Celtic long cist cemetery first discovered in 1867. At that time the finds were re-covered and written records were scant, so with the exact location not being known it was almost forgotten about. It wasn't until 1975 that it would once more be the talk of the town. Archaeologists were called to the garden of a newly built house on Hallow Hill where human bones had been found. The building work at 12 Hallow Hill had uncovered the bones in the grounds and a visit by the archaeologists was to spark a two year dig on the hill and much excitement in the town.

I was at Canongate primary school at the time in 1975 just near the hill and can still remember the buzz that went around about bones and graves being found at the newly built house.

145 burial sites were uncovered in total across the hill, a high proportion of which were children. What they uncovered was an early Christian burial plot from around the 6th to the 8th centuries. The church that was here pre-dates St. Mary on the Rock situated by the Cathedral and Harbour. It is believed the population of the region was buried here well before St. Rule arrived on the scene. Also discovered was a cobbled road and signs of buildings. Once they had completed their finds, the cists were filled in, but 7 cists were left for the public to view. The popularity of the find had captured the imagination of the residents and the stone coffins of some of the earliest settlers in the region can still be seen on the hill today.

## The Lamond Drive Fishermen

In the new town of St. Andrews, a council house midway along the mile stretch of road known as Lamond Drive is now a B&B. Years ago this was John Marini's family home. His mother told me in the early 1980s about an experience she had there one night in the 1970s. She came down stairs during the night to get a drink of water. The rest of the family were fast asleep upstairs at the time. She walked through the living room to go to the kitchen and saw in the middle of the room a table. Seated at this table were four men playing cards. "They looked like fishermen of long ago" she said. No sound was made by these unwelcome visitors and the display was very brief!

## Roundhill Road

### The Unexpected Call

Every Saturday the mother of a couple of my school friends would receive a phone call that her mother was ready to be picked up and taken out for shopping and tea in the town with her grandson. Every Saturday as regular as clockwork this would happen. The phone would ring a certain number of times. It was always at the same time and it was always the same amount of rings. So they always knew who it was on the other end and that she was ready to be picked up. There was never any need to pick up the phone which also saved on the phone bills.

Eventually this lovely elderly woman died. Her passing was sorely missed by her family and all who knew her. That following Saturday, at exactly the same time as she had always called - the phone rang, it gave the same number of rings as it had always done then stopped. The mother and her son both sitting in the living room looked at each other – they both knew straight away it was her mother and his granny who had called them a few days after her passing.

As technology advances there are a growing number of cases relating to such phenomenon, but this case is unusual. Generally there is some form of communication such as the phone ringing and the person answering having a conversation, say with a friend or family member. Often when this happens they don't realise at the time the person they are speaking with has died. It also works reciprocally, they call someone, the phone is picked up and a conversation takes place. Again it is only later when they find the person they called and spoke with had passed away before they made the call.

Research into phone calls from the dead was conducted by D. Scott Rogo and Raymond Bayless culminating in a publication about their findings in 1979. Recently Callum E. Cooper (Cal) a parapsychologist based at the

University of Northampton in the UK has furthered their researches of the time. When I met him he had not long published a fascinating and highly recommended book on the subject through Tricorn Books called *Telephone calls from the dead*, (2012). Cal is part of the new generation of parapsychologists, opening the field of research in refreshing new directions.

The house the elderly lady stayed at along Bridge Street also had its own phenomenon once she passed away. The window of one of the rooms would often be found open when the occupants knew it had been closed. This had been her bedroom and she liked to keep the room aired.

## The Mystery of the Blue Girl

There is heard tell of a house in central St. Andrews believed to be haunted by a ghostly figure known as the 'Blue Girl'. The exact locality is not stated although the ghost of a woman has been seen in Queen Mary's House wearing a blue dress and Linskill also writes about the ghost of a blue girl, or rather a young woman.

### Linskill at a glance
He gives acknowledgment to a 'blue girl' and also devotes a tale to a young woman dressed in blue in a house in St. Andrews and connects her to the Maiden Rock which he says was named after her.[lxiii]

## The Maiden Rock
### and the Weeping Woman
*Ghosts of St. Andrews Location Ref. 70*

The Maiden Rock is a large natural sea stack of rock, standing quite apart from the cliff face. Rising to a height of some thirty feet it can be found a short distance along the picturesque coastal walk from the East Sands. This ancient landmark around which a legend seems to have developed is known as the Maiden Rock, but these stories are maybe but fanciful tales simply born out of the word 'maiden', as this is also another form of the old Cymric or Celtic word for rock or stone.

### Linskill at a glance
Linskill has a couple of different stories about the ghost seen hereabouts. The chapter concerning the maiden is found in *The Bewitched Ermentrude*, p.309 It

---

[lxiii] Refer also to *The Ghosts of Queen Mary's House*, p.140

seems Ermentrude who he describes as wearing a blue dress was bewitched, and killed the lover of her husband to be then disappeared. She was never seen or heard of again and was supposed to have drowned herself at the Maiden Rock — hence the name it bears.

He also made a brief entry regarding the Maiden Rock in the *St. Andrews Citizen* on January 5th 1929 with a variation saying. 'A young woman, very sad looking, crouching and weeping may be seen at night mourning and wailing for her lost sweetheart who was shipwrecked.'[124]

Interestingly this last story is very similar to the woman who Linskill relates went to her lost husband 'Piper Jock' at the Pipers cave. In his story *The Smothered Piper of the West Cliffs,* p.331 he says; 'For years after, the small crouching figure of a woman could be seen on moonlight nights perched on the rock balcony of the fatal cave, dim, shadowy, and transparent.'

# Kinkell Castle
## & the Castle Golf Course
### *Ghosts of St. Andrews Location Ref. 71*

Kinkell Castle

It is hard to believe now that in the 17th century, just to the south of St. Andrews, high on the cliffs overlooking St. Andrews Bay stood a fortified mansion known as Kinkell Castle. It stood a little inland on the cliff top above Kinkell Cave and the Rock and Spindle, or Spindle Rock as it is known. A large volcanic plug, set between the cliffs and the sea and is so named because of its shape.

The castle had a long gallery, a courtyard and a private chapel. A few illustrious Fifeshire families have been resident here over the years; amongst them were the 'Moubrays, then by marriage the Hepburns, the Monipennies of Pitmilly (of Pitmilly House fame)[lxiv], the Hamiltons and John Ramsay esq.'[125]

No trace is to be found of this castle today which drew large numbers to its illegal Presbyterian meetings. When Archbishop Sharpe of St. Andrews asked the provost to send the militia to break up the meetings, the provost said he could not, since the militia had also gone to hear the preaching!

Kinkell takes its name from the chapel of St. Anna built here by Kellach, Bishop of St. Andrews around AD 875 and means ceann coille or head of the wood. This area including Kinkell was once called Muckross from muic; meaning boar and ross being a promontory. From the 12th century the land was called Cursus Apri meaning Boar's Chase and was the hunting ground for wild boars by the early Scottish Kings and nobility. Sibbald wrote 'Anciently all round it [St. Andrews] was forest and infested with boars...They tell of one boar that was of a vast bulk and fierceness, and that two of his teeth, each sixteen inches long and four thick, were chained to St. Andrews alter in the cathedral church.'[126] The chains were believed to have been made of silver.

The following has been taken from a brief article written by W. T. Linskill which included Kinkell Castle and appeared in the St. Andrews Citizen dated 5th January 1929 as part of his last entry before his death:

'It was believed to be haunted by the apparition of Lady Kinkell who silently roamed the area of the chapel. The original coastal road to Crail ran by the cliffs edge past this old castle, but the constant bombardment on the coastline from the elements has resulted in many landslides along these cliffs, ensuring that no trace may now be found of the castle, nor indeed most of the original coastal route baring on old maps of the area marking its original position.'[127]

In June 2008 a new 18 hole golf course was opened at Kinkell on what was much of Kinkell and neighbouring Brownhills Farm land, extending to the Kinkell Braes – or steep slopes leading down to the sea. The northern edge of the course runs along by the cliff tops and the public footpath.

Becoming the newest in the portfolio of St. Andrews courses, (this being number 7) it is appropriately called the Castle Course. The castle stood in the proximity of the new Castle Club House, amid grounds which the local farmers when it was a field once called Castle Park.

There has never been a regular occupancy on this spot since the time of the castle itself, so with staff and visitors now being here from sunrise to sunset it is far more likely for sightings of the Lady of Kinkell to be seen once again. Either

---

[lxiv] Refer to *Pitmilly House* in the book *Ghosts of Fife* (2013) by the author

in the Castle Club House building or to be seen wandering across the grass land when looking out of the restaurant window – commanding as it does unrivalled panoramic views across St. Andrews Bay.

Ghosts tend to be impressed upon the atmosphere, as a snapshot in time, so they are not generally disturbed by changes taking place to either landscape or architecture. This is why ghosts appear to walk through walls where doors once stood or above ground when the level has since dropped.

## *The Phantom Cavalier and the Ghostly Steed*

This area is also haunted by something else. As I have mentioned this area was once known as the Boar's Chase and now gives its name to the 12th hole of the Castle Golf Course, it was also the illegal meeting place of the Presbytery. The location of the following story recounted by James Wilkie isn't mentioned, but in all likelihood it is this area, which would never be obvious unless the historical connections were made:

'There hung till recently in the house of Lingo[lxv], which once belonged to the Priory of Pittenweem, a portrait of General Dalzell, "with his bald head and his beard to his girdle," although these lands only came in the family a few years before the '45. Beneath it were suspended the great riding-boots of him who, with Grierson of Lagg (Scott's Sir Robert Redgauntlet) and wild Bonshaw, Sir James Turner and Claverhouse, peopled the inferno of the Whigs. Legends yet linger concerning these boots. On nights when the moon shone in fitful gleams, as the clouds scudded over the sky, or when the stars of winter alone burned in the heavens, they would disappear from their accustomed place. Out on the moors that of old comprised the Boar's Chase flew a ghostly steed, the boots striking spurred heels into its flanks, and the feet of a bearded phantom filling them. It was the shade of the fierce old cavalier in wild pursuit of invisible Whigs, as in the days when word was brought in of an unlawful gathering in some remote hollow,[lxvi] and the general buckled on the broadsword, ever by his chair, and leaped on his ready bridled horse, calling on his men to follow.'[128]

---

[lxv] Lingo House is a large white country mansion just off the B940 north east of West Lingo.

[lxvi] This is referring to 'illegal' meetings held at the Castle

# Craigtoun
## Ghosts of St. Andrews Location Ref. 74

*Craigtoun House and Country Park*

Craigtoun and the Mount Melville estate are situated a couple of miles southwest of St. Andrews on the Pitscottie road. The ownership of the lands at Craigtoun is today somewhat fragmented. This area, once all part of Mount Melville farm land comprises the Duke's Golf complex with an 18 hole championship course, a country park, a holiday park with lodges and caravans, and Mount Melville House, together with a late Victorian mansion built in 1900 for Dr James and Mrs Annie Younger. They were part of the famous Scottish Brewers based in Edinburgh. Younger Hall in North Street, St. Andrews was donated by Annie Younger to the University in 1929 as a Graduation Hall.

Mount Melville House together with 47 acres of Mount Melville ground was bought by Fife council in 1947. The landscaped grounds were then turned into Craigtoun Country Park. For many years this has been a major attraction for locals and visitors to Fife alike. The park even hosted a couple of Live Aid inspired music festivals called Fife Aid in the 1980s.

The grounds of the house have a number of follies, as well as landscaped gardens, all built by the Younger family to entertain guests. The unusual Dutch village is one such folly, a white walled mock village set in the middle of a boating lake. It was designed in the 1920s by the Younger's and has been one of the central features in drawing people to the park since it became public ground. The village has a boathouse, tower, pavilion, a gatehouse and a long stone bridge spanning the land and the village.

The park is haunted by a tall dark figure standing near the entrance of this bridge on the landward side. The ghostly figure has also been seen within the fairly circular grass courtyard of the village which is flanked by white buildings and a wall. Nothing appears to be known about this solitary apparition, nor why it would be haunting this particular spot.

Craigtoun Country Park has always been a buzzing place for families – especially when the sun is shining. Like many others in St. Andrews, I used to finish work of a summer evening and head for the park for a couple of hours. Apart from the ghost, the parks attractions also include a miniature renovated steam railway for rides around the park, a performance stage, crazy golf and putting, an Italian garden and trampolines etc. I always remember the small café in the middle of the Dutch village serving ice cream and tea. The area has suffered neglect over the years despite the volume of people visiting each year, but it has finally had a facelift and the park was re-launched in March 2013 after a major financial revamping of its tired looking services, and is set once more to become the attraction it deserves to be. The Victorian mansion of Mount Melville House which stands in the grounds was named Craigtoun House when the Fife Council bought it and in 1949 they turned it into the local maternity hospital for St. Andrews and surrounding districts.

The building closed as a maternity hospital in the 1980s as it was proving too costly to run. Its loss was felt throughout the town as a piece of history where many were born closed its doors. The building lay empty for a time, until the council could find a use for it. It temporarily became a residential home for the elderly then closed its doors once again in 1992. The council retained the country park but sold the house to the American investor Kohler Co, the farm estate sold a massive 330 acres of Mount Melville land to them also. Kohler also has the Old Course Hotel and Hamilton Hall (Hamilton Grand) in St. Andrews. They turned the land into the Duke's Golf Course in 1995. The mansion was left empty for 16 years before redeveloped slowly began to breathe life into the old building again and 2008 saw it starting to turn into a private luxury residence for golfers and guests.

When the mansion was a maternity hospital the hairs on the back of the neck of its occupants would often be alerted by its resident ghosts. A woman I spoke with who had a baby here when it was a maternity hospital told me that around lunchtime the cries of a baby were sometimes heard, baffling those who would search for its source. It was heard on occasions by the staff, patients and visitors alike and after eliminating the more obvious of sources no satisfactory explanation would ever been found in tracing its whereabouts. The building is also haunted by a mother looking for her baby. Both had apparently died here when she was in labour and she now roams the large empty corridors in perpetuity, searching for the child she never saw whilst alive. A place of this size and history will have a few other haunts and stories to tell I have no doubt. So many mansions find their fate in ruins and decay. The mansion at Craigtoun is both imposing and beautiful. With a new lease of life from the high end golfing market its future as a building of stature is now guaranteed for many years to come.

# A background story of the Phantom Coaches

## The Bloody Murder of Archbishop Sharpe
## at Magus Muir
*Ghosts of St. Andrews Location Ref. 75*

Archbishop James Sharpe

The following is a most gruesome episode in the history of this area with a culmination in horrific and graphic displays that St. Andrews and the surrounding shire have never forgotten.

While we make light the notions of phantom coaches and speculate upon their occupancy it is easy to forget the causes of how such macabre spectacles can come into manifestation. The Devil takes on many guises when the righteous convictions of man contrive to enact the most abominable of atrocities in the name of God. In this there is none more delighted in both their accusations and actions in knowing there is only ever one winner in the outcome of fate - the Devil himself.

On the morning of Saturday 3rd May 1679, a most ghastly murder took place at Magus Muir. A lonely wooded spot sited half a mile from the village of Strathkinness and three miles from St. Andrews. The following is the story of that fateful bloody day and the consequences to befall those involved. Included here also are some passages written in some detail from the time with a personal graphic account from Hackston of Rathillet following his involvement.

Two land owners – David Hackston of Rathillet and his brother-in-law John Balfour of Kinloch (Known as Burley) and seven other catholic Covenanters set out in the morning with the intention of conspiring against William Charmichael, a former magistrate of Edinburgh, who after being promoted by the Protestant Archbishop Sharpe to Sheriff Depute of Fife had constantly set himself against them with brutality and extortion. They assigned themselves not to kill him but to severely chasten him for his involvement in their persecution.

After being given information he was to be hunting at Tarvet Hill that morning they rode at full speed. On arrival they found their plans thwarted as Charmichael had been notified of possible danger by a shepherd and had immediately fled in safety to Cupar some six miles away. Unknown to the party at the time a far bigger fish was about to fall into their hands.

A woman who believed in the cause of the Covenanters discovered that Archbishop James Sharpe was journeying his way back from Edinburgh after conducting business and had briefly stopped in Ceres to visit the minister there. The woman sent her son to notify the party that Sharpe's coach would at some point during the day be in the vicinity of Magus Muir. The unexpectedness of this somewhat revelatory news didn't help to serve them in the situation about to unfold. Sharpe was not the original intention of these men, however their grievance against Charmichael although strong, had been slight in comparison to that for the Primate of Scotland. One year earlier James Mitchell, a fellow covenanter had been tricked by Sharpe into confessing he had conspired against him six years previously, making his confession on the promise his life would be spared, Sharpe never kept his word, and in a display of how ruthless he could be he had Mitchell executed.

The Covenanters felt the scenario now being presented had been guided to them from a divine source, raising them to near hysterical fever. The prospect of the Archbishop appearing over the horizon was leading them to an almost inevitable conclusion, and the weight of what they were about to do would cause repercussions they will also have been aware of. They chose Hackston to be their leader, although he hated Sharpe, he could not let his judgement influence him like the others as his was a personal matter against Sharpe and not a matter of the cause, so he declined the offer. Although wanting no part in the proceedings he could not stand in the way of the others so John Balfour took up the position himself. So it was then, with mixed feelings and no planning the party now led by John Balfour rode to Magus Muir in anticipation of the arrival of Sharpe's coach.

It was midday when he appeared over the horizon of Magus Muir. Sharpe was accompanied on this particular journey by his eldest daughter, four servants, a coachman and a postilion. Once the coachman saw the band approaching on this lonely moor nothing could be done to evade them.[lxvii] A pistol shot was fired through the window of the coach missing its target, then once stopped the servants were restrained and the horses cut loose. It was then demanded that Sharpe leave the carriage, but refusing to comply with their demands they fired further shots into the carriage and thrust their swords at him where he sat. Badly wounded and bloody he eventually emerged falling to his knees.

This depiction of Sharpe's brutal murder appeared in an early newspaper; 'The Manner of the Barbarous Murder of James, Late Lord Arch-Bishop Sharp of St. Andrews, Primate and Metropolitan of all Scotland, and one his Majesties most Honourable Privy-Council of that Kingdom; May 3. 1679.'

In the previous plate Sharpe is depicted just in front of the coach dressed in black, with his hand raised as gun shot was fired at him, and in the bottom right, Isabel Sharpe is seen pleading with the men.

Hackston during the frenzied bloodshed was still mounted on his horse some distance away, like a mysterious highwayman watching the maddening slaughter with his cloak covering the lower half of his face. Sharpe begged them to spare his life that theirs may be spared also, but with the death of James Mitchell in their minds and by virtue of who they had before them, they

---

[lxvii] Refer also to *The Spectral Coachman and the Postilion,* p.111 The Novum Hospitium (The New Inn)

ignored him. At one point it seems Hackston even tried to intercede but to no avail, and amid the panic and the adrenaline of the moment his daughter Isabel Sharpe in great distress implored and pleaded with the persecutors to stop harming her father. With this she was seriously wounded herself in the merciless attack for her trouble. Entreating them to stop, her father raised his left hand as they fired yet more shots and plunged their swords into his bloodied body as he then slumped forward and lay still.

A stone pyramid cairn stands in the woods at Magus Muir marking the spot where Archbishop Sharpe met his final end.

Following a post-mortem and a report by four surgeons, in all there were sixteen great wounds found on his body. In his back, head, one above his left eye, three in his left hand that he raised in desperation and a shot above his right breast which was found to be powder.

Before the perpetrators fled 'they took nothing from him but his tobacco-box and bible, and a few papers. With these they went to a barn nearby. Upon the opening of his tobacco-box a living humming bee flew out. This either Rathillet or Balfour called his familiar, and some in the company not understanding the term, they explained it to be a devil. In the box were a pair of pistol balls, parings of nails, some worsit or silk, and some say a paper with some characters, but that is uncertain.'[129]

As famous as the above account of the tobacco-box and its contents is, there is another account of the box which sounds all the more plausible, as the one above is from a catholic perspective. 'they found on the bishop a box with some pistol-ball, threads of worsted, and other odd things in it, which they knew not what to make of.'[130]

After this barbaric display the descriptions of the perpetrators were given to the appropriate authorities, and a major hunt ensued for their capture with a reward of 10,000 merks for the apprehension of any involved. Andrew Guillan a weaver from Balmerino was one of the first to be found and slain, although it was believed that he, like Hackston had taken no part in the actual murder. At his trial in Edinburgh 'it was noticed that he endured the torture he was put to with a great deal of courage. In cutting off his hands the hangman, being drunk, or affecting to appear so, mangled him fearfully, and gave him nine strokes before he got them off. He endured all with invincible patience, and it is said, when his right hand was cut off, he held up the stump in the view of the spectators, crying as one perfectly easily, "My blessed Lord sealed my salvation with his blood and I am honoured this day to seal his truths with my blood." After his body was hung in chains for some time, some people came and took it down for which the country about was brought to no small trouble. On May

27th, 1684, "The council granted a commission to the earl of Balcarras to pass sentence of banishment on the persons who took down Andrew Guillan's body from Magus-muir, as being owners of the horrid murder of the Archbishop of St Andrews.'"[131]

While Andrew was originally from Balmerino he lived at Magus Muir. He was a sympathiser for the Covenanters cause, but it was by the unfortunate circumstance of already being in the area that was to be his downfall on this day. For all his suffering following the murder of Sharpe as relayed above, the account in the *History of the Sufferings of the Church of Scotland* of 1829 concerning Andrew Guillan writes of the actual part he played that resulted in his gruesome death:

'...all his share in the action was, that being called out of his house [by the Covenanters], he held their horses, and was witness to what was done.'[132]

He had found himself not only in the wrong place at the wrong time but had been killed as an example of the wrath against the Covenanters and the fate that awaited all who dared join in their cause.

In a nearby field Andrew Guillan is remembered on a tombstone with this inscription:

A faithful martyr here doth lye
A witness against perjury
Who cruelly was put to death
To gratify proud prelate's wrath
They cut his hands ere he was dead
And after that struck off his head
To Magus Muir then did him bring
His body on a pole did hing
His blood under the alter cries
For vengeance on Christs enemies

His head was displayed in Cupar but this stone marks where his body parts were hung by chains. The site of the grave is also close to where he lived and worked as a simple weaver, so those who knew him in the area would have certainly seen the aftermath of his death in Edinburgh. So it may not have been so much sympathising Covenanters who set free what was left of his mutilated remains bound in chains, but sympathising friends who couldn't bear to see the horror of his fate in being hung and not buried. His ghost is said to roam the area around his grave.

*The Horrors Awaiting David Hackston of Rathillet*

A little over a year after the murder of Sharpe, on the 22$^{nd}$ of July 1680 the Joint Sheriff-Depute of Dumfriesshire; Bruce of Earlshall[lxviii] and around 120 Dragoons found and surprised Hackston and his men at Airds Moss, a moorland in East Ayrshire. The ensuing conflict resulted in the capture of Hackston.

The following which is said to have been written in his own hand is a graphic account of his capture and what then followed in Edinburgh as relayed from the ages of Wodrow in 1829.

*Hackston's Account*

'I was stricken down with three on horseback behind me, and received three sore wounds on the head, and so falling saved my life, which I submitted to. They searched me, and carried me to their rear, and laid me down, where I bled much, where were brought several of their men sorely wounded. They gave us all testimony of brave resolute men. What more of our men were killed I did not see, nor know, but as they told me after the field was theirs. I was brought towards Douglas. They used me civilly, and brought me drink out of a house by the way. At Douglas, Janet Clellan was kind to me, and brought a surgeon to me, who did but little to my wounds, only stanched the blood. Next morning I was brought to Lanark, and brought before Dalziel, Lord Ross, and some others, who asked many questions at me: but I not satisfying them with answers, Dalziel did threaten to roast me; and carrying me to the tolbooth, caused to bind me most barbarously, and cast me down, where I lay till Saturday morning, without any, except soldiers, admitted to speak to me, or look at my wounds, or give me any ease whatsoever. And next morning they brought me and John Pollock, and the other two of us, near two miles on foot, I being without shoes, to where that party, which had broken us at first, received us. They were commanded by Earlshall. We were horsed, civilly used by them on the way, and brought to Edinburgh, about four in the afternoon, and carried about the north side of the town, to the foot of the Canongate, where the town magistrates were who received us; and setting me on an horse with my face backward, and the other three bound on a goad of iron, and Mr.

---

[lxviii] This is Bloody Bruce. So named for tracking down the Covenanters and from an incident at the Battle of Bothwell Bridge on the 22$^{nd}$ of June 1679 where he cut the head and hands off Richard Cameron and took them for display to Edinburgh. Refer also to Earlshall Castle home of Bloody Bruce in the authors companion work *Ghosts of Fife*.

Cameron's head carried on an halbert before me, and another head in a sack, which I knew not, on a lad's back; and so we were carried up the street to the parliament-cross, where I was taken down, and the rest loosed.'[133]

Although like Andrew Guillan he had not actually taken part in the murder, he found himself an accessory nonetheless and suffered the same fate.

His ghost haunts Sharpe's old residence Strathtyrum House[lxix] in remorse of the events of that day in not being able to prevent what occurred. Hackston knew Sharpe, it was said: 'Hackston was the tutor for a cousin's children [of Sharpe], and had been made responsible for disbursements made by Sharp (from a forced sale of property for rents owed him).'

As graphic and sickening as Hackston's account is, it is still slim to the gruesome reality of the manner in which he was to spend the last moments of his life, as the arrangements for his death were laid out and followed in detail. They were drawn up by the Privy Council so as to inflict the most painful death as possible on Hackston. Both the arrangements of his actual death and what was then to befall his body was recorded in great detail as follows:
'That his body be drawn backward on a hurdle to the Mercat Cross; that there be an high scaffold erected a little above the Cross, where, in the first place, his right hand is to be struck off and, after some time, his left hand; then he is to be hanged up, and cut down alive, his bowels to be taken out, and his heart shown to the people by the hangman; then his heart and his bowels to be burned in a fire prepared for that purpose on the scaffold; that, afterwards, his head be cut off, and his body divided into four quarters; his head to be fixed on the Netherbow; one of his quarters with both his hands to be affixed at St. Andrews,[lxx] another quarter at Glasgow, a third at Leith, a fourth at Burntisland; that none presume to be in mourning for him, or any coffin brought; that no person be suffered to be on the scaffold with him, save the two bailies, the executioner and his servants; that he be allowed to pray to God Almighty, but not to speak to the people; that Hackston's and Cameron's heads be fixed on higher poles than the rest.

Privy Council.' [134]

---

[lxix] Refer to *Strathtyrum House*, p.205

[lxx] They were displayed in St. Andrews at the Tolbooth, also known as the Town House. This was a double storied building that stood in the middle of Market Street toward the Mercat Cross. It once housed a Charter of the town from King Malcolm II and a very large axe used for royalist executions at the tolbooth in 1645. It was pulled down in 1862 and was not replaced by another building. Its removal extended the street to what it is today.

Although not being present at Magus Muir on that day, five of the Covenanters caught at Bothwell Bridge were 'hanged' in chains on Christmas Day 1679 at Magus Muir for not speaking up about the identity of the perpetrators. Their bodies were left there to rot away as an example to others for nine years. At Magus Muir there is also a grave to these men in a field not far from that of Andrew Guillan's stone.

## A Foreboding Atmosphere on Magus Muir

It isn't surprising something supernatural should be associated with this location. Having this bloody piece of history attached to its name lends a strange eerie atmosphere and along with the ghost of Guillan the bodies that languished here for so many years linger even on bright summer days.

As the mind is cast back to that fateful day in 1679 with Sharpe's death and the fate of the Covenanters it becomes a reminder of how all found themselves caught in the horrors of conviction and circumstance. The isolation of this moor known afterwards as 'Bishop's Wood' appears all the more desolate when it is realised how close it is to the slim haven of Strathkinness, yet still distant enough that none could hear the shouts and screams.

## Further reports of the Phantom Coach

The coach that drove Sharpe to his death has been seen a few times between Strathkinness and St. Andrews careering along the road from Magus Muir. As with other cases of phantom coaches around the British Isles, the Archbishops coach when heard traditionally foretells death or some other adequately auspicious misfortune. Linskill recounts the full story in *A True Tale of the Phantom Coach*, p.340.

Another with a connection to the Phantom Coaches being passed down by the annals of legend is David Beaton, is as follows:

# Cardinal David Beaton and the Devil – East Sands
### *Ghosts of St. Andrews Location Ref. 69*

"Have you heard how the Cardinal's coach goes by,
At the dead of night when the tide is high?
And the morn has hid, and the wind is shrill,
And all the city lies dark and still?!"[135]

A story or rather a legend on the Phantom Coach posted in the National Observer in 1893 concerns Cardinal David Beaton and the Devil. Beaton we have already met as being one of the more regular ghosts to haunt the castle of St. Andrews.

'Whenever the tide is full on the East Sands between midnight and the first hour of morning David Beaton drives down by the old Abbey Wall into the Sea. They are many that have seen his white face pleading at the coach window; he cannot speak – mutely he must implore your prayers; for the Devil sits with him and holds him by the arm. His outriders are skeletons, his coachman is headless, and thus he drives to his doom.'[136]

One legend tells how this spectral coach and four is seen passing through the area, vanishing in a puff of blue smoke and leaving only the reek of sulphur.

Refer also to *St. Andrews Castle Ghosts*, p.68

## Have you heard the Phantom Coach go by?

The phenomenon of the Phantom Coach is a strange one. It is rare to see though not to hear. I am sure many have heard it over the years, careering its way along roads and forgotten lanes in and around St. Andrews. As Andrew Green says; 'people are a wee bit canny about talking on such things.' With this I have to say people are also a wee bit canny about thinking on such things. The sounds are rarely heard amid the general montage of street noises being carried by the wind, but listen very carefully when the souls of the town are at rest, and the sounds of the day are stilled. Then you will hear the faint rumblings of a coach in old St. Andrews town.

## The Body Snatchers

Before we take our leave of that bloody day when Sharpe met his end on a desolate moor and the relentless Protestant hounds tracked and tortured the Covenanters and any connected with the Covenanters deeds. In the Holy Trinity Church in South Street there stands a large black and white marble tomb. Erected by Sharpe's son, it marks where Archbishop Sharpe was interred in 1679. In 1725 the tomb was raided and it was rumoured at the time his body had been taken. Generations would pass before any would know for sure if this were true. In 1849, with 124 years of rumours and speculation the tomb was opened, his body was missing. To this day no one knows who was responsible for its removal or what then happened to it. So with a twist in the tale, is the Phantom Coach carrying the corpse of Sharpe to his former dwelling once he had been killed at Magus Muir, or as the Catholics supposed at the time, in having him in league with the Devil, with no resting place on hallowed ground is it indeed like Beaton carrying him to Hell.

# Strathtyrum House
*Ghosts of St. Andrews Location Ref. 68*

The beautiful and grand building of Strathtyrum Mansion House set amid 400 acres of landscaped grounds sits around one mile from the centre of St. Andrews on the north western edge of St. Andrews. The entrance to the grounds is just beyond the edge of Station Park and the St. Andrews boundary sign on the A91 St. Andrews to Guardbridge road. James Cheape bought Strathtyrum House and Estate in 1782 for the Cheape family who still retain it to this day. In 1827 he bought the St. Andrews Links, saving it from the rabbit farmers! Archbishop Hamilton in 1552 had granted the golfers the right to use the land, but unfortunately at the same time he also granted the land to the rabbit farmers. The land the course was on was dually divided in half. Today small marker stones can be found down the middle of the course painted green. On one side is the letter 'G' denoting golfers and on the other; 'R' for rabbits. The resulting competition between the two raged for nearly 300 years! James buying the links in 1827 for the golfers meant the rabbit farmers had to move and the sanity of the golfers after so many years was once again preserved. This secured the very extensive tract of ideal golfing ground we have today, and in so doing there were no further distractions from rabbits (who had been employed to keep the grass short) running off with the balls. From now on the golfers had to do it themselves so the course was eventually bought by the Royal and Ancient or the R & A as it is known, in 1892, which was then sold to the town in 1893 and taken over by the Links Trust to maintain.

The Cheape family who are related to the Royal family have a large bunker named after them on the famous Old Course golf course. Its name is Cheape's Bunker and doubles across the 2nd and 17th fairways.

The National Observer of 1893 published a number of stories, accounts and tales regarding St. Andrews under the heading of *St. Andrews Ghosts*. Four of these accounts have been included throughout this book. The following concerns the ghost of Strathtyrum House and is as follows:

'A Mile from St. Andrews in a certain country house, now the property of an eminently respectable person, once the Palace of Archbishop Sharpe. Long afterwards and during the tenancy of Mr Brook of Sheffield: (that eminent publisher), a certain member of the Royal and Ancient went out to dine and stay the night. Going to bed he knew nothing more till he was awakened suddenly by hearing someone in his room. He sat up, and through the curtains at his feet he saw a figure passing softly to and fro. Now he had particularly desired to be called at 7am; it was daylight but he didn't know what time it was so he called to his servant as he supposed in good time, and turned to look at his watch. It was not yet 5am and at that moment the man went silently by the bed into a closet in the chamber wall; and as he passed, that golfer saw his face, and marked it in his mind. Then he leapt out of bed and ran after; but the closet stood empty. There upon he slept no more. When the servant eventually came in at 7 he was told and sworn to secrecy about the incident. Years went by and eventually he was once more a guest in the house. This time his host was a great collector of old prints and showed them to him – chamber after chamber filled with antique portraits. One morning he saw something that brought his heart into his mouth. There in a little old dirty print, but unmistakably identical, was the face of the man who had woken him in his room that summer morning years ago. Breathless he asked the name. "Hackston of Rathillet"!'[137]

Although the story doesn't mention directly which house it pertains to, there is little doubt the dwelling is Strathtyrum. Archbishop Sharpe mentioned at the start of the story had been the proprietor of this house, as well as having his official residence at The New Inn in the Pends in the 17th century. With the Cheape family also owning the Links course it makes sense why a member of the Royal and Ancient Club House in St. Andrews who administer the rules of the game of golf would stay here of a night.

In 1986 Mrs Gladys Cheape sold part of the estates land across the main A91 road from the house to the Links Trust. Following extensive landscaping the Strathtyrum Golf Course was created, and in 1993 it become the 5th golf course in St. Andrews.

The house is now a wedding venue as well as providing accommodation for bespoke golfers playing the nearby courses. It also has a very popular farm shop and cafe called the Balgove Larder which is open to the public during the day.

For Hackston of Rathillet to haunt Sharpe's former dwelling it would have to be as I mentioned earlier, in remorse that he does so. He had personal grievances against Sharpe and had not directly taken part in the murder, feeling any personal intervention would detract from the cause the Covenanters were pursuing. Consequently at one stage he seems to have shown compassion for the Archbishop and tried to prevent his murder, as he knew Sharpe and had tutored one of Sharpe's cousins – probably in this house, which would link his association with the house. Following his execution in a most barbaric and painful way as an example to others for the crime committed, parts of Hackston's body were displayed at the Tolbooth which once stood in Market Street.

### Linskill at a glance
Linskill only makes a brief reference to this ghost by calling it 'the wraith of Hackston of Rathillet'. He also makes reference to this Covenanter as being a possible occupant of the Phantom Coach.

For Linskill's reference to Hackston refer to The Veiled Nun of St. Leonards, p.344<br>
For Linskill's account of Sharpe and the Phantom Coach refer to<br>
The True Tale of the Phantom Coach, p.340<br>
For a ghostly sighting of Hackston on horseback in Fife refer to my book<br>
Ghosts of Fife – Rathillet.

## The Station Park Monks
### Ghosts of St. Andrews Location Ref. 67

When coming into the town on the Guardbridge to St. Andrews road. The road sweeps in a long left hand arc around a large open field of grass known as Station Park. The area was named after the first railway station in St. Andrews which opened in 1852 and stood on the grounds of the Old Course Hotel.

'In the autumn of 1979 a St. Andrews student walking across the playing fields of Station Park one night saw three ghostly monks walking above the present ground level; when they were about ten feet away from him they completely disappeared.'[138] This is the only account I have thus far heard concerning any form of disturbance at Station Park.

# The Library Window
## A Victorian Ghost Story by Mrs Oliphant, 1896

### Introduction by Richard Falconer

Mrs (Margaret) Oliphant (1828 – 1897)

The following is by way of a brief introduction to Mrs Oliphant and her Victorian Ghost Story. The Library Window is a fictional tale featuring the hidden window of the haunted James VI library. Facing onto South Street in St. Andrews the library is part of the St. Mary's Quad.

Mrs (Margaret) Oliphant was a Scottish historical writer and novelist who became quite famous in her day. She led a difficult life though, trying to look after her children and her ill husband. In a bid to improve her husband's health they moved to the warmer climate of Rome, but alas both her husband and one of her children died there. All her family died before herself, with three of her six children dying in infancy. *The Library Window* was published in 1896, only a year before her own death. This is a somewhat melancholic Victorian ghostly tale, with a number of psychological levels involving 19th century St. Andrews society life, youthful obsession and unrequited love. The story mentions the Abbey and the West Port as incidental points of reference, however the town's name has been changed to St. Rules and South Street has become the High Street. The characters feature names of prominent ancient and wealthy Fife families such as Pitmilly, Carnbee and Balcarres.

# The Library Window

A Victorian Ghost Story
By
Mrs (Margaret) Oliphant
1896

## A Story of the Seen and the Unseen

I WAS not aware at first of the many discussions which had gone on about that window. It was almost opposite one of the windows of the large old-fashioned drawing-room of the house in which I spent that summer, which was of so much importance in my life. Our house and the library were on opposite sides of the broad High Street of St Rule's, which is a fine street, wide and ample, and very quiet, as strangers think who come from noisier places; but in a summer evening there is much coming and going, and the stillness is full of sound – the sound of footsteps and pleasant voices, softened by the summer air. There are even exceptional moments when it is noisy: the time of the fair,[lxxi] and on Saturday nights sometimes, and when there are excursion trains. Then even the softest sunny air of the evening will not smooth the harsh tones and the stumbling steps; but at these unlovely moments we shut the windows, and even I, who am so fond of that deep recess where I can take refuge from all that is going on inside, and make myself a spectator of all the varied stories out of doors, withdraw from my watch-tower. To tell the truth, there never was very much going on inside. The house belonged to my aunt, to whom (she says, Thank God!) nothing ever happens. I believe that many things have happened to her in her time; but that was all over at the period of which I am speaking, and she was old, and very quiet. Her life went on in a routine never broken. She got up at the same hour every day, and did the same things in the same rotation, day by day the same. She said that this was the greatest support in the world, and that routine is a kind of salvation. It may be so; but it is a very dull salvation, and I used to feel that I would rather have incident, whatever kind of incident it might be. But then at that time I was not old, which makes all the difference. At the time of which I speak the deep recess of the drawing-room window was a great comfort to me. Though she was an old lady (perhaps

---

[lxxi] This is the Lammas Market, the oldest surviving street fair and market in Scotland.

because she was so old) she was very tolerant, and had a kind of feeling for me. She never said a word, but often gave me a smile when she saw how I had built myself up, with my books and my basket of work. I did very little work, I fear – now and then a few stitches when the spirit moved me, or when I had got well afloat in a dream, and was more tempted to follow it out than to read my book, as sometimes happened. At other times, and if the book were interesting, I used to get through volume after volume sitting there, paying no attention to anybody. And yet I did pay a kind of attention. Aunt Mary's old ladies came in to call, and I heard them talk, though I very seldom listened; but for all that, if they had anything to say that was interesting, it is curious how I found it in my mind afterwards, as if the air had blown it to me. They came and went, and I had the sensation of their old bonnets gliding out and in, and their dresses rustling; and now and then had to jump up and shake hands with someone who knew me, and asked after my papa and mamma. Then Aunt Mary would give me a little smile again, and I slipped back to my window. She never seemed to mind. My mother would not have let me do it, I know. She would have remembered dozens of things there were to do. She would have sent me up-stairs to fetch something which I was quite sure she did not want, or downstairs to carry some quite unnecessary message to the housemaid. She liked to keep me running about. Perhaps that was one reason why I was so fond of Aunt Mary's drawing-room, and the deep recess of the window, and the curtain that fell half over it, and the broad window-seat where one could collect so many things without being found fault with for untidiness. Whenever we had anything the matter with us in these days, we were sent to St Rule's to get up our strength. And this was my case at the time of which I am going to speak.

Everybody had said, since ever I learned to speak, that I was fantastic and fanciful and dreamy, and all the other words with which a girl who may happen to like poetry, and to be fond of thinking, is so often made uncomfortable. People don't know what they mean when they say fantastic. It sounds like Madge Wildfire or something of that sort. My mother thought I should always be busy, to keep nonsense out of my head. But really I was not at all fond of nonsense. I was rather serious than otherwise. I would have been no trouble to anybody if I had been left to myself. It was only that I had a sort of second-sight, and was conscious of things to which I paid no attention. Even when reading the most interesting book, the things that were being talked about blew in to me; and I heard what the people were saying in the streets as they passed under the window. Aunt Mary always said I could do two or indeed three things at once – both read and listen, and see. I am sure that I did not listen much, and seldom looked out, of set purpose – as some people do who notice what bonnets the ladies in the street have on; but I did hear what I couldn't help hearing, even when I was reading my book, and I did see all sorts of things, though often for a whole half-hour I might never lift my eyes.

This does not explain what I said at the beginning, that there were many discussions about that window. It was, and still is, the last window in the row, of the College Library, which is opposite my aunt's house in the High Street. Yet it is not exactly opposite, but a little to the west, so that I could see it best from the left side of my recess. I took it calmly for granted that it was a window like any other till I first heard the talk about it which was going on in the drawing-room. "Have you never made up your mind, Mrs Balcarres," said old Mr Pitmilly, "whether that window opposite is a window or no?" He said Mistress Balcarres - and he was always called Mr Pitmilly, Morton: which was the name of his place.

"I am never sure of it, to tell the truth," said Aunt Mary, "all these years."

"Bless me!" said one of the old ladies, "and what window may that be?"

Mr Pitmilly had a way of laughing as he spoke, which did not please me; but it was true that he was not perhaps desirous of pleasing me. He said, "Oh, just the window opposite," with his laugh running through his words; "our friend can never make up her mind about it, though she has been living opposite it since ---"

"You need never mind the date," said another; "the Library window! Dear me, what should it be but a window? up at that height it could not be a door."

"The question is," said my aunt, "if it is a real window with glass in it, or if it is merely painted, or if it once was a window, and has been built up. And the oftener people look at it, the less they are able to say."

"Let me see this window," said old Lady Carnbee, who was very active and strong-minded; and then they all came crowding upon me - three or four old ladies, very eager, and Mr Pitmilly's white hair appearing over their heads, and my aunt sitting quiet and smiling behind.

"I mind [remember/know] the window very well," said Lady Carnbee; "ay: and so do more than me. But in its present appearance it is just like any other window; but has not been cleaned, I should say, in the memory of man."

"I see what ye mean," said one of the others. "It is just a very dead thing without any reflection in it; but I've seen as bad before."

"Ay, it's dead enough," said another, "but that's no rule; for these hizzies of women-servants in this ill age ---"

"Nay, the women are well enough," said the softest voice of all, which was Aunt Mary's. "I will never let them risk their lives cleaning the outside of mine.

And there are no women-servants in the Old Library: there is maybe something more in it than that."

They were all pressing into my recess, pressing upon me, a row of old faces, peering into something they could not understand. I had a sense in my mind how curious it was, the wall of old ladies in their old satin gowns all glazed with age, Lady Carnbee with her lace about her head. Nobody was looking at me or thinking of me; but I felt unconsciously the contrast of my youngness to their oldness, and stared at them as they stared over my head at the Library window. I had given it no attention up to this time. I was more taken up with the old ladies than with the thing they were looking at.

"The framework is all right at least, I can see that, and painted black ----"

"And the panes are painted black too. It's no window, Mrs Balcarres. It has been filled in, in the days of the window duties: you will mind, Lady Carnbee."

"Mind!" said that oldest lady. "I mind when your mother was marriet, Jeanie: and that's neither the day nor yesterday. But as for the window, it's just a delusion: and that is my opinion of the matter, if you ask me."

"There's a great want of light in that muckle room at the college," said another. "If it was a window, the Library would have more light."

"One thing is clear," said one of the younger ones, "it cannot be a window to see through. It may be filled in or it may be built up, but it is not a window to give light."

"And who ever heard of a window that was no to see through?" Lady Carnbee said. I was fascinated by the look on her face, which was a curious scornful look as of one who knew more than she chose to say: and then my wandering fancy was caught by her hand as she held it up, throwing back the lace that dropped over it. Lady Carnbee's lace was the chief thing about her - heavy black Spanish lace with large flowers. Everything she wore was trimmed with it. A large veil of it hung over her old bonnet. But her hand coming out of this heavy lace was a curious thing to see. She had very long fingers, very taper, which had been much admired in her youth; and her hand was very white, or rather more than white, pale, bleached, and bloodless, with large blue veins standing up upon the back; and she wore some fine rings, among others a big diamond in an ugly old claw setting. They were too big for her, and were wound round and round with yellow silk to make them keep on: and this little cushion of silk, turned brown with long wearing, had twisted round so that it was more conspicuous than the jewels; while the big diamond blazed underneath in the hollow of her hand, like some dangerous thing hiding and sending out darts of light. The hand, which seemed to come almost to a point, with this strange ornament underneath, clutched at my half-terrified imagination. It too seemed to mean far more than was said. I felt as if it might clutch me with sharp claws, and the lurking, dazzling creature bite - with a sting that would go to the heart.

Presently, however, the circle of the old faces broke up, the old ladies returned to their seats, and Mr Pitmilly, small but very erect, stood up in the midst of them, talking with mild authority like a little oracle among the ladies. Only Lady Carnbee always contradicted the neat, little, old gentleman. She gesticulated, when she talked, like a Frenchwoman, and darted forth that hand of hers with the lace hanging over it, so that I always caught a glimpse of the lurking diamond. I thought she looked like a witch among the comfortable little group which gave such attention to everything Mr Pitmilly said.

"For my part, it is my opinion there is no window there at all," he said. "It's very like the thing that's called in scientific language an optical illusion. It arises generally, if I may use such a word in the presence of ladies, from a liver that is not just in the perfect order and balance that organ demands - and then you will see things - a blue dog, I remember, was the thing in one case, and in another ---"

"The man has gane gyte [delirious]," said Lady Carnbee; "I mind the windows in the Auld Library as long as I mind anything. Is the Library itself an optical illusion too?"

"Na, na," and "No, no," said the old ladies; "a blue dog would be a strange vagary: but the Library we have all kent [known] from our youth," said one. "And I mind when the Assemblies were held there one year when the Town Hall was building," another said.

"It is just a great divert to me," said Aunt Mary: but what was strange was that she paused there, and said in a low tone, "now"; and then went on again, "for whoever comes to my house, there are aye discussions about that window. I have never just made up my mind about it myself. Sometimes I think it's a case of these wicked window duties, as you said, Miss Jeanie, when half the windows in our houses were blocked up to save the tax. And then, I think, it may be due to that blank kind of building like the great new buildings on the Earthen Mound in Edinburgh, where the windows are just ornaments. And then while I am sure I can see the glass shining when the sun catches it in the afternoon."

"You could so easily satisfy yourself, Mrs Balcarres, if you were too --"

"Give a laddie a penny to cast a stone, and see what happens," said Lady Carnbee.

"But I am not sure that I have any desire to satisfy myself," Aunt Mary said. And then there was a stir in the room, and I had to come out from my recess and open the door for the old ladies and see them down-stairs, as they all went away following one another. Mr Pitmilly gave his arm to Lady Carnbee, though she was always contradicting him; and so the tea-party dispersed. Aunt Mary came to the head of the stairs with her guests in an old-fashioned gracious way, while I went down with them to see that the maid was ready at the door. When I came back Aunt Mary was still standing in the recess looking out. Returning to my seat she said, with a kind of wistful look, "Well, honey: and what is your opinion?"

"I have no opinion. I was reading my book all the time," I said.

"And so you were, honey, and no' very civil; but all the same I ken [know] well you heard every word we said."

## II

IT was a night in June; dinner was long over, and had it been winter the maids would have been shutting up the house, and my Aunt Mary preparing to go upstairs to her room. But it was still clear daylight, that daylight out of which the sun has been long gone, and which has no longer any rose reflections, but all has sunk into a pearly neutral tint--a light which is daylight yet is not day. We had taken a turn in the garden after dinner, and now we had returned to what we called our usual occupations. My aunt was reading. The English post had come in, and she had got her 'Times,' which was her great diversion. The 'Scotsman' was her morning reading, but she liked her 'Times' at night.

As for me, I too was at my usual occupation, which at that time was doing nothing. I had a book as usual, and was absorbed in it: but I was conscious of all that was going on all the same. The people strolled along the broad pavement, making remarks as they passed under the open window which came up into my story or my dream, and sometimes made me laugh. The tone and the faint sing-song, or rather chant, of the accent, which was "a wee Fifish," was novel to me, and associated with holiday, and pleasant; and sometimes they said to each other something that was amusing, and often something that suggested a whole story; but presently they began to drop off, the footsteps slackened, the voices died away. It was getting late, though the clear soft daylight went on and on. All through the lingering evening, which seemed to consist of interminable hours, long but not weary, drawn out as if the spell of the light and the outdoor life might never end, I had now and then, quite unawares, cast a glance at the mysterious window which my aunt and her friends had discussed, as I felt, though I dared not say it even to myself, rather foolishly. It caught my eye without any intention on my part, as I paused, as it were, to take breath, in the flowing and current of undistinguishable thoughts and things from without and within which carried me along. First it occurred to me, with a little sensation of discovery, how absurd to say it was not a window, a living window, one to see through! Why, then, had they never seen it, these old folk? I saw as I looked up suddenly the faint greyness as of visible space within - a room behind, certainly dim, as it was natural a room should be on the other side of the street - quite indefinite: yet so clear that if someone were to come to the window there would be nothing surprising in it. For certainly there was a feeling of space behind the panes which these old half-blind ladies had disputed about whether they were glass or only fictitious panes marked on the wall. How silly! when eyes that could see could make it out in a minute. It was only a greyness at present, but it was unmistakable, a space that went back into gloom, as every room does when you look into it across a street. There were no curtains to show whether it was inhabited or not; but a room -oh, as distinctly as ever a room was! I was pleased with myself, but said nothing, while Aunt Mary rustled her paper, waiting for a favourable moment to announce a discovery which settled her problem at once. Then I was carried away upon the stream again, and forgot the window, till somebody threw unawares a word from the outer world, "I'm goin' hame; it'll soon be dark." Dark! what was the fool thinking of? it never would be dark if one waited out, wandering in the soft air for hours longer; and then my eyes, acquiring easily that new habit, looked across the way again.

Ah, now! nobody indeed had come to the window; and no light had been lighted, seeing it was still beautiful to read by - a still, clear, colourless light; but the room inside had certainly widened. I could see the grey space and air a little deeper, and a sort of vision, very dim, of a wall, and something against it; something dark, with the blackness that a solid article, however indistinctly seen, takes in the lighter darkness that is only space - a large, black, dark thing coming out into the grey. I looked more intently, and made sure it was a piece of furniture, either a writing-table or perhaps a large book-case. No doubt it must be the last, since this was part of the old library. I never visited the old College Library, but I had seen such places before, and I could well imagine it to myself. How curious that for all the time these old people had looked at it, they had never seen this before!

It was more silent now, and my eyes, I suppose, had grown dim with gazing, doing my best to make it out, when suddenly Aunt Mary said, "Will you ring the bell, my dear? I must have my lamp."

"Your lamp?" I cried, "when it is still daylight." But then I gave another look at my window, and perceived with a start that the light had indeed changed: for now I saw nothing. It was still light, but there was so much change in the light that my room, with the grey space and the large shadowy bookcase, had gone out, and I saw them no more: for even a Scotch night in June, though it looks as if it would never end, does darken at the last. I had almost cried out, but checked myself, and rang the bell for Aunt Mary, and made up my mind I would say nothing till next morning, when to be sure naturally it would be more clear.

Next morning I rather think I forgot all about it - or was busy: or was more idle than usual: the two things meant nearly the same. At all events I thought no more of the window, though I still sat in my own, opposite to it, but occupied with some other fancy. Aunt Mary's visitors came as usual in the afternoon; but their talk was of other things, and for a day or two nothing at all happened to bring back my thoughts into this channel. It might be nearly a week before the subject came back, and once more it was old Lady Carnbee who set me thinking; not that she said anything upon that particular theme. But she was the last of my aunt's afternoon guests to go away, and when she rose to leave she threw up her hands, with those lively gesticulations which so many old Scotch ladies have. "My faith!" said she, "there is that bairn[lxxii] there still like a dream. Is the creature bewitched, Mary Balcarres? and is she bound to sit there by night and by day for the rest of her days? You should mind that there's things about, uncanny for women of our blood."

I was too much startled at first to recognise that it was of me she was speaking. She was like a figure in a picture, with her pale face the colour of ashes, and the big pattern of the Spanish lace hanging half over it, and her hand held up, with the big diamond blazing at me from the inside of her uplifted palm. It was held up in surprise, but it looked as if it were raised in malediction; and the diamond threw out darts of light and glared and twinkled at me. If it had been in its right place it would not have mattered; but there, in the open of the hand! I started up, half in terror, half in wrath. And then the old lady laughed, and her hand dropped. "I've wakened you to life, and broke the spell," she said, nodding her old head at me, while the large black silk flowers of the lace waved and threatened. And she took my arm to go down-stairs, laughing and bidding me be steady, and no' tremble and shake like a broken reed. "You should be as steady as a rock at your age. I was like a young tree," she said, leaning so heavily that my willowy girlish frame quivered – "I was a support to virtue, like Pamela, in my time."

"Aunt Mary, Lady Carnbee is a witch!" I cried, when I came back.

"Is that what you think, honey? well: maybe she once was," said Aunt Mary, whom nothing surprised.

---

[lxxii] Child

And it was that night once more after dinner, and after the post came in, and the 'Times,' that I suddenly saw the Library window again. I had seen it every day and noticed nothing; but to-night, still in a little tumult of mind over Lady Carnbee and her wicked diamond which wished me harm, and her lace which waved threats and warnings at me, I looked across the street, and there I saw quite plainly the room opposite, far more clear than before. I saw dimly that it must be a large room, and that the big piece of furniture against the wall was a writing-desk. That in a moment, when first my eyes rested upon it, was quite clear: a large old-fashioned escritoire, standing out into the room: and I knew by the shape of it that it had a great many pigeon-holes and little drawers in the back, and a large table for writing. There was one just like it in my father's library at home. It was such a surprise to see it all so clearly that I closed my eyes, for the moment almost giddy, wondering how papa's desk could have come here - and then when I reminded myself that this was nonsense, and that there were many such writing-tables besides papa's, and looked again - lo! it had all become quite vague and indistinct as it was at first; and I saw nothing but the blank window, of which the old ladies could never be certain whether it was filled up to avoid the window-tax, or whether it had ever been a window at all.

This occupied my mind very much, and yet I did not say anything to Aunt Mary. For one thing, I rarely saw anything at all in the early part of the day; but then that is natural: you can never see into a place from outside, whether it is an empty room or a looking-glass, or people's eyes, or anything else that is mysterious, in the day. It has, I suppose, something to do with the light. But in the evening in June in Scotland - then is the time to see. For it is daylight, yet it is not day, and there is a quality in it which I cannot describe, it is so clear, as if every object was a reflection of itself.

I used to see more and more of the room as the days went on. The large escritoire stood out more and more into the space: with sometimes white glimmering things, which looked like papers, lying on it: and once or twice I was sure I saw a pile of books on the floor close to the writing-table, as if they had gilding upon them in broken specks, like old books. It was always about the time when the lads in the street began to call to each other that they were going home, and sometimes a shriller voice would come from one of the doors, bidding somebody to "cry upon the ladies" to come back to their suppers. That was always the time I saw best, though it was close upon the moment when the veil seemed to fall and the clear radiance became less living, and all the sounds died out of the street, and Aunt Mary said in her soft voice, "Honey! will you ring for the lamp?" She said honey as people say darling: and I think it is a prettier word.

Then finally, while I sat one evening with my book in my hand, looking straight across the street, not distracted by anything, I saw a little movement within. It was not any one visible - but everybody must know what it is to see the stir in the air, the little disturbance - you cannot tell what it is, but that it indicates someone there, even though you can see no one. Perhaps it is a shadow making just one flicker in the still place. You may look at an empty room and the furniture in it for hours, and then suddenly there will be the flicker, and you know that something has come into it. It might only be a dog or a cat; it might be, if that were possible, a bird flying across; but it is someone, something living, which is so different, so completely different, in a moment from the things that are not living. It seemed to strike quite through me, and I gave a little cry. Then Aunt Mary stirred a little, and put down the huge newspaper that almost covered her from sight, and said, "What is it, honey?" I cried "Nothing," with a little gasp, quickly, for I did not want to be disturbed just at this moment when somebody was coming! But I suppose she was not satisfied, for she got up and stood behind to see what it was, putting her hand on my shoulder. It was the softest touch in the world, but I could have flung it off angrily: for that moment everything was still again, and the place grew grey and I saw no more.

"Nothing," I repeated, but I was so vexed I could have cried. "I told you it was nothing, Aunt Mary. Don't you believe me that you come to look - and spoil it all!"

I did not mean of course to say these last words; they were forced out of me. I was so much annoyed to see it all melt away like a dream: for it was no dream, but as real as - myself or anything I ever saw.

She gave my shoulder a little pat with her hand. "Honey," she said, "were you looking at something? Is't that? Is't that?" "Is it what?" I wanted to say, shaking off her hand, but something in me stopped me: for I said nothing at all, and she went quietly back to her place. I suppose she must have rung the bell herself, for immediately I felt the soft flood of the light behind me, and the evening outside dimmed down, as it did every night, and I saw nothing more.

It was next day, I think, in the afternoon that I spoke. It was brought on by something she said about her fine work. "I get a mist before my eyes," she said; "you will have to learn my old lace stitches, honey - for I soon will not see to draw the threads."

"Oh, I hope you will keep your sight," I cried, without thinking what I was saying. I was then young and very matter-of-fact. I had not found out that one may mean something, yet not half or a hundredth part of what one seems to mean: and even then probably hoping to be contradicted if it is anyhow against one's self.

"My sight!" she said, looking up at me with a look that was almost angry; "there is no question of losing my sight - on the contrary, my eyes are very strong. I may not see to draw fine threads, but I see at a distance as well as ever I did - as well as you do."

"I did not mean any harm, Aunt Mary," I said. "I thought you said----But how can your sight be as good as ever when you are in doubt about that window? I can see into the room as clear as –" My voice wavered, for I had just looked up and across the street I could have sworn that there was no window at all, but only a false image of one painted on the wall.

"Ah!" she said, with a little tone of keenness and of surprise: and she half rose up, throwing down her work hastily, as if she meant to come to me: then, perhaps seeing the bewildered look on my face, she paused and hesitated—"Ay, honey!" she said, "have you got so far ben as that?"

What did she mean? Of course I knew all the old Scotch phrases as well as I knew myself; but it is a comfort to take refuge in a little ignorance, and I know I pretended not to understand whenever I was put out. "I don't know what you mean by 'far ben,'" I cried out, very impatient. I don't know what might have followed, but someone just then came to call, and she could only give me a look before she went forward, putting out her hand to her visitor. It was a very soft look, but anxious, and as if she did not know what to do: and she shook her head a very little, and I thought, though there was a smile on her face, there was something wet about her eyes. I retired into my recess, and nothing more was said.

But it was very tantalising that it should fluctuate so; for sometimes I saw that room quite plain and clear - quite as clear as I could see papa's library, for example, when I shut my eyes. I compared it naturally to my father's study, because of the shape of the writing-table, which, as I tell you, was the same as his. At times I saw the papers on the table quite plain, just as I had seen his papers many a day. And the little pile of books on the floor at the foot - not ranged regularly in order, but put down one above the other, with all their angles going different ways, and a speck of the old gilding shining here and there. And then again at other times I saw nothing, absolutely nothing, and was no better than the old ladies who had peered over my head, drawing their eyelids together, and arguing that the window had been shut up because of the old long-abolished window tax, or else that it had never been a window at all. It annoyed me very much at those dull moments to feel that I too puckered up my eyelids and saw no better than they.

Aunt Mary's old ladies came and went day after day while June went on. I was to go back in July, and I felt that I should be very unwilling indeed to leave until I had quite cleared up - as I was indeed in the way of doing - the mystery of that window which changed so strangely and appeared quite a different thing, not only to different people, but to the same eyes at different times. Of course I said to myself it must simply be an effect of the light. And yet I did not quite like that explanation either, but would have been better pleased to make out to myself that it was some superiority in me which made it so clear to me, if it were only the great superiority of young eyes over old - though that was not quite enough to satisfy me, seeing it was a superiority which I shared with every little lass and lad in the street. I rather wanted, I believe, to think that there was some particular insight in me which gave clearness to my sight -which was a most impertinent assumption, but really did not mean half the harm it seems to mean when it is put down here in black and white. I had several times again, however, seen the room quite plain, and made out that it was a large room, with a great picture in a dim gilded frame hanging on the farther wall, and many other pieces of solid furniture making a blackness here and there, besides the great escritoire against the wall, which had evidently been placed near the window for the sake of the light. One thing became visible to me after another, till I almost thought I should end by being able to read the old lettering on one of the big volumes which projected from the others and caught the light; but this was all preliminary to the great event which happened about Midsummer Day - the day of St John, which was once so much thought of as a festival, but now means nothing at all in Scotland any more than any other of the saints' days: which I shall always think a great pity and loss to Scotland, whatever Aunt Mary may say.

## III

IT was about midsummer, I cannot say exactly to a day when, but near that time, when the great event happened. I had grown very well acquainted by this time with that large dim room. Not only the escritoire, which was very plain to me now, with the papers upon it, and the books at its foot, but the great picture that hung against the farther wall, and various other shadowy pieces of furniture, especially a chair which one evening I saw had been moved into the space before the escritoire, - a little change which made my heart beat, for it spoke so distinctly of someone who must have been there, the someone who had already made me start, two or three times before, by some vague shadow of him or thrill of him which made a sort of movement in the silent space: a movement which made me sure that next minute I must see something or hear something which would explain the whole - if it were not that something always happened outside to stop it, at the very moment of its accomplishment. I had no warning this time of movement or shadow. I had been looking into the room very attentively a little while before, and had made out everything almost clearer than ever; and then had bent my attention again on my book, and read a chapter or two at a most exciting period of the story: and consequently had quite left St Rule's, and the High Street, and the College Library, and was really in a South American forest, almost throttled by the flowery creepers, and treading softly lest I should put my foot on a scorpion or a dangerous snake. At this moment something suddenly called my attention to the outside, I looked across, and then, with a start, sprang up, for I could not contain myself. I don't know what I said, but enough to startle the people in the room, one of whom was old Mr Pitmilly. They all looked round upon me to ask what was the matter. And when I gave my usual answer of "Nothing," sitting down again shamefaced but very much excited, Mr Pitmilly got up and came forward, and looked out, apparently to see what was the cause. He saw nothing, for he went back again, and I could hear him telling Aunt Mary not to be alarmed, for Missy had fallen into a doze with the heat, and had startled herself waking up, at which they all laughed: another time I could have killed him for his impertinence, but my mind was too much taken up now to pay any attention. My head was throbbing and my heart beating. I was in such high excitement, however, that to restrain myself completely, to be perfectly silent, was easier to me then than at any other time of my life. I waited until the old gentleman had taken his seat again, and then I looked back. Yes, there he was! I had not been deceived. I knew then, when I looked across, that this was what I had been looking for all the time - that I had known he was there, and had been waiting for him, every time there was that flicker of movement in the room - him and no one else. And there at last, just as I had expected, he was. I don't know that in reality I ever had expected him, or anyone: but this was what I felt when, suddenly looking into that curious dim room, I saw him there.

He was sitting in the chair, which he must have placed for himself, or which someone else in the dead of night when nobody was looking must have set for him, in front of the escritoire - with the back of his head towards me, writing. The light fell upon him from the left hand, and therefore upon his shoulders and the side of his head, which, however, was too much turned away to show anything of his face. Oh, how strange that there should be someone staring at him as I was doing, and he never to turn his head, to make a movement! If anyone stood and looked at me, were I in the soundest sleep that ever was, I would wake, I would jump up, I would feel it through everything. But there he sat and never moved. You are not to suppose, though I said the light fell upon him from the left hand, that there was very much light. There never is in a room you are looking into like that across the street; but there was enough to see him by - the outline of his figure dark and solid, seated in the chair, and the fairness of his head visible faintly, a clear spot against the dimness. I saw this outline against the dim gilding of the frame of the large picture which hung on the farther wall.

I sat all the time the visitors were there, in a sort of rapture, gazing at this figure. I knew no reason why I should be so much moved. In an ordinary way, to see a student at an opposite window quietly doing his work might have interested me a little, but certainly it would not have moved me in any such way. It is always interesting to have a glimpse like this of an unknown life - to see so much and yet know so little, and to wonder, perhaps, what the man is doing, and why he never turns his head. One would go to the window - but not too close, lest he should see you and think you were spying upon him - and one would ask, Is he still there? is he writing, writing always? I wonder what he is writing! And it would be a great amusement: but no more. This was not my feeling at all in the present case. It was a sort of breathless watch, an absorption. I did not feel that I had eyes for anything else, or any room in my mind for another thought. I no longer heard, as I generally did, the stories and the wise remarks (or foolish) of Aunt Mary's old ladies or Mr Pitmilly. I heard only a murmur behind me, the interchange of voices, one softer, one sharper; but it was not as in the time when I sat reading and heard every word, till the story in my book, and the stories they were telling (what they said almost always shaped into stories), were all mingled into each other, and the hero in the novel became somehow the hero (or more likely heroine) of them all. But I took no notice of what they were saying now. And it was not that there was anything very interesting to look at, except the fact that he was there. He did nothing to keep up the absorption of my thoughts. He moved just so much as a man will do when he is very busily writing, thinking of nothing else. There was a faint turn of his head as he went from one side to another of the page he was writing; but it appeared to be a long long page which never wanted turning. Just a little inclination when he was at the end of the line, outward, and then a little inclination inward when he began the next. That was little enough to keep one gazing. But I suppose it was the gradual course of events leading up to this, the finding out of one thing after another as the eyes got accustomed to the vague light: first the room itself, and then the writing-table, and then the other furniture, and last of all the human inhabitant who gave it all meaning. This was all so interesting that it was like a country which one had discovered. And then the extraordinary blindness of the other people who disputed among themselves whether it was a window at all! I did not, I am sure, wish to be disrespectful, and I was very fond of my Aunt Mary, and I liked Mr Pitmilly well enough, and I was afraid of Lady Carnbee. But yet to think of the - I know I ought not to say stupidity - the blindness of them, the foolishness, the insensibility! discussing it as if a thing that your eyes could see was a thing to discuss! It would have been unkind to think it was because they were old and their faculties dimmed. It is so sad to think that the faculties grow dim, that such a woman as my Aunt Mary should fail in seeing, or hearing, or feeling, that I would not have dwelt on it for a moment, it would have seemed so cruel! And then such a clever old lady as Lady Carnbee, who could see through a millstone, people said - and Mr Pitmilly, such an old man of the world. It did indeed bring tears to my eyes to think that all those clever people, solely by reason of being no longer young as I was, should have the simplest things shut out from them; and for all their wisdom and their knowledge be unable to see what a girl like me could see so easily. I was too much grieved for them to dwell upon that thought, and half ashamed, though perhaps half proud too, to be so much better off than they.

All those thoughts flitted through my mind as I sat and gazed across the street. And I felt there was so much going on in that room across the street! He was so absorbed in his writing, never looked up, never paused for a word, never turned round in his chair, or got up and walked about the room as my father did. Papa is a great writer, everybody says: but he would have come to the window and looked out, he would have drummed with his fingers on the pane, he would have watched a fly and helped it over a difficulty, and played with the fringe of the curtain, and done a dozen other nice, pleasant, foolish things, till the next sentence took shape. "My dear, I am waiting for a word," he would say to my mother when she looked at him, with a question why he was so idle, in her eyes; and then he would laugh, and go back again to his writing-table. But He over there never stopped at all. It was like a fascination. I could not take my eyes from him and that little scarcely perceptible movement he made, turning his head. I trembled with impatience to see him turn the page, or perhaps throw down his finished sheet on the floor, as somebody looking into a window like me once saw Sir Walter do, sheet after sheet. I should have cried out if this Unknown had done that. I should not have been able to help myself, whoever had been present; and gradually I got into such a state of suspense waiting for it to be done that my head grew hot and my hands cold. And then, just when there was a little movement of his elbow, as if he were about to do this, to be called away by Aunt Mary to see Lady Carnbee to the door! I believe I did not hear her till she had called me three times, and then I stumbled up, all flushed and hot, and nearly crying. When I came out from the recess to give the old lady my arm (Mr Pitmilly had gone away some time before), she put up her hand and stroked my cheek. "What ails the bairn?" she said; "she's fevered. You must not let her sit here in the window, Mary Balcarres. You and me know what comes of that." Her old fingers had a strange touch, cold like something not living, and I felt that dreadful diamond sting me on the cheek.

I do not say that this was not just a part of my excitement and suspense; and I know it is enough to make any one laugh when the excitement was all about an unknown man writing in a room on the other side of the way, and my impatience because he never came to an end of the page. If you think I was not quite as well aware of this as anyone could be! but the worst was that this dreadful old lady felt my heart beating against her arm that was within mine. "You are just in a dream," she said to me, with her old voice close at my ear as we went down-stairs. "I don't know who it is about, but it's bound to be some man that is not worth it. If you were wise you would think of him no more."

"I am thinking of no man!" I said, half crying. "It is very unkind and dreadful of you to say so, Lady Carnbee. I never thought of----any man, in all my life!" I cried in a passion of indignation. The old lady clung tighter to my arm, and pressed it to her, not unkindly.

"Poor little bird," she said, "how it's strugglin' and flutterin'! I'm not saying but what it's more dangerous when it's all for a dream."

She was not at all unkind; but I was very angry and excited, and would scarcely shake that old pale hand which she put out to me from her carriage window when I had helped her in. I was angry with her, and I was afraid of the diamond, which looked up from under her finger as if it saw through and through me; and whether you believe me or not, I am certain that it stung me again - a sharp malignant prick, oh full of meaning! She never wore gloves, but only black lace mittens, through which that horrible diamond gleamed.

I ran up-stairs - she had been the last to go and Aunt Mary too had gone to get ready for dinner, for it was late. I hurried to my place, and looked across, with my heart beating more than ever. I made quite sure I should see the finished sheet lying white upon the floor. But what I gazed at was only the dim blank of that window which they said was no window. The light had changed in some wonderful way during that five minutes I had been gone, and there was nothing, nothing, not a reflection, not a glimmer. It looked exactly as they all said, the blank form of a window painted on the wall. It was too much: I sat down in my excitement and cried as if my heart would break. I felt that they had done something to it, that it was not natural, that I could not bear their unkindness - even Aunt Mary. They thought it not good for me! not good for me! and they had done something - even Aunt Mary herself - and that wicked diamond that hid itself in Lady Carnbee's hand. Of course I knew all this was ridiculous as well as you could tell me; but I was exasperated by the disappointment and the sudden stop to all my excited feelings, and I could not bear it. It was stronger than I.

I was late for dinner, and naturally there were some traces in my eyes that I had been crying when I came into the full light in the dining-room, where Aunt Mary could look at me at her pleasure, and I could not run away. She said, "Honey, you have been shedding tears. I'm loath, loath that a bairn of your mother's should be made to shed tears in my house."

"I have not been made to shed tears," cried I; and then, to save myself another fit of crying, I burst out laughing and said, "I am afraid of that dreadful diamond on old Lady Carnbee's hand. It bites - I am sure it bites! Aunt Mary, look here."

"You foolish lassie," Aunt Mary said; but she looked at my cheek under the light of the lamp, and then she gave it a little pat with her soft hand. "Go away with you, you silly bairn. There is no bite; but a flushed cheek, my honey, and a wet eye. You must just read out my paper to me after dinner when the post is in: and we'll have no more thinking and no more dreaming for tonight."

"Yes, Aunt Mary," said I. But I knew what would happen; for when she opens up her 'Times,' all full of the news of the world, and the speeches and things which she takes an interest in, though I cannot tell why - she forgets. And as I kept very quiet and made not a sound, she forgot to-night what she had said, and the curtain hung a little more over me than usual, and I sat down in my recess as if I had been a hundred miles away. And my heart gave a great jump, as if it would have come out of my breast; for he was there. But not as he had been in the morning - I suppose the light, perhaps, was not good enough to go on with his work without a lamp or candles - for he had turned away from the table and was fronting the window, sitting leaning back in his chair, and turning his head to me. Not to me - he knew nothing about me. I thought he was not looking at anything; but with his face turned my way. My heart was in my mouth: it was so unexpected, so strange! though why it should have seemed strange I know not, for there was no communication between him and me that it should have moved me; and what could be more natural than that a man, wearied of his work, and feeling the want perhaps of more light, and yet that it was not dark enough to light a lamp, should turn round in his own chair, and rest a little, and think - perhaps of nothing at all? Papa always says he is thinking of nothing at all. He says things blow through his mind as if the doors were open, and he has no responsibility. What sort of things were blowing through this man's mind? or was he thinking, still thinking, of what he had been writing and going on with it still? The thing that troubled me most was that I could not make out his face. It is very difficult to do so when you see a person only through two windows, your own and his. I wanted very much to recognise him afterwards if I should chance to meet him in the street. If he had only stood up and moved about the room, I should have made out the rest of his figure, and then I should have known him again; or if he had only come to the window (as papa always did), then I should have seen his face clearly enough to have recognised him. But, to be sure, he did not see any need to do anything in order that I might recognise him, for he did not know I existed; and probably if he had known I was watching him, he would have been annoyed and gone away.

But he was as immovable there facing the window as he had been seated at the desk. Sometimes he made a little faint stir with a hand or a foot, and I held my breath, hoping he was about to rise from his chair - but he never did it. And with all the efforts I made I could not be sure of his face. I puckered my eyelids together as old Miss Jeanie did who was shortsighted, and I put my hands on each side of my face to concentrate the light on him: but it was all in vain. Either the face changed as I sat staring, or else it was the light that was not good enough, or I don't know what it was. His hair seemed to me light - certainly there was no dark line about his head, as there would have been had it been very dark - and I saw, where it came across the old gilt frame on the wall behind, that it must be fair: and I am almost sure he had no beard. Indeed I am sure that he had no beard, for the outline of his face was distinct enough; and the daylight was still quite clear out of doors, so that I recognised perfectly a baker's boy who was on the pavement opposite, and whom I should have known again whenever I had met him: as if it was of the least importance to recognise a baker's boy! There was one thing, however, rather curious about this boy. He had been throwing stones at something or somebody. In St Rule's they have a great way of throwing stones at each other, and I suppose there had been a battle. I suppose also that he had one stone in his hand left over from the battle, and his roving eye took in all the incidents of the street to judge where he could throw it with most effect and mischief. But apparently he found nothing worthy of it in the street, for he suddenly turned round with a flick under his leg to show his cleverness, and aimed it straight at the window. I remarked without remarking that it struck with a hard sound and without any breaking of glass, and fell straight down on the pavement. But I took no notice of this even in my mind, so intently was I watching the figure within, which moved not nor took the slightest notice, and remained just as dimly clear, as perfectly seen, yet as indistinguishable, as before. And then the light began to fail a little, not diminishing the prospect within, but making it still less distinct than it had been.

Then I jumped up, feeling Aunt Mary's hand upon my shoulder. "Honey," she said, "I asked you twice to ring the bell; but you did not hear me."

"Oh, Aunt Mary!" I cried in great penitence, but turning again to the window in spite of myself.

"You must come away from there: you must come away from there," she said, almost as if she were angry: and then her soft voice grew softer, and she gave me a kiss: "never mind about the lamp, honey; I have rung myself, and it is coming; but, silly bairn, you must not aye be dreaming - your little head will turn."

All the answer I made, for I could scarcely speak, was to give a little wave with my hand to the window on the other side of the street.

She stood there patting me softly on the shoulder for a whole minute or more, murmuring something that sounded like, "She must go away, she must go away." Then she said, always with her hand soft on my shoulder, "Like a dream when one awaketh." And when I looked again, I saw the blank of an opaque surface and nothing more.

Aunt Mary asked me no more questions. She made me come into the room and sit in the light and read something to her. But I did not know what I was reading, for there suddenly came into my mind and took possession of it, the thud of the stone upon the window, and its descent straight down, as if from some hard substance that threw it off: though I had myself seen it strike upon the glass of the panes across the way.

## IV

I AM afraid I continued in a state of great exaltation and commotion of mind for some time. I used to hurry through the day till the evening came, when I could watch my neighbour through the window opposite. I did not talk much to any one, and I never said a word about my own questions and wonderings. I wondered who he was, what he was doing, and why he never came till the evening (or very rarely); and I also wondered much to what house the room belonged in which he sat. It seemed to form a portion of the old College Library, as I have often said. The window was one of the line of windows which I understood lighted the large hall; but whether this room belonged to the library itself, or how its occupant gained access to it, I could not tell. I made up my mind that it must open out of the hall, and that the gentleman must be the Librarian or one of his assistants, perhaps kept busy all the day in his official duties, and only able to get to his desk and do his own private work in the evening. One has heard of so many things like that - a man who had to take up some other kind of work for his living, and then when his leisure-time came, gave it all up to something he really loved - some study or some book he was writing. My father himself at one time had been like that. He had been in the Treasury all day, and then in the evening wrote his books, which made him famous. His daughter, however little she might know of other things, could not but know that! But it discouraged me very much when somebody pointed out to me one day in the street an old gentleman who wore a wig and took a great deal of snuff, and said, That's the Librarian of the old College. It gave me a great shock for a moment; but then I remembered that an old gentleman has generally assistants, and that it must be one of them.

Gradually I became quite sure of this. There was another small window above, which twinkled very much when the sun shone, and looked a very kindly bright little window, above that dullness of the other which hid so much. I made up my mind this was the window of his other room, and that these two chambers at the end of the beautiful hall were really beautiful for him to live in, so near all the books, and so retired and quiet, that nobody knew of them. What a fine thing for him! and you could see what use he made of his good fortune as he sat there, so constant at his writing for hours together. Was it a book he was writing, or could it be perhaps Poems? This was a thought which made my heart beat; but I concluded with much regret that it could not be Poems, because no one could possibly write Poems like that, straight off, without pausing for a word or a rhyme. Had they been Poems he must have risen up, he must have paced about the room or come to the window as papa did - not that papa wrote Poems: he always said, "I am not worthy even to speak of such prevailing mysteries," shaking his head - which gave me a wonderful admiration and almost awe of a Poet, who was thus much greater even than papa. But I could not believe that a poet could have kept still for hours and hours like that. What could it be then? perhaps it was history; that is a great thing to work at, but you would not perhaps need to move nor to stride up and down, or look out upon the sky and the wonderful light.

He did move now and then, however, though he never came to the window. Sometimes, as I have said, he would turn round in his chair and turn his face towards it, and sit there for a long time musing when the light had begun to fail, and the world was full of that strange day which was night, that light without colour, in which everything was so clearly visible, and there were no shadows. "It was between the night and the day, when the fairy folk have power." This was the after-light of the wonderful, long, long summer evening, the light without shadows. It had a spell in it, and sometimes it made me afraid: and all manner of strange thoughts seemed to come in, and I always felt that if only we had a little more vision in our eyes we might see beautiful folk walking about in it, who were not of our world. I thought most likely he saw them, from the way he sat there looking out: and this made my heart expand with the most curious sensation, as if of pride that, though I could not see, he did, and did not even require to come to the window, as I did, sitting close in the depth of the recess, with my eyes upon him, and almost seeing things through his eyes.

I was so much absorbed in these thoughts and in watching him every evening - for now he never missed an evening, but was always there - that people began to remark that I was looking pale and that I could not be well, for I paid no attention when they talked to me, and did not care to go out, nor to join the other girls for their tennis, nor to do anything that others did; and some said to Aunt Mary that I was quickly losing all the ground I had gained, and that she could never send me back to my mother with a white face like that. Aunt Mary had begun to look at me anxiously for some time before that, and, I am sure, held secret consultations over me, sometimes with the doctor, and sometimes with her old ladies, who thought they knew more about young girls than even the doctors. And I could hear them saying to her that I wanted diversion, that I must be diverted, and that she must take me out more, and give a party, and that when the summer visitors began to come there would perhaps be a ball or two, or Lady Carnbee would get up a picnic. "And there's my young lord coming home," said the old lady whom they called Miss Jeanie, "and I never knew the young lassie yet that would not cock up her bonnet at the sight of a young lord."

But Aunt Mary shook her head. "I would not listen much to the young lord," she said. "His mother is sore set upon siller[lxxiii] for him; and my poor bit honey has no fortune to speak of. No, we must not fly so high as the young lord; but I will       gladly take her about the country to see the old castles and towers. It will perhaps rouse her up a little."

"And if that does not answer we must think of something else," the old lady said.

---

[lxxiii] Silver

I heard them perhaps that day because they were talking of me, which is always so effective a way of making you hear - for latterly I had not been paying any attention to what they were saying; and I thought to myself how little they knew, and how little I cared about even the old castles and curious houses, having something else in my mind. But just about that time Mr Pitmilly came in, who was always a friend to me, and, when he heard them talking, he managed to stop them and turn the conversation into another channel. And after a while, when the ladies were gone away, he came up to my recess, and gave a glance right over my head. And then he asked my Aunt Mary if ever she had settled her question about the window opposite, "that you thought was a window sometimes, and then not a window, and many curious things," the old gentleman said.

My Aunt Mary gave me another very wistful look; and then she said, "Indeed, Mr Pitmilly, we are just where we were, and I am quite as unsettled as ever; and I think my niece she has taken up my views, for I see her many a time looking across and wondering, and I am not clear now what her opinion is."

"My opinion!" I said, "Aunt Mary." I could not help being a little scornful, as one is when one is very young. "I have no opinion. There is not only a window but there is a room, and I could show you," I was going to say, "show you the gentleman who sits and writes in it," but I stopped, not knowing what they might say, and looked from one to another. "I could tell you - all the furniture that is in it," I said. And then I felt something like a flame that went over my face, and that all at once my cheeks were burning. I thought they gave a little glance at each other, but that may have been folly. "There is a great picture, in a big dim frame," I said, feeling a little breathless, "on the wall opposite the window."

"Is there so?" said Mr Pitmilly, with a little laugh. And he said, "Now I will tell you what we'll do. You know that there is a conversation party, or whatever they call it, in the big room to-night, and it will be all open and lighted up. And it is a handsome room, and two-three things well worth looking at. I will just step along after we have all got our dinner, and take you over to the party, madam--Missy and you---"

"Dear me!" said Aunt Mary. "I have not gone to a party for more years than I would like to say--and never once to the Library Hall." Then she gave a little shiver, and said quite low, "I could not go there."

"Then you will just begin again to-night, madam," said Mr Pitmilly, taking no notice of this, "and a proud man will I be leading in Mistress Balcarres that was once the pride of the ball!"

"Ah, once!" said Aunt Mary, with a low little laugh and then a sigh. "And we'll not say how long ago;" and after that she made a pause, looking always at me: and then she said, "I accept your offer, and we'll put on our braws[lxxiv]; and I hope you will have no occasion to think shame of us. But why not take your dinner here?"

That was how it was settled, and the old gentleman went away to dress, looking quite pleased. But I came to Aunt Mary as soon as he was gone, and besought her not to make me go. "I like the long bonnie night and the light that lasts so long. And I cannot bear to dress up and go out, wasting it all in a stupid party. I hate parties, Aunt Mary!" I cried, "and I would far rather stay here."

"My honey," she said, taking both my hands, "I know it will maybe be a blow to you, but its better so."

"How could it be a blow to me?" I cried; "but I would far rather not go."

"You'll just go with me, honey, just this once: it is not often I go out. You will go with me this one night, just this one night, my honey sweet."

I am sure there were tears in Aunt Mary's eyes, and she kissed me between the words. There was nothing more that I could say; but how I grudged the evening! A mere party, a conversazione (when all the College was away, too, and nobody to make conversation!), instead of my enchanted hour at my window and the soft strange light, and the dim face looking out, which kept me wondering and wondering what was he thinking of, what was he looking for, who was he? all one wonder and mystery and question, through the long, long, slowly fading night!

It occurred to me, however, when I was dressing--though I was so sure that he would prefer his solitude to everything - that he might perhaps, it was just possible, be there. And when I thought of that, I took out my white frock though Janet had laid out my blue one - and my little pearl necklace which I had thought was too good to wear. They were not very large pearls, but they were real pearls, and very even and lustrous though they were small; and though I did not think much of my appearance then, there must have been something about me - pale as I was but apt to colour in a moment, with my dress so white, and my pearls so white, and my hair all shadowy perhaps, that was pleasant to look at: for even old Mr Pitmilly had a strange look in his eyes, as if he was not only pleased but sorry too, perhaps thinking me a creature that would have troubles in this life, though I was so young and knew them not. And when Aunt Mary looked at me, there was a little quiver about her mouth. She herself

---

[lxxiv] Best clothes

had on her pretty lace and her white hair very nicely done, and looking her best. As for Mr Pitmilly, he had a beautiful fine French frill to his shirt, plaited in the most minute plaits, and with a diamond pin in it which sparkled as much as Lady Carnbee's ring; but this was a fine frank kindly stone, that looked you straight in the face and sparkled, with the light dancing in it as if it were pleased to see you, and to be shining on that old gentleman's honest and faithful breast: for he had been one of Aunt Mary's lovers in their early days, and still thought there was nobody like her in the world.

I had got into quite a happy commotion of mind by the time we set out across the street in the soft light of the evening to the Library Hall. Perhaps, after all, I should see him, and see the room which I was so well acquainted with, and find out why he sat there so constantly and never was seen abroad. I thought I might even hear what he was working at, which would be such a pleasant thing to tell papa when I went home. A friend of mine at St Rule's - oh, far, far more busy than you ever were, papa! - and then my father would laugh as he always did, and say he was but an idler and never busy at all.

The room was all light and bright, flowers wherever flowers could be, and the long lines of the books that went along the walls on each side, lighting up wherever there was a line of gilding or an ornament, with a little response. It dazzled me at first all that light: but I was very eager, though I kept very quiet, looking round to see if perhaps in any corner, in the middle of any group, he would be there. I did not expect to see him among the ladies. He would not be with them, - he was too studious, too silent: but, perhaps among that circle of grey heads at the upper end of the room--perhaps----

No: I am not sure that it was not half a pleasure to me to make quite sure that there was not one whom I could take for him, who was at all like my vague image of him. No: it was absurd to think that he would be here, amid all that sound of voices, under the glare of that light. I felt a little proud to think that he was in his room as usual, doing his work, or thinking so deeply over it, as when he turned round in his chair with his face to the light.

I was thus getting a little composed and quiet in my mind, for now that the expectation of seeing him was over, though it was a disappointment, it was a satisfaction too - when Mr Pitmilly came up to me, holding out his arm. "Now," he said, "I am going to take you to see the curiosities." I thought to myself that after I had seen them and spoken to everybody I knew, Aunt Mary would let me go home, so I went very willingly, though I did not care for the curiosities. Something, however, struck me strangely as we walked up the room. It was the air, rather fresh and strong, from an open window at the east end of the hall. How should there be a window there? I hardly saw what it meant for the first moment, but it blew in my face as if there was some meaning in it, and I felt very uneasy without seeing why.

Then there was another thing that startled me. On that side of the wall which was to the street there seemed no windows at all. A long line of bookcases filled it from end to end. I could not see what that meant either, but it confused me. I was altogether confused. I felt as if I was in a strange country, not knowing where I was going, not knowing what I might find out next. If there were no windows on the wall to the street, where was my window? My heart, which had been jumping up and calming down again all this time, gave a great leap at this, as if it would have come out of me - but I did not know what it could mean.

Then we stopped before a glass case, and Mr Pitmilly showed me some things in it. I could not pay much attention to them. My head was going round and round. I heard his voice going on, and then myself speaking with a queer sound that was hollow in my ears; but I did not know what I was saying or what he was saying. Then he took me to the very end of the room, the east end, saying something that I caught - that I was pale, that the air would do me good. The air was blowing full on me, lifting the lace of my dress, lifting my hair, almost chilly. The window opened into the pale daylight, into the little lane that ran by the end of the building. Mr Pitmilly went on talking, but I could not make out a word he said. Then I heard my own voice, speaking through it, though I did not seem to be aware that I was speaking. "Where is my window? - where, then, is my window?" I seemed to be saying, and I turned right round, dragging him with me, still holding his arm. As I did this my eye fell upon something at last which I knew. It was a large picture in a broad frame, hanging against the farther wall.

What did it mean? Oh, what did it mean? I turned round again to the open window at the east end, and to the daylight, the strange light without any shadow, that was all round about this lighted hall, holding it like a bubble that would burst, like something that was not real. The real place was the room I knew, in which that picture was hanging, where the writing-table was, and where he sat with his face to the light. But where was the light and the window through which it came? I think my senses must have left me. I went up to the picture which I knew, and then I walked straight across the room, always dragging Mr Pitmilly, whose face was pale, but who did not struggle but allowed me to lead him, straight across to where the window was - where the window was not;- where there was no sign of it. "Where is my window? --where is my window?" I said. And all the time I was sure that I was in a dream, and these lights were all some theatrical illusion and the people talking; and nothing real but the pale, pale, watching, lingering day standing by to wait until that foolish bubble should burst.

"My dear," said Mr Pitmilly, "my dear! Mind that you are in public. Mind where you are. You must not make an outcry and frighten your Aunt Mary. Come away with me. Come away, my dear young lady! and you'll take a seat for a minute or two and compose yourself; and I'll get you an ice or a little wine." He kept patting my hand, which was on his arm, and looking at me very anxiously. "Bless me! bless me! I never thought it would have this effect," he said.

But I would not allow him to take me away in that direction. I went to the picture again and looked at it without seeing it: and then I went across the room again, with some kind of wild thought that if I insisted I should find it. "My window--my window!" I said.

There was one of the professors standing there, and he heard me. "The window!" said he. "Ah, you've been taken in with what appears outside. It was put there to be in uniformity with the window on the stair. But it never was a real window. It is just behind that bookcase. Many people are taken in by it," he said.

His voice seemed to sound from somewhere far away, and as if it would go on forever; and the hall swam in a dazzle of shining and of noises round me; and the daylight through the open window grew greyer, waiting till it should be over, and the bubble burst.

## V

IT was Mr Pitmilly who took me home; or rather it was I who took him, pushing him on a little in front of me, holding fast by his arm, not waiting for Aunt Mary or anyone. We came out into the daylight again outside, I, without even a cloak or a shawl, with my bare arms, and uncovered head, and the pearls round my neck. There was a rush of the people about, and a baker's boy, that baker's boy, stood right in my way and cried, "Here's a braw ane!"[lxxv] shouting to the others: the words struck me somehow, as his stone had struck the window, without any reason. But I did not mind the people staring, and hurried across the street, with Mr Pitmilly half a step in advance. The door was open, and Janet standing at it, looking out to see what she could see of the ladies in their grand dresses. She gave a shriek when she saw me hurrying across the street; but I brushed past her, and pushed Mr Pitmilly up the stairs, and

---

[lxxv] Lovely one

took him breathless to the recess, where I threw myself down on the seat, feeling as if I could not have gone another step farther, and waved my hand across to the window. "There! there!" I cried. Ah! there it was - not that senseless mob - not the theatre and the gas, and the people all in a murmur and clang of talking. Never in all these days had I seen that room so clearly. There was a faint tone of light behind, as if it might have been a reflection from some of those vulgar lights in the hall, and he sat against it, calm, wrapped in his thoughts, with his face turned to the window. Nobody but must have seen him. Janet could have seen him had I called her up-stairs. It was like a picture, all the things I knew, and the same attitude, and the atmosphere, full of quietness, not disturbed by anything. I pulled Mr Pitmilly's arm before I let him go,--"You see, you see!" I cried. He gave me the most bewildered look, as if he would have liked to cry. He saw nothing! I was sure of that from his eyes. He was an old man, and there was no vision in him. If I had called up Janet, she would have seen it all. "My dear!" he said. "My dear!" waving his hands in a helpless way. "He has been there all these nights," I cried, "and I thought you could tell me who he was and what he was doing; and that he might have taken me into that room, and showed me, that I might tell papa. Papa would understand; he would like to hear. Oh, can't you tell me what work he is doing, Mr Pitmilly? He never lifts his head as long as the light throws a shadow, and then when it is like this he turns round and thinks, and takes a rest!"

Mr Pitmilly was trembling, whether it was with cold or I know not what. He said, with a shake in his voice, "My dear young lady--my dear---" and then stopped and looked at me as if he were going to cry. "It's peetiful, it's peetiful," he said; and then in another voice, "I am going across there again to bring your Aunt Mary home; do you understand, my poor little thing, my I am going to bring her home - you will be better when she is here." I was glad when he went away, as he could not see anything: and I sat alone in the dark which was not dark, but quite clear light - a light like nothing I ever saw. How clear it was in that room! not glaring like the gas and the voices, but so quiet, everything so visible, as if it were in another world. I heard a little rustle behind me, and there was Janet, standing staring at me with two big eyes wide open. She was only a little older than I was. I called to her, "Janet, come here, come here, and you will see him,--come here and see him!" impatient that she should be so shy and keep behind. "Oh, my bonnie young leddy!" she said, and burst out crying. I stamped my foot at her, in my indignation that she would not come, and she fled before me with a rustle and swing of haste, as if she were afraid. None of them, none of them! not even a girl like myself, with the sight in her eyes, would understand. I turned back again, and held out my hands to him sitting there, who was the only one that knew. "Oh," I said, "say something to me! I don't know who you are, or what you are: but you're lonely and so am I; and I only--feel for you. Say something to me!" I neither hoped that he would hear, nor expected any answer. How could he hear, with the street between us, and his window shut, and all the murmuring of the voices and the people standing about? But for one moment it seemed to me that there was only him and me in the whole world.

But I gasped with my breath that had almost gone from me, when I saw him move in his chair! He had heard me, though I knew not how. He rose up, and I rose too, speechless, incapable of anything but this mechanical movement. He seemed to draw me as if I were a puppet moved by his will. He came forward to the window, and stood looking across at me. I was sure that he looked at me. At last he had seen me: at last he had found out that somebody, though only a girl, was watching him, looking for him, believing in him. I was in such trouble and commotion of mind and trembling, that I could not keep on my feet, but dropped kneeling on the window-seat, supporting myself against the window, feeling as if my heart were being drawn out of me. I cannot describe his face. It was all dim, yet there was a light on it: I think it must have been a smile; and as closely as I looked at him he looked at me. His hair was fair, and there was a little quiver about his lips. Then he put his hands upon the window to open it. It was stiff and hard to move; but at last he forced it open with a sound that echoed all along the street. I saw that the people heard it, and several looked up. As for me, I put my hands together, leaning with my face against the glass, drawn to him as if I could have gone out of myself, my heart out of my bosom, my eyes out of my head. He opened the window with a noise that was heard from the West Port to the Abbey. Could anyone doubt that?

And then he leaned forward out of the window, looking out. There was not one in the street but must have seen him. He looked at me first, with a little wave of his hand, as if it were a salutation - yet not exactly that either, for I thought he waved me away; and then he looked up and down in the dim shining of the ending day, first to the east, to the old Abbey towers, and then to the west, along the broad line of the street where so many people were coming and going, but so little noise, all like enchanted folk in an enchanted place. I watched him with such a melting heart, with such a deep satisfaction as words could not say; for nobody could tell me now that he was not there, - nobody could say I was dreaming any more. I watched him as if I could not breathe - my heart in my throat, my eyes upon him. He looked up and down, and then he looked back to me. I was the first, and I was the last, though it was not for long: he did know, he did see, who it was that had recognised him and sympathised with him all the time. I was in a kind of rapture, yet stupor too; my look went with his look, following it as if I were his shadow; and then suddenly he was gone, and I saw him no more.

I dropped back again upon my seat, seeking something to support me, something to lean upon. He had lifted his hand and waved it once again to me. How he went I cannot tell, nor where he went I cannot tell; but in a moment he was away, and the window standing open, and the room fading into stillness and dimness, yet so clear, with all its space, and the great picture in its gilded frame upon the wall. It gave me no pain to see him go away. My heart was so content, and I was so worn out and satisfied - for what doubt or question could there be about him now? As I was lying back as weak as water, Aunt Mary came in behind me, and flew to me with a little rustle as if she had come on wings, and put her arms round me, and drew my head on to her breast. I had begun to cry a little, with sobs like a child. "You saw him, you saw him!" I said. To lean upon her, and feel her so soft, so kind, gave me a pleasure I cannot describe, and her arms round me, and her voice saying "Honey, my honey!"- as if she were nearly crying too. Lying there I came back to myself, quite sweetly, glad of everything. But I wanted some assurance from them that they had seen him too. I waved my hand to the window that was still standing open, and the room that was stealing away into the faint dark. "This time you saw it all?" I said, getting more eager. "My honey!" said Aunt Mary, giving me a kiss: and Mr Pitmilly began to walk about the room with short little steps behind, as if he were out of patience. I sat straight up and put away Aunt Mary's arms. "You cannot be so blind, so blind!" I cried. "Oh, not to-night, at least not to-night!" But neither the one nor the other made any reply. I shook myself quite free, and raised myself up. And there, in the middle of the street, stood the baker's boy like a statue, staring up at the open window, with his mouth open and his face full of wonder - breathless, as if he could not believe what he saw. I darted forward, calling to him, and beckoned him to come to me. "Oh, bring him up! bring him, bring him to me!" I cried.

Mr Pitmilly went out directly, and got the boy by the shoulder. He did not want to come. It was strange to see the little old gentleman, with his beautiful frill and his diamond pin, standing out in the street, with his hand upon the boy's shoulder, and the other boys round, all in a little crowd. And presently they came towards the house, the others all following, gaping and wondering. He came in unwilling, almost resisting, looking as if we meant him some harm. "Come away, my laddie, come and speak to the young lady," Mr Pitmilly was saying. And Aunt Mary took my hands to keep me back. But I would not be kept back.

"Boy," I cried, "you saw it too: you saw it: tell them you saw it! It is that I want, and no more."

He looked at me as they all did, as if he thought I was mad. "What's she wantin' wi' me?" he said; and then, "I did nae harm, even if I did throw a bit stane at it - and it's nae sin to throw a stane."

"You rascal!" said Mr Pitmilly, giving him a shake; "have you been throwing stones? You'll kill somebody some of these days with your stones." The old gentleman was confused and troubled, for he did not understand what I wanted, nor anything that had happened. And then Aunt Mary, holding my hands and drawing me close to her, spoke. "Laddie," she said, "answer the young lady, like a good lad. There's no intention of finding fault with you. Answer her, my man, and then Janet will give ye your supper before you go."

"Oh speak, speak!" I cried; "answer them and tell them! you saw that window opened, and the gentleman look out and wave his hand?"

"I saw nae [no] gentleman," he said, with his head down, "except this wee gentleman here."

"Listen, laddie," said Aunt Mary. "I saw ye standing in the middle of the street staring. What were ye looking at?"

"It was naething [nothing] to make a wark [work] about. It was just yon windy [window] yonder in the library that is nae windy. And it was open as sure's death. You may laugh if you like. Is that a' [all] she's wantin' wi' [with] me?"

"You are telling a pack of lies, laddie," Mr Pitmilly said.

"I'm tellin' nae lees [no lies] - it was standin' open just like ony [any] other windy [window]. It's as sure's death. I couldna believe it mysel'; but it's true."

"And there it is," I cried, turning round and pointing it out to them with great triumph in my heart. But the light was all grey, it had faded, it had changed. The window was just as it had always been, a sombre break upon the wall.

I was treated like an invalid all that evening, and taken up-stairs to bed, and Aunt Mary sat up in my room the whole night through. Whenever I opened my eyes she was always sitting there close to me, watching. And there never was in all my life so strange a night. When I would talk in my excitement, she kissed me and hushed me like a child. "Oh, honey, you are not the only one!" she said. "Oh whisht, whisht [be quiet], bairn [child]! I should never have let you be there!"

"Aunt Mary, Aunt Mary, you have seen him too?"

"Oh whisht, whisht, honey!" Aunt Mary said: her eyes were shining - there were tears in them. "Oh whisht, whisht! Put it out of your mind, and try to sleep. I will not speak another word," she cried.

But I had my arms round her, and my mouth at her ear. "Who is he there? - tell me that and I will ask no more---"

"Oh honey, rest, and try to sleep! It is just - how can I tell you? - a dream, a dream! Did you not hear what Lady Carnbee said? - the women of our blood"

"What? what? Aunt Mary, oh Aunt Mary----"

"I canna tell you," she cried in her agitation, "I canna tell you! How can I tell you, when I know just what you know and no more? It is a longing all your life after - it is a looking - for what never comes."

"He will come," I cried. "I shall see him to-morrow - that I know, I know!"

She kissed me and cried over me, her cheek hot and wet like mine. "My honey, try if you can sleep - try if you can sleep: and we'll wait to see what to-morrow brings."

"I have no fear," said I; and then I suppose, though it is strange to think of, I must have fallen asleep - I was so worn-out, and young, and not used to lying in my bed awake. From time to time I opened my eyes, and sometimes jumped up remembering everything: but Aunt Mary was always there to soothe me, and I lay down again in her shelter like a bird in its nest.

But I would not let them keep me in bed next day. I was in a kind of fever, not knowing what I did. The window was quite opaque, without the least glimmer in it, flat and blank like a piece of wood. Never from the first day had I seen it so little like a window. "It cannot be wondered at," I said to myself, "that seeing it like that, and with eyes that are old, not so clear as mine, they should think what they do." And then I smiled to myself to think of the evening and the long light, and whether he would look out again, or only give me a signal with his hand. I decided I would like that best: not that he should take the trouble to come forward and open it again, but just a turn of his head and a wave of his hand. It would be more friendly and show more confidence - not as if I wanted that kind of demonstration every night.

I did not come down in the afternoon, but kept at my own window up-stairs alone, till the tea-party should be over. I could hear them making a great talk; and I was sure they were all in the recess staring at the window, and laughing at the silly lassie. Let them laugh! I felt above all that now. At dinner I was very restless, hurrying to get it over; and I think Aunt Mary was restless too. I doubt whether she read her 'Times' when it came; she opened it up so as to shield her, and watched from a corner. And I settled myself in the recess, with my heart full of expectation. I wanted nothing more than to see him writing at his table, and to turn his head and give me a little wave of his hand, just to show that he knew I was there. I sat from half-past seven o'clock to ten o'clock: and the daylight grew softer and softer, till at last it was as if it was shining through a pearl, and not a shadow to be seen. But the window all the time was as black as night, and there was nothing, nothing there.

Well: but other nights it had been like that: he would not be there every night only to please me. There are other things in a man's life, a great learned man like that. I said to myself I was not disappointed. Why should I be disappointed? There had been other nights when he was not there. Aunt Mary watched me, every movement I made, her eyes shining, often wet, with a pity in them that almost made me cry: but I felt as if I were more sorry for her than for myself. And then I flung myself upon her, and asked her, again and again, what it was, and who it was, imploring her to tell me if she knew? and when she had seen him, and what had happened? and what it meant about the women of our blood? She told me that how it was she could not tell, nor when: it was just at the time it had to be; and that we all saw him in our time--" "that is," she said, "the ones that are like you and me." What was it that made her and me different from the rest? but she only shook her head and would not tell me. "They say," she said, and then stopped short. "Oh, honey, try and forget all about it - if I had but known you were of that kind! They say - that once there was one that was a Scholar, and liked his books more than any lady's love. Honey, do not look at me like that. To think I should have brought all this on you!"

"He was a Scholar?" I cried.

"And one of us, that must have been a light woman, not like you and me But maybe it was just in innocence; for who can tell? She waved to him and waved to him to come over: and yon ring was the token: but he would not come. But still she sat at her window and waved and waved--till at last her brothers heard of it, that were stirring men; and then - oh, my honey, let us speak of it no more!"

"They killed him!" I cried, carried away. And then I grasped her with my hands, and gave her a shake, and flung away from her. "You tell me that to throw dust in my eyes - when I saw him only last night: and he as living as I am, and as young!"

"My honey, my honey!" Aunt Mary said.

After that I would not speak to her for a long time; but she kept close to me, never leaving me when she could help it, and always with that pity in her eyes. For the next night it was the same; and the third night. That third night I thought I could not bear it any longer. I would have to do something if only I knew what to do! If it would ever get dark, quite dark, there might be something to be done. I had wild dreams of stealing out of the house and getting a ladder, and mounting up to try if I could not open that window, in the middle of the night - if perhaps I could get the baker's boy to help me; and then my mind got into a whirl, and it was as if I had done it; and I could almost see the boy put the ladder to the window, and hear him cry out that there was nothing there. Oh, how slow it was, the night! and how light it was, and everything so clear no darkness to cover you, no shadow, whether on one side of the street or on the other side! I could not sleep, though I was forced to go to bed. And in the deep midnight, when it is dark dark in every other place, I slipped very softly down-stairs, though there was one board on the landing-place that creaked - and opened the door and stepped out. There was not a soul to be seen, up or down, from the Abbey to the West Port: and the trees stood like ghosts, and the silence was terrible, and everything as clear as day. You don't know what silence is till you find it in the light like that, not morning but night, no sunrising, no shadow, but everything as clear as the day.

It did not make any difference as the slow minutes went on: one o'clock, two o'clock. How strange it was to hear the clocks striking in that dead light when there was nobody to hear them! But it made no difference. The window was quite blank; even the marking of the panes seemed to have melted away. I stole up again after a long time, through the silent house, in the clear light, cold and trembling, with despair in my heart.

I am sure Aunt Mary must have watched and seen me coming back, for after a while I heard faint sounds in the house; and very early, when there had come a little sunshine into the air, she came to my bedside with a cup of tea in her hand; and she, too, was looking like a ghost. "Are you warm, honey - are you comfortable?" she said. "It doesn't matter," said I. I did not feel as if anything mattered; unless if one could get into the dark somewhere - the soft, deep dark that would cover you over and hide you - but I could not tell from what. The dreadful thing was that there was nothing, nothing to look for, nothing to hide from - only the silence and the light.

That day my mother came and took me home. I had not heard she was coming; she arrived quite unexpectedly, and said she had no time to stay, but must start the same evening so as to be in London next day, papa having settled to go abroad. At first I had a wild thought I would not go. But how can a girl say I will not, when her mother has come for her, and there is no reason, no reason in the world, to resist, and no right! I had to go, whatever I might wish or any one might say. Aunt Mary's dear eyes were wet; she went about the house drying them quietly with her handkerchief, but she always said, "It is the best thing for you, honey - the best thing for you!" Oh, how I hated to hear it said that it was the best thing, as if anything mattered, one more than another! The old ladies were all there in the afternoon, Lady Carnbee looking at me from under her black lace, and the diamond lurking, sending out darts from under her finger. She patted me on the shoulder, and told me to be a good bairn. "And never believe what you see from the window," she said. "The eye is deceitful as well as the heart." She kept patting me on the shoulder, and I felt again as if that sharp wicked stone stung me. Was that what Aunt Mary meant when she said yon ring was the token? I thought afterwards I saw the mark on my shoulder. You will say why? How can I tell why? If I had known, I should have been contented, and it would not have mattered any more.

I never went back to St Rule's, and for years of my life I never again looked out of a window when any other window was in sight. You ask me did I ever see him again? I cannot tell: the imagination is a great deceiver, as Lady Carnbee said: and if he stayed there so long, only to punish the race that had wronged him, why should I ever have seen him again? for I had received my share. But who can tell what happens in a heart that often, often, and so long as that, comes back to do its errand? If it was he whom I have seen again, the anger is gone from him, and he means good and no longer harm to the house of the woman that loved him. I have seen his face looking at me from a crowd. There was one time when I came home a widow from India, very sad, with my little children: I am certain I saw him there among all the people coming to welcome their friends. There was nobody to welcome me, - for I was not expected: and very sad was I, without a face I knew: when all at once I saw him, and he waved his hand to me. My heart leaped up again: I had forgotten who he was, but only that it was a face I knew, and I landed almost cheerfully, thinking here was someone who would help me. But he had disappeared, as he did from the window, with that one wave of his hand.

And again I was reminded of it all when old Lady Carnbee died - an old, old woman - and it was found in her will that she had left me that diamond ring. I am afraid of it still. It is locked up in an old sandal-wood box in the lumber-room in the little old country-house which belongs to me, but where I never live. If anyone would steal it, it would be a relief to my mind. Yet I never knew what Aunt Mary meant when she said, "Yon ring was the token," nor what it could have to do with that strange window in the old College Library of St Rule's.

# Appendix
## The Ghost Criteria

*Do you believe in ghosts?*
Walking through walls or locked doors, becoming transparent, gliding above ground or moving silently are all familiar aspects of hauntings that may be accompanied by dramatic drops in temperature, strong winds, unusual sounds, and the movement of objects. Ghosts usually appear solid in form and can cast shadows, the reflection of a ghost can be seen in mirrors and telepathic communication can occur with spirits of the departed.

Alongside the stereotypical and more obvious experiences we are unable to explain away, there are additional experiences we don't realise are attributable to the paranormal. Ghosts can appear so real in every detail we might see them all the time in the street and not realise they are no longer flesh and blood living beings of our own time.

In many cases they have only given themselves away when the usual sensory information which ordinarily accompanies the presence of the living is either distorted or absent; making no sound when passing, not being seen by others, obnoxious smells, drops in temperature or they are wearing unusual clothing.

Without the sensory interaction it is only when they display something out of the ordinary that we are alerted to their unusual nature. Due to the realism of an encounter we typically only realise their supernatural origin after the event, when we start thinking of the impossibility of what has just occurred. Despite our tendency to look for even the most tenuous of physical or indeed psychological of explanations to account for our experiences, it is this impossibility that alerts us to the unusual nature of what we have just experienced. Like the account mentioned earlier by Greta Boyd in her account of the monk at St. Rules Tower where the apparition manoeuvred past her on the stairway, then in retrospect she realised this would have proved impossible without the figure squeezing past.

Ghosts within themselves can only cause slight physical harm. On brushing past they have caused rashes to appear. Among the feign of heart they have caused mild psychological disturbances, but nothing matching the malign potential created by their counterpart – the Poltergeist.

To be psychic or to be a medium is to be aware of a deeper reality not picked up by those with a mind fully absorbed in the everyday aspects of life. We can get so caught up with life it is easy to forget what life is all about. Also, if we were more educated in what constitutes paranormal phenomenon out with the stereotypical concepts we are accustomed to, we would be more open to the realisation of what has always been waiting in the sidelines for us to recognise.

It is believed 1 in 10 people will have an experience they are unable to account for. The figure is actually quite a bit higher than this.

In the main it is only our conformity, prejudice and our lacking in understanding that prevents what should be a natural ability for receiving a greater influx of potential to the unseen than we are currently aware of.

As unusual as supernatural phenomenon appears to be, it is still natural phenomenon. With this in mind we are all gifted with so termed 'psychic' tendencies or abilities that enable us at times to perceive, and sometimes interact a little more with the generally hidden elements of reality. In our expression we can say paranormal activity stems from a different realm or realms. In this we would be correct, but we would also be correct in saying all realms are aspects of a greater or deeper reality we are all part of. Everything fits squarely in the same reality we exist within. This may be thought of as being a greater reality existing alongside and through the familiarity of our own. With this there is a potential hidden from our physical nature. Our conscious mind has been conditioned to suppress our deeper awareness to such things, and all is reinforced by those sciences which primarily fall short of acknowledging this greater existence. There is more than meets the eye to our reality, and to perceive a little more of it we just need to be a little more open within ourselves.

Some seem to be more open than others and this often translates into a recipient being prone to attracting phenomenon more readily than others but not knowing why. Often I am asked why this might be. Why do some attract more unusual activity than others? Well the answer is held within the nature of the attraction itself, which by degrees is directly linked to how open and receptive we are.

Without realising it we are all constantly exposed to phenomenon all the time – because our existence coincides with this greater deeper reality we tend not to be aware of. However without it, nothing would exist. The more receptive or in-tune our awareness is, i.e.; the more open we are, the more we will then perceive. So we don't attract phenomenon so much as we have the ability to perceive what many miss. We can acknowledge it, and we are able to observe it. We are often unaware of the conditions or requirements for this to happen because our level and depth of awareness is just simply part of the natural level of who we are. None of us are more special in this regard as we all have our own abilities which partly define us, and make us who we are. As I say, we all have the ability to develop our receptivity to more of what we are constantly being exposed to without realising.

Greta in this respect is certainly one gifted with this particular receptivity for the unseen.

Over the years a tremendous amount of case data has been collected from all areas of the world, compiled and researched by such eminent bodies as the Society for Psychical Research established in 1882. The subject is finally gaining respect not only with the layman but within particular scientific circles, with the study of this subject being developed by parapsychology. In many ways paranormal research is still a new subject of study, hampered in many ways by the constraints of a physical quantification than by its illusive nature. As more ground is covered however so too are the barriers of separation becoming that little bit less daunting. Research is not so confined as it was in its early days to the laboratory. More research graduates are conducting field work alongside psychical researchers, but investigations can – and should be very time consuming. This often presents the additions of cost, coupled with no guarantees of immediate or long term success in witnessing any such phenomenon, let alone then being able to quantify it in some way.

A concrete foundation of validity has been laid by a mass of accumulated data from all over the globe. The independent correlations far outweigh the theories of speculation or mass fabrication – be it knowingly or tricked in some psychological fashion. This vast subject area has been dismissed out of hand for far too long as superstitious nonsense. A dismissive that should now be unworthy of any intelligent enquirer in our present age. There are and will always be those who will seek to deceive or trick for whatever reason, but no longer can the question be asked "does phenomenon exist?" It must surely be one of enquiring how and why it exists.

As the Society for Psychical Research developed and data was amassed, it became apparent that patterns were emerging that could be quantified into more specific relationships or category types of phenomenon. Mr G. N. M. Tyrell, President of the Society for Psychical Research from 1945-6 divided apparitions into four categories as follows:

**Experimental Ghosts:** Astral Projection

**Crisis Ghosts:** Appearing around the time of great crisis such as severe illness or death.

**Post-Mortem Ghosts:** Appearing after death to somebody known.

**Ghosts:** Habitual hauntings.

What follows in brief are categories for the phenomenon incorporating Mr Tyrell's formula, although his 'Ghosts' category is too much of a generalisation, as it amalgamates all habitual hauntings. I have therefore found it necessary to break it down and substitute it with further classifications.

### Experimental Apparitions
Appearances of people still alive, caused by astral projection and crisis phenomenon.

Experiments have been conducted through astral projection with the aim of one person appearing in front of another who may or may not be miles away. The 'agent' concentrates the mind on appearing in front of the 'recipient' for which results have shown marked degrees of success.

### Crisis Apparitions
Seen, heard or felt by somebody known to the apparition. The appearances are triggered by very powerful emotions projected as associative energies to the recipient in a time of extreme crisis. Occurring some twelve hours before or after death or a severe illness, but appearing sometimes up to four days after.

Accounts are on record that during the First World War, soldiers appeared to their loved ones when they were many hundreds of miles away, suffering the primitive and barbaric carnage taking place on the battle fields. The timing of their appearances being around the same time they either died or were seriously wounded in action. Crucially the recipient has no idea they may have died.

### Post-Mortem Apparitions
The apparition of someone close that has passed away may appear in times of great stress or to warn of some impending danger that may still befall them. One of the most common post-mortem sightings is when a close member of the family having passed away comes back to comfort the loved ones and deliver a message of reassurance that they are ok. These are similar to Crisis Apparitions but rather than just appearing they tend to warn or impart something and can appear long after they have died. Unlike Crisis the recipient knows they are no longer alive. They are only seen once they are dead, whereas Crisis can appear during near death experiences such as the time of a serious illness.

### Impressionistic/Recurrent Apparitions
Ghosts of these two types are the most durable, lasting for many centuries.

## Impressionistic Ghosts

As far as ghostly phenomenon goes this is the most common type witnessed.

Everything comprises of energy, everything generates energy and everything at every moment – every action and every expression including thought, emotion etc, is permanently recorded on the atmosphere. This is a continual infusing of impressions on the energy make-up comprising the 'space' of the locality, as a continual record of unfolding of events. It is possible for these to be picked up. We do it all the time. We are continually walking into an 'atmosphere'. It could be at work or socially where we just sense or feel something. It could be elation, or foreboding, it could be sorrow or feelings of joy. Places affect our emotions and so too our moods, our happiness, and our thoughts can be directed by them. Consequently they are very powerful forces.

We pick up the residues of past and present events all the time. The general air of a church or the collective feeling experienced at a concert, or just walking into a room, or an old building. A hospital or police station can be dramatic, even if we are not ill ourselves or have done nothing wrong. Everything is impacting upon us in a great many obvious and subtle ways. The obvious gives us our immediate evaluation and the subtle may change our mood.

When we are in a space of apparent neutrality – emotionally speaking, and there is no obvious suggestive psychological emotion that we might gather from a police station or a hospital, it is only the very powerful emotional impressions of events past such as at times of great stress, illness or death – especially violent death that will generally impact with enough energetic force to then attract our awareness. This attraction is through our acknowledgment of them. This is then translated to our level of susceptibility to phenomenon, which is through a determination of how it then affects us psychologically etc. Extreme emotional or traumatic events such as a gruesome murder or an intense sense of fear can blast the 'space' of the locality with a very intense energy. Remember all is energy and the energy we pick up is altering our own energetic field causing changes to our perception.

It is also possible for an event repeated many times over to also gradually build up this same intensity; perhaps a person with a great love for a certain place or area visiting it many times. Or the repartition of a particular act such as prayer – which is one of the reasons the inordinate amount of peace can be felt when entering into a church. Coupled with this is often that deep sense of sorrow as we empathise with the 'space' acutely and so more deeply.

The force; be it sudden or repetitive carries with it such an outburst of energy that it can be perceived. The recipient acts as a trigger, unlocking the impression held within the energy makeup, like unlocking an embedded period in time, a capsule locked in the reality fabric of the locality.

The imbedded sequence or impression is a 'none participatory' re-enactment of prior events. The phenomenon perceived is not aware. There is no intelligence, so there can be no interaction. In the same way characters in a film are not aware of you when you watch them. So it is much in the same way as walking into a room and starting a projector in motion, then watching a certain sequence of events unfold. This is what we call ghosts.

## Recurrent Ghosts

These appear at the same place and time at certain times of the years, perhaps on the anniversary of their death.

Because these two types are impressions left on the energetic atmosphere it explains why a ghost may haunt various places at the same time. Especially those of the famous who either haunt many places around the country, or at least have been attributed to do so. Before moving on to the next category it is worth noting how the attribution of a haunting is usually to that of the most famous patronage that fits the description. While some certainly are those of the Kings and Queens etc, that haunt the many locations, those attributions stemming from a one off visit of an afternoon are highly unlikely to be of those they are purported to be. The impression they leave is simply not dramatic enough to leave its mark, especially after a few hundred years. On the opposite side of the coin to this, it is wholly possible for the most famous person to be haunting a locality even with a very brief visit. The residue is initiated by them, and reinforced by those who were there at the time, followed by a reinforcing and strengthening over time by others aware of their associations with the location. We have all heard of charisma. Mary Queen of Scots had it in abundance. Within charisma is an intensity of energy, almost magical in the way it draws and attracts. There are many other aspects to this but space must dictate it be given on another occasion.

## Ghosts of the Living

The living persons double is also known as a doppelganger. There are many cases of people observing, sometimes even speaking with somebody they know or are familiar with that were elsewhere at the time, although they appear real in every detail to them. Unlike Experimental Ghosts, no explanation is ever forthcoming as to why they are appearing, other than historical associations correlating an appearance as being portents of death or as a sign of longevity.

## Wandering Spirits

These are of people who don't realise they have died or they cannot rest and move on until unfinished business has been completed; a grave injustice, or a murderer for example, and wander the earth or rather the locality of where they died in a kind of limbo between this world and the next. These kinds of spirits are intelligent and communicate with mediums. They can be the cause of the most frightful occurrences to be witnessed in order for their presence to be made known. This has resulted in either mediums or more dramatically in exorcists being called to put the unhappy spirits at rest. The medium is always more preferable than the exorcist. The medium is a lot gentler with the spirits, far more in-tune, receptive and responsive to their requests. They can find out what ails them and maybe see about rectifying an injustice. If the spirit doesn't realise they have passed on, they can diplomatically and sensitively inform them of their situation and guide them gently rather forcefully (in the case of the exorcist) to the light of the energy realm where they need to be.

## The Mirage Effect

The mirage effect is caused when the difference in temperature between layers of air cause differences in density, and these in turn cause light rays to travel in curved paths. The light rays reach the eye as if they have travelled in straight lines – and as the mirage appears above or below the true image. The mirage frequently appears magnified and with a greater clarity.

Cases have been known for whole towns to appear in this way, often many miles from where they actually are. People have also been seen and battles re-enacted in the sky. The latter phenomenon may have occurred many years previously. The explanation for this is more complex than that just mentioned above. They can be formed; unlocked and witnessed in the same manner as impressionistic ghosts (where the impression has left its mark on the space of the locality), coupled with the distortion of a mirage it then appears in the sky.

This doesn't take account of all sightings and can never be a definitive. While we may look for one line answers to cover what we look to understand, nothing in reality is ever black and white. Individual circumstance will always dictates the nature of the explanation.

An example of the mirage effect from an experience I had many years ago can be read in my book *Ghosts of Fife*, under *Crail: The Pans.*

## Poltergeist Activity

As with other aspects of the unknown it has always been easy to place the odd occurrence within the category of the paranormal rather than looking for the rational explanation for say – the mislaid object or the odd bang. Within buildings a whole host of natural occurrences have been mistaken for being supernatural in origin; windows rattling, strange noises, groans, creaks, bangs, doors closing etc can all be caused by a dwelling expanding and contracting, by hot water pipes, by vibrations from heavy traffic, by the wind, by changes in air pressure, by underground streams, and a surprising amount by rodents knocking objects off shelves etc. While these count for many reported disturbances and need to be eliminated before a metaphysical explanation is sought they don't account for all disturbances.

Along with this and often adding to the physical possibilities there is the more delicate matter of the many psychological aspects of an involvement requiring its own consideration. This may include any potential motivation afoot for anything untoward such as attention seeking or fraud. An example of this would be claims of poltergeist activity masking a family looking to be re-housed by the council because of bad neighbours. These are an all too common feature of many reports having been collated and studied over the years. With researchers of the Society for Psychical Research (SPR) and its Scottish arm the Scottish Society for Psychical Research (SSPR) along with Parapsychology units across the country finding the same. Recipients of supposed disturbances are often – if not always surprised when the line of questioning is initially directed toward them before being directed to any of their reported disturbances.

The word 'poltergeist' is an old German word meaning 'noisy ghost' or spirit. A term still used by investigators to describe such phenomenon, although not all phenomena can be placed within this category.

Not always destructive but always mischievous, poltergeist activity has been thought of as an external invisible force notorious for all manner of trouble. Characteristics of which include the moving or throwing of furniture and objects and a dangerous reputation for pyromania. Unlike other forms of ghostly phenomenon poltergeist activity has also caused physical injuries to occur both directly and indirectly. Indirectly by way of flying objects etc and although uncommon, directly, causing wheal marks, scratches, rashes and human teeth marks to appear on its victims body and arms. There does seem to be an unwritten rule where any serious harm is attributed to the psychological rather than to the physical. Cases are on record of kitchen objects such as knives, cutlery, plates and pots being hurtled across the kitchen but they seem to aim to miss. There has never to my knowledge ever been any deaths directly caused by such activity.

This mischievous behaviour of manifestation coupled with incidences such as human teeth marks may lend a brief insight to their nature. When the possibilities of natural causes and the elements of deception or psychological intrusions have been eliminated, there are two main categories: Psychokinesis and External Paranormal Phenomenon or EPP I call it, with the latter fitting the term Poltergeist more accurately.

Psychokinesis is a form of energy building in the soul or spirit of the individual and streaming from the subconscious mind of an individual to physical manifestation. When it is consciously applied it has positive and beneficial attributes as it is controlled by the host. When the host is unaware of its generation and especially manifestation it is a chaotic, negative and often destructive force. The destructive aspects more often stem from an individual experiencing a very traumatic period in their life, one filled with great emotional tension and stress. Instead of physically releasing the spent up emotional energies, psychokinetic energy or PK is generated from within the individual that is added to by the natural energies in the locality – more on that in a moment.

Through this great build up of emotional pressure a very powerful force can gather, and when it finds its release, the psychokinetic energy can cause all manner of phenomenon. Simple objects can disappear – often generally important objects such as door or car keys, objects moving or flying across the room akin to the spontaneity of physically throwing an object as a way of releasing built up emotion and anger. The release of psychokinetic energy is often just as spontaneous and just as uncontrollable as a fit of anger. The only difference being the host is rarely (if ever) aware of how the outbursts are caused. When not aware they may be the cause of the phenomenon themselves it is not controllable so the somewhat violent and unstable manifestations can be a very frightening ordeal for any involved, and understandably the phenomenon leads to the conclusion of the location being haunted.

As will have been noted, the behaviour of the poltergeist appears in many circumstances to mimic that of a young mischievous child, it may not be surprising then to find the age of individuals concerned range from around ten years to their early twenties. The latter is uncommon, with activity tending to cease altogether when maturity is reached, due in part to the extreme pressures and stresses of youth becoming more balanced and easier to cope with in adulthood, growing out of puberty and all the difficulties the teen years can bring – especially when physical or psychological abuse is involved and unfortunately as is so often the case, these forms of abuse tend to be coupled with a threat if silence isn't maintained. With this silence comes pain, confusion and can build into a tremendous force that causes great personal damage to the psyche and can manifest itself through psychological problems in later life. So PK is one way of releasing this spent up anger and frustration.

Usually outbreaks are confined to the home where most stress is generated, and in the main it all only lasts a few months. If the host moves to another address the change in both surroundings and circumstance have often been sufficient to alter the emotional stance, thus laying to rest any of the former activity; whether aware or not of causing the disturbances (albeit indirectly) themselves.

When the disturbances do still continue, it has sometimes led to the first intimation that the cause may lay with a particular individual as opposed to the previous place being haunted per se. In these circumstances psychologists, parapsychologists, mediums and priests have often been sought. Only around one percent of known poltergeist outbreaks have resulted in an exorcism by a priest. In the main the phenomenon does not respond to exorcism because it is being generated by the host rather than by an external agency. Equally, if there is abuse issues a priest is likely to exacerbate them through attributing the wrong diagnosis as it were to the cause of the phenomenon. Exorcisms have never succeeded in ridding a house from the abuse by others. An exorcism is an extreme form of trying to deal with such manifestations, not least because the priests are going in blind as to the causes they are looking to dispel. It is possible for the dramatic nature to change the temperament of both an individual and others who suffer the phenomenon, but I have to say when it is poltergeist activity stemming from an individual and not an external agency, an exorcism is rarely enough to allay any proceedings. At best they give a temporary abeyance through the equally temporary peace of mind, brought about by the surreal situation at hand, and the faith that can also bring. Queen Mary's House in St. Andrews was such a case; "'the Bishop was brought, with bell, book, and candle; now, it appears, Queen Mary's and the adjacent house are undisturbed.'[139][lxxvi] In reality however, the exorcism succeeded it seems in allaying for a time more the fears of the occupants than the disturbances."

External paranormal phenomenon can display the same characteristics as Psychokinesis but the phenomenon has its cause from an external energetic agency, force or spirit – this is the classic poltergeist activity that is often

---

[lxxvi] Refer to *The Ghosts of Queen Mary's House*, p.140

associated with the 'classic haunting' where ghosts and spirits are also in accompaniment.

The energies causing a disturbance can remain external or in the case of the former where it feeds off a host, it latches onto, and works through an individual by taking possession of the individuals raw energies to strengthen its own ends. The outbursts are then released in like manner to Psychokinesis, but they can last for much longer and become much more violent and disturbed, and indeed then result in possession. These are the situations where exorcisms have worked in riding the individuals of the entities having latched onto them.

Being of the nature of energy they feed off the charged energies of a host and the energies imbued in the atmosphere of the locality, concentrating the energy for manifestations to occur, which brings us to the following:

*External phenomenon associated with the 'Classic Haunting'*
When the cause is purely external and the energies are operating without using the energies of an individual, they may last for many years utilising the energies of the locality. For an agency to affect physical objects it often needs to utilise physical energy to produce the manifestations concurrent with paranormal phenomenon. So it needs to collect physical energy to then be able to utilise it. A great deal of energy is required. The agency is able to couple physical energy with its own to affect the physical by energetic means. The process it uses to do this is similar to the initial process of a dehumidifier. With a dehumidifier the air is attracted into the fans, the water condenses on the cold surface of the refrigeration unit and the moisture is collected, the dry cold air is then warmed up and returns to the air of the location. In the case of how an agency gathers additional energy to cause manifestations, it utilises the energy in the heat of the location. Rather than dissipating the warm energy by cooling the air down, the agency extracts the warm energy out of the atmosphere – or rather it collects the electromagnetic energy, focuses it and along with its own form of psychokinetic energy it creates what we would call paranormal phenomenon. All that is left in the atmosphere is the moisture as a residue which then forms the puddles of water on the ground we see so often in accompaniment to a great deal of disturbances. Unlike a dehumidifier the air is not then warmed up again, so the air becomes cold but also dry and produces the customary cold spots that are also common aspects of phenomenon. With the energy being extracted as a concentration it is often why these cold spots can just be localised to the space of a foot or a few feet. The more humidity in the air, the more energy there is available to create 'physical' phenomenon. In a haunted location the dampest area is often where a lot of the phenomenon will stem from, even though the

phenomenon may manifest elsewhere – when in the field researching phenomenon, it is the dampest area associated with a disturbance that the humidity meter needs to be placed in.

The inherent energies of an agency have similar characteristics to those we associate with physical energy, but they are not the same and should not be confused as being such. They are not dependent on any physical energetic constraint for their own existence, but when they affect physical objects, they have to use a physical means to affect them. We call their displays 'super' natural though with them using physical energy, what they produce is natural phenomenon, science just don't know enough about it yet to switch categories to encompass it all under the umbrella term 'natural'. When we eventually do, we might just keep the 'super' bit to highlight how extraordinary it really is – extraordinary because of its rarity but natural all the same.

*Phenomenon and Energy Centres*
Phenomenon is more prevalent at particular energy centres which attract these raw and often destructive energies. These are known as energy lines or ley lines which cover the earth like a web of energy. The crossing of ley lines accentuates the energy and a building on these sites will often have the familiar aspects of the 'classic haunting' in residence. With unexplained noises, footsteps, doors locking and unlocking, banging, heavy knocks and faint music etc all being characteristic of its display. Essentially the veils between worlds at these points are more tenuous. Stone circles often mark the crossing of leys, standing stones have also been used for this purpose but they are far less common, singular standing stones are usually placed as markers along ley lines rather than at the crossing points. Importantly the configuration of stones have all been placed in these locations marking this web of energy that it can then be accentuated and put to service in positive ways – always positive ways, never negative.

If a house is built on the crossing of a number of leys chances are it will suffer greater disturbances. The phenomenon at these centres may be accompanied by, or be associated with spectral visitations or intelligent spirits having departed this earth generally under violent or sudden circumstances. Other types of intelligent phenomenon are also attracted to these centres of energy as they are natural conduits between realms of existence. The opening in the veil can be almost like a seepage of sorts, where they can move more freely between this realm and their own. In these latter cases it is possible for mediums to communicate with the departed, allowing them to then continue their journey and bring an end to at least their involvement in whatever is taking place.

Iron stakes have been placed around such locations where it has been possible to do so. The energies are then diverted around the house instead of through it. This technique has had marked degrees of success in allaying disturbances – so long as the stakes are not then removed! It must be remembered the line of energy doesn't disappear, it is just re-routed.

These energies are not exclusive to ley lines, electricity pylons also convey degrees of electromagnetism and again exposure to phenomenon is increased accordingly when underneath them – especially when living underneath them, but unlike the energetic properties of ley lines, the residue from electricity pylons can cause damage to the physical health.

## The Residual Impact of Energy

Interestingly a number of the places displaying poltergeist activity in St. Andrews are former hotels or larger dwellings. The Star Hotel (now shops and flats), the Britannia Hotel (now The West Port Bar and Kitchen – although still with rooms to let), the Grand Hotel (now Hamilton Grand), Chattan Hotel (now McIntosh Hall) and the St Leonards – St Katherine's Junior School for girls in North Street (now the Crawford Arts Centre). The activity displayed is all part of the 'classic haunting' phenomenon and while they have *not* been caused by a 'living and breathing' adolescent they often bear testimony to all the same hallmarks.

It is not exclusive to hotels by any means, but why hotels? With such a high turnover of occupants and the diversity they bring, there is an equally high turnover of energy. This energy is increased when the occupants suffer physical and mental difficulties, the resulting turmoil can – and often does attract its own phenomenon. It is also more than possible for the occasional person to die while in residence and however imperceptible, everything leaves an impacting residue of energy on the locality. This is impressed on the atmosphere of the location to then be picked up at a later date. Given the right conditions it can and does manifest into poltergeist type phenomenon, as well as apparitional.

# Part Two

W. T. Linskill's Classic Work

# *St. Andrews*
# *Ghost Stories*
1911

Introduced and annotated by
Richard Falconer

The Dean of Guild William Thomas Linskill

*William Thomas Linskill*
Born in 1855, he was the son of Captain William T. Linskill of Tynemouth Lodge, Northumberland, educated at Harrow he was the Captain of the 5th Dragoon Guards and the Honourable Mrs Frances Arthur Charlotte Linskill, daughter of Arthur Annesley the 10th Viscount Valentia. Viscount Valentia is a title in the Peerage of Ireland. The family had their origins as a powerful Anglo-Irish family between the County of Buckinghamshire and the County of Armagh.

The above photograph of Dean Linskill was taken in Cambridge on one of his golf outings. In the background are members wearing the blue blazers and crest of the Cambridge Golf Club he founded. He was a very keen golfer and had been tutored in St. Andrews by the 'Young' Tom Morris featured in the earlier account *The Ghostly Golfers of the Old Course.*

Besides *St. Andrews Ghost Stories*, Linskill wrote one of the earliest books about golf. Simply titled *Golf* it was published in 1889. Written very much from a St. Andrews and Old Course perspective it includes 19<sup>th</sup> century techniques and rules of play as they stood in Victorian times.[lxxvii]

Linskill studied at the Jesus College, Cambridge and was known at the time as both 'Tommy' Linskill and 'Mr Cambridge'. It was Linskill who formalised the game of golf in Cambridge. After becoming a member of the Royal and Ancient Club House in 1875 he founded the Cambridge University Golf Club (CUGC) in the same year from an existing unofficial body created some 6 years previous, and which had subsequently folded. He was Captain of the Club and Honorary Secretary for 20 years. He also united Oxford and Cambridge in golfing tournaments forming the Oxford and Cambridge Golfing Society. With their first 'Varsity' match being played on the 6<sup>th</sup> March 1878, the society is known to be the oldest golfing society in the world.

Linskill had visited St. Andrews when young and stayed here on many occasions, but he never moved here until 1877. Whilst in St. Andrews he continued to travel for matches in Cambridge and to carry out his official duties with the club and society.

He was a well known and well respected character both in Cambridge and St. Andrews – well, as much as any Victorian Gentleman of standing can be, although his stern enthusiasm and joviality was known to ruffle the odd feather or two!

### Linskill's Ghost Book

Linskill found St. Andrews was indeed an ancient treasure trove of history, myth and legend, with many a tale to be explored and told. In Linskill's book a wealth of stories will be found adding a touch of colour to the subtle grey and sandy stonework the town is furnished with. His ghost book is primarily a collection of Victorian supernatural fiction – or so at first glance it would appear. It transports the reader back to a time when the many ruins preserved throughout the town were buildings of great stature, commanding enormous political as well as spiritual influence and importance. A time when the Cathedral was a major hub of ecclesiastical life affecting the inhabitants, not only of St. Andrews as a site of personal pilgrimage and worship, but of the

---

[lxxvii] Refer to an anthology by the current author called *St. Andrews Golf*, Obsidian Publishing, (2014). The book includes some of the early commentaries to have been written about the game of Golf. The period featured is from 1801 to 1899, centred on St. Andrews it makes fascinating reading for any interested in the game and its early development in the town.

surrounding land as a spiritual governance and seat of Scotland and beyond. All this had a great affect on Linskill.

Whilst in St. Andrews he contributed much to the furtherance and well being of the town. For over twenty years he was a town councillor - the Dean of Guild and President of the Antiquarian Society. He had a great passion for golf but he is known more in St. Andrews for his ghost stories, which he prided himself on relaying at every opportunity, especially as after dinner speeches.

Deeply interested in the supernatural throughout his life he was a great collector of supernatural tales. Even though his book on golf proved popular at the time, his success and reputation came with the publication of his *St. Andrews Ghost Stories* in 1911, which remained in print up until 1978. Filling homes with blood curdling tales it became somewhat of a classic around St. Andrews, with almost every household having leafed through its pages at one time or another. Published through J & G Innes for many years both he and his *St. Andrews Ghost Stories* have been great companions to the residents of St. Andrews now for over 100 years. With his Victorian charm and his charismatic ability as an author, his style has captured the imagination of generations; locals, students and visitors alike.

Dean of Guild Linskill lived for a time in Deans Court opposite the Cathedral and spent many a night wandering its precincts in search of the ghosts he so lovingly wrote about. He also lived in Murray Park with his wife and two daughters.

A number of the visitations he writes about predate his publication which he then encompassed in story form. Although they command all the airs and graces of Victorian fireside storytelling, liberally mixed with his humorous style, a number of the phantoms mentioned have been substantiated in more recent times. There are present day reports of the White Lady, the phantom monks, the floating head, phantom coaches and other occurrences he passionately speaks about as tales in his book.

Within his pages you will learn of how he was present at the 1888 opening of the Haunted Tower in the imposing Cathedral ruins, which was to further open a mystery that is – unlike the occupancy of the tower still relatively intact to this day, and forms one of St. Andrews greatest mysteries.

His stories have been criticised in the past. Rather than giving him the freedom an author deserves, critics seem to believe comparisons should be made resulting in his work being praised or decried according to the merits of more noted and more prominent ghost writers of the time, All this is subjective and dependent on the opinion and preferred style of the critic, and has little to do with the subject matter itself.

So it is with great privilege that I present his work to you here. I have hand transcribed it, so unlike a couple of other versions appearing in 2010 which have been through an ocr process or have been rapidly scanned with no care for the actual words contained, there are no errors resulting in jumbled words or ill-read computer faded passages etc. I have also annotated his work throughout with photos – some rare, including the above photo of the man himself. Also included is additional information about the people, the locations and the ghosts he mentions throughout with what I hope is interesting asides and pertinent references etc., to his work.

I have also cross-referenced his work with the related accounts throughout this book which I am sure you will have noted as you wove your way through the previous pages.

Interestingly, Linskill wrote two short pieces for the *Fife Herald and Journal*, dated 13th and 27th January 1904, some seven years before publication of his book. The first is the introductory build up to what would become *The Smothered Piper of the West Cliffs* and is as follows:

### Local Ghost Stories, St. Andrews

'Some wonderful bogie stories ... of the ghost of Thomas Platter, who murdered Prior Robert of Montrose on the dormitory staircase before vespers: of the negro in a Fifeshire house, who is invisible himself[lxxviii], but maps out his bare footmarks on the floor of the painted gallery [cf. Baft Barefoot, ante}:[lxxix] of [Archbishop] Sharp's [phantom] coach, which being heard, betokens a death; of haunted old Balcomie Castle; of the murdered pedlar in our own South Street, who sweeps down with a chilly hand the cheeks of invaders to his haunted cellar [location never found]; of the ghost that appeared in the house of Archbishop Ross, mentioned in Lyon's History; and of the terrible ghost in the Novum Hospitium, which so alarmed the people that it had to be pulled down; and only a fragment now remains.'[1]

The version in his book of 1911 then continues: '...but they wanted to hear the tale of the "Ghostly Piper of the West Cliffs"; so I told them the legend as I had heard it years ago.'[lxxx]

---

[lxxviii] If the ghost was invisible why say it is a negro? What it doesn't say here is the ghost in question is of a negro servant boy who had also been seen as well as heard.

[lxxix] Baft or Baff Barefoot is referring to the ghostly footsteps heard in Grangemuir Mansion House in Fife which has been recounted in my companion book *Ghosts of Fife*,

[lxxx] Refer to Linskill, *The Smothered Piper of the West Cliffs* p.331

His second entry of 27th January 1904, with only a slight variation was to be encompassed in his story *The True Tale of the Phantom Coach* of 1911 and read: 'The tale goes that the phantom coach finishes its nocturnal journey in the waves of St. Andrews Bay . . . [and] has been seen from time to time on the roads round St. Andrews.'[2]

Of the stories he mentions it is interesting he gives preference to a couple of the more obscure hauntings such as Baff Barefoot or the murdered pedlar with no mention of the White Lady, which being one of the more famous of ghostly attractions I found quite odd.

In places I have added footnotes which pertain to later versions of his stories. Some of the material changed over the years, small details such as names were omitted, or whole paragraphs were changed or excluded altogether for subsequent editions. One prominent alteration was concerning a particular ghost he mentions on occasion throughout his book. In his original book he called the ghost of a black boy a 'nigger'. I have adjusted this throughout to the term 'negro', which is the term that was adopted for later editions, and mention the variance here for historical accuracy. Also the order of the stories changes with later versions. The original had them as a collection of stories, almost jumbled together, whereas with later versions have them in an order which flows sometimes from one to the next with related stories sitting next to each other. I have adopted Linskill's original order for this book, there may or may not be a reason for the order in which they originally appeared, but I have felt it important to preserve its original integrity.

Playing on his antiquarian nature and the romantic ideals embedded in Victorian folklore, Linskill brings the legends about the many ghosts to life through the characters, with many humorous Dickensian styled names and nicknames he partly took from his compatriots at Cambridge.

His tales were told as after dinner stories in Cambridge, St. Andrews and no doubt, wherever he happened to reside over the years, both setting the scene in the narrative and the tale being told. He loved to promote a conducive and congenial atmosphere for the telling of a good ghost story with a friend or a few friends, relaxing over a pipe or a cheroot by a blazing hot fire of a customary wild and stormy evening.

Setting the scene to create the atmosphere for a ghostly tale was certainly all part of Linskill's formula, and a ghost story wouldn't be a ghost story if it didn't have a storm complete with strong icy winds, thunder, lightning and a rolling cloud before an ever present full moon! The manner of Linskill in this respect is always pleasant to the senses and warming to the imagination. His humour is both entertaining and fanciful and always filled with a gentlemanly Victorian appeal. The settings are for the most part local to St. Andrews – if they can be pinpointed to a location that is, although there is the odd one he has included out with the town for its associations with St. Andrews and the odd one he includes because it is a good ghost story. Interestingly with this he could easily have written them as St. Andrews stories and omitted or changed the location and I often wonder why he didn't. Unless he was conveying truths mixed with his fiction, which to a degree I believe he was doing, it would then point to his gentlemanly morality maintaining a particular integrity of privacy for those they involved. How would we ever know the difference you may ask? Well, we wouldn't, a lot of his material is far too obscure for most if not all to pick up on today, but in his day there were those who he knew and who were still alive at the time. Some would have relayed aspects of these stories to him. So his work has a number of underlying themes and contexts to grapple with. His book is not a long volume, but he spent a long time writing it, and within its pages he placed a number of red herrings in his stories – along with these he also placed a number of clues to various locations and events.

Captain Chester is a character who crops up throughout the book and appears very much as being Linskill's alter ego. Linskill writes that he met him in Cambridge in September 1875, when he was an undergraduate at Cambridge University. The way Captain Chester carries himself in his many adventures and exploits conveys an idealism of the encounters he would dearly loved to have experienced himself. The Captain for example prefers to bag ghosts than to bag exotic animals in some far off jungle, as Victorian gentleman of the day were prone to do it seems. The Captain also refers to astral projection and to other spiritual pursuits which fascinated Linskill. He was sceptical to some of the aspects of Victorian spiritualism, as were many with exposés of fraudulent practice being publicised in the press. He also knew this overshadowed genuine accounts, testimony and mediumship abilities which he had a firm conviction for as to their reality. He would dearly have loved to have seen a ghost himself though, but alas they were always to be as illusive to his experiences as his conviction to their reality was to the sceptic. He attributed his lacking in direct experience to simply not being psychic himself.

Despite his lacking in personal experience his conviction for their existence never diminished over the years. For him they were very real indeed, as were the labours of many of his other antiquarian pursuits and enquiries which he endeavoured always with conviction to explore to their full.

Right up to his death in 1929 he strongly believed in the existence of subterranean passages under the town and especially under the cathedral precincts. He never managed to find them when alive and occasionally when work was being carried out in the old town and new discoveries were being made he would excitedly rush to the scene of a new find. There are three occasions where his enthusiasm would reach new but short lived heights: The opening of the haunted tower, the tunnel under the Pends and the tunnels under the castle. Alas the discoveries of the tunnels were not to confirm his theories about subterranean passageways. The tunnel under the Pends turned out to be a large mediaeval sewage pipe, and the subterranean passageways in the castle grounds was the mine and counter mine from the siege of the castle by the French in 1547.

As well as Linksill writing in his book a number of variations to some of his stories in different pages, he also encompassed a number of them into one story entitled *The Beckoning Monk*, p.303. The background to the story centres on these elusive subterranean passages which can be likened to a labyrinth containing all he never found. He populated them with some of St. Andrews famed ghostly inhabitants. The 'beckoning monk' it might be imagined was modelled on Robert De Montrose whose spirit helps the unsure of foot up the steep stone steps of St. Rules Tower. He imagined the monk to be one guiding the unwary – including himself – through this labyrinth under the Cathedral where the secrets were to be found. The passageways were inhabited by skeleton monks clothed in white. The famed White Lady also makes an appearance, with beautiful features and a long flowing white dress, and who he had searched for in the Cathedral grounds to no avail. The scene of the story is even complete with the sounds of chanting monks and the bells of the Cathedral ringing out in their once former glory. The latter I mentioned in the section on the Cathedral is taken from a legend that when the Cathedral was ransacked, the bells were taken aboard a ship which then sank in a storm in St. Andrews Bay and can still be heard to this day. This story in particular can be likened to his own personal journey as he romanticises about what he longed to encounter, as if reminiscing upon his own experiences past.

The town itself is also a labyrinth. While it is no longer the political or spiritual seat of Scotland, when wandering through the old town, each corner turned reveals a new encounter with its spiritual, political and royal past. St. Andrews is so steeped in history it is easy to be lost in a sense of timelessness, just as Linskill's character in the story of the *Beckoning Monk* also becomes lost to his senses. So there are a number of parallels to be drawn between the town, Linskill and his stories. This is all part and parcel of the ways in which St. Andrews imbues its own natural charm upon all who arrive within its precincts

– and once experienced, its magnetism stays with the mind as its own companion, drawing each who fall in love with the town back for another visit.

One thing is for sure with Linskill, he loved his ghostly yarns and he was renowned for knowing how to tell them. On this note I finish this brief introduction of one of St. Andrews most enduring and endearing characters, by saying as my own personal tribute to him – if one person were to haunt the old town of St. Andrews it would surely be fitting if it were he.

Just before handing the reigns over to Mr Linskill for the final part of this book, if this is your first encounter with his work other than those brief snippets I relayed earlier, then it is best you understand there are a number of requirements to lend atmosphere to his writing before you begin.

In-keeping with Linskill's desires, firstly be sure you have had a hearty meal in a congenial setting, then on retiring to your homely comforts, be sure it is dark, that the moon is full, and there is a suitably brewing storm to rattle the windows and chill the bones. Dim the lights, put another log on the fire, and once certain you are perfectly alone; sit back, relax, and enjoy a trip back to Victorian St. Andrews in the company of the Dean of Guild – Mr W. T. Linskill himself – as your ever present ghostly guide.

Richard Falconer

# St. Andrews Ghost Stories

By
## W. T. Linskill
(Dean of Guild)


There are ghosts and phantoms round us,
On the mountains, on the sea;
Some are cold and some are clammy,
Some are hot as hot can be.
They can creep, and crawl, and hover,
And can howl, and shriek, and wail,
But those who want to hear of them
Must read this little tale.
W. T. L.


First published by
J. & G. Innes, *St. Andrews Citizen* Office.

————

1911

Dedicated to my old Friends,

John L. Low
(Laing)

and

Charles Blair MacDonald.

*

*Note by Richard Falconer*
These dedications for the book by Linskill were dropped for some
of the later editions. So who were his old friends?

John L. Low or John Laing Low was the British Amateur Golf Championship
runner-up in the 1901 at the St. Andrews Links. He was regarded as the
greatest authority on British Amateur Golf at the time and wrote a number of
early books on the subject.

Charles Blair MacDonald
1855-1939

He was a golfing architect. In 1893 he
designed the first 18 hole golf course
in the USA

# Contents

# A Haunted Manor House and the Duel at St. Andrews;

## or

## The Old Brown Witch.[lxxxi]

This can hardly be termed a St. Andrews ghost story, but it is so remarkably strange and weird that I have been specially requested to add it to the series, and there is an allusion to St Andrews in it after all.

Several years ago we had in the Golf Club at Cambridge a Russian Prince who took up golf, and the questions of spirits, bogies, witches, banshees, death warnings, and the like, equally strongly. He was a firm disbeliever in all of them, and belonged to a Phantasmalogical Research Society[lxxxii] to inquire into and expose all such things. I frequently have long letters from him from all sorts of remote parts of the world where he is investigating tales of haunted houses, churchyards, and so on; but from this, his last letter, he seems to have contrived to meet a *genuine* and very unpleasant sort of spectre. Of course I suppress all names.

"X------ x Manor,

Feb. -----, 1905.

Dear W. T. L., – Well, here I am, actually in a really haunted manor house at last, and I have had a most horribly, weird, and uncanny experience of a most loathsome appearance. I have been here a fortnight now – such a queer, great old house, all turrets and towers, and damp wings covered with ivy and creepers, and such small, narrow windows. It is on a slight elevation, and has in bygone days had a moat around it. It is surrounded by dense woods, and there is a black-looking lake at the back. The staircases are all stone and very narrow, and there is an old chapel and a coffin room in the house. In the garden, in a yew avenue, is a vault and a tombstone, and thereby hangs my curious tale.

It seems that centuries ago a very unpleasant old widow lady, and a very unpleasant son, had the old house. She was a very ugly and eccentric creature, and a miser, and was nicknamed by the village folk "The Brown Witch." The tales about her on goings told to this day are most remarkable. It seems her son,

---

[lxxxi] Later editions drop the title 'The Old Brown Witch'.
[lxxxii] The Society for Psychical Research

who, according to all accounts, was a shocking bad lot, was killed in a duel, and the old lady died shortly afterwards a *raving maniac.*

She seems to have left a very curious will. I deal with only two details in it. One was that the chamber in which she lived and died was forever to be left *untouched and undisturbed,* but *unlocked,* or the disturber would be cursed with instant blindness and ultimately death. The second was that she was to be buried in the vault in the yew avenue that she had specially made for her remains; that she was to be dressed in her usual clothes and bonnet, and that she must be placed in a tightly-sealed *glass coffin,* so as to be visible to any intruder. My host told me the chamber or the vault in the grounds had never been interfered with, but that her appearances had been very frequent to most credible witnesses, and that such appearances all portended some dire calamity to someone.

She had appeared and terrified many visitors, both in the house and in the grounds. She had also been seen by the village pastor and by the servants. He had never seen her himself, but he had taken every measure he could think of to unravel the mystery, but in vain. The outdoor servants were terrified, and would never remain, and one lady visitor had been nearly driven mad by seeing her peering in at the window at dusk.

Of course, I laughed the tale to scorn, and also the story of the alarm bell which tolled at intervals without any apparent or human agency. Not even the bravest would dare to walk down the yew avenue after nightfall.

Well, I had been ten days in the house before anything happened. I must say, the wind and the rats, and owls and bats, and the tapping noise of the ivy on the old windows at night were rather creepy, but nothing really out of the common happened till the other night.

My room was in a long, narrow, old gallery. After cards and billiards, and at about 12.30, I was going off to my well-earned rest, and was getting near my door in the gallery, when I saw a faint light coming towards me round a corner. I went into my room and waited to see who was wandering about so late at night. Then a figure stopped at my door, evidently carrying a lighted old lantern. I raised my candle to have an inspection, and then, oh! horror! – I staggered back for a moment, for before me clearly stood the horrible figure of the old "Brown Witch," A cold sweat broke out all over me.

Far, far worse than the description. I saw her brown robe and the poke bonnet, the horrible face, the huge black sockets of the eyes without eyeballs, the nose gone, and, worst of all, that fearful grin, the cruel grin of a maniac, a wicked, terrible face.

I opened my drawer and seized my always loaded revolver. I shouted loudly, and fired *once, twice, thrice*. She never moved; only the horrible mocking smile grew wider and more devilish. I rushed forward, slammed my door to shut out the awful sight, and then collapsed back into a chair.

I must have hit it each time for certain. An offensive charnel house smell pervaded the air. Then the door flew open, and my host and several men and servants rushed into the room, anxiously asking what was the matter, and why I fired? I told them everything. We found the three bullet shots in the wall opposite my door. They *must* have passed through that abominable horror.

Need I say I spent a wretched night? In fact, I sat up and never went to bed at all. I resolved to leave next day early, but before doing that I determined at all hazards, to go into that vault and see what it contained, and also to carefully investigate the "Brown Witch's" chamber without disturbing anything in it. I told my host next day at breakfast what I proposed doing, and he offered no objection whatever, but declined absolutely to go near the vault or chamber himself, or to let any of his household do so.

"Oh! by-the-by, did you ring the alarm bell in the tower last night?" he asked me. "It was the sound of your shots and the great bell ringing immediately afterwards that brought me along so quickly to your room. We all heard it."

I told him I knew nothing of it and never even heard the bell.

"I thought that," he said, "for you were nearly off in a faint when we all came in and hardly knew us for a bit."

"I can't make out the bell," said my host, "or what on earth can make it ring so. It has no rope, and it cannot possibly be the wind. I must have it removed. Last time it rung loudly like that, my old housekeeper was found dead in her bed in the morning."

To make a long story short, the next thing I did was to get a couple of labourers to shovel away the earth and find the lid of the old vault in the yew avenue. This was soon done, and we quickly descended into the place with lights. We found ourselves in a large-built, clammy chamber, and on the floor lay a tattered and broken old lantern. At first we thought the chamber was empty, but all of a sudden we noticed a niche at one end and at once went forward to it. In this singular alcove was a large glass box, or coffin, standing on its end, and in it standing upright was the horrible eyeless mummy (still arrayed in the brown robe and poke bonnet) of the terrible creature I had seen in the gallery, and with the same mocking, grinning mouth and the huge ugly teeth. The same smell I have told you of before pervaded the whole place.

She was hermetically sealed up in this ghastly glass coffin and preserved. We were all very glad to leave that charnel-house and cover it up out of sight, but not out of memory. That would be perfectly impossible to any of us. I can't get that smell out of my nose yet. It would sicken you.

Next, I went to the chamber with a friend and my bicycle lantern to investigate. It was up a long, narrow stone stair. The old oak door (it was unlocked, as I said before) soon yielded to our combined efforts and creaked open, and we stood in a room of the Middle Ages. The old shutters were tightly closed. The ceiling, which had once been handsomely painted, was rapidly falling away and the tapestry was rotting off the walls. It had evidently once been a splendid apartment, but now it was given up to rats and moths and spiders and damp. It chilled one to the very marrow, and it had that same horrible smell. There was a four-poster bed in one corner with rags and shreds of curtains, probably where the old creature had died. The tables and chairs were covered with the dust of ages. There was no carpet of any kind. An old spinet stood against the wall; and papers were lying all over the place inches deep in dust. A few charred logs of wood lay in the gaping old fireplace with its old-time chimney corners, and there seemed to be bits of valuable old china and bric-a-brac about the place. Many pictures had fallen off the walls, but a few faded pencil drawings were still in their places. Just guess my surprise and astonishment when I found they were Scottish views – one of Edinburgh, one of Crail Church, and three of St. Andrews, including the old College and Chapel, the Castle, and St Leonards College, with date 1676. Here was another most curious thing I determined to ask about before I left. However, I touched nothing in the room, as I had promised my host, and besides – you will laugh – I had no wish to be stricken with the "Brown Witch's" promised curse of blindness and ultimate death to any intruder who touched her things. I dreaded her far too much since I had seen her in the gallery and in her tomb, and heard of her bewitched alarm bell, which portended death to someone.

Before I left, I mentioned the Scottish drawings in the witch's room to my host, and asked him if he could throw any light on how they came there.

Briefly, it seems that she (the witch) sent her son far away in those old days to a Scottish University, and St. Andrews was her choice. It seems he was very quarrelsome in his cups, and frequently fought duels, and generally proved the victor. One of the last he fought at Sauchope Stone, near Crail, with a nephew of the Laird of Balcomie Castle, and they fought with broadsword and buckler, and again the "Witch's" son killed his man. His last duel was fought on St. Andrews sands with rapiers, and he was run through the heart – a good job.

Now I must conclude. I am determined to investigate further the whole most mysterious affair. If you ever visit this place, my host, Mr -------, says he will let you explore the vault in the yew avenue, and see the coffin and the old witch, and you may also go and look at the chamber. If you ever do, take the advice of an old friend and do not *dare* to touch anything therein.

YOUR FRIEND TO COMMAND.

# A Spiritualistic Seance

THE M'Whiskers, whom I met at Oban, were very jolly old people. Papa M'Whisker had made a big fortune teaplanting in Ceylon, and had bought, and added to Dramdotty Castle in the far, far north. They were perfectly full of ghosts and spiritualism, and at Dramdotty they seemed to have a ghost for every day in the week. On Monday there was the "Spotted Nun," on Tuesday the "Floating Infant," on Wednesday the "Headless Dwarf," on Thursday the "Vanishing Negro," on Friday the "Burnt Lady," and on Saturday the "Human Balloon," and on Sunday the whole lot attended on them, and, I daresay, went to the kirk with them.

M'Whisker himself was a jovial soul, fond of his toddy, and very much resembled the Dougal Cratur in "Rob Roy." My friend, John Clyde, should have seen him. He had a furious red head of hair and beard of the same colour, and the street boys used to call after him the song, "The folks all call me Carroty, What, what, what, oh! Carroty," etc. Mrs M'Whisker was a stout lady with eyes like small tomatoes and a gimlet nose. They had a son, a boy of ten, called Fernando M'Whisker, because he was born in Spain. When they came to St. Andrews they had purchased a number of my "Ghost Books." (These ghosts at present chiefly haunt the *Citizen* Warehouse, booksellers' shops, and the railway bookstall.) That is the reason perhaps that the M'Whiskers invited me to a spiritualistic seance at their house in South Street. They generally came to St. Andrews for the winter, partly to get away from the cold of their northern home, and partly because they thought the history and atmosphere of St. Andrews lent itself to an all-pervading presence of ghosts, spooks, and spirits. I had only been to two such shows before - one at Helensburgh and one at Cambridge - and was, and still am, very doubtful of the genuineness of spiritualism. On the day appointed I went to the M'Whiskers' house in South Street, and was shown in by a Highlander in the M'Whisker tartan. It was early in the afternoon, but I found the shutters in the large room all shut, and a few dim lights only were burning. On a sideboard in the comer stood plenty of refreshments and everything else to comfort the inner man. In the centre of the room there was a round table covered with a M'Whisker tartan tablecloth, which touched the floor all round: this in itself was suspicious to my mind. I was introduced to the chief medium, one Mr Peter Fancourt, who looked as if he had been buried and dug up again. He was in tight, sleek black clothes, and resembled in every way "Uriah Heep" in "David Copperfield." The other medium was a Mrs Flyflap Corncockle. They were supposed not to know each other, but I am as certain that they were accomplices as that the Bell Rock is near St. Andrews Bay. A number of chairs encircled the table. We had all to seat ourselves on these chairs, with our thumbs and little fingers touching round the edge of the table. The first thing that happened was a kind of "squish," and then a huge bouquet of flowers descended on the table from somewhere. It was a clever trick, but the flowers were of the commonest sort, and what I had seen in all the greengrocers' shops that

morning. The lights were now turned very low, and a spirit arm and hand appeared floating about, which shone a good deal. It hovered about from the ceiling to above our heads, and when I got a chance I jumped on a chair and seized it with both hands. It seemed to shrink up, and was torn through my hands very forcibly, and in such a material manner that I was forced to let go. I don't know where the hand and arm went to, but it was simply a juggling trick. After this "Mr Heep" (I beg his pardon, Mr Fancourt) said that there was an unbeliever present, and as I was that unbeliever I was relegated to an armchair by the fireplace with one of M'Whisker's muckle cigars. From that point of vantage I watched the whole affair, and they assured me they would tell me all that was going on. The next very curious thing was that they suddenly all took their hands off the table, and their eyes slowly followed something ceilingwards. It was funny to see them all lying back staring up at the roof. Then very slowly their heads and eyes resumed their normal position.

"Did you see that?" said the M'Whisker triumphantly. "I saw nothing whatever," I remarked. "What! did you not see the table float up to the ceiling? It remained there quite half a second, and then came down as lightly as a feather." "I was watching the table the whole time," I said, "and it never moved an inch from its place."

"Oh! you are an unbeliever," said Mrs M'Whisker sadly, "but later on when it is darker you will see Mr Fancourt float out of one of the windows and come in at the other." I fervently hoped if he did anything of the kind he would come a cropper on the pavement below and break some of his ribs. The table then started to dance about and move along, but this, I am certain, was simply engineered by those two mediums.

After some tomfoolery of this kind they all agreed that "Ouija" should be brought out. A large oblong yellow board was then produced and laid on the table. On it were the letters of the alphabet and a number of figures, also the sun, moon, and stars, and some other fantastic symbols. On this board was placed a small table with a round body and round head, it had three hind legs and a front, which was the pointer. These legs had little red velvet boots on. The two mediums then placed their hands on each side of this curious table, which immediately began to run about to the letters and figures, spelling out things and fixing dates in answer to questions asked. It was not the least like a planchette, which is on wheels. The first thing they informed me it had said was that a spirit called Clarissa was present, and for many years she had lain dying in that room. She maintained that she was some distant relation of the White Lady of the Haunted Tower. It then rushed into poetry. Its first effort was the "Legend of Purple James and his Girl," a comic thing which reminded me of the "Bab Ballads." They afterwards gave me a copy of this poem, which I still possess. Next the spirit gave us a Scotch poem about a haggis, and then one called "Edward and the Hard-Boiled Egg." It then devoted its attention to me, whom it characterised as the "Unbeliever." It stated that if the Antiquarian Society would dig a pit four feet square by six feet deep between the two dungeons in the Kitchen Tower of the castle, and if the rock were cut through, a cave would be found full of casks of good red wine. On no condition whatever would I, on such evidence, recommend the Society to strike a pick in there. The next spirit that turned up was one Jaspar Codlever. He alluded to me as "the Cambridge man in the chair with the cigar." He said that if excavations were made between the two last trees in Lawpark Wood a stone cist would be found full of Pictish ornaments.[lxxxiii] Again he told us that within a cave on the cliffs there was a chalice of great value placed there by Isabella the Nun, who still guarded it by night and day, and was very dangerous to approach. This spirit then went away, and his place was taken by a monk named Rudolph, who informed us that the entrance to the Crypt or sub-Chapel was between two of the pillars in the Priory. As there are a lot of pillars there, it is impossible to know which he meant.[lxxxiv] He said this entrance was near Roger's tomb. Who Roger may be I know not.[lxxxv] He then told us about this Crypt. He said there was something so horrible in it that it turned him sick. Curiously enough, some

---

[lxxxiii] Law Park Wood is situated at the end of the Lade Braes by an ancient Mill Pond. This is by Hallow Hill, the site of a Celtic long cist cemetery where over 140 graves were uncovered by archaeologists in 1975. The site was first discovered in 1867 and is believed to be the site of one of the earliest chapels and perhaps communities of the town. (Refer to *Hallow Hill*, p.188)

[lxxxiv] The logical place would be between the last and second last pillars of the South Transept by the old Priory, on the far right when looking from the direction of the Cathedral entrance which is where I saw the white lady on two occasions.

[lxxxv] Bishop Roger De Beaumont was Bishop of St. Andrews from 1189. Dying in 1202 he was buried in the Cathedral grounds. Building of the new Cathedral had begun in 1160 to replace St. Regulus Cathedral. Bishop Roger continued overseeing its construction and also built the Castle as an Episcopal Palace shortly before his death.

thought-reading people told us the same story in the Town Hall some years ago, but they said the underground Chapel was at the east end of the Cathedral. The monk then went on to tell us of this place in the Priory. He said it had Purbeck marble pillars, a well of clear water, and three small costly altars, and a number of books of the Vincentian Canons. There was a short interval now, and the lights were turned up. I was anxious to get away, but they implored me to stay and see the cabinet and the spirits therein. I told them in my most dramatic fashion that I was late already, and I had a meeting on. M'Whisker then begged me, if I would not stay to see the spirits, to taste some, and he mixed me an excellent whisky-and-soda, which he called a "Blairgowrie." I then made my adieu, and was very glad to get once more into the street and also into a world of sense. The M'Whiskers informed me some days afterwards that they were very sorry at my leaving, as, after I had gone, Fancourt had floated out of the window, and numerous wonderful spirits had appeared in the cabinet. I am glad I went when I did, as I should certainly have taken a poker to that cabinet.

# A Very Peculiar House

Last time I visited Cambridge I was invited by a friend to meet a party of merry undergraduates. They had all nicknames, and what their real names were I cannot remember. There was Mike, and Whiffle, Toddie, Bulger, the Infant, Eddie Smith from Ramsgate, and the Coal Scuttle. We had a most sumptuous repast, as only can be supplied by first-class Cambridge kitchens, and to which we did ample justice. We were smoking after lunch when they informed me that they had taken the liberty of making an engagement for me to go to tea with such a dear old lady called Sister Elfreda at a house in Bridge Street, opposite St Clement's Church, on the following day at 4.30, as she wished to tell me some ghostly experiences she had had at St Andrews. Of course I said I would very gladly go. They asked me before I went if I could take them behind the scenes that night at the Cambridge Theatre. This I had to flatly refuse, as no undergraduates are allowed within the sacred precincts of the stage door. Next day was a damp, raw, typical Cambridge day. I wended my way to Bridge Street, and easily found the house I was going to, as I had once lodged there. The rooms were kept by two old women who might be called decayed gentlewomen. Their name was Monkswood, and they had been nicknamed "The Cruets," namely, "Pepper" and "Vinegar." Very different from them was their niece, a lovely young actress, who was known on the stage as Patricia Glencluse, who was quite the rage in musical comedy, and who, it was rumoured abroad, would soon become a Duchess. The door was opened by Patricia herself, who said, "Oh, I thought it might be you. Sister Elfreda told me you were coming to tea. You will like her she is such a darling    just like the "Belle of New York," only grown older. If you write anything about what she tells you, mind you send it to me, to the Whittington Company, Theatre, Birmingham." "Of course I will," I said, "and I will put you in it." "Now come along upstairs and I will introduce you to her," she said. She tapped at a door and then opened it, and ushered me into the presence of the Sister. "Look here. Sister," said Patricia, "I have brought the ghost man from St. Andrews to see you. Here he is." "Very good of you," said the Sister as she shook hands with me warmly. "You know," she said, "I have read all your ghost tales." She then told Patricia to run downstairs and send the servant up with tea. Then we seated ourselves down to tea and muffins, and the old lady related her story. She said: - "I wanted very much to tell you of a little experience I had some months ago. I was asked to come up for a short time to look after an invalid lady who lived at St. Andrews. Well, I arrived safely there, and went from the station to the house in a bus. It was an old house, and when I entered I felt a queer sort of creepy sensation come over me such as I had never experienced before. I was ushered into the presence of my host and hostess and the invalid lady. He was a splendid example of an old British soldier, and his wife was a pretty, fragile-looking old piece of china. The invalid lady I found only suffered from nerves, and very little wonder, I thought, in such a peculiar house. I had always a fancy that some other human being resided in the house; but if so, it only remained a feeling. The name of the cook was Timbletoss, the butler was Corncockle, and oddly enough they both came from Cambridge." "What curious names there are here," I said to the Sister; "when I first went to Cambridge I thought the names over the shops must be some gigantic joke – a man once suggested to me that someone must have been specially engaged to come to Cambridge and invent those wonderful names." "Well," continued the Sister, "it really was a most extraordinary house. I had never seen anything out of the common before, and I have never seen anything like that house since. The servants told me most remarkable tales – how the bedclothes were twitched off the bed in the night by unseen hands, and how the tables and chairs rattled about over the floor, and the knives and forks flew off the table. Curious little coloured flames known there as 'Burbilangs' used to float about in the air at night, and Corncockle, the butler, said the beer taps in the cellar were constantly turned on and the gas turned off. The servants had to have their wages considerably raised to keep them in the house. At luncheon on several occasions the lady used to jump up and run out of the room in great haste, and did not reappear till dinner, when she looked very white and shaky. On two occasions I was ordered to go at once to my room and lock the door and remain there until the old Squire sounded the hall gong. They seemed very much perturbed when I got down again. I will only mention one or two curious things I saw. One was a quaint creature called the 'Mutilated Football,' which stotted downstairs in front of me, and when it reached the lobby a head and a pair of arms and legs appeared, and it pattered off down the cellar stairs at a breakneck speed. The story goes that this creature was once a great athlete and football player, and when he got old and fat would insist on still playing, though warned not to do so. He got such a severe kick that his ribs were broken, and he died on the field. I never heard the true story of the 'Animated Hairpin,' but I saw it once seated in an armchair in the dining-room. It looked as if it had on black tights and a close-fitting black jersey. It had a very long white face, with great round eyes like an owl's and black hair standing on end to a great height. When it saw me it got up quickly from the chair, bowed very low till its head nearly touched the ground, and then walked in a most stately manner out of the room. Then I saw 'The Green

Lady' – a tall, beautiful girl with very long hair and a rustling green brocaded dress. She glided along as if on wheels. That this was no imagination of mine may be drawn from the fact that one day when I had a little girl to tea she suddenly clutched my arm and asked me who that beautiful lady in green with the long hair was, who had gone past the door on roller skates. I will not enlarge now on the bangings, crashes, thumpings, and tappings that resounded through the rooms at all times of day and night, sometimes on the ceilings, sometimes on the walls, and sometimes on the floors. The doors and windows, too, had a nasty habit of suddenly opening without any visible cause; and another very curious thing was that one might be sitting by a very bright fire when, without any apparent cause, it would suddenly go out, and leave nothing but inky blackness. The first night I slept in my room in this peculiar house I examined it most thoroughly, but there was nothing out of the common to be seen. My door, which I most carefully locked, flew open with a bang, though the bolt still remained out. I again closed and relocked the door, and put a chair against it, but to my astonishment the door once more flew open and hurled the chair across the room. After that I decided to leave the door wide open and see what would happen next. I got quite accustomed to the 'Burbilangs' or flying lights – they were like pretty fireworks. Nothing more happened to me for several days, till one morning I awoke about two o'clock to find a youngish-looking monk seated in an arm- chair, 'Fear not,' he said, 'Sister Elfreda, I left this earth many years ago. In life my name was Walter Desmond, but when I became a monk at St. Anthony I was known as Brother Stanilaus. As a rule I am invisible, but can assume my bodily shape if necessary. In life I was at St. Andrews, Durham, and Cambridge.' 'When in Cambridge,' I asked, 'did you know the writer of St. Andrews ghost stories?' 'No, I only knew him by sight. I was very young then, and was somewhat afraid of him, as I heard when getting on the Links he used to become very violent if he missed a putt, topped a drive, foozled an iron shot, or got into any of the numerous ditches which intersect the Cambridge Links. But I came specially to see you tonight to tell you how to rid this house of the evil influence there is over it. I have here a manuscript regarding it which I took from a foreign library, and which I wish you to read and act upon, and so purify this house and render it habitable, but I must impose the strictest secrecy on you in regard to what you read; reveal it to no one.' 'But how will you get that paper back?' I asked the brother. 'Oh, time and space are nothing to us – I got this paper from that distant library only a few seconds ago, and when you have digested it, it will be immediately replaced from whence it came; only follow all the directions carefully, or my visit will have been of no avail. We read the paper over together most carefully, but of that I may say no more.' 'Having told you what to do,' said the monk, 'I fear I must hie hence. I have much to do tonight after replacing the paper.' 'I will fulfil all that you have asked me brother,' I said, 'and hope that it will make this house less fearsome. But before you go, brother,' I said, 'as you are a Cambridge man, why do you not pay a visit to the author of St. Andrews Ghost Stories?' 'He would not see me because I would not materialise myself there, I could only appear as a puff of smoke, or, as it were, a light fog.' ('Thanks, Sister,' I said, 'do not ask any nasty damp fogs to come and call on me.' She laughed.) The monk, in vanishing, said, 'Remember, Sister, no bolts, locks, or bars can keep us from going where we choose.'"

I got up and thanked her, and proceeded to put on a greatcoat. "I never wear greatcoats," I said, "in Scotland, but I am afraid of the Cambridge damp, so I borrowed this topcoat from Colonel Churchtimber."

"You have dropped something out of the pocket," said the Sister.

"Hullo," I said, "this is a piece of classical music which must belong to Macbeth Churchtimber, the Colonel's son. Now, goodnight, and many thanks. Sister Elfreda."

I descended the stairs and said goodnight to the Cruets and Patricia. As I wandered down the street to the theatre in the damp foggy evening I pondered over what Sister Elfreda had told me, and as I lit my pipe I kept thinking of those people – "The Mutilated Football," "The Animated Hairpin," and the "Monk Brother Stanilaus," to whom locks, bolts and bars were as nothing, and who had the nasty habit of appearing to his friends as a damp cloud – a habit, I think, not to be encouraged.

\*       \*       \*       \*       \*       \*

Sister Elfreda now informs me that the peculiar house is now quite "normal," and that all the "bogies" have vanished into thin air.

# Concerning More Appearances
## of the White Lady

I HAD been invited, and was sitting at tea with a very dear old lady friend of mine not long ago. It may seem strange, but tea is, I consider, an extra and an unnecessary meal. It does not appeal to me in the least, and only spoils one's dinner and digestion. The reason I went to tea was because in her note to me the lady mentioned that she had read my book of ghost tales, and that she was interested in ghosts in general and St. Andrews ghosts in particular, and that she knew lots of such stories in the days of her girlhood in St Andrews, now about 85 years ago. That is why I went to eat cakes with sugar, hot buttered toast, and drink tea as black as senna or a black draught. She had also informed me in the note that she could tell me a lot about the Haunted Tower and the Beautiful White Lady.

It took some time to get her to that point. She would talk about Archbishop Sharpe and his haunted house in the Pends Road, of the ghost seen by Archbishop Ross, of my friend the Veiled Nun, of the Cathedral and Mr John Knox, of Hungus, King of the Picts, of Constantine, Thomas Plater, and various others. She told me a long tale of the Rainham Ghost in Norfolk, known as "The Brown Lady of Rainham," whom her father Captain Marryat both saw, and so on.

At last we got near the subject I wished information on.

"In my young days," she said, "St Andrews was quite a wee bit place with grass-grown streets, red-tiled houses, outside stairs, queer narrow wynds, not over clean, only a few lights at night - here and there, an old bowet or oil lamp hanging at street corners. Everyone believed in Sharpe's Phantom Coach in those good old days."

"Did you ever see it?" I queried.

"No," she said, "but I have heard it rumble past, and I know those who have seen it, and many other things too."

"But tell me about the White Lady, please," I said.

"I will. Few people in those days cared to pass that haunted tower after nightfall. If they did they ran past it and also the castle. Those new-fangled incandescent gas lamps have spoiled it all now.[lxxxvi] The White Lady was one of the *Maries*, one of the maids of honour to poor martyred Mary of Scotland,

---

[lxxxvi] This is quite a humorous in-joke of Linskill's, as it was he who had them installed when he was Dean of Guild for the town.

they said then. She was madly in love with the French poet and minstrel, 'Castelar,' and he was hopelessly in love, like many others, with Marie's lovely mistress, 'the Queen of Scots.'"

"Was she supposed to be the girl seen in the built-up haunted tower?" I asked.

"That I really can't say," she said. "There was a story often told in the old days that a beautiful embalmed girl in white lay in that tower, and it was there and near the castle that she used to appear to the people.[lxxxvii] You know poor Castelar, the handsome minstrel, said and did some stupid things, and was beheaded[lxxxviii] at the castle, and was probably buried near there. Get me from that shelf Whyte Melville's novel, 'The Queen's Maries.'"[lxxxix]

I did as she bade me.

"Well, you will see there that the night before Castelar was to be beheaded kind Queen Mary sent one of her Maries, the one who loved Castelar, at her own special request to the castle with her ring to offer him a pardon if he left this country for ever.[xc] This Marie did see Castelar, showed him the Queen's ring, and pleaded with him to comply, but he refused - he preferred death to banishment from his beloved Queen's Court, and the fair messenger left him obstinate in his dungeon.

This faithful Marie paced up and down all that night before the castle; then at dawn came the sound of a gun or culverin, a wreath of smoke floated out to sea, and Castelar was gone. Whyte Melville says she did not start, she did not shriek, nor faint, nor quiver, but she threw her hood back and looked wildly upward, gasping for air. Then as the rising sun shone on her bare head, Marie's raven hair was all streaked and patched with grey. When Mary Stuart fled to

---

[lxxxvii] This is a distortion of Linskill attributing the White Lady to all sightings in this area. There are ghosts of three White Ladies on the Scores path side of the Cathedral alone. Only one is the White Lady of the Haunted Tower. The others are Lady Buchan between the Castle and the convergence of the Scores path from Gregory Place leading to the Haunted Tower, and the White Lady of the castle who is possibly Marion Ogilvy. Refer also to *The Ghost of a Woman – Marion Ogilvy?*, p.78, *The Ghost of Lady Buchan and her Cave*, p.86, *The White Lady of the Haunted Tower* p.130 and the book *A St. Andrews Mystery* by the author (2014)

[lxxxviii] He was hanged at the Mercat Cross in Market Square (now Market Street) in St. Andrews on the 20th February 1563.

[lxxxix] The book was a work of fiction published in 1862 by Major George John Whyte Melville, a novelist, poet and a golfing friend of Linskill's.

England, this faithful Marie, now no more needed, became a nun in St Andrews.

Look at page 371 of Whyte Melville's book," she said. So I read – "It was an early harvest that year in Scotland, but e'er the barley was white, Marie had done with nuns and nunneries, vows and ceremonies, withered hopes and mortal sorrows, and had gone to that place where the weary heart can alone find the rest it had so longed for at last."[xci]

The pathetic and the comic often go together. Just at this interesting point a cat sprang suddenly up and upset a cup of tea in the lap of my genial hostess. This created a diversion. Old ladies are apt to wander, which is annoying. She got clean away from her subject for a bit. She asked me if I knew Captain Robert Marshall, who wrote plays and "The Haunted Major." [xcii] I said I knew Bob well, and that he was an old Madras College boy.

She then wanted to know if I knew how to pronounce the name of Mr Travis's American putter, and if Mr Low or I had ever tried it. She also wanted to know if I knew anything of the new patent clock worked on gramophone principles which shouted the homes instead of striking them.

Having answered all these queries to her satisfaction, and taken another cup of senna — I mean tea — I got her back to the White Lady.

"Oh, yes, my dear," she said, "I saw her, I and some friends. *A lot of us* had been out at Kinkell Braes one afternoon and stayed there long past the time allowed us. It was almost dark, and we scuttled up the brae from the Harbour rather frightened. Just near the turret light we saw the lady gliding along the top of the old Abbey wall. She was robed in a grey white dress with a veil over her head. She had raven black hair, and a string of beads hanging from her waist. We all huddled together, with our eyes and mouths wide open, and watched the figure. 'It's a girl sleep-walking,' I murmured.

---

[xci] Refer to my book *A St. Andrews Mystery,* (2014)

[xcii] Captain Robert Marshall was indeed from St. Andrews, like myself he went to Madras and Linksill knew him. He was a Captain in the 71$^{st}$ Highland Light Infantry. He was a Scottish author and playwright and his story *The Haunted Major* was a ghostly golfing yarn he published in 1902. It features a game of golf played at St. Magnus (St. Andrews) where the prize is the hand in marriage to a woman. The hero of the story is one Major John Gore who is playing very badly until the ghost of the Scottish Prelate Cardinal Smeaton comes to his aid against Gore's opponent called Lindsay. This is an inference on St. Andrews history. Smeaton is Beaton who was killed at the Castle. Lindsay is described by the ghost in the book as one of his most determined foes and bewitches Gore's clubs to win the game against his arch enemy.

'It's a bride,' whispered another. 'Oh! she'll fall,' said a little boy, grasping my arm. But she did not. She went inside the parapet wall at the Haunted Tower and vanished completely.

'It's a ghost; it's the White Lady,' we all shrieked, and ran off trembling home. My sister also saw her on one of the turrets in the Abbey wall, where she was seen by several people. Some months after, as I was doing my hair before my looking-glass, the same face looked over my shoulder, and I fainted. I have always felt an eerie feeling about a looking- glass ever since, even now, old woman as I am. Her lovely face is one never, never to be forgotten, having once seen it, but your new fashioned lamps have altered everything."

"And what do you think about it now" I asked her.

"I have told you all I know. The Lady used to be seen oftenest between the castle and that old turret. Perhaps she came to look at the last resting-place of her much loved and wayward minstrel, Castelar. Maybe she came to revisit the favourite haunts of her beloved girl Queen - truly called the Queen of the Roses; but to my dying day I shall never forget that face, that lovely, pathetic face I saw years ago, and which may still be seen by some. What! must you really go now; won't you have another cup of tea? Very well, good bye."

As I wended my way Clubwards I could not but think of the strange tale I had just heard and of Castelar's sad end, and I could not help wondering if I should ever be favoured with a sight of this beautiful White Lady.[xciii]

---

[xciii] This whole story is a mix of Chastelard's infatuation with the Queen and who was executed because of it and the fictitious ballad of Mary Hamilton and a woman who may have been a chamber maid and executed for sleeping with the Queens second husband Lord Darnley. All is mixed with inspiration from the fictitious story by Whyte Melville.

# Related by Captain Chester

In my travels I have met many extraordinary and remarkable people with hobbies and fads of various kinds, but I never met a man of such curious personality as this old friend of mine, Captain Chester. All his methods and ideas were purely original. Everyone has some hobby; his hobby was ghost and spook-hunting.

We were sitting one lovely September evening in the gardens of one of the hotels at Bonn, which stretched down to the river Rhine, listening to the band and watching the great rafts coming down the river from the Black Forest.

"By Jove, sir," said the old man, "I have shot big game in the Rockies, and hunted tigers and all that sort of thing; but, zooks! sir, I prefer hunting ghosts any day. That Robert de Montrose was the first I saw. There are shoals of these shades about, a perfect army of them everywhere, especially in St. Andrews. Gad, sir, you should hear the banshees shrieking at night in the Irish bogs. I don't believe in your infernal sea serpents, but I've seen water kelpies in the Scottish and American lakes."

I told him I had never heard a banshee or seen a water kelpie.

"Very likely, sir, very probable. Everyone can't see and hear these things. *I can.*"

I told him I had never seen a disembodied spirit, and didn't want to.

"Gad, zooks! sir, I consider disinspirited bodies far worse. They are quite common. I allude to human bodies that have lost their spirits or souls, and yet go about among us. Zounds! sir, my cousin is one of them."

"Ah," he continued, "detached personality is a curious thing. I can detach my personality, can you?"

"Most certainly not," I said, "what the deuce do you mean?"

"Mean," he said, "I mean my spirit can float out of my body at will. My spirit becomes a sort of mental balloon. I can then defy destiny."[xciv]

"How in thunder do you manage to do it anyway?"

"By practice, sir, of course. When my spirit floats out of my body, I can see my own old body sitting in my arm-chair and an ugly old wreck of a body it is. It is bad for one, I admit; it is very weakening. Another thing may happen; another wandering spirit may suddenly take possession of one's body, and then

---

[xciv] By this Linksill is implying that through astral projection, he is as he shall be in death – still aware and alive in spirit.

one's own spirit can't get back again, and it becomes a wandering spirit, and is always trying to force itself into other people's bodies. Then one's spirit gets into a mental bunker, you see."

"I don't see a bit. It is most unpleasant. Tell me about ghosts you have seen, and about that dagger you gave Major Montrose."

"Oh! so then you are not interested in eliminated personality?"

"Not a bit," I said, "I don't know what it is. Tell me about that dagger for a change."

"Oh! ah! Well, the dagger Robert of Montrose gave me proved of great use to my old friend. Bob Montrose, on *many* occasions. It had a wonderful power of its own. Once he got into a broil with a lot of Spanish fellows one night, and as he was unarmed at the time he was in a remarkably tight corner. Suddenly something slipped into his hand, and, by Jove, sir, it was the dagger, and that dagger saved his life. Another time he found himself in an American train with a raving lunatic, and if it had not been for the protecting dagger he'd have been torn limb from limb. After that he took it everywhere with him."

"Where is it now?"

"Well, there's an odd thing if you like. Bob died in the Isle of France, where Paul and Virginia used to be. He was killed by a fall, and is buried there. He left the dagger to me in his will, but no human eyes have ever seen that dagger since his death. It may have been stolen, or it may have gone back to where it came from into Robert of Montrose's stone kist in the old Chapter-House at St Andrews Cathedral. Probably its usefulness was at an end, and it was needed no more. Bob told me one queer thing about that dagger. *Once a year* near Christmastide (the dagger hung on the wall of his bedroom) it used to exude a thick reddish fluid like blood, which used to cover the blade in large drops, and it remained so for several hours – and, again, sometimes at night it used to shine with a bright light of its own."

"That is indeed wonderful," I said, lighting another cheroot, "but tell me more about the St Andrews bogles. Astral bodies, dual personality, and things of that kind depress me a bit."

"Well, that is odd," said old Chester, "I love them. When I was in St. Andrews I rented a fine old house, with huge thick walls, big fireplaces, funny corkscrew stairs, such rum holes and corners, and big vaulted kitchens. It's all pulled down now, I believe, and a brand new house built; but I hear the vaulted rooms below are left exactly as they were. People didn't take to the old house; they heard noises and rappings, and saw things in the night, and so on. *We all saw things.* My brother met the ghost of a horrible looking old witch, quite in the orthodox dress, on the Witch Hill above the Witch Lake. It upset him terribly at the time – made him quite ill – nerves went all to pot – would not sleep in a room by himself after that. He made me devilish angry, sir, I can tell you."[xcv]

"Perhaps it was Mother Alison Craik, a well-known witch, who was burnt there."

"Likely enough, sir, it may have been the old cat you mention, an old hag. Then my nephew and I saw that phantom coach in the Abbey Walk one windy moonlit night. It passed us very quickly." but made a deuced row, like a lifeboat carriage."

"What was it like?"

"Like a huge black box with windows in it, and a queer light inside. It reminded me of a great coffin. Ugly looking affair; very uncanny thing to meet at that time of night and in such a lonely spot. It was soon gone, but we heard its muffled rumbling noise for a long time."

"What were the horses like, eh?"

"Shadowy looking black things, like great black beetles with long thin legs."

"And what was the driver like?" I asked.

"He was a tall thin, black object also, like a big, black, lank lobster, with a cocked hat on the top. That's all I could see. On the top of the coach was an object that looked like a gigantic tarantula spider, with a head like a moving gargoyle. I can't get at the real history of that mysterious old coach yet. I don't believe it has anything whatever to do with the murdered prelates, Beaton or Sharpe. However, the coach does go about. [xcvi] Another wraith I saw at the Castle of St. Andrews was that of James Hepburn, Earl of Bothwell, third husband of Mary Queen of Scots. He lies buried in the crypt of Faarveile Church, close to the Cattegat. Before his death he was a prisoner at Malmo; then he was sent to Denmark, and died in the dungeon of the State prison at Drachsholm."

"I am awfully interested," I said, "about those times and in Bothwell and Mary in particular."

"Odd's fish, sir," said Chester, "so am I. I went to Faarveile to see Bothwell's well-preserved body. The verger took me down a trap-door near the altar, and there it lies in a lidless box, a very fine face, with a cynical and mocking mouth. He murdered Darnley, and he was treated and buried as a murderer in those bygone days. At Malmo folks say he was tormented by the ghosts of his mad wife, Jane Huntly, and by Darnley. He ended his days in misery, and serve him

---

[xcv] Refer to *Witch Hill and Lake*, p.38
[xcvi] Refer to p.147

devilish well right, say I. I love and revere lovely Mary Stuart. Damn it, sir, he deserted her when she was in a fix at Carberry Hill, the curmudgeon."

"But what of the appearances of the Earl you saw?"

"Met him twice at the castle – no mistaking him – a big, knightly, handsome fellow. Spirits can easily at times assume their earthly form and dress. I recognised him at once — the sneering lips and all, just like his pictures, too. When he glided past me his teeth were chattering like a dice-box, and the wind was whistling through his neck bones. I addressed him boldly by name, but he melted away. One sees these apparitions with one's mental eyes. I saw him again leaning against the door that leads to that oubliette in the Sea Tower of the castle. Egad, sir, he *exactly* resembled the body I saw in the old crypt at Faarviele. He often appears there, and at Hermitage Castle also. No mistake, sir, that was Hepburn, the Earl of Bothwell. I must turn into bed now. I go to the service at the Cathedral here early to-morrow."

Then the tall figure of Captain Chester strode away and left me alone to my meditations.

Well! I suppose if *I had been* Captain Chester, left alone there in those gardens, I'd have seen a ghost or two with my mental eyes; but, instead, I saw a fat waiter approaching, who told me my supper awaited me.[xcvii]

---

[xcvii] Refer to *Two Appearances of James Hepburn, 4ᵗʰ Earl of Bothwell,* p.144

# The Apparition of
## Sir Roger de Wanklin

I AM very fond indeed of Christmas time. There has been little snow this season. I think it has forgotten how to snow in these days. Still, I always feel Christmassy. I think of the good old coaching days, when there was really snow, of Washington, Irving, and good old Dickens and Scott, of the yule log and the family gatherings and reunions, of the wassail bowl, of frumenty and plum porridge, and mince pies, plum puddings, and holly and mistletoe and big dances in the servants' hall, of good old ancestral ghosts and hearty good cheer.

I am sitting to-day in a cosy armchair (of the old school, no modern fake) talking to my old friend, Theophilus Greenbracket. Filus, as I call him, is a clever man of many parts; he is a great traveller and sportsman, and takes a deep interest in every mortal thing. There is nothing of the kill joy or fossil about Greenbracket; he is up-to-date and true blue.

He is sitting opposite me smoking a gigantic cigar and imbibing rum punch, and talking hard; he always talks hard, but is never a bore, and never palls on one in the slightest degree. He has an enormous dog at his feet, with a fierce, vindictive expression, which belies its real nature, as it is gentle with everything and everybody, except cats and rats. Greenbracket is, among many other things, a great spiritualist and visionary, and possesses all kinds of mediumistic appliances, such as pythos, planchettes and ouijas, which he works with his old butler, Amos Bradleigh, who is another spirit hunter.

"By the bye," said Greenbracket, "I am at present taking lessons in music with Mr Easeboy." He says this so suddenly that he makes me jump, as we were talking about sea serpents and the probability of their existence.

"Are you indeed, old chap," I said.

"Yes, thorough bass, and consecutive fifths and harmony and all that sort of thing, you know. He has a pupil, Macbeth Churchtimber, who has just written a thundering pretty waltz called "Eleanor Wynne."

"I thought Churchtimber," I mildly suggested, "only played severe classical stuff."

"Oh, yes," replied my friend, "but he occasionally touches on a lighter theme, and has even written a comic song, called, 'I lay beside a milestone with a sunflower on my brow.'"

"I must try it someday," I said, "but how about your ghosts? Have you seen any lately?"

"There was one here a few minutes ago," said Greenbracket, "a tall man in armour sitting in that corner over there."

"What rubbish," I said, quite crossly, "you dream things, or drink, or eat too much."

"No I don't," said Greenbracket, "do you really mean to tell that you felt no sensation just now, no pricking or tingling feeling, or a chilly sensation down your back?"

"Certainly not, nothing of the kind," I replied.

"Well, that is queer," he said, "I know you don't see these things, but I fancied you would have felt a strange presence in some way. I don't know who the man in armour was. I have not seen him before, but my butler has, at all events. It was not Sir Roger de Wanklyn."

'Who the ------ is he?" I queried.

"Oh," said my host, "he is the earth-bound spirit of an architect who lived in St. Andrews at the time that James the Fifth married Mary of Lorraine in the Cathedral; he says he was present at the ceremony and can describe it all. A gay pageant it was and much revelry."

"If you can get all this sort of curious information, which I don't exactly credit, why on earth can't you find out something practical and useful, for instance, where the secret underground hiding place is, and where all the tons of valuable ornaments, papers, and vestments are concealed?"

"My dear friend," said Greenbracket solemnly, "these people won't be pumped; they only tell you what they choose to, or are permitted to reveal."

"If they really do turn up and talk to you as you say they do, why on earth can't you get them to talk some useful sense?"

"I really can't force their confidence," said Greenbracket, "all they do tell me voluntarily is most interesting and absorbing. This Sir Rodger planned numerous very important structural alterations in the Cathedral and elsewhere."

"It is all very odd to me," I said, "one meets people with strange ideas. I met a man years ago at Aberystwyth who was a firm believer in the transmigration of souls. He said he quite remembered being a cab horse in Glasgow, and was certain when he left this planet he would become a parrot in Mars."

"I don't understand that sort of thing a bit," said my extraordinary friend, Greenbracket, "but Sir Rodger de Wanklyn has sometimes to visit the Valley of Fire and Frost, where there are mighty furnaces on one side of him and ice and snow on the other and it is very painful."

"I had that sort of experience the other day," I remarked, "at a meeting. On one side was a furnace of a fire and on the other a window wide open with a biting frost wind blowing in."

"Tuts," said Greenbracket "that's here; I am talking of the spirit world."

"Hang! your spirit stuff. Has your butler, Amos Bradleigh, seen any spooky things lately?"

"Yes, he is much annoyed by the spirit of an evil old housekeeper here who lost her life by falling downstairs, and she is continually pushing him down my cellar stairs. He is furious."

"Is this butler of yours any connection of Jeremiah Anklebone?" I asked.

"Yes, he is a cousin," said Greenbracket; "all that family have second sight, and see and dream strange things."

"And who," I asked, "may this housekeeper be who pitched your butler down stairs?"

"Oh," said Greenbracket, "she's a badly constituted wraith, and her name is Annibal Strongthorn. She was housekeeper ages ago to this Sir Roger de Wanklyn in this very old house we are in."

"What happened to this Sir Roger? Has he told you?"

"Oh! yes he fell over the cliffs."

"Bless me, and did this old housekeeper woman push him over. Was she a murderess?"

"Oh, how can I tell," said Greenbracket peevishly, "he has told me nothing of the kind."

"Well, old fellow," I said, "you really do not get much interesting information out of your ghostly friends, but what I like about you is that all your numerous ghosts come straight to you, straight to head-quarters at once – you don't go fooling about with chairs and tables and sideboards and other pieces of timber in an idiotic way. If, as some people say, they can get chairs and tables and other articles of furniture to follow them about, why don't they go in for cheap furniture removals at night when the streets are empty?"

"Don't make a joke of everything," said Greenbracket, "I do see and converse with departed spirits. I do not ask them to come; they come to me, and half of them I have never heard of before or thought of either."

"May I ask, my good friend Greenbracket, what sort of clothes they wear when they pay you these visits; for instance, what does your latest apparition. Sir Rodger, clothe himself in?"

"Bless me!" said Theophilus, "why in the dress of his times, of course – a jerken, doublet, and hose, a rapier, and all that sort of thing; sometimes he wears a sort of coarse fustian cassock with a double breast."

"I can't make out," I said to my spiritualistic friend, "where these clothes come from. Have they got a sort of theatrical wardrobe wherever they are existing? If so, why can't the ghosts of old world clothes come alone? In such a case you might see a modern suit of evening togs, or armour, or boots and spurs, or military dress walk into your room without anything inside them; or you might, with a stretch of imagination, see a suit of pyjamas, or a pair of slippers going about the place."

"Shut up talking like that," said Theophilus, "you don't possess the sense – I mean the extra sense to see these beings; but read this document I have written out. Surely it will convince you that I really do get valuable inspirations from other worlds, but, mind, keep it a strict secret at present."

"All right, I promise you," I murmured placidly. Then I perused carefully the more than extraordinary document he had handed me.

"It is very curious," I said, "if it be one bit true; and if genuine, might be extremely useful. Mind my lips are sealed. But from whom did you obtain this remarkable story?"

"From Sir Rodger de Wanklyn, the Cathedral architect," he replied, and off I went quite full of my queer friend. Greenbracket, and of Annabel Strongthorn, Amos Bradleigh, and his cousin Anklebone, and particularly Rodger de Wanklyn.

# The Apparition of the Prior of Pittenweem

It was in September, 1875, that I first met dear old Captain Chester (now gone to his rest); and it was very many years before that date that he rented his fearsomely haunted old house in St. Andrews.

I was a Cambridge boy when I met him – how the undergraduates scorn that term "boy." He told me the following queer tales in the Poppledorf Avenue at Bonn when I was on holiday.

The house he rented at St. Andrews, from his accounts, must have been a most unpleasant and eerie dwelling. Rappings and hammerings were heard all over the house after nightfall, trembling of the walls, quiverings. Heavy falls and ear-piercing shrieks were also part of the nightly programme.

I suggested bats, rats, owls, and smugglers as the cause, which made the old man perfectly wild with rage, and caused him to use most unparliamentary language.

I pointed out that such language would probably have scared away any respectable ghost. However, let me tell the story in his own peculiar way.

"My brother and I took the house, sir," he said, "and we had a nephew and some nieces with us. There were also three middle-aged English servants at the time; and, gadsooth, sir, they had strange names. The cook possessed the extraordinary name of Maria Trombone, the housemaid was called Jemima Podge, and the other old cat was called Teresa Shadbolt.

"One evening I was sitting smoking in my study, when the door flew open with a bang and Maria rushed in.

"'Zounds! Mrs Trombone,' I said, 'how dare you come into my room like this?'

"'Well, sir,' she said, 'there are *hawful* things going on tonight. I'm *frighted* to death. I was washing hup, please sir, when something rushed passed me with a rustle, and I got a great smack on the cheek with a damp, cold hand, and then the place shook, and all the things clattered like anything.'

"'Nonsense, Trombone,' I said, 'you were asleep, or have you been drinking, eh?'

"'Lor' bless you, sir, no! never a drop; but last night, sir, Teresa Shadbolt had all the bedclothes pulled off her bed twice, sir, and Jane said a tall old man in a queer dressing-gown came into her room and brushed his white beard over her face, and, lor', sir, didn't you hear her a-screamin'?'

"'No, I'm hanged if I did. You must all be stark, staring mad, you know.'

"'Not a bit of us, master,' continued Mrs Trombone. 'There is something wrong about this blessed house – locked doors and windows fly wide open, and the bells keep ringin' at all hours of the night, and we hear steps on the stairs when everyone is in bed, and knocks, and crashes, and screams. Then the tables and things go moving about. No Christian could put up with it, please sir. *We must all leave.*'

"Well, I got all those women up, and they told me deuced queer things, but I squared them up at last."

"How?" I inquired.

"I doubled their wages, sir, and I told them they might all sleep in one room upstairs together, and I promised them a real good blow-out at Christmas, and so on.

"Next my nephew and little nieces saw the old man with the long white beard at various times in the passages and on the stairs. Oddly enough, my little nieces got quite accustomed to see the aged man with the grey beard, and were not a bit timid. They said he was just like the pictures of old Father Christmas, and he looked kind.

"I never saw him," continued Chester, "till one All Hallows Night, or Hallowe'en as they termed it in St. Andrews; but I will speak of that later on."

"Go on," I said, "it is very interesting indeed to me."

"The servants all saw him at times, and that old arch fiend, Trombone, was constantly getting frightened, and breaking things and fainting. I was myself annoyed by strange unearthly sounds when sitting smoking at night late. There were curious rollings and rumblings under the house, like enormous stone balls being bowled along, then a heavy thud followed by intolerable silence. Then there was a curious sound like muffled blinds being quickly drawn up and down; that and a sort of flapping and rustling seemed to pervade the air.

"This perplexed me, and I got in a detective; but he found out nothing at all. After much trouble and research I learned of the legend of the Prior of Pittenweem and his connection with the old house.

"It seems when Moray and his gang of plunderers shut up St Monance Church and the old Priory of Pittenweem, the last Prior (not Forman or Rowles), a very old man, was cut adrift, and for some months lay hidden at Newark Castle, food being brought him by some former monks. Newark Castle was burned, and this old Prior fled to Balcomie Castle. From there he went to Kinkell Cave near St Andrews."

"I know all those places well," I said.

"After some weeks, and when winter came, he took refuge in the very old house in which I lived. He seems to have been among both friends and foes there, and brawls were quite common things within those walls.

"One night those long dead and forgotten old-world inhabitants were startled from their slumbers by shots, the clashing of arms, and wild yells. To make a long tale short, that old Prior of Pittenweem was never seen by human eyes after that fearful night.

"Many suspected foul play, but in those times it was deemed best to keep one's mouth shut tight, and what mattered it if an old Prior disappeared?"

"They were awful times those," I said. "Glad we live in these days."

"Well, now," said the Captain, "I must come to the night of All Hallows E'en, or Holy Even, when the spirits of the night are said to wander abroad. We dined early in those days, and after dinner I walked down to an old Clubhouse in Golf Place, of which I was an hon. member, to play cards. It was a perfect night, and a few flakes of snow had begun to fall, and the wind was keen and sharp. When I left the Club later the ground was well covered with snow, but the storm had ceased, and the moon and stars were shining brightly in a clear sky. By Jove, sir, it was like fairyland, and all the church towers and house tops were glittering in the moonbeams.

"I wandered about the old place for fully an hour. It was lovely. I was reluctant to go indoors. Gad, sir, I got quite sad and poetical. I thought of my poor sister who died long ago and is buried in Stefano Rodundo at Rome, and lots of other things. Then I thought of St Andrews as it is and what it might have been. I thought of all its holy temples, erected by our pious forefathers, and its altars and statues lying desolate, ruined and profaned.

"At last I arrived at my own door, and entered – in a thoughtful mood. I went to my study and put on my slippers and dressing gown. I had just sat down and commenced reading when there came a most tremendous shivering crash. I involuntarily cowered down. I thought the roof had fallen – at least, gad, sir, I was flabbergasted. It woke everyone. The crash was followed by a roaring sound."

"It must have been an earthquake. Captain Chester,"
I said.

"Zounds, sir, I don't know what it was. I thought I was killed. Then my nephew and I got a lamp and examined the house.

"Everything was right – nothing to account for the fearful noise. Finally, we went downstairs to the vaulted kitchens. Zounds, sir, all of a sudden my nephew gripped my arm, and with a cry of abject terror pointed to the open kitchen door. 'Oh, look there, look there!' he almost screamed.

"I looked, and, gad, I got a queer turn. There facing us in the open doorway was a very tall, shaven-headed old man with a long grey beard. He had a white robe or cassock on, a linen rocket, and, above all, an almuce or cloak of black hue lined with ermine – *The Augustinian habit.* In one hand he held a very large rosary, and he lent on a stout cudgel.

"As I advanced he retreated backwards, always beckoning to me – and I followed lamp in hand. I *had* to follow – could not help myself. Do you know the way a serpent can fascinate or hypnotise its prey before it devours them?"

"Yes," I said, "I have seen the snakes at the Zoo do that trick."

"Well, sir, I was hypnotised like that – precisely like that. He beckoned and I followed.

"Suddenly I saw a little door in the comer of the kitchen standing open – a door I had never noticed before. The shadowy vision backed towards it. Still I followed. Then he entered its portals. As I advanced he grew more and more transparent, and finally melted away, and the heavy door shut upon him with a tremendous crash and rattle. The lamp fell from my trembling hand and was shattered to fragments on the stone floor. I was in pitch darkness – silence reigned – I don't remember how I got out to the light again.

"Next morning early I got in some workmen and took them down to the kitchen, direct to the corner where the door was through which the apparition vanished the previous night.

"Zounds, sir, there was *no door there* – only the white plastered wall. I was dumfounded. 'Mrs Trombone,' I said to the cook, 'where the devil has that door gone?'"

"'The door, sir,' said the cook, 'there ain't no door there that I ever saw.'

"'Trombone,' I replied, 'don't tell falsehoods – you're a fool.'

"I made the men set to work and tear down the plaster and stuff, and, egad, sir, in an hour we found the door – a thick oak, nail studded, iron clamped old door. It took some time to force it open, and then down three steps we found ourselves in a chamber with mighty thick walls and with a flagged floor, about six feet square, lit by a small slit of a window.

"'Tear up the flags,' I said.

"They did so, and there was only earth below.

"'Dig down,' I said, 'dig like thunder,'

"In about an hour we came to a huge flag with a ring in it. Up it came, and below it was a dryly-built bottle-shaped well.

"We went down with lights. What do you think we found at the bottom of it?"

"Perhaps water," I suggested.

"Water be d------- ," said Captain Chester, "we found the mouldering skeleton of a very tall man in a sitting posture. Beside him lay a large rosary and a stout oak cudgel – the rosary and cudgel I had seen in the phantom's hands the previous night. My friend, I *had solved the problem* – that was the skeleton of the old Prior of Pittenweem who vanished in that house hundreds of years ago."

# The Beautiful White Lady
## of the Haunted Tower

"How very, very lovely she was to be sure!"

"Of whom are you speaking?" I asked. "Of some of the Orchid or Veronique people, or of some of your own company? I did not know you were hard hit old chap." I was sitting in the smoking-room of the Great Northern Hotel, King's Cross, talking to an old friend, an Oxford man, but now the manager of a big theatrical company, when he suddenly made the above remark.

"No, no! Of none of those people," he replied; "but our talking of St. Andrews reminded me of a ghost, a phantom, or a spectre - call it what you choose - I saw in that ancient city several years ago - no horrid bogie, but a very lovely girl, indeed."

"By Jove," I said, "tell me about it; I want a new ghost tale very badly indeed. I know a lot of them, but perhaps this is something new and spicy."

"I am sure I do not know if it be new," he replied. "I have never seen anything spectral before or since, but I saw that lovely woman three different times. It must be fully ten years ago. I saw her twice on the Scores and once in an old house."

"Well, I must really hear all about it," I said. "Please fire away."

"All right, all right!" he said. "Now for her *first* appearance. I was living in St. Andrews at the time. It must have been the end of January or beginning of February, and I was strolling along to the Kirkhill after dinner and enjoying the fine evening and the keen sea breeze, and thinking about the old, old days of the Castle and Cathedral, of Beaton's ghost, and many other queer tales, when a female figure glided past me. She was in a long, flowing white dress, and had her beautiful dark hair hanging down past her waist. I was very much astonished to see a girl dressed in such a manner wandering about alone at such an hour, and I followed her along for several yards, when lo! just after she had passed the turret light she completely vanished near the square tower, which I was afterwards informed was known as the 'Haunted Tower,' I hunted all round the place carefully, but saw nothing more that night. Queer, wasn't it?"

"Certainly it was," I remarked; "but I know dozens of weird stories connected with that old tower. But what more have you to tell me?"

"Well," he continued, "as you may imagine, the whole affair worried and puzzled me considerably, but it was gradually vanishing from my mind when near the same place I saw her again. I had my sister with me this time, and we both can swear to it. It was a lovely night with a faint moon, and as the white lady swept past quite silently we saw the soft trailing dress and the long, black wavy hair. There was something like a rosary hanging from her waist, and a cross or a locket hanging round her throat. As she passed she turned her head towards us, and we both noticed her beautiful features, especially her brilliant eyes. She vanished, as before, near that old tower. My sister was so awfully frightened that I had to hurry her off home. We were both absolutely convinced we had seen a being not of this world — a face never to be forgotten."

"How strange," I said. "You know, several people saw a girl in that built-up old turret lying in her coffin. A former priest of the Episcopal Church here saw some masons repairing the wall of that tower, and their chisel fell into the turret through a chink. On removing a stone, they came upon a chamber within, and they saw a girl dressed in white, with long hair, lying in a coffin, wanting the lid. The hole was built up again at once. I know, and have often talked to persons who saw her there. One of them was a mason employed at the work. The doorway of the tower is opened up now, and a grill put in, but there is no sign of the girl. Queer stories arose. Some said it was the remains of Princess Muren, daughter of Constantine. Others said it was the embalmed body of some sweet girl Saint concealed there in times of trouble, and so on; but finish your story."

"I have little more to tell," he answered. "Some months afterwards I was a guest in an old house in Fifeshire, and was given the turret room. On the second night I went to bed early, as I had been at golf all day and felt awfully dead beat. I must have fallen asleep suddenly, as I left my candle burning on the table. All of a sudden I woke up with a start to find the now familiar figure of the "White Lady" at the foot of my bed. She was gazing at me intently. When I sat up she glided away behind the screen at the door. I jumped up, put on my dressing-gown, seized the candle, and made for the door. The lady was gone, and the door was as I left it when I went to bed — locked. I unlocked it, flung it open, and looked into the passage. There she was. I saw the white dress, the splendid hair, the rosary, and the gold locket quite plainly. She turned her lovely face to me and smiled a sweet, pathetic smile; gently raised her hand, and floated away towards the picture gallery. Now for the end. Next day my kind hostess took me through the old gallery. I saw pictures of all ages, sorts, and sizes ; but imagine my amazement when I saw 'The White Lady' - the same white dress, the lovely sweet face and splendid eyes, the rosary, and a locket, which I now saw had on it the arms of Queen Mary and Lord Darnley. 'Who on earth is that?' I asked.

"'You seem interested in that painting,' said Mrs ------.

"Well, that is a portrait of one of the lovely Mary Stuart's Maries. She was madly in love with Castelar, the French minstrel, and after he was beheaded at St Andrews she became a nun, and it is said died of grief in her nunnery."

"That is all, old boy," he said, "and it is late. I think it seems right; *that* girl I and my sister saw *must* have been the spirit of Marie --- ; and perhaps it was she who was the occupant of that haunted tower - who knows? but I shall never, never see such a divinely beautiful face on this earth again."

# The Beckoning Monk

MANY years ago, about the time of the Tay bridge gale, I was staying at Edinburgh with a friend of mine, an actor manager. I had just come down from the paint-room of the theatre, and was emerging from the stage-door, when I encountered Miss Elsie H ------, a then well-known actress.

"You are just the very person I wanted to meet," she said. "Allow me to introduce you to my friend, Mr Spencer Ashton. He's not an actor, he's an artist, and he's got such a queer story about ghosts and things near your beloved St. Andrews."

I bowed to Mr Ashton, who was a quiet-looking man, pale and thin, rather like a benevolent animated hairpin. He reminded me somehow of *[Fred Vokes.]*[xcviii] We shook hands warmly.

Fred Vokes

"Yes," he said, "my story sounds like fiction, but it is a fact, as I can prove. It is rather long, but it may possibly interest you. Where could we foregather?"

"Come and dine with me at the Edinburgh Hotel to-night at eight. I'll get a private room," I said.

"Right oh!" said he, and we parted.

That evening at eight o'clock we met at the old Edinburgh Hotel (now no longer in existence), and, after dinner, he told me his very remarkable tale.

"Some years ago," he said, "I was staying in a small coastal town in Fife, not very far from St. Andrews. I was painting some quaint houses and things of the sort that tickled my fancy at the time, and I was very much amused and excited by some of the bogie tales told me by the fisher folk. One story particularly interested me."

"And what was that?" I asked.

"Well, it was about a strange, dwarfish, old man, who, they swore, was constantly wandering about among the rocks at nightfall; a queer, uncanny

---

[xcviii] Fred or Frederick Vokes was a famous Drury Lane Theatre actor and dancer. 1846 – 1888, which Linskill based this character on. His name isn't mentioned in some later editions of this book, being substituted for '*a friend*'.

creature they said, who was 'aye beckoning to them' and who was never seen or known in the daylight. I heard so much at various times and from various people about this old man that I resolved to look for him and see what his game really was. I went down to the beach times without number, but saw nothing worse than myself, and I was almost giving the job up as hopeless, when one night 'I struck oil,' as the Yankees would say."

"Good," I said, "let me hear."

"It was after dusk," he proceeded, "very rough and windy, but with a feeble moon peeping out at times between the racing clouds. I was alone on the beach. Next moment I was *not* alone."

"Not alone," I remarked, "Who was there?"

"Certainly not alone," said Ashton. "About three yards from me stood a quaint, short, shrivelled, old creature. At that time the comic opera of 'Pinafore'[xcix] was new to the stage-loving world, and this strange being resembled the character of 'Dick Deadeye' in that piece. But this old man was much uglier and more repulsive. He wore a tattered monk's robe, had a fringe of black hair, heavy black eyebrows, very protruding teeth, and a pale, pointed, unshaven chin. Moreover, he possessed only one eye, which was large and telescopic looking [penetrating]."

"What a horrible brute," I said

"Oh! he wasn't half so bad after all," said Ashton, "though his appearance was certainly against him. He kept beckoning to me with a pale, withered hand, continually muttering, 'Come.' I felt compelled to follow him, and follow him I did."

I lit up another pipe and listened intently.

"He took me," resumed Ashton, "into a natural cave, a cleft in the rocks, and we went stumbling over the rocks and stones, and splashing into pools. At least I did. He seemed to get alone all right. At the far end of this clammy cave, a very narrow stair, cut out of solid rock, ascended abruptly about twenty or thirty steps, then turned a corner and descended again into a large passage. Then a mighty queer thing happened."

"What might that be?" I enquired.

"Well, my guide somehow or other suddenly became possessed of a huge great candlestick with a lighted candle in it, about three feet high, which lit up the vaulted passage.

"'We now stand in the monk's sub-way,' he said.

---

[xcix] HMS Pinafore by Arthur Sullivan and W. S. Gilbert. May 1878. Some 18 months before the Tay Bridge disaster.

"'Indeed, and who may you be? Are you a man or a ghost?'

"The queer figure turned, 'I am human,' he said, 'do not fear me. I *was* a monk years ago, now I am reincarnate – time and space are nothing whatever to me. I only arrived a short while ago from Naples to meet you here.'

"Good heavens, Ashton," I said, "is this all true?"

"Absolutely true, my dear fellow," said Ashton. "I was in my sound senses, not hypnotised or anything of that sort, I assure you. On and on we went, the little man with his big candle leading the way, and I following. Two or three times the sub-way narrowed, and we had a tight squeeze to get through, I can tell you."

"What a rum place," I interjected.

"Yes, it was that," said Ashton, "but it got still rummer as we went up and down more stairs, and then popped through a hole into a lower gallery, and I noticed side passages branching off in several different directions.

"'Walk carefully and look where you tread,' said my monkish guide. 'There are pitfalls here; be very wary.'

"Then I noticed at my feet a deep, rock-hewn pit about two feet wide right across the passage. 'What is that for?' I asked. 'To trap intruders and enemies,' said the little monk. '*Look down.*' I did so, and I saw at the bottom, in a pool of water, a whitened skull and a number of bones. We passed four or five such shafts in our progress."

"Upon my word, this beats me altogether," I interpolated.

"It would have beaten me altogether if I had fallen into one of those traps," said Ashton. "Suddenly the close, damp, fungus sort of air changed and I smelt a sweet fragrant odour. 'I smell incense,' I said to the monk.

"'It is the wraith, or ghost, of a smell,' he said. 'There has been no incense hereaway since 1546. There are ghosts of sounds and smells, just as there are ghosts of people. We are here surrounded by spirits, but they are transparent, and you cannot see them unless they are materialised, but you can feel them.'

"'Hush, hark!' said the monk, and then I heard a muffled sound of most beautiful chiming bells, the like I had never heard before.

"'What is that?'

"'The old bells of St. Andrews Cathedral. That is the ghost of sounds long ago ceased,' and the monk muttered some Latin. Then all of a sudden I heard very beautiful chanting for a moment or more, then it died away.

"'That is the long dead choir of monks chanting vespers,' remarked my guide, sadly.

"At this moment the monk and I entered a large, rock-hewn chamber, wide and lofty. In it there were numerous huge old iron clamped chests of different sizes and shapes.

"'These, said the monk, 'are packed full of treasures, jewels and vestments. They will be needed again someday. Above us *now* there are ploughed fields, but long ago right over our heads there existed a church and monastery to which these things belonged.' He pointed with a skinny claw of a hand to one corner of the chamber. 'There,' he said, 'is the stair that once led to the church above.'"

Ashton stopped and lit a cigar, then resumed.

"well, on we went again, turning, twisting, going up steps, round corners, through more holes, and stepping over pitfall shafts. It was a loathsome and gruesome place.

"Out of a side passage I saw a female figure glide quickly along. She was dressed as a bride for a wedding; then she disappeared.

"Fear not, said the monk, 'that is Mirren of Hepburn's Tower,[c] the White Lady. She can materialise herself and appear when she chooses, but she is not re-incarnate as I am.'

"Well, after we had gone on it seemed for hours, as I have described, the monk paused.

"'I fear I must leave you,' he said, suddenly. 'I am wanted. Before I go, take this,' and he placed in my hand a tiny gold cup delicately chased; 'it is a talisman and will bring you good luck always,' he said. 'Keep it safe, I may never see you again here, but do not forget.'

"Then I was alone in black darkness. He and his candle had vanished in a second. Quite alone in that awful prison, heaven only knows how far below the ground, I could never have gone back, and I feared to go forward. I was entombed in a worse place that the Roman Catacombs, with no hope of rescue, as it was unknown and forgotten by all."

"What a fearful position to be in," I said.

"I should think it was," said Ashton, "The awful horror of it I can never forget as long as I live. I was absolutely powerless and helpless. I had lost my nerve, and I screamed aloud in an agony of mind. I had some matches, and these I used at rare intervals, crawling carefully and feeling my way along the slimy floor of the passage. I had a terrible feeling, too, that something intangible, but horrible, was crawling along after me and stopping when I

---

[c] His reference here is to Princess Mirren. She was a Pictish Princess who is said to be the first to have been buried …refer to the White Lady of the Haunted Tower, p.130

stopped. I heard it breathing. I struck a match, and it was lucky, for I just missed another of those pitfalls. By the light of the match I saw a small shrine in an alcove which had once been handsomely ornamented. My progress forward was suddenly stopped by a gruesome procession of skeleton monks all in white. They crossed the main sub-way from one side passage and entered another. Their heads were all grinning skulls, and in their long bony fingers they bore enormous candles, which illuminated the passage with a feeble blue glare."

"It's awful," I remarked.

"On, and on, I slowly went. It seemed hours and hours. I was exhausted and hungry and thirsty. After a time I passed through open oak and nail-studded doors that were rotting on their hinges, and then – *then*, I saw a *sight so horrible* that I would never mention it to anyone. I dare not, I may know its meaning someday – I hope so –"

"What on earth was it?" I inquired eagerly.

"For heaven's sake let me go on and do not ask about it," said Ashton, turning ghastly pale. "The horror of the whole thing so upset me that my foot slipped, and I fell down what seemed to be a steep stairway. As I struck the bottom I felt my left wrist snap, and I fainted. When I regained my senses for a brief moment, I found that the White Lady, bearing a taper, was bending kindly over me. She had a lovely face, but as pale as white marble. She laid an icy cold hand on my hot brow, and then all was darkness again.

"Now listen! Next time I came to myself and opened my eyes I was out of the accursed passage. I saw the sky and the stars, and I felt a fresh breeze blowing. Oh! Joy, I was back on the earth again, that I knew. I staggered feebly to my feet, and where on earth do you think I found I had been lying?"

"I cannot guess," I said.

"Just inside the archway of the Pends gateway at St. Andrews,"[ci] said Ashton. "How on earth did you get there?"

"Heaven knows," said Ashton. "I expect the White Lady helped me somehow. It all seemed like a fearful nightmare, but I had the gold cup in my pocket and my broken wrist to bear testimony to what I had gone through. To make a long story short, I went home to my people, where I lay for six long weeks suffering from brain fever and shock. I always carry the cup with me. I am not superstitious; but it brings me good luck *always*."

Ashton showed me the monk's gold cup. It was a beautiful little relic.

---

[ci] His reference here is to the tunnel which was discovered in 1894. Linskill was desperately hoping its discovery would be the subterranean passageways he had always longed to discover, but alas it turned out to be a mediaeval latrine!

"Did you ever examine the place where you entered the passage?" I asked.

"Oh, yes," he replied, "I went there some years afterwards and found the cave, but it has all fallen in now."

"By Jove! It's very late, thanks for the dinner, I must be off. Good night."

I lit a pipe and pondered over that curious story. The entrance to the passage in the cave has fallen in; the exit from it in St. Andrews is unknown to Ashton – only the White Lady knows.

On the whole, the story is wrapped in mystery, and does not help one much to unravel the wonders that lie in underground St. Andrews. We may know some day or never.

# The Bewitched Ermentrude

Very many years ago now I was sauntering down historic old South Street one November afternoon, my object being to lunch in one of the quaint houses with my old time friend, Harold Slitherwick. Lunch was not, however, the main object of my visit, but to meet a man called Reginald Saedegar, an ex-Indian judge, who had actually seen a genuine spirit or ghost.

It is a sad, nay, a melancholy fact (for I have been told this by the very best authorities) that *I am not Psychic*, despite the fact that I have spent days and nights in gloomy, grimly-haunted chambers and ruins, and even a lonesome Halloween night on the summit of St Rule's ancient Tower (my only companions being sandwiches, matches, some cigars, and the necessary and indispensable flask), yet, alas! I have *never* heard or seen anything the least abnormal, or felt the necessary, or much-talked-of mystic presence.

Arriving at the old mansion, I was duly ushered in by Slitherwick's butler, one Joe Bingworthy, a man with the manner and appearance of an archbishop, and from whom one always seemed to expect a sort of pontifical blessing.

There were several fellows there, and I was speedily made known to Saedeger, a very cheery, pleasant little person, with dark hair and big eyebrows.

There was a very heated discussion going on when I entered as to what was really a properly constituted Cathedral. Darkwood was shouting, "No Bishop's Chair, *no* Cathedral." "If," he said, "a Bishop had his chair in a tiny chapel, it was a Cathedral, but if a religious building was as big as the Crystal Palace, and there was no Bishop's Chair there, it was not one bit a Cathedral."

I stopped this discussion suddenly by asking Saedegar about his ghost, and was told I would hear the whole story after lunch.

Before we adjourned to the smoke room Saedeger was telling us he felt a bit knocked up with his long journey. He had a thirty-six hours' journey after he left good old Tony-Pandy. Visions of "Tony Lumpkin," and "Tony Faust," in "My Sweetheart," flitted through my brain, then I suddenly remembered, luckily, that "Tony-pandy" was a town in Wales.

Once comfortably seated in the smoke-room with pipes, cigars, and whisky, Reginald Saedeger became at once the centre of all the interest.

"Lots of years ago," he said, in a quiet legal voice, "I came to visit some friends in St. Andrews, and I had a most unaccountable experience. I will tell you all about it. I never saw anything supernatural before, and have never seen anything the least remarkable since; but one night, my first night in that house, I undoubtedly saw the wraith of the 'Blue Girl.'"

"What had you for supper that evening?" I mildly asked.

"Only chicken and salad," was the reply. "I was not thinking of anything ghostly. If you fix your mind *intently* on one thing, as some folk can, you can self-hypnotise yourself. I had no idea but golf in my mind when I went off to roost."

"Well, drive ahead," said I.

"I had a charming, comfortable, big old-world room given me, nice fire, and all that sort of thing," continued Saedeger, "and as I was deuced tired I soon went to bed and to sleep.

"I woke suddenly, later, with the firm conviction that a pair of eyes were fixed on me. I suppose everyone knows that if you stare fixedly at any sleeping person, they will soon awake. I got a start when I half-opened my eyes, for leaning on the mantelpiece staring hard at me in the mirror was a most beautiful girl in a light blue gauzy dress, her back, of course, was to the bed, and I saw she had masses of wavy, golden-brown hair hanging down long past her waist.

"I was utterly astonished, and watched the movements of this beautiful creature with my eyes almost closed. I felt sure it was someone in the house having a lark at my expense, so pretended to be asleep. As I watched, the girl turned round and faced me, and I marvelled at the extraordinary loveliness of her figure and features. I wondered if she was a guest in the house, and what she was doing wandering about at that time of night, and if she was sleep-walking? She then glided – it certainly *was not walking* – to a corner of the room, and then I noticed that her feet were bare. She seemed to move along above the carpet – not on it – a curious motion. She drifted, and stood beneath a big picture, took out a key and opened a small aumbrey, or cupboard, in the wall quite noiselessly. And from this receptacle she took out some small things that glittered in her pretty fingers, long taper fingers."

"How on earth did you contrive to see all that in a dark bedroom?" I sarcastically inquired.

"The room wasn't dark," said Saedeger. "I always keep the light burning in a strange house and in a strange room."

"Oh, I see," I replied. "Go on."

"Well," continued Reginald Saedeger, "she then turned and came towards the bed, and I got a more distinct view of her. I had never seen anyone a bit like her before; it was an utterly unforgettable face. I have certainly never before, or since, seen anyone as pretty as she was – yet it was a strange, unearthly beauty, and her huge forget-me-not blue eyes were a perfection of pathos. Nearer, and yet nearer, she came, and when quite close to the bed, she bent over me and raised her hand with the glittering thing in it high over my head. Then I made a tremendous spring out of bed, crying loudly, 'Now I'll see who is trying to frighten me.' I flung out my arms to grasp her, but they closed on nothing, and to my utter astonishment I saw her standing smiling at me on the opposite side of the room.

"That was odd and uncanny enough, but then she gradually began to disappear, dissolving into a thin blue-grey mist, until nothing whatever remained – I was absolutely alone in the room and dumfoundered"

"What next?" I asked.

"Well! what could I do or think?" said Saedeger. "I was fairly flabbergasted at the unexpected turn of events. I admit I felt shaky, so I took a stiff whisky and soda, smoked a pipe, and went back to bed to reflect on the matter, and fell asleep. I was wakened in the morning by my host, Harold Slitherwick, walking into the room carrying a pony brandy for me."

"Well, old blighter, how have you slept?" he asked.

"Then I told him about the blue girl."

"Bless my heart! Have you seen her too? Lots of people, my wife among the number, declare they have seen her; but as you have seen her now, I really begin to believe there is some truth in the tale."

"I then told my host there was no dubiety about the matter, and pointed out the place under the picture where there was a cupboard. We both went and looked. There was no cupboard to be seen."

"Very rum thing," said my host; "there was a murder once took place in this room ages ago. Perhaps the blue lady had something to do with it; but let us hunt for your cup- board."

"On rapping with our knuckles on the wall we found a hollow spot, scraped off the paper, and there sure enough was the little door I had seen. We soon forced it open, and discovered a receptacle, about a foot square, going very deep into the thick stone wall. There were a lot of things in that place, scissors, a thimble, a dagger, a work-box, and a lot of old musty, dusty papers. And then we found a long tress of ruddy-gold hair in an envelope and a beautiful miniature magnificently painted on ivory of the blue girl I had seen – every detail, the face, the dress, the hair, and the bare feet, were perfectly exact. On both the envelope and the miniature were written the names 'Ermentrude Ermengarde Annibal Beaurepaire,' with the date 1559.

"We then examined the old documents which gave us some clue to the mystery. It was a very long story that we had to read over, but I will tell it to you briefly. Long ages ago this ancient house was the property of a Frenchman, Monsieur Louis Beaurepaire. He had an only and lovely daughter of twenty, named Ermentrude Ermengarde Annibal Beaurepaire, who was intended to be a bride of the Church, otherwise a nun. This idea, apparently, did not appeal to her views. She passionately loved a young student, and was equally beloved by him, whose name was Eugene Malvoisine.

"All went well it seems, for two years, and they were to be married in the Cathedral at Easter. All the arrangements were complete for the nuptials; but fortune is a fickle jade, and willed it otherwise. A rival turned up on the scene in the person of Marie de Mailross, a cousin of the Beaurepaires, and a frequent guest at their house. Ermentrude found that her beloved Eugene had proved faithless, and transferred his youthful affections to the lovely Marie, and that a speedy elopement was pending.

"Ermentrude went and consulted a wise woman, otherwise a witch, who resided in Argyll, outwith the Shoegate Port.[cii] This witch, by name 'Alistoun Brathwaite,' used her evil powers on the fair Ermentrude, and enraged her jealousy to fury and a desire for revenge, and presented her with a potion, and a cunning, well-wrought dagger.

"The witch threw a spell over Ermentrude, and took all the good within her away, and implanted evil passions within her breast. It seems that Marie of Mailross slept in this old room, and one night Ermentrude, willed by the witch, went to Marie's bedside, and planted the dagger in her heart, and she died. It seems Ermentrude disappeared, and was never seen or heard of again, and was supposed to have drowned herself at the Maiden Rock — hence the name it bears.

"That," said Saedeger, "is my quaint tale. The room I slept in was the very room in which in ages past, Marie was done to death by Ermentrude, and it seems to have been my lot to see Ermentrude and discover the secret that lay in that old cupboard."

We all thanked Saedeger, and after thoughtfully consuming a few more whiskies and sodas, and a few more cigars, went off to the Links pondering deeply.

---

[cii] The West Port. The Shoegate was an old name for South Street.

A brief introduction to Linskill's next story
# The Hauntings and Mysteries of Lausdree Castle

This next tale is all about Lausdree Castle near St. Andrews. If you have read this story before you will realise there is a problem – or perhaps not so much a problem as a niggling in the back of the mind as there is when reading much of Linskill's work. We know Lausdree Castle doesn't exist and Linskill's story is a work of fiction, yet I am sure many over the years have wondered if it could be based on an existing castle – and if this were the case, what castle might it be?

So as an exercise, I thought I would see if there was a real Lausdree Castle, if there was something close by that Linskill might have used as partial inspiration for his story. There are no castles or any dwellings in Fife that pack in the ghosts and ghouls in quite the same way as Linskill does here, but I did find one castle not far from St. Andrews which does share in a few correlations – albeit tentatively. So as a suggestive and quite possibly romantic candidate for Linskill's Lausdree Castle I propose Earlshall Castle near Leuchars.

I have found Balgonie Castle south east of the Lomond Hills to be the most haunted castle in Fife and indeed the most haunted dwelling in Fife, but the associations there are different; it doesn't fit the bill with some of what Linskill writes here quite as closely.

It does give another angle to a story Linskill wrote as a piece of fictionalised fireside entertainment. On one level he didn't necessarily mean to be taken seriously, but having researched Linskill, he had a habit of masking truth in fiction, and he was subtle with his references. A lot of them are too obscure to spot as they will have been in-jokes for those he knew, and some of his inferences might have made complete sense at the time, but a century later are now lost. It is all there for the taking though and what I have missed I am sure others will pick up on. As I mention in my analysis of the White Lady,[ciii] his stories occasionally include clues as to his sources of inspiration, and these could well be shared between a mix of fiction and fact. I have included seven possible correlations with Earlshall through seven pages of the chapter. Alongside the correlations with Earlshall, he draws his inspiration from Lordscairnie Castle together with a well known Demon from the old grimoires and a South Street apparition. One of the inferences in his book which supports the theory of Earlshall being an inspiration for Lausdree is from a later Linskill chapter called *The Spectre of the Castle* which begins with a letter to Linskill as follows:

---

[ciii] Refer to *A St. Andrews Mystery* (2014)

Lausdree Castle,

SIR, - Yours to command. Sir, I have not forgot our pleasant talk on that snowy night up in the far north, when you were pleased to be interested in my experiences of Lausdree. Could you very kindly meet me any day and time you choose to fix at Leuchars? And oblige. Your obedient servant,

Jeremiah Anklebone

Further details of Earlshall Castle can be found in my companion book *Ghosts of Fife* (2013)

# The Hauntings and Mysteries of Lausdree Castle

It is many years ago since I was on a walking tour in the Highlands, far to the north of Bonnie Glenshee; and when on the moorlands I was overtaken for my sins, by a regular American snowstorm – a genuine blizzard of the most pronounced type. I struggled along as well as I could for some considerable time, and then I became aware that someone was beside me. It was a young Highland lassie with a plaid over her head. I was pleased to learn from her that her name was "Jean," that she was the niece of a neighbouring innkeeper, and that she would speedily convey me to his haven of rest. We trudged along in the blinding snow without a word, and I was more than thankful to the lassie when I at last found myself out of the snow in a nice little sanded parlour with a glorious fire of peat and logs blazing on the hospitable hearth. A glass of something hot, brought by mine host, was most welcome.

I found there was one other storm-stayed traveller in the wee house, an old family butler, whose name I discovered was Jeremiah Anklebone[civ]. He had been on a visit to relations in the North, *[and had been caught in the snow like myself. We were both]* thankful to find such a warm, cosy shanty on such an inclement evening, and, to use a Scots term, we foregathered at the ingle inside.

He asked me if I knew much about spirits, to which I replied that I had just had a glass, but he at once explained that although not averse to toddy, he alluded to spirits of another nature, viz., ghosts, banshees, boggards, and the like.

I told him I had frequently been in so-called haunted places in various countries, but had never seen or heard anything except owls, bats, rats, and mice.

He ventured the remark I had often heard before, that I could not be receptive, and I told him I was thankful that I was not.

---

[civ] As I mentioned in the introduction to this book regarding Linskill, he has a particular Dickensian touch when it comes to dishing out the humorous names. The name anklebone however through this story may have a clue as an inference to something else. The ghost of 'Bloody' Bruce at Earlshall Castle is said to 'snatch at your ankle in the gloaming, as you go up or down the worn turret stair.' It is one of the most famous paranormal features of the castle. Was he giving us a clue by calling the butler of his fictitious castle Anklebone?

He was a fine old fellow, an ideal family butler, and doubtless the recipient of many family secrets. He had big mutton-chop whiskers and a bald head, and looked as if he had served turtle soup all his life; but it was *not* soup he was soaked with – he seemed fairly saturated with spook lore. He informed me, quite calmly, that he was gifted with the remarkable faculty of seeing apparitions, demons, etc.

I could not help remarking that it seemed a very unpleasant faculty to possess, but he quite differed with me, and got as warm as his toddy on the subject. I shall not in a hurry forget that wild evening in the Highland inn before that blazing fire, or the wonderful narrations I heard from Butler Anklebone. Space precludes me from putting down here *all* the marvels he revealed to me.

It seemed all his life – he was 62 – he had been gasping like a fish on a river's bank to get into a really well-haunted house, but had utterly failed till he took the post of head butler at Lausdree Castle, which he informed me was but a short distance from St. Andrews. He gave me a most tremendous description of the old castle, and from his account it seemed to be the asylum and gathering place of *all* the bogies in Britain and elsewhere. Congregated together there were the Ice Maid, the Brown Lady, a headless man, a cauld lad, a black maiden, the Flaming Ghost, the Wandering Monk, a ghost called Silky, auld Martha, a radiant boy, an iron knight, a creeping ghost, jumping Jock, old No-legs, Great Eyes, a talking dog, the Corbie Craw, a floating head,[cv] a dead hand, bleeding footprints, and many other curious creatures far too numerous to mention.

The castle, he said, was full of uncouth and most peculiar sights and sounds, including rappings, hammerings, shrieks, groans, crashings, wailings, and the like.

"What a remarkable place," I said to Mr Butler Anklebone, "and how do you account for so many spectres in so limited an area?"

"Oh! there is no time or space for them," he said, "they are earth-bound spirits, and can go from one part of the globe to another in a second; but they have their favourite haunts and meeting places just as we folks have, and Lausdree seems to appeal to their varied tastes."

He then went on to tell me some details of the Haunted Castle. "There are supposed to be," he said, "beneath the castle splendid old apartments, dungeons, winding passages, and cellars; but history states that any of those

---

[cv] This is probably a reference to *the floating Head in a South Street flat*. Refer to p.165

persons who tried to investigate these mysteries *returned no more*, so the entrances were walled up, and are now completely lost sight of.

"There is a built-up chamber, but no one durst open it, the penalty being total blindness or death, and such cases are on record. There is also a coffin room shaped exactly like its name; but one of the queerest places at Lausdree is a small apartment with a weird light of its own. At night this room can be seen from the old garden, showing a pale, uncanny, phosphorescent glow.[cvi]

"Mr Snaggers – that's the footman - and I unlocked the door and examined the place carefully. There was a table, a sofa, and a few old chairs therein, and an all-pervading sickly light equally diffused. The furniture throws no shadows whatever. The room seemed very chilly, and there was a feeling as if all one's vitality was being sucked out of one's body, and drawing one's breath caused pain. Snaggers felt the same. No one could live long in that eerie apartment. I know we were glad to lock it up again.

"Then there is a spiral stair, called 'Meg's Leg.' I don't know the legend, but almost every night one hears her leg stumping up these steps."[cvii]

"What a creepy place it must be, to be sure," I murmured, gravely.

"Yes!" said Anklebone, "and I tell you sir, Snaggers and I generally arranged to go up to bed together; one always felt there was something coming up the stairs behind one. When a person stopped, it stopped also, and one could hear it breathing and panting, but nothing was to be seen. Snaggers, one night when the candle went out, said he saw monstrous red eyes, but I saw nothing then. The creeping creature I only saw twice, it was like an enormous toad on spider's legs. They say it has a human head and face, but I only saw its back.[cviii] Some folks say it is alive and not a ghost, and that it hides somewhere in the cellars, but we never could get a trace of it. One night I was going down to the service room when my way was barred by a ghastly, tall figure, with great holes where eyes should have been, so I just shut my eyes and rushed through it downstairs. When I got down, I found all my clothes were covered with a vile, sickly-smelling, sticky sort of oil, and I had to destroy them all."

"Go on, please," I said, "you astonish me vastly,"

---

[cvi] At Earlshall strange blue lights have been seen within the castle with no apparent source.

[cvii] Also at Earlshall heavy footsteps have been heard on the turret stairwell.

[cviii] This is somewhat reminiscent of the Demon Baal. One of the 7 Princes of Hell. Described in *Dictionnarie Infernal* by Collin de Plancy, 1818, as having three heads and spiders legs. The three heads are of a man, a toad and a cat. If this demon does indeed have any reality it is certainly no ghost – Linskill was an antiquarian and will have known this.

"Yes," he said slowly, "It's all very queer. Lausdree is haunted and no mistake. Snaggers and I shared the same room. One night a great blood-stained hand and arm came round the corner of the bed curtain and tried to grab me. It was dead ice-cold too. Then a thing, an invisible thing, used to patter into the room, puffing and groaning, and get under the bed and heave it up, but we looked and there was never anything there, *[and the door locked too]*. We saw a great black corkscrew thing one night fall from the ceiling on to the floor and disappear, and then there was a mighty rush along the passage. Outside the door a great crash, a yell, and a groan dying away far below. There was a humorous spirit also, the Iron Knight. We called him 'Uncle.' He was up to tricks. We didn't mind him. When the fat cook was sitting down to a meal, he'd pull back her chair, and down she would come with a rare crash. If any of the maids upset a tray of tea-things, or fell downstairs with the kettle, or knocked over the great urn, they used to say – 'Oh! That's Uncle again!'"

I told him (Mr Anklebone) that I was delighted there was a touch of comedy in such a gruesome place, as I preferred comedians to ghosts any day. One thing I learnt from his story, and that was, that if he was head butler at Lausdree Castle, the head ghost was Sir Guy Ravelstocke, whose portrait still hung in the old picture gallery. The castle dated back to Norman times,[cix] but about 1457 it fell into the hands of this Sir Guy Ravelstocke, who had been educated at the "Stadium Generale," or University of Saint Andrews. He and his two friends, Geoffrey De Beaumanoir and Roger Le Courville, held high revel and carnival in the old halls of Lausdree, and were the terror of the whole countryside. Sir Guy was a dissolute fellow, a gambler, and everything else bad. The neighbours alleged that he had sold himself to Old Nick.[cx] He would spill blood as if it was water, and he and his white steed, "Nogo," were well known all over Fife and the Lothians. He was held to be a free-booter, a wizard and a warlock, a highwayman, a pirate, and a general desperado. He had slain many men in mortal combat, and was found invulnerable.[cxi]

"He must have been a sort of Michael Scott of Balwearie," I remarked.

"He must have been a holy terror," said the butler. "I've seen him often, exactly like his portrait in the picture gallery. I've seen him in his old-world

---

[cix] While Earlshall Castle is not of Norman origin, the nearby Church of St. Athernase in Leuchars village dating back to the 12th century is of Norman origin.

[cx] This is a reference to Earl Beardie of a different castle; Lordscairnie Castle whose legend has him playing cards with the Devil and on losing the Devil takes his soul. Refer to my companion book *Ghosts of Fifes* (2013).

[cxi] This is quite possibly the 16th century Sir Andrew 'Bloody' Bruce of Earlshall.

dress with his sword hanging at his side, sometimes on his white horse and sometimes on foot.

"There were always terrible knockings, shrieks, and crashes before he appeared, and all our dogs showed the greatest terror. I slept in an old four-poster bed, and he used to draw aside the curtain and glare at me constantly. He nearly always was accompanied by the spectre of a negro carrying his head under his arm. Sir Guy was a great traveller in foreign lands, and, I have been told, used to bring back all sorts of curious animals and insects with him.[cxii] Perhaps that great toad thing I saw was one of the creatures. I've heard toads live for ages."

I said I believed that was quite true.

"I found a queer place one day," said Anklebone. "I was going up the turret staircase, and found some of the steps moved back. I got Mr Snaggers and Darkgood, the gardener, and we tugged them out. We called the master, and then we found narrow steps going down to a locked door. We forced it open, and got into a stone chamber. There were skulls and bones all over the place. Most of them belonged to animals, but there was a horrible thing on the floor, a sort of mummified vampire bat, with huge teeth and enormous outstretched wings, like thick parchment, and four legs. Perhaps it was a regular vampire. They fanned folks to sleep with their great wings, and then sucked their blood dry. We cleared out the room, and buried all the things in a wood.

"Now," said Anklebone, "I will tell you the end of Sir Guy Ravelstocke. He brought back with him from them foreign parts a negro servant, and they called him the 'Apostle'. Well, one night," he and his chums were dining, and full of wine, and the 'A – Postal' offended them somehow, and Sir Guy stabbed him. Then they chained his hands and feet together, took him to the dungeon, and filled his mouth, nose, and ears full of clay and left him. That is the negro ghost I saw always with Sir Guy – the murdered negro.

"About two years after, Sir Guy and his friends were in the same room drinking when there came a great hammering at the castle door. Sir Guy drew his sword, flung open the door, and plunged out into the darkness. A few moments passed then his friends rushed out on hearing wild unearthly shrieks, but there was no Sir Guy to be seen, he had totally disappeared, and was never

---

[cxii] The Long Hall of Earlshall Castle was described by Russell Kirk as having a 'strange panelled hall with its painting of Princes and marvellous beasties.'

heard of or seen in life again.[cxiii] We found his remains three years ago, but I will tell you of that directly. One day Snaggers and I had gone to St. Andrews to buy things. We were just at the end of South Street when a horseman dashed past us at full gallop. 'Heavens,' said Snaggers, 'it's Sir Guy as I live.' He went bang into the big iron gates at the Cathedral. When we came up the great gates were locked, and there was Sir Guy leaning up against the west gable scowling at us, but the white horse had gone, and he melted away as we looked. I saw him again with the negro at Magus Muir, and alone one dark night in North Street.

"I was alone one evening in the room below the banquet hall at Lausdree and heard a pattering on the table. On looking up I saw a stain in the ceiling, and drops of blood were dropping down on the table and the floor. The room above was the very place where the negro was stabbed. Next morning we went into the room where I saw the blood drip, and there was the mark of a bloody hand on the table, but no stain on the roof.

"Now for the discovery. I had often dreamed about an old overgrown well there was in the gardens, and felt very suspicious of what might be therein.[cxiv] Then the gardener and the woodman told me they had frequently seen the awful spectre of Sir Guy and the 'Apostle' hovering round about the thicket that enclosed what was known as the haunted well, and then vanish in the brushwood without disturbing it. I felt sure that there lay the mystery of Sir Guy Ravelstocke. This idea was soon after confirmed by a curious occurrence. One morning Snaggers was dusting an old oil painting over the huge mantelpiece, and above the weeping stone in the great hall, when somehow or other he contrived to touch a secret spring and the painting flew back and revealed a chamber beyond.

"We sent for Master, and got down by some steps into the room. Such a queer place! It was octagonal in shape, and there had been either a great fire or an explosion there. The vaulted stone roof and floor were all blackened and cracked, and the fireplace and wood-panelling were all burnt and charred."

"Perhaps the chapel," I remarked.

"That is what Master said," replied the butler, "and there were remains of burnt tapestry, charred wood, and documents all over the stone floor. Master

---

[cxiii] This again is a reference to Earl Beardie when the Devil first appeared to him in his castle and he reached for his sword. At the end of the night when he had lost at cards, the Devil had his soul and Earl Beardie disappeared from mortal gaze.

[cxiv] Earlshall Castle has an ancient well in the garden with a very elaborate iron well head.

got one piece of burnt paper with faded writing on it in some foreign tongue. The odd thing was the big picture. The eyes were sort of convex like, and two holes were bored in the pupil of each of its eyes, so that anyone standing up on top of the stone stairs could see all that took place in the great hall below, and hear also.

"Master took the piece of parchment and managed to make out a few words. They were – 'I am sure that Ravelstocke lies in the old Prior's Well, with the dead negro servant we placed there. I would not go near that spot for my life. Heaven grant *it* may not come for me, I must leave the place.' That was all he could decipher on the burnt paper.

"'We must explore that Prior's Well (evidently that is its name) tomorrow morning,' said our Master. We were all up at dawn, and got all the men available to cut down the shrubs, bushes, and the undergrowth round the well, the growth of ages. When the well was exposed it looked very like the holy well at St. Andrews, only it had been very finely carved and ornamented at one time. The entrance was a Norman archway, and the remains of an oak door still hung there. We found a shallow bath shaped pool of muddy water inside, and a lot of broken stones and bits of old statues and glass. At the far end was a large square opening a few feet above the pool of water. We, of course, made for this, and found there was a cell beyond. The whole wall on one side was riven and rent, either by lightning or the effects of an earthquake shock. If that ancient well could have spoken it would have told us as queer tales as St Rule's Tower at St. Andrews.[cxv] There was a most curious, overpowering, sickening odour inside the place, like a vault or charnel house."

I remarked that I knew no smells worse than acetylene gas or the awful smell I unearthed when digging, long ago, opposite the St. Andrews Cathedral.[cxvi]

"Well," said Anklebone, "I can't imagine a worse odour than there was beside that Prior's Well. It turned us all so faint. We had to get some brandy. We got into the far cell, and there were two skeleton bodies on the flagged floor. One was a blanched skeleton as far as the neck, but the skull was well preserved, and matted black hair still clung on it and round the jaw. All the teeth were in their place. Some rings had fallen from the bony fingers, and a sword, all eaten away by rust, lay beside the skeleton. The other was of a dark

---

[cxv] Referring to the murder of Robert De Montrose.
[cxvi] Meaning maybe the ancient latrine at the top of the Pends Linskill mistook for a subterranean passage, mentioned in my footnote to the end of the last chapter and elsewhere. Perhaps he was meaning the re-opening of the Haunted Tower in 1888.

oak colour, the nails on the fingers and toes being quite perfect. Chains, also almost worn away, hung round the feet and hands.

"'Good Heavens,' said Master, 'it is Sir Guy Ravelstocke and the murdered Apostle!' There was no doubt of that whatever. We had them removed and buried at once. The mystery was solved after all these long years.

"The negro had been placed there, but the mystery of Sir Guy was inexplicable. *Who came for him* that night when he rushed out of the door of Lausdree Castle, centuries ago, with his sword, and who carried him to his doom in the Prior's Well? No one can answer that terrible question now. Oh! that the old well could speak and reveal its secret."[cxvii]

---

[cxvii] Along with the legend of Earl Beardie (Alexander Lindsay, 4th Earl of Crawford and the Devil at Lordscairnie Castle, a parallel legend exists at Glamis Castle in Angus. Alexander Lyon, 2nd Lord Glamis was also known as Earl Beardie and the same story is told there. A secret room was found at Glamis, when towels were hung from all the windows of the castle. They found one window without a towel and traced this to a secret room hidden in the thickness of the castle wall. This is where Earl Beardie was believed to have played cards with the Devil and his bones may still be within the sealed chamber. The ghosts of the Earl Beardie's roam the area of both Glamis and Lordscairnie Castles.

# The Monk of St. Rule's Tower

Some years ago I was perfectly surrounded with crowds of bonny children in the St Albans Holborn district of London. I fancy they belonged to some guild or other, and they enacted the parts of imps, fairies, statues, &c., in various pantomimes in neighbouring theatres.

I had been invited there to amuse the kiddies with songs and imitations, and now they were all shrieking and yelling at the top of their voices for a ghost story. "It's getting near Christmas," they all shouted, "and we all want to hear about ghosts, real creepy ghosts." I pointed out the fact that most ghost stories were bunkum, and that such tales were very apt to keep wee laddies and lassies awake at night; but, bless you, they wouldn't listen to that one bit. They wanted ghosts, and ghosts they would have.

Well, in about an hour I had yarned off most of my best bogie stories. I had used up most of my tales regarding Scottish, English, and Continental castles, and the banshees, water kelpies, wraiths, &c., connected therewith; but still those children, like Oliver Twist, demanded more. I really was fairly stumped, when, all of a sudden, my mind flew back to 1875, when a strange story was told me by Captain Chester in the Coursal grounds at beautiful Baden-Baden. I first fell in with this dear old warrior in Rome, and we became firm friends, and travelled together for many cheery weeks. He told me his queer tale in the very strongest of military language, which I must omit. The language would be suitable to use in bunkers, but not on paper. It was a sultry day. So were his remarks.

It would seem that many years before, he had visited Scotland and England to try and see a ghost or two. He had been to Cumnor Hurst House in order to investigate the appearances of ill-fated Amy Robsart. He went to Rainham Hall to interview the famous Brown Lady, and he journeyed to Hampton Court to hear the Shrieking Ghost, and also went to Church Strelton to see if he could fix the ghost at the Copper Hole. In Scotland he followed the scent of various ghosts, and finally landed in St. Andrews.

"By Jove, sir," he said, "that's the place for ghosts. Every blessed corner is full of them – bang full. Look at those fellows in the castle dungeons, and Beaton and Sharpe and the men that got hanged and burned, and the old dev -- – I mean witches."

*I saw my ghost there.* Years and years ago I took an old house in St. Andrews, which was a small place then. Very little golf was played, and there was very little to do. But, gad, sir, the ghosts were thick, and the quaint old bodies in the town were full of them. They could spin yarns for hours about phantom coaches, death knells, corpse candles, people going about in winding sheets, phantom hearses, and Lord knows what else. I loved it; it took me quite back to the middle ages."

So I told these children Captain Chester's tale, as nearly as possible in his own words, minus the forcible epithets. I managed to hit off his voice and manner, and this in particular seemed to amuse the bairns. "Egad, sir," he said, "it was a curious time. Of all the tales I heard, the one that pleased and fascinated me most was the legend of the monk that looks over St. Regulus's Tower on moonlight nights. I went thither every night, and constantly fancied I saw a figure peering over the edge, but was not certain. Then I got hold of a very old man, who related to me the old legend. It seems that years ago there was a good Prior of St. Andrews named Robert de Montrose. He ruled well, gently, and wisely, but among the monks there was one who was always in hot water, and whom Prior Robert had often to haul over the coals. He played practical jokes, often absented himself from the daily and nightly offices of Holy Kirk, and otherwise upset the rules and discipline. Finally, when Earl Douglas and his retinue came to St. Andrews to present to the Cathedral a costly statue, long known as the Douglas Lady, this monk made desperate love to one of the waiting women of Lady Douglas. For this he was imprisoned in the Priory Dungeon for some days. It was the custom of Robert de Montrose almost every fine night to ascend the tower of St Rule and admire the view. The summit was reached in those days by means of ladders and wooden landings – not, as it is now, by a stair. In those days, too, the apse and part of the nave were still standing, and the summit of the solemn old tower was crowned by a small spire. One evening just before Yuletide, when the Prior, as usual, was on the top of the tower, the contumacious monk slyly followed him up the ladders, stabbed him in the back with a small dagger, and flung him over the north side of the old tower."

"I thought, Captain Chester," I said, "that the murder took place on the Dormitory stairs."

"Gad, Zooks, and Oddbodkins, sir, I am telling you what I was told, and what I can prove, sir."

"All right," I replied, "please fire away."

"Well," continued Chester, "they told me the Prior had often been seen since peeping over the tower, and at times he was seen to fall, as he did years ago, from the summit. By the bye, his assassin was starved to death and buried in some old midden. One moonlight night as my brother and I were standing on the Kirkhill, to our horror and amazement we saw a figure appear suddenly on the top of the tower, leap on to the parapet, and deliberately jump over. Zounds, sir, my blood ran cold."

"We did not hesitate long, but jumped the low wall of the Cathedral. It was easily done in those days, and we were young and active, and hurried to the grim old tower. Just as we neared it, a monk passed us in the Augustinian habit, his cowl was thrown back, and for just one second we had a view of his pallid, handsome face and keen penetrating eyes. Then he disappeared as suddenly as he had appeared. We were alone in the moonlight, nothing stirring."

"That is very odd," I said.

"Zooks! sir, I have odder things still to tell you. We went home to the old house, had supper, and retired to bed thoughtfully. I woke about 2 a.m. The blinds were up and it was as clear as day with the moonlight. Imagine my blank astonishment when I clearly perceived, leaning up against the mantelpiece, the pallid monk I had seen a few hours before near the Square Tower. He leaned on his elbow and was gazing intently at me, while in his hand he held some object that had a blue glitter in the moonbeams.

"He smiled. 'Fear not, brother,' he said, 'I am Prior Robert of Montrose who quitted this earth many years syne, [cxviii] and of whom you have been talking and thinking so much of late days. I saw you tonight in our cruelly ruined Abbey Kirk. Alas! alas! but I come from ayont [cxix] the distant hills and have far to go tonight.'

"'What do you want, Holy Father?' I said, 'and what of your murder?'

"'That is forgiven and forgotten long syne,' he said, 'and I love to revisit, *at times*, my old haunts, and so does he. You have in your regiment, methinks, one named Montrose, a scion of our family.'

"'Yes,' I said, 'I know Bob Montrose well.'

"'See you this dagger I hold,' said Prior Robert, 'it was with this I lost my life on this earth many years syne on the tower of blessed St Rule. They buried it with me in my stone kist; I will leave it here with you to give to my kinsman, for it will prove of use to him e'er he pass hence – mark my words.'

"He raised his hand as in act of blessing, and melted away. I fell back in a sleep or in a faint. When I woke the morning sun was streaming into my bedroom. At first I thought I had eaten too much supper and had a nightmare, but there on the table by my bed lay an old dagger of curious workmanship – the dagger that slew the Prior years and years ago. I faithfully fulfilled my vow,

---

[cxviii] Since
[cxix] Beyond

and my friend, Major Bob Montrose, has now got his monkish ancestor's dagger."

"That's all Captain Chester told me, dear children. Goodbye, don't forget me, and do not forget old St. Andrews Ghosts, the Tower of St Rule, and the Spectre of Prior Robert of Montrose."

Then a modern hansom whirled me away to King's Cross.[cxx]

---

[cxx] Refer to *The Phantom Monks*, p.126

# The Screaming Skull of Greyfriars

I NEVER met a better fellow in the world than my old friend, Allan Beauchamp. He had been educated at Eton, and Magdalene at Oxford, after which he joined a crack regiment, and later on took it into his head to turn doctor. He was a great traveller and a magnificent athlete. There was no game in which he did not excel. Curiously enough, he hated music; he had no ear for it, and he did not know the difference between the airs of "Tommy, make room for your uncle" and "The Lost Chord." He was tremendously proud of his pedigree; he had descended from the de Beauchamps, and one of his ancestors, he gravely informed people, had helped Noah to get the wasps and elephants into the Ark. Another of them seems to have been not very far away in the Garden of Eden. In fact, they seem to have been quite prehistoric. He was quite cracked on the subject of brain transference, telepathy, spiritualism, ghosts, warnings, and the like, and on these points he was most uncanny and fearsome. The literature he had about them was blood curdling. He believed in dual personality, and in visions, horoscopes, and dreams. He showed me a pamphlet he had written, entitled "The Toad-faced Demon of Lone Devil's Dyke." He was always flitting about Britain exploring haunted houses and castles, and sleeping in haunted rooms when it was possible. Some years ago Beauchamp and myself, accompanied by his faithful valet, rejoicing in the name of Pellingham Truffles, went to the Highlands for a bit of quiet and rest, and it was there I heard his curious story of the skull.

We were sitting over a cosy fire after dinner. It was snowing hard outside, and very cold. Our pipes were alight and our grog on the table, when Allan Beauchamp suddenly remarked – "It's a deuced curious thing for a man to be always followed about the place by a confounded grinning skull."

"Eh, what," I said, "who the deuce is being followed about by a skull? It's rubbish, and quite impossible."

"Not a bit," said my friend, "I've had a skull after me more or less for several years."

"It sounds like a remark a lunatic would make," I rejoined rather crossly. "Do not talk bunkum. You'll go dotty if you believe such infernal rot."

"It is not bunkum or rot a bit," said Allan, "It's gospel truth. Ask Truffles, ask Jack Weston, or Jimmy Darkgood, or any of my south country pals."

"I don't know Jack Weston or Jimmy Darkgood," I said, "but tell me the whole story, and some day, if it's good, I'll put it in the *St. Andrews Citizen*."

"It's mostly about St. Andrews," said Beauchamp, "so here goes, but shove on some coals first."

I did so, and then requested him to fire away.

"It was long, long ago, I think about the year 1513, that one of my ancestors, a man called Neville de Beauchamp, resided in Scotland. It seems he was an uncommonly wild dog, went in for racing and cards, and could take his wine and ale with any of them even in those hard-drinking days. He was known as Flash Neville. Later on he married a pretty girl, the daughter of a silk mercer in Perth, who, it seems, died (they said of a broken heart) two years later. Neville de Beauchamp was seized with awful remorse, and became shortly after a monk in Greyfriars Monastery at St. Andrews. After Neville's wife's death, her relations seem to have been on the hunt after him, burning for revenge, and the girl's brother, a rough, wild dog in those stormy days, at last managed to track his quarry down in the monastery at St. Andrews."

"Very interesting," I said, "that monastery stood very nearly on the site of the present infant school, and we found the well in 1880. Well, what did this brother do, eh?"

"It seems that one afternoon after vespers he forced his way into the Monastery Chapel, sought out Neville de Beauchamp, and slashed off his head with a sword in the aisle of the Kirk. Now a queer thing happened – his body fell on the floor, but the severed head, with a wild scream, flew up to the chapel ceiling and vanished through its roof."

"Mighty queer that," I said.

"The body was reverently buried," went on Allan, "but the head never was recovered, and, whirling through the air over the monastery, screaming and groaning most pitifully, it used to cause great terror to the monks and others o' nights. It was a well-known story, and few cared to venture in that locality after nightfall. The head soon became a skull, and since that time has always haunted some member of the house of Beauchamp. Now comes a strange thing. I went a few years ago and lived in rooms at St. Andrews for a change, and while there I heard of my uncle's death somewhere abroad. I had never seen him, but I had frequently heard that he was very much perplexed and worried by the tender attentions paid to him by the skull of Neville de Beauchamp, which was always turning up at odd times and in unexpected places."

"This is a grand tale," I said.

"Now I come on the job," said Allan, ruefully. "That uncle was the very last of our family, and I wondered if that skull would come my way. I felt very ill and nervous after I got the news of my uncle's death. A strange sense of depression and oppression overcame me, and I got very restless. One stormy evening I felt impelled by some strange influence to go out. I wandered about the place for several hours and got drenched. I felt as if I was walking in my sleep, or as if I had taken some drug or other. Then I had a sort of vision - I had just rounded the corner of North Bell Street."

"Now called Greyfriars Garden," I remarked.

"Yes! Well, when I got around that corner I saw a large, strange building before me. I opened a wicket gate and entered what I found to be the chapel; service was over, the lights were being extinguished, and the air was laden with incense. As I knelt in a corner of the chapel I saw the whole scene, the tragedy of which I had heard, enacted all over again. I saw that monk in the aisle, I saw a man rush in and cut off his head. I saw the body fall and the head fly up with a shriek to the roof. When I came to myself I found I was sitting on the low wall of the school.[cxxi] I was very cold and wet, and I got up to go home. As I rose I saw lying on the pavement at my feet what appeared to be a small football. I gave it a vicious kick, when to my horror it turned over and I saw it was a skull. It was gnashing its teeth and moaning. Then with a shriek it flew up in the air and vanished. A horrible thing. Then I knew the worst. The skull of the monk Neville de Beauchamp had attached itself to me for life, I being the last of the race. Since then it is almost always with me."

"Where is it now?" I said, shuddering.

"Not very far away, you bet," he said.

"It's a most unpleasant tale," I said. "Good night, I'm off to bed after that"

I was in my first sleep about an hour afterwards, when a knock came to my door, and the valet came in.

"Sorry to disturb you, sir," he said, "but the skull has *just come back*. It's in the next room. Would you like to see it?"

"Certainly not," I roared. "Get away and let me go to sleep."

Then and there I firmly resolved to leave next morning. I hated skulls, and I fancied that probably it might take a fancy to me, and I had no desire to be followed about the country by a skull as if it was a fox terrier.

Next morning I went in to breakfast. "Where is that beastly skull?" I said to Allan.

"Oh, it's off again somewhere. Heaven knows where; but I have had another vision, a waking vision."

"What was it?"

---

[cxxi] This was the old infant school, now a council building in Alexandra Place, and site of the former chapel.

"Well," said Allan, "I saw the skull and a white hand which seemed to beckon to me beside it. Then they slowly receded and in their place was what looked like a big sheet of paper. On it in large letters were the words – *Your friend, Jack Weston, is dead.* This morning I got this wire telling me of his sudden death. Read it."

That afternoon I left the Highlands and Allan Beauchamp.

Since then I have constant letters from him from his home in England. He has tried every means possible to get rid of that monk's skull; but they are of no avail, it always returns. So he has made the best he can of it, and keeps it in a locked casket in an empty room at the end of a wing of the old house. He says it keeps fairly quiet, but on stormy nights wails and gruesome shrieks are heard from the casket in that closed apartment.

I heard from him last week. He said: -

"Dear W. T. L. – I don't think I mentioned that twice a year the skull of Neville de Beauchamp vanishes from its casket for a period of about two days. It is never away longer.

"I wonder if it still haunts its old monastery at St. Andrews where its owner was slain. Do write and tell me if anyone now in that vicinity hears or sees the screaming skull of my ancestor, Neville de Beauchamp."[cxxii]

---

[cxxii] Refer to The Old Monastery of Greyfriars, p.168, *The Mysterious Head on the Scores*, p.87

# The Smothered Piper of the West Cliffs

*"Hush! hush! hush! Here comes the Bogie Man."*

This was shouted out to me very loudly by a cheery golfing "Johnny," as I entered the merry smoking-room of the old 'Varsity Golf Club at Coldham Common, Cambridge, some years ago. "Draw in your arm-chair, light a cigar or a pipe, and tell us all [many celebrated actors were present] some of those wonderful bogie stories about dear St Andrews. It is the bogie time of the year, and you must remember I played the 'Bogie Man' for you in one of your big burlesques at St. Andrews and Cupar some years ago, so fire away with the bogies, please, and be quick."

Then I reeled off a big lot of yarns: of the ghost, Thomas Plater, who murdered Prior Robert of Montrose on the dormitory staircase before vespers; of the negro in a Fifeshire house, who is invisible himself, but maps out his bare footmarks on the floor of the painted gallery; of Sharpe's coach, which, being heard, betokens a death; of haunted old Balcomie ruined Castle; of the murdered pedlar in our own South Street, who sweeps down with a chilly hand the cheeks of invaders to his haunted cellar; of the ghost that appeared in the house of Archbishop Ross, mentioned in Lyon's History; and of the terrible ghost in the Novum Hospitium, which so alarmed people that its dwelling had to be pulled down, and only a fragment of the building now remains. But they wanted to hear the tale of the "Ghostly Piper of the West Cliffs"; so I told them the legend as I had heard it years ago.

It seems that in the old days no houses existed on the Cliffs from the old Castle of Hamilton to the modem monument near the Witch Hill. It was all meadow land, much used for the grazing of cattle and sheep, and also much frequented as a playground for bygone children. On and over the face of the cliffs, slightly to the westward of Butts Wynd, existed then the entrance to a fearsome cave, or old ecclesiastical passage, which was a terror to many, and most people shunned it. It had many names, among them the "Jingling Cove," "The Jingling Man's Hole," "John's Coal Hole," and later "The Piper's Cave, or Grave." A few of the oldest inhabitants still remember it. A few knew a portion of it; none dared venture beyond this well-known portion. Like the interior of an old ice-house, it was dark, chilly, and clammy; its walls ran with cold sweat. It was partly natural, but mostly artificial - a most dark, creepy, and fearsome place.

In a description which I got of it many years ago, and which appeared in the *St Andrews Citizen*, I learn that "the opening of this cliff passage was small and triangular; it was situated on a projecting ledge of rock, and it was high enough, after entering, to enable a full-sized man to stand upright. From the opening it was a steep incline down for a distance of 49 feet, thereafter it proceeded in a level direction for over 70 feet, when it descended into a chamber. At the further end of this chamber were two, if not more, passages branching off from it. Between the passages was cut out in the rock a Latin cross." This would seem to point to an ecclesiastical connection, and had nothing whatever to do with the more modern smugglers' cave near the ladies' bathing place.

But enough of description. In bygone days, in a small cottage, little better than a hovel, situated in Argyle, lived an old dame named Goodman. She occupied one room, and her son and his young wife tenanted the other little chamber. He was a merry, dare-devil, happy-go-lucky lad, and he was famed as one of the best players on the bagpipes in all Fife; he would have pleased even Maggie Lauder[cxxiii]. Of nights at all hours he would make the old grass-grown streets lively with his music. "Jock the Piper," was a favourite among both young and old. He was much interested in the tale of the old West Cliff cave, and took a bet on with some cronies that on a New Year's night he would investigate the mysteries of the place, and play his pipes up it as far as he could go. His old mother, his wife, and many of his friends tried hard to dissuade him from doing so foolish and so foolhardy a thing; but he remained obdurate, and firmly stuck to his bet. On a dark New Year's night he started up the mysterious cavern with his pipes playing merrily; and they were heard, it is said, passing beneath Market Street, then they died away. They suddenly ceased, and were never more heard. He and his well-known pipes were never seen again.

Somewhere beneath St. Andrews lies the whitened bones of that by-gone piper lad, with his famous pipes beside him. Attempts were made to find him, but without avail; no one, not even the bravest, dared to venture into that passage full of damp foul air. His mother and wife were distracted, and the young wife used to sit for hours at the mouth of that death - trap cave. Finally, her mind gave way, and she used to wander at all hours down to the mouth of the cave where her husband had vanished. The following New Year's night she left the little cottage in Argyle, and putting a shawl over her wasted shoulders, turned to the old woman and said, "I'm going to my Jock" Morning came, but

---

[cxxiii] Maggie Lauder is attributed to an ancient anonymous Scottish folk song about a Fife maiden and her meeting with Rob the Ranter, the best piper she had heard play in all of Fife.

she never returned home. She had, indeed, gone to her lost "Jock." For years after, the small crouching figure of a woman could be seen on moonlight nights perched on the rock balcony of the fatal cave, dim, shadowy, and transparent. Wild shrieks and sounds of weird pipe music were constantly heard coming from out of that entrance.

In after years, when the houses were built, the mouth of this place was either built or covered up, and its memory only remains to us.

But what of "Piper Jock?" He, it is said, still walks the edge of the old cliffs; and his presence is heralded by an icy breath of cold air, and ill be it for anyone who meets or sees his phantom form or hears his pipe music. He seems to have the same effect as the ghost of "Nell Cook" in the dark entry at Canterbury, mentioned in the "Ingoldsby Legends," from which I must quote a few verses -

"And tho' two hundred years have flown,
Nell Cook doth still pursue
Her weary walk, and they who cross her path
The deed may rue.

Her fatal breath is fell as death!
The simoon's blast is not
More dire (a wind in Africa
That blows uncommon hot).

But all unlike the simoon's blast,
Her breath is deadly cold,
Delivering quivering, shivering shocks
Upon both young and old.

And whoso in the entry dark
Doth feel that fatal breath,
He ever dies within the year
Some dire untimely death."

So it is with him who meets "Piper Jock."

"By Jove," interrupted the golfing "Johnny," "has anyone seen him lately?"

"I only know of one man," I said, "who told me that one awful night in a heavy thunderstorm he had heard wild pipe music, and seen the figure of a curiously dressed piper walking along the cliff edge, *where no mortal could walk*, at a furious speed."

"What do you think of it all?" asked my golfing friend.

"I don't know, I'm sure; I am not receptive and don't see ghosts, but if I could only find now the mouth of that place, I bet another 'Jock' and I would get along it and find out the whereabouts of 'Jock the Piper' and his poor little wife. Here is my hansom. Good night, don't forget the Piper."

And they haven't.

# The Spectre of the Castle

Several years had elapsed since I met the butler of Lausdree Castle in the Highland Inn. I had just come up from the south of England for some golf and fresh air, and was looking over my letters one morning at breakfast when I opened the following missive: -

Lausdree Castle,

………..

SIR, - Yours to command. Sir, I have not forgot our pleasant talk on that snowy night up in the far north, when you were pleased to be interested in my experiences of Lausdree. Could you very kindly meet me any day and time you choose to fix at Leuchars? And oblige.

Your obedient servant,

JEREMIAH ANKLEBONE.

*P.S.* - I have something to divulge to you connected with St Andrews that may absorb your mind.

Accordingly, I fixed up arrangements and met Mr Anklebone at Leuchars, where we went to the nearest hostelry and ordered the best lunch they had there. Jeremiah looked thinner, older, and whiter than when I last saw him, doubtless owing to his frequent communing with spirits.

"How is Lausdree getting on?" I meekly inquired," and what of the ghosts?"

"It is getting on fine, sir. I have had a number of new experiences since I had the pleasure of seeing you last. You must understand, sir, that my family for generations have been favoured with occult powers. My father was a great seer, and my great-grandfather, Mr Concrikketty Anklebone, of the Isle of Skye, was a wonderful visionary."

Now, Anklebone was an interesting old fellow, but he had a tiresome habit of wandering away from his theme, and, as it were, getting off the main road into a labyrinth of bye -ways, and one had, metaphorically, to push him out of these side lanes and place him on his feet again in the main road.

"Before I come to St Andrews Castle," he said, "I must tell you about a queer episode of an astral body at Lausdree, a disentangled personality, as it were."

"Push along," I said, "and tell me."

"Well, one afternoon after luncheon the master and I were in the dining hall, when we saw a gentleman crossing the lawn towards the castle. He was a tall man in a riding dress, with curly hair and a large flowing moustache. He came up to the window and looked in earnestly at us, and then walked along the gravel-walk round to the castle door. 'Hullo!' said the master, 'that is my old friend, Jack Herbert, to whom I have let Lausdree for this summer. What on earth can bring him here? I'll go to the door myself and let him in. He never said he was coming.'

"In a minute or two the master came back looking bewildered. 'Anklebone,' he said, 'that's a *very* queer thing; there is nobody there! 'Perhaps,' I suggested, 'the gentleman has gone round to the stables'; so we both hurried off to look, but not a sign of anyone could be seen, and we stared blankly at each other. We could not make it out. Two days after, the master got a letter from Mr Jack Herbert telling him he had had a bad fall off his horse, had injured his spine, and was confined to bed.

"Mr Herbert went on to say that two days before, while he was asleep, he dreamt vividly that he was at Lausdree; that he crossed the lawn to the window of the dining hall, and, looking in, saw my master and the butler (that's me) in the room. He was going round to the front door when he awoke. Now that was his *astral body* that my Master and I saw. He loved Lausdree, and during sleep he came and paid us that visit. Queer, isn't it? Ten days after, he died. He wanted to see the old castle before he died, and his force of will power brought his double self, or astral body, to visit us. It is not so *uncommon* as people think.

"Numbers of people are seen in two places at once far apart. Look at Archbishop Sharpe of St Andrews. He was in Edinburgh, at Holyrood I think, and sent his servant over post haste to St. Andrews to bring back some papers he had forgotten there. When his trusty servant went up to his study in the Novum Hospitium to get the papers from the desk, lo! there was the Archbishop sitting in his usual chair and scowling at him. He told the Archbishop this when he returned with the papers to Edinburgh, but his Grace sternly bade him be silent and mention the matter to no one on pain of death.[cxxiv]

---

[cxxiv] Refer also to *The Doppelganger of Archbishop Sharpe*, p.108

"Now, sir, it seems that my master is able to see astral bodies, for he saw Mr Jack Herbert, but I doubt if he could see a *real spirit*. Perhaps, sir," suggested Anklebone, politely, "you might be able to see astral bodies?"

"Thank you very much indeed," I replied, "but I'm ------ if I want to see anything of the sort; but I have heard a tale of an eminent man in London who took a nap in his armchair every afternoon, and while asleep appeared to his friends in different parts of the country, but I doubt the fact very much."

"Ah! "said the butler, very solemnly, "only about one in a thousand has the power of visualising real spirits. Many ordinary persons have *long* sight, and some have *short* sight, but most people are short-sighted when ghosts are visible. The ghosts are really there all the time. Some people cannot see them, but can feel their presence or touch only. Most animals can see spirits; sometimes they are killed with terror when they see the spirits."

I pulled the bell rope and ordered some spirits for the butler.

"I don't think that will kill you with terror," I said when it arrived.

He looked grateful, and remarked that talking was dry work, however interesting the subject might be.

"Now, look here, Mr Anklebone," I said, "you know, I daresay, the stories about the Cathedral, the Haunted Tower, and all that. Please tell me what your experiences have been there."

Anklebone's whole appearance suddenly changed; he gripped my arm violently, shivered and shuddered, and turned ghastly pale. I thought he was going to have a fit.

"For pity's sake, sir," he said, trembling, "ask me nothing about that. There is something *too terrible* there, but I dare not reveal what I know and have seen to anyone. Do not allude to it again or it will drive me mad."

He lay back in his chair for a few moments with his eyes closed and shaking all over, but he gradually recovered his usual appearance.

"I wish to tell you about the castle Spectre," he said, weakly.

I must confess that I felt nonplussed and disappointed at the turn the conversation had taken, as whatever my private opinion was regarding the worthy Jeremiah's curious statements, still I felt anxious to find out his experiences at the Cathedral particularly. However, I swallowed my disappointment like a Trojan, and begged him to proceed.

He gulped down his spirits and informed me he felt better again, but he did not seem quite himself for some time.

"Well, sir," he said, "I often used to climb over the castle wall after dusk, and smoke my pipe and meditate on all the grand folk that must have been there in bygone days before the smash-up. I thought of lovely young Queen

Mary, of Mary Hamilton, and her other Maries, of Lord Darnley, of the poet Castelar, of Lord Arran, and the Duke of Rothesay, and all the Stuart Kings that used to be there. Then I thought of Prior Hepburn and poor murdered Cardinal Beaton, and of monks, knights, and lovely wenches that used to frequent the old place. I loved it, for I have read history a lot. One could not help thinking of the feasting, revelry, and pageants of those interesting old times, and the grand services in the churches, and what fine dresses everybody wore."

I saw he was going bang off the subject again, and when he began to tell me there were lots of Anklebones in Norman times about Fifeshire, I had to pull him back with a jerk to his ghost at the castle.

"Very well, sir, I was in the castle one evening, and I was sitting on the parapet of the old wall when I saw a head appearing up the old broken steps on the east side of the castle that once led down to the great dining hall. I knew no one could now come up that way without a ladder from the sea beach, and when the figure got to the level ground it came right through the iron railing just as if obstruction were there. I stared hard and watched the advancing figure. It looked like a woman. I had heard of the Cardinal's ghost, and wondered if it could be his Eminence himself. Nearer and nearer it came, and although it was a gusty evening, I noticed the flowing garments of the approaching figure were quite still and unruffled by the wind. It was like a moving statue. As it passed me slowly a few yards away, I saw they were not the robes of a Cardinal, but those of an Archbishop. I am a Churchman, and know the garments quite well. I saw all his vestments clearly, and I shall never forget the pale, ashen set face, and the thin determined mouth. Then I noticed one *very very* strange thing - the statuesque tall figure had a thick rope round the neck, and the end of the rope was trailing along the grass behind it, but there was no sound whatever. On it went and began to climb the stairs to the upper apartments. I tried to follow, but could not move for a bit. I felt as if I was mesmerised or paralysed. I was all in a cold sweat, too, and I was glad to get away from the castle at last and hurry home. I haven't gone so fast for many years. When I went next day to Lausdree I made a clean breast of the whole affair to Master.

"'Would you know him again?' he asked me.

"'Aye,' I replied, 'I would know that face and figure among a thousand.'

"'Come to the study,' said the master, 'and I will show you some pictures.'

"We went, and I looked over a number of them. At last I came to one that fairly transfixed me. There was no mistaking the face. Before me was the picture of the spectre I had seen the previous night in the ruined castle of Saint Andrews.

"'Well, Anklebone,' said the master, 'this is *really wonderful,* and you actually saw the rope round the neck?'

"'I did,' I said, 'as I am a living man, but who is it? It is not the Cardinal?'

"'No,' said the master very gravely, '*this man* was publicly hanged by his enemies on a gibbet at the Market Cross of Stirling on April 1st, 1571.'

"'But who was he?' I asked, imploringly.

"'The man, or ghost, you saw,' said master, 'was Archbishop John Hamilton of St Andrews – in his own castle grounds where he once reigned supreme.'"

I said farewell to Mr Anklebone, and as I thought over his extraordinary story journeying home in the train, I could not help repeating over and over again to myself that very curious name that seemed to rhyme with the motion of the train - Concrikketty Anklebone.

# The True Tale of the Phantom Coach

The great curtain had fallen after the pantomime, and I was standing chatting on the stage of the theatre at Cambridge when one of the stage men came to tell me I was wanted at the stage door and I must hurry up at once. Thither I proceeded, and found a lot of golfing boys, hunting boys, dramatic boys, who shouted out "Come along quick to the Blue Pig" (the "Blue Pig" is a Cambridge name for the Blue Boar Hotel), "We want you to meet a fellow called Willie Carson, and there is to be supper, and he has something to tell us. The 'Bogie Man' has gone on there now, so come right away."

Well off we went to the Blue Boar Hotel, and we found Carson sitting over a blazing fire, with a capital supper set in his nice old fashioned room, lit up with candles only, the picture of comfort – outside it was snowing hard and bitterly cold.

THE LOUNGE, "BLUE BOAR HOTEL, CAMBRIDGE.

The photo in this postcard is of the lounge of the Blue Boar Hotel in Cambridge. The photo was taken at the turn of the twentieth century around the time Linskill visited the hotel to set the scene for his tale of the Phantom Coach.

After a talk over merits of the pantomime, we did full justice to a most excellent supper, and then crowded round the blazing hearth to hear a story our host wanted to tell us.

"Did you ever hear of the Phantom Coach at St. Andrews?" he asked, turning to me suddenly and removing his cigar.

"Often," I replied, "I have heard most extraordinary yarns about it from lots of people; but why do you ask?"

"Because *I've seen it*," he replied, softly and thoughtfully. "Some five years ago. It was very, very strange, not to be forgotten and quite unexplainable; that is why I asked you here tonight. I wanted to talk to you about it." He stopped over the fire and was silent for a few minutes.

"Tell us all about it," we all shouted at once, "we won't make fun of it."

"There is nothing to make fun of; indeed, it's a true, solemn fact," he said. "Listen and I will try to tell you what I saw, but I can't half picture it properly. Five years ago I had just come home from America. I went to stay at St. Andrews for some golf. I think it was the latter half of August, and I must have been in the town about week at least, when one night – it was hot and stuffy, and about midnight – I determined to take a good long country walk, and struck out right along the road to Strathkinness.

"It was a hot, dark, and stormy night, not wet; fitful black clouds floated now and again at a rapid pace over the moon, which now and then shone out brightly; in the distance the sea made a perpetual moan, and at intervals the dark eastern sky was lit up by flashes of summer wildfire lighting over the distant Cathedral towers.

"Now and again I could hear the mutter of far-away thunder, and there were incessant gusts of wind. I must have been about two miles along the road, when I could discern some very large object approaching me rapidly. As it came nearer I noticed it resembled a coach, dark, heavy, primitive; it seemed to have four large black horses, and the driver was a muffled, shapeless figure. It approached with a low humming or buzzing sound, which was most peculiar and unpleasant to hear. The horses made a hollow kind of ticking sound with their feet, otherwise it was noiseless.

"No earthly coach of the kind could go without any ordinary sound. It was weird and eerie in the extreme. As it passed me the moon shone out brightly, and I saw for a second a ghastly white face at the coach window; but I saw those four strange, silent black horses, the more extraordinary, tall, swaddled-up shapeless driver, and the quaint black, gloomy old coach, with a coffin-shaped box on the roof, only far, far too well. One most remarkable thing was that it *threw no shadow* of any kind.

"Just as it passed me there was a terrific roar of thunder, and a blaze of lightning that nearly blinded me, and in the distance I saw that horrible ghastly receding coach; then clouds came over the moon and all was black – a darkness one could feel, a darkness of shut-up smothering vault. I felt sick and dazed for a minute or two. I could not make out if I had been struck by the lightning or was paralysed. However, after a bit it passed off; it was a horrible deathly feeling while it lasted. I never experienced a similar sensation before or since, and hope I never may again. *[Another very curious thing was the behaviour of my collie dog, usually frightened at nothing, on the approach of the phantom (for phantom it was). He crouched down, shivering and whining, and as it drew nearer fled with a bark like a screech, and cowered down in the ditch at the roadside and gave forth low growls.]*

"I tell you, boys, it's all right in this room to talk about it, but none of you would have liked to be in my place that queer, uncanny night on that lonely road. That it was supernatural, I am convinced; it is a very thin veil between us and the unseen world of spirits.

"They say I possess a seventh sense, namely, second sight, and I know I shall never forget night's experience.

"But listen – the story is not ended yet. Next morning a telegram arrived from my brother in Kent, 'Are you alright?' I wondered much, and wired back that I was very well.

"The following day a letter came from my brother giving me a very curious explanation.

"The following afternoon of the day I saw the coach, my brother was looking out of one of the old manor house windows in Kent, when he and several others noticed a large bird, having most peculiar plumage, seated on the garden wall. No one had ever seen a bird of the kind before. He was rushing off for a gun to shoot it, when our father, who looked very white and scared, stopped him. 'Do not shoot,' he said, 'it would be of no use. That is the bird of ill omen to all our race, it only appears before a death. I have only once seen it before – that week your dear mother died.'

"My brother was so alarmed at this that he sent the wire I have mentioned to me at St. Andrews. By the next mail from Australia we learned that our eldest brother had died there the very day I saw the coach at St. Andrews and my brother saw the bird at our home in Kent. Very odd, is it not; but what do you know about that coach?

"Only tales," I said. "Many people swear they have heard it, or seen it, on stormy nights. I know a girl who swears to it, and also a doctor who passed it on the road, and it nearly frightened his horse to death and him too.

"The tale of the two tramps is funny. They were trudging into St. Andrews one wild stormy night when this uncanny coach overtook them. It stopped; the door opened, and a white hand beckoned towards them. One tramp rushed up and got in, then suddenly the door noiselessly shut and the coach moved off, leaving the other tramp alone in the pitiless wind and rain. 'I never saw my old mate again,' said the old man when he told the tale, 'and I never shall – that there old coach was nothing of this here world of ours, it took my old mate off to Davy Jones's locker mighty smart, poor fellow.'

"They say his body was found in the sea some months afterwards, and the tale goes that the phantom coach finishes its nocturnal journey in the waves of St. Andrews Bay."

"Whose coach is it?" asked all that were in the room.

"I cannot say; some say Bethune, others Sharpe, and others Hackston; I do not know who is supposed to be the figure inside, unless it is his Satanic Majesty himself. At all events, it seems a certain fact that a phantom coach has been seen from time to time on the roads round St. Andrews. I have never seen any of these things myself."

"Well," said Carson, "that awful coach *does appear*, it appeared to me, and, doubtless, in the course of time will appear to many others. It bodes no one any good, and I pity with all my heart anyone who meets it. Beware of those roads late at night, or, like me, you may some day to your injury meet that ghastly, uncanny, old phantom coach. If so, you will remember it to your dying day."

"Curious thing that about seeing the coach and the bird at the same time, and in two places so far apart." Murmured the golfing Johnny, "and then Carson's brother dying too."

*["I'd sooner see the bird than the coach," said one.*

*"Guess I'd rather not see either of them," said an American present, "glad we have no phantom coaches in Yankeeland."]*

# The Veiled Nun of St. Leonards

Curiously enough, although I have been in many old haunted castles and churches (at the exact correct hour, viz., midnight) in Scotland, England, Wales, and the Rhine country, yet I have never been able to either see or hear a ghost of any sort. The only experience of the kind I ever had was an accidental meeting with the far-famed "Spring-heeled Jack" in a dark lane at Helensburgh. It was many years ago, and as I was then very small and he was of immense proportions, the meeting was distinctly unpleasant for me.

Now, from legends we learn that St. Andrews is possessed of a prodigious number of supernatural appearances of different kinds, sizes, and shapes – most of them of an awe-inspiring and blood curdling type. In fact, so numerous are they – 80 in number they seem to be – that there is really no room for any modern aspirants who may want a quiet place to appear and turn people's hair white. It might be well to mention a few of them before telling the tale of "The Veiled Nun of St Leonards Church Avenue."

We will put aside ordinary banshees and things that can only be heard. Well, there is the celebrated Phantom Coach that Willie Carson told us of. It has been heard and seen by many. There is also a white lady that used to haunt the Abbey Road, the ghost of St Rule's Tower, the Haunted Tower ghost, the Blackfriars ghost, the wraith of Hackston of Rathillet, the spectre of the old castle, the Dancing Skeletons, the smothered Piper Lad, the Phantom Bloodhound, the Priory Ghost, and many, many more. The Nun of St Leonards is as curious and interesting as any of them, though a bit weird and gruesome. In the time of charming Mary Stuart, our white Queen, there lived in the old South Street a very lovely lady belonging to a very old Scottish family, and her beauty and wit brought many admirers to claim her hand, but with little or no success. She waved them all away. At last she became affianced to a fine and brave young fellow who came from the East Lothian country, and for some months all went merrily as a marriage bell, but at last clouds overspread the rosy horizon. She resolved that she would never become an earthly bride, but would take the veil and become a bride of Holy Church – a nun, in point of fact. When her lover heard that she had left home and entered a house of Holy Sisters, he at once announced his intention of hastening to St. Andrews, seizing her, and marrying her at once. In this project it would seem the young lady's parents were in perfect agreement with the devoted youth. He did hasten to St. Andrews almost immediately, and there received a terrible shock. On meeting this once lovely and loved maiden, he discovered that she had actually done what she had threatened to do. Sooner than be an earthly bride she had mutilated her face by slitting her nostrils and cutting off her eyelids and both her top and bottom lips, and had branded her fair cheeks with cruel hot irons.

The poor youth, on seeing her famous beauty thus destroyed, fled to Edinburgh, where he committed suicide, and she, after becoming a nun, died from grief and remorse. That all happened nearly 400 years ago; but her spirit with the terribly marred and mutilated face still wanders o' nights in the peaceful little avenue to old St Leonards iron kirk gate down the Pends Road. She is all dressed in black, with a long black veil over the once lovely face, and carries a lantern in her hand. Should any bold visitor in that avenue meet her, she slowly sweeps her face veil aside, raises the lantern to her scarred face, and discloses those awful features to his horrified gaze. Here is a curious thing that I know happened there a few years ago.

I knew a young fellow here who was reading up theology and Church canon law. I also knew a great friend of his, an old Cambridge man. The former I will call Wilson, and the latter Talbot, as I do not want to give the exact names. Well, Wilson had invited Talbot up to St. Andrews for a month of golf, and he arrived here on a Christmas day. He came to my rooms for about ten minutes, and I never saw anyone merrier and brighter and full of old days at Cambridge. Then he hurried off to see the Links and the Club. Late that evening Wilson rushed in. "Come along quick and see Talbot; he's awfully ill, and I don't know what's up a bit." I went off and found Talbot in his lodgings with a doctor in attendance, and he certainly looked dangerously ill, and seemed perfectly dazed. Wilson told me that he had to go to see some people on business that evening down by the harbour, and that he took Talbot with him down the Pends Road. It was a fine night, and Talbot said he would walk about the road and enjoy a cigar till his friend's return. In about half-an-hour Wilson returned up the Pends Road, but could see Talbot nowhere in sight. After hunting about for a long time, he found him leaning against the third or fourth tree up the little avenue to St Leonards kirk gate.

He went up to him, when Talbot turned a horrified face towards him, saying, "Oh, my God, have you come to me again?" and fell down in a fit or a swoon. He got some passers-by to help to take poor Talbot to his rooms. Then he came round to me. We sat up with him in wonder and amazement; and, briefly, this is what he told us. After walking up and down the Pends Road, he thought he would take a survey of the little avenue, when at the end he saw a light approaching him, and turned back to meet it. Thinking it was a policeman, he wished him "Good evening," but got no reply. On approaching nearer he saw it to be a veiled female with a lantern. Getting quite close, she stopped in front of him, drew aside her long veil, and held up the lantern towards him. "My God," said Talbot, "I can never forget or describe that terrible, fearful face. I felt choked, and I fell like a log at her feet. I remember no more till I found myself in these rooms, and you two fellows sitting beside me. I leave this place tomorrow" – and he did by the first train. His state of panic was terrible to see. Neither Wilson nor Talbot had ever heard the tale of the awful apparition of the St Leonards nun, and I had almost forgotten the existence of the strange story till so curiously reminded of it. I never saw Talbot again, but I had a letter from him a year after written from Rhienfells, telling me that on Christmas day he had had another vision, dream, or whatever it was, of the same awful spectre. About a year later I read in a paper that poor old Talbot had died on Christmas night at Rosario of heart failure. I often wonder if the dear old chap had had another visit from the terrible Veiled Nun of St Leonards Avenue.[cxxv]

---

[cxxv] Refer to *The Veiled Nun of St. Leonards*, p.116, and *A St. Andrews Mystery* (2014)

# References

## Introduction

[1] Howie, John, *Biographia Scoticana*, John Bryce; Glasgow, 1775, p.28

[2] Leighton, John, M, *History of the County of Fife* Vol.11, Joseph Swan; Glasgow, 1840, p.9

[3] Holder, Geoff, *Haunted St. Andrews*, The History Press, 2012

[4] Mackay, J. G, *The County Histories of Scotland, Fife and Kinross,* W. Blackwood & Sons, 1896


## *Part One*
### Ghosts of St. Andrews Tour

[1] Lang, Andrew, from a poem about St. Andrews written by Lang entitled *Almae Matres*, 1862


## An Introduction to the Old Grey Toun

[1] Brown, Charles (ed), *Seekers after a City*, story of the same title by Robert. L Mackie. Ballantyne, Hanson & Co; Edinburgh, 1911, pp.1-7


## The Ghost Tour

[1] *The StAndard*, University of St. Andrews Staff Magazine, Issue 17, Philippa Dunn, November 2009. pp.18-19. Also available as a PDF online: https://www.st-andrews.ac.uk/media/press-office/standard/StAndard-Issue17.pdf

[2] Grierson, James, *Delineations of St. Andrews,* Cupar; 1807, p.180

[3] Photo housed in the St. Andrews Museum

[4] Wessels, Chelsea, Online article about the cinema: http://cinemastandrews.org.uk/exhibition/opening-of-the-cinema-house/

[5] Wilkie, James, *Bygone Fife: From Culross to St. Andrews,* Blackwood; Edinburgh, 1931, pp.333-334

[6] Foxe. John, *Foxe's Book of Martyrs*, 1563, chapter XV

[7] Ibid

[8] Grierson, James, *Delineations of St. Andrews;* Cupar, 1807, pp.150-151

[9] Howie, John, *Biographia Scoticana*, John Bryce; Glasgow, 1775, p.28

[10] thestudentroom.co.uk /wiki/University_of_St_Andrews, titled PH Cobbles and the May Dip.

[11] *St. Andrews Citizen*, 4th August 1928. p.5

References continued

[12] Fleming, David Hay, *Handbook to St. Andrews and Neighbourhood*, J. & G. Innes, St. Andrews Citizen Office; St. Andrews, 1897, p.94

[13] Wilkie, James, *Bygone Fife, From Culross to St. Andrews*, Blackwood; Edinburgh, 1931, pp.296-298

[14] Alger, Leclaire G, *Gaelic Ghosts*, Holt, Rinehart & Winston; New York, 1963

[15] Beveridge, David, *Culross and Tulliallan or Perthshire on Forth. It's History and Antiquities*. William Blackwood; Edinburgh, 1885, Vol. II, p.160

[16] *The Sunday Mail*, 15th June 1980

[17] *The Scotsman*, 25th May 2010

[18] *The StAndard*, University of St. Andrews Staff Magazine: Issue 17, Philippa Dunn, November 2009, P.18-19.

[19] Wilkie, James, *Bygone Fife, From Culross to St. Andrews*, Blackwood; Edinburgh, 1931, pp.359-360

[20] Chalmers, Alexander, The General Biographical Dictionary Vol. IV, Nichols, Son & Bentley; London,1812, pp.240-241

[21] Ibid, p.242

[22] The Topographical, Statistical and Historical Gazetteer of Scotland, Vol.2, A Fullarton and Co, 1856, pp.523-524

[23] Lesley, John, *History of Scotland*, book 10, Cody ed., (1895) p.296: Thomson ed., (1830), Edinburgh, p.195

[24] Knox, John, *History of the Reformation*, vol.1, Blackie, Fullarton & Co; Edinburgh, 1831, p.61

[25] Chambers, Robert, *The Scottish Songs collected and Illustrated*, Ballantyne & Co for William Tait; Edinburgh, 1829, pp.19-20

[26] Kirkton, Rev. James, *The Secret and True History of the Church of Scotland*. Edited from the MS By Charles Kirkpatrick Sharpe; Edinburgh 1817, p.407

[27] *National Observer, St. Andrews Ghosts*: 7th Jan 1893.

[28] Wilkie, James, *Bygone Fife, From Culross to St. Andrews*, Blackwood; Edinburgh, 1931, pp.366-367

[29] Lyon, The Rev, Charles Jobson, *History of St. Andrews*, Vol.1, William Tait; Edinburgh, 1838, p. 202

[30] Ibid

[31] Grierson, James, *Delineations of St. Andrews;* Cupar, 1807, p.147

[32] Ibid

[33] http://thehistorylady.wordpress.com/2012/05/15/historic-st-andrews-queen-marys-great-escape-from-loch-leven/

[34] Linskill, W. T, *St. Andrews Citizen*, 24th Nov 1928. p.7

[35] Fleming, David Hay, *Handbook to St. Andrews and Neighbourhood*, J. & G. Innes, St. Andrews Citizen Office; St. Andrews, 1897, p.53

[36] Lang, Andrew, *John Knox and the Reformation*, Longmans, Green & Co; London, New York and Bombay, 1905.

[37] Lyon, The Rev, Charles Jobson, *History of St. Andrews*, Vol.1, William Tait; Edinburgh, 1838, p.193

[38] Fleming, David Hay, *Handbook to St. Andrews and Neighbourhood*, J. & G. Innes, St. Andrews Citizen Office; St. Andrews, 1897, p.51

[39] Ibid, p.53

[40] Ibid, p.52

[41] Ibid, p.51

[42] Groome, Francis, H (Ed): *Ordnance Gazetteer of Scotland: A Survey of Scottish Topography, Statistical, Biographical and Historical,* originally published in parts by Thomas C. Jack, Grange Publishing Works, Edinburgh between 1882 and 1885.

[43] Grierson, James, Delineations of St. Andrews Cupar, 1807, p.219

[44] Fleming, David Hay, *Handbook to St. Andrews and Neighbourhood*, J. & G. Innes, St. Andrews Citizen Office; St. Andrews, 1897, p.52

[45] Grierson, James, *Delineations of St. Andrews;* Cupar, 1807, p.219

[46] Groome, Francis, H (Ed): *Ordnance Gazetteer of Scotland: A Survey of Scottish Topography, Statistical, Biographical and Historical,* originally published in parts by Thomas C. Jack, Grange Publishing Works, Edinburgh between 1882 and 1885. p.297

[47] Geddie, John, *The fringes of Fife*, David Douglas; Edinburgh, 1894, p.196

[48] Pennant, Thomas: *Tour through Scotland*, B. White; London, 1769

[49] Lyon, The Rev, Charles Jobson, *History of St. Andrews*, Vol.1, William Tait; Edinburgh, 1838, pp.161 - 162

[50] Ibid, p.185

[51] Fleming, David Hay, *Handbook to St. Andrews and Neighbourhood*, J. & G. Innes, St. Andrews Citizen Office; St. Andrews, 1897, p.52

[52] Lyon, The Rev, Charles Jobson, *History of St. Andrews*, Vol.1, William Tait; Edinburgh, 1838, p.191

[53] Groome, Francis, H (Ed): *Ordnance Gazetteer of Scotland: A Survey of Scottish Topography, Statistical, Biographical and Historical,* originally published in parts

by Thomas C. Jack, Grange Publishing Works, Edinburgh between 1882 and 1885. p.297

[54] Ibid

[55] Ibid

[56] Robertson, James, K, About St. Andrews and About, Citizen Office; St. Andrews,1973, p.73

[57] Lamont, Stewart, *Is Anybody There,* Mainstream Publishing, 1980, p.38

[58] Kirk, Russell, *St. Andrews,* B. T. Batsford Ltd, 1954, pp.48-49

[59] Lamont, Stewart, *Is Anybody There,* Mainstream Publishing, 1980, p.37

[60] Cook, Helen: *Scots Magazine. Haunted St. Andrews,* November 1978.

[61] Fleming, David Hay, *Handbook to St. Andrews and Neighbourhood,* J. & G. Innes, St. Andrews Citizen Office; St. Andrews, 1897, p.48

[62] Ibid, p.43

[63] Grierson, James, *Delineations of St. Andrews;* Cupar, 1807, pp.135-136

[64] Fleming, David Hay, *Handbook to St. Andrews and Neighbourhood,* J. & G. Innes, St. Andrews Citizen Office; St. Andrews, 1897, p.43

[65] Ibid, p.69

[66] Fleming, David Hay, *Handbook to St. Andrews and Neighbourhood,* J. & G. Innes, St. Andrews Citizen Office; St. Andrews, 1897, p.47

[67] Martine, George: *Reliquiae divi Andreae, or The state of the venerable and primitial see of St. Andrews,* 1683. Published 1797 by James Morison, Printer to the University, p.190

[68] Ibid, p.47

[69] Wilkie, James, *Bygone Fife: From Culross to St. Andrews,* Blackwood; Edinburgh, 1931, pp.340-341

[70] *Fife Herald and Journal,* 13th January, 1904

[71] Simpkins, John, Ewart, *Folklore of Fife,* Sidgwick; London, 1914

[72] Wodrow, Rev Robert: *Analecta: Or Materials for a History of Remarkable Providences Mostly relating to Scotch Ministers and Christians.* 1842 by the Maitland Club and reproduced from manuscripts dating 1721-1722.

[73] Fleming, Dr. Hay LL.D, *Handbook to St. Andrews and Neighbourhood,* New Edition, St. Andrews Citizen Office; St. Andrews, 1902, p.68

[74] Ibid, pp.68-69

[75] Green, Andrew, Website - Mystical World Wide Web – Article: *The unexplained explained.*

[76] Kirk, Russell, *St. Andrews,* B. T. Batsford Ltd, 1954, p.140

[77] Lyon, The Rev, Charles Jobson, *History of St. Andrews*. Vol. II, William Tait; Edinburgh, 1843, pp.398-9 (From private letters addressed to Mr Wodrow)

[78] Ibid

[79] Wodrow, Robert: *The History of the Sufferings of the Church of Scotland*. Vol. III. 1721-1722. Reproduced by Blackie Fullerton & Co; Glasgow, 1829. p.43

[80] Henry, David, F.S.A. Scot: *Knights of St. John with other Mediaeval Institutions and their Buildings in St. Andrews*. W. C. Henderson. K. Son, University Press, 1912, p.183

[81] Lamont, Stewart, *Is Anybody There*, Mainstream Publishing, 1980, p.37

[82] Wilkie, James, *Bygone Fife: From Culross to St. Andrews*, Blackwood; Edinburgh, 1931, pp.339-340

[83] *National Observer - St. Andrews Ghosts*, 7th Jan 1893.

[84] From the Special Collections of the University of Glasgow

[85] Wormald, Jenny, *Mary, Queen of Scots; Politics, Passion and a Kingdom Lost*, George Philip; London, 1988, p.90

[86] Wilkie, James, *Bygone Fife: From Culross to St. Andrews*, Blackwood; Edinburgh, 1931, pp.360-361

[87] Fleming, David Hay, *Handbook to St. Andrews and Neighbourhood*, J. & G. Innes, St. Andrews Citizen Office; St. Andrews, 1897, p.43

[88] Ibid, p.41

[89] Cook, *Excursionists Guide to St. Andrews*, J. Cook & Son, 1896, p.8

[90] Lyon, The Rev, Charles Jobson, *History of St. Andrews*, Vol.1, William Tait; Edinburgh, 1838, pp.188 -190

[91] Wilkie, James, *Bygone Fife: From Culross to St. Andrews*, Blackwood; Edinburgh, 1931, pp.343-344

[92] Lamont, Stewart, *Is Anybody There*, Mainstream Publishing, 1980, pp.38-39

[93] Underwood, Peter: *Gazetteer of Scottish Ghosts*, Harper Collins, 1973, p.169

[94] Wilkie, James, Bygone *Fife: From Culross to St. Andrews*, Blackwood; Edinburgh, 1931, p.342

[95] Lamont, Stewart, *Is Anybody There*, Mainstream Publishing, 1980, pp.37-38

[96] Lyon, The Rev, Charles Jobson, *History of St. Andrews*. Vol. 2, William Tait; Edinburgh, 1843, pp.155-156 and Fleming, Dr. Hay, *Handbook to St. Andrews and Neighbourhood*, New Edition, St. Andrews Citizen Office; St. Andrews, 1902. p.60

[97] Linskill, W. T, *St. Andrews Citizen*, 29th Jan 1927. p.3

[98] Brown, Charles (ed), *Seekers after a City, The Virgin's Necklet* by David Scott, Ballantyne, Hanson & Co; Edinburgh, 1911, pp.36-48

[99] Lang, Theo, *The Kingdom of Fife*, 1951, Hodder & Stroughton; London, p.205

[100] Wilkie, James, *Bygone Fife: From Culross to St. Andrews*, Blackwood; Edinburgh, 1931, pp.354

[101] Kirk, Russell, *St. Andrews*, B. T. Batsford Ltd, 1954, p.88

[102] Wilkie, James, *Bygone Fife, From Culross to St. Andrews*, Blackwood; Edinburgh, 1931, p.355

[103] Ibid, p.354-5

[104] Wilkie, James, *Bygone Fife, From Culross to St. Andrews*, Blackwood; Edinburgh, 1931, pp.354-355

[105] Ibid, p.360

[106] Paterson, A. B, *The Byre Theatre – Through the Years,* The Theatre, 1983

[107] Lewis, Roy Harley, *Theatre Ghosts,* David & Charles, 1988

[108] Brown, Raymond Lamont, *Phantoms of the Theatre*, Satellite Books, 1977, p.135.

[109] *St. Andrews Citizen*, 1st January 1938. p.2

[110] Groome, Francis, H (Ed): *Ordnance Gazetteer of Scotland: A Survey of Scottish Topography, Statistical, Biographical and Historical,* originally published in parts by Thomas C. Jack, Grange Publishing Works, Edinburgh between 1882 and 1885.

[111] Brown, Charles (ed), Seekers after a City: *Alma Mater* by L. P. Steele-Hutton, Ballantyne, Hanson & Co; Edinburgh, 1911, p.16

[112] Lang, Theo, *The Kingdom of Fife*, 1951, Hodder & Stroughton; London, pp.200-201

[113] Kirk, Russell, *St. Andrews*, B. T. Batsford Ltd, 1954, pp.121-122

[114] Reid, Norman, *The StAndard,* 2008, pp.38-39

[115] Lyon, The Rev, Charles Jobson, *The History of St. Andrews: Ancient and Modern*, William Tait; Edinburgh, 1838, pp.218-219

[116] Fleming, David Hay, *Handbook to St. Andrews and Neighbourhood*, J. & G. Innes, St. Andrews Citizen Office; St. Andrews, 1897, p.40

[117] Kirk, The Rev. Robert, *The Secret Commonwealth*, 1691, p.14

[118] Scott, Sir Walter, *Letters on Demonology and Witchcraft*, 1830. This edition George Routledge & Sons; London, 1884.

[119] Proudfoot, E, *St Andrews Citizen*, 22 October 1982

[120] Lang, Theo, *The Kingdom of Fife*, 1951, Hodder & Stroughton; London, pp.202-3

[121] Leighton, John, M, *History of the County of Fife*, Vol. III, Joseph Swan, Glasgow,1840, p.23

[122] Fleming, Dr. Hay LL.D, *Handbook to St. Andrews and Neighbourhood*, New Edition, St. Andrews Citizen Office; St. Andrews, 1902.

[123] Bord, Janet and Colin: *Modern Mysteries of the World*, Harper Collins, 1990, p.349

[124] Linskill, W. T, *St. Andrews Citizen*, January 5th, 1929

[125] Sibbald, Robert, *History of Fife and Kinross*, 1710, pp.348-349

[126] Ibid, p.349

[127] *St. Andrews Citizen*, 5th January 1929

[128] Wilkie, James, *Bygone Fife, From Culross to St. Andrews*, Blackwood; Edinburgh, 1931, p.202

[129] Smellie, Alexander: *Men of the Covenant*, 1908, p.226

[130] Wodrow, Robert, *The History of the Sufferings of the Church of Scotland*. Vol. III. 1721-1722. Reproduced by Blackie Fullerton & co; Glasgow, 1829. p.45

[131] Ibid, p.463

[132] Ibid, p.462

[133] Ibid, p.219

[134] Smellie, A (1908), *Men Of The Covenant*, London, p.340

[135] Robertson, James K, *About St. Andrews and About*, Citizen Office; St. Andrews,1973, p.73

[136] *National Observer, St. Andrews Ghosts*, 7th Jan 1893.

[137] Ibid.

[138] Bord, Janet and Colin, *Modern Mysteries of the World*, Harper Collins, 1990, p.349

References continued next page

## *Appendix*
## The Ghost Criteria

[139] Kirk, Russell: *St. Andrews.* 1954, p.88

## *Part Two*
## W. T. Linskill's St. Andrews Ghost Stories

### Introduction

[1] Fife Herald and Journal, 13th January, 1904
[2] Fife Herald and Journal, 27th January, 1904

Lightning Source UK Ltd.
Milton Keynes UK
UKOW04f1725050715

254638UK00002B/23/P